FE
SUCCESS
STORIES

CÉLÉBRONS
NOS RÉUSSITES
FÉMINISTES

FEMINIST SUCCESS STORIES

CÉLÉBRONS NOS RÉUSSITES FÉMINISTES

Edited by / Sous la direction de

Karen A. Blackford
Marie-Luce Garceau
Sandra Kirby

ACTEXPRESS

UNIVERSITY OF OTTAWA PRESS
LES PRESSES DE L'UNIVERSITÉ D'OTTAWA

Canadian Cataloguing in Publication Data

Main entry under title:
Feminist success stories = Célébrons nos réussites féministes
(Actexpress)
Includes bibliographical references.
Text in English and French.
ISBN 0-7766-0511-9

1. Feminism–Canada. 2. Women–Education–Canada. 3. Women–Health and hygiene–Canada. 4. Women–Employment–Canada. 5. Volunteers–Canada. I. Blackford, Karen, 1944- II. Garceau, Marie-Luce, 1951- III. Kirby, Sandra L. (Sandra Louise), 1949- IV. Title: Célébrons nos réussites féministes. V. Series.

HQ1453.F47 1999   305.42'0971   C99-901331-9E

Données de catalogages avant publication (Canada)

Vedette principale au titre :
Feminist success stories = Célébrons nos réussites féministes
(Actexpress)
Comprend des références bibliographiques.
Textes en anglais et en français.
ISBN 0-7766-0511-9

1. Féminisme–Canada. 2. Femmes–Éducation–Canada. 3. Femmes–Santé et hygiène–Canada. 4. Femmes–Travail–Canada. 5. Femmes bénévoles–Canada. I. Blackford, Karen, 1944- II. Garceau, Marie-Luce, 1951- III. Kirby, Sandra L. (Sandra Louise), 1949- IV. Titre: Célébrons nos réussites féministes. V. Collection.

HQ1453.F47 1999   305.42'0971   C99-901331-9F

University of Ottawa Press gratefully acknowledges the support extended to its publishing programme by the Canada Council and the University of Ottawa.
We acknowledge the financial support of the Government of Canada through the Book Publishing Industry Development Program for this project.
Les Presses de l'Université d'Ottawa remercient le Conseil des Arts du Canada et l'Université d'Ottawa de l'aide qu'ils apportent à leur programme de publication.
Nous reconnaissons l'aide financière du gouvernement du Canada par l'entremise du Programme d'aide au développement de l'industrie et de l'édition pour nos activités d'édition.

 UNIVERSITY OF OTTAWA
UNIVERSITÉ D'OTTAWA

Cover illustration/Illustration de couverture: Élise Palardy

© University of Ottawa Press, 1999
Les Presses de l'Université d'Ottawa, 1999
542 King Edward, Ottawa, Ont. Canada K1N 6N5
press@uottawa.ca   http://www.uopress.uottawa.ca

Printed in Canada / Imprimé au Canada

À la mémoire de Monique Hébert

Contents — Sommaire

Acknowledgements — Remerciements

Originally, this book was intended to identify institutional barriers to women's equality, demonstrate through examples how women have overcome these barriers, and explain how these transformations occurred. There was no formal plan to inform readers about the experience of living with a disability. Yet, through the process of publication, the book has become a telling example of how disability is inherently a part our lives — in this case, a part of women's lives.

Threads of the disability experience first emerged as articles were submitted. A call for papers from women in a variety of life's locations meant that, inevitably, because fifteen percent of the population has some form of disability, the theme of disability would be part of some women's stories. For instance, we see in the portrayal of Franco-Ontarian women that disability is often a part of the aging process. In a description of the institutional forces facing women with breast cancer, we read about the disabling effects of medical practices that value objectivity over personhood. Some First Nations women in an economic development project demonstrate the disabling effects of racism and sexism. Also illustrated is the ironic potential for enablement of families when a parent has multiple sclerosis (MS). Even discussion of an educational union's transformation addresses the importance of establishing accessibility and accommodation for workers with disabilities.

The book's progress was slow because of a number of factors. One was the fact that many Canadian publishers who otherwise wanted to produce the book were reluctant to risk publishing and marketing a bilingual book. Another was the time demanded in weaving together each chapter in such a way as to allow each author to write in her own official language. The changeable nature of Canadian women's lives was another barrier, as many authors and editors experienced the distracting forces of the competitive economy on one hand and inadequate social supports on the other. Finally, the publication process was slowed down by an extended, seriously disabling event in the life of one of the editors. This woman's experience of disability brought uncertainty to the process of completion.

While the book is thus partly about women and disability, it is also about life's reality. The unpredictable natures of our bodies and of our lives is part of being human. At the same time, partly because feminism, disability, humanness, and unpredictability are part of the book's fabric, the processes and final outcomes of this publication are clear demonstrations of empowerment of and by women. In this sense, the book has fulfilled the editors' original intentions. The book identifies institutional barriers to women's equality, and shows how barriers can be overcome. These examples of empowerment can be of benefit to all marginalized groups.

Publication of this book would not have been possible without the generous contributions of a number of organizations and individuals. The book is sponsored by the Canadian Centre on Disability Studies in Winnipeg, Manitoba. Funding was provided by Human Resources Development Canada and Laurentian University. External anonymous reviewers generously provided editorial suggestions for each chapter. The Canadian Sociology and Anthropology Association agreed to have two of their anonymous reviewers to read and comment on the manuscript as a whole. Our editors and authors are sincerely grateful for all of these contributions. In each case, authors made revisions in response to suggestions made by these readers and showed incredible patience with what became a lengthy publishing process. The editors appreciate the cooperation of every author.

Finalement, nous aimerions remercier chaleureusement les personnes qui ont révisé le manuscrit et qui ont bien voulu apporter leurs commentaires et leurs suggestions : Julie Boissonneault, Lorraine Carter et Leda Culliford de l'Université Laurentienne, Marc Charron et Pierre Lemelin, travailleurs autonomes. Merci aussi à Jo-Ann Philipow et à Léo Duquette de Concepts médiatiques Inc., à Élyse Pallardy pour l'oeuvre de la couverture et à Jean-Marc Bélanger, Ken Clamain et Jennifer Keck pour la lecture finale du manuscrit.

Karen Blackford, Marie-Luce Garceau, Sandra Kirby

INTRODUCTION
Celebrating Success — Célébrons nos réussites

The main purpose of this book is to recognize advances made by feminists in Canada. Increasing international corporate power, withdrawal of state services, and regressive legislation impoverish women and ravage the quality of their everyday lives. Women have reason to be demoralized. Recognizing this challenging and unfortunate situation, this text establishes as its mandate something different. Specifically, it is a review of women's successes, intended to hearten the Women's Movement and to show that the potential for feminist change still exists.

The use of both French and English throughout this text is deliberate as we want to provide opportunities for authors to tell their stories in their own official languages. We also want to demonstrate that issues for feminists in Canada cross linguistic and other differences.

The body of the book organizes papers according to various contexts out of which the authors have discovered women's experiences of oppression. In Part I, we have articles which address the oppression of women in a broad variety of fields within education. Part II, called *Women at Work*,

Reconnaître et célébrer les réussites des féministes canadiennes, voilà le but de ce livre. Pourtant, en cette ère de changements économiques et politiques — mondialisation, restructuration, privatisation, adoption de lois rétrogrades au niveau social et coupures drastiques — la vie des femmes est jalonnée de conditions difficiles. Dans ce contexte, de nombreuses femmes sont inquiètes. Or, ce livre, par la célébration de nos réussites, tente de contrer la morosité ambiante. Ces réussites sont une force vive à laquelle nous pouvons puiser.

Ce livre tente aussi, par l'utilisation de la langue officielle de chacune des auteures, de montrer que leurs réussites traversent les frontières linguistiques et culturelles.

Chacun des textes, contextualise, à partir de l'expérience des femmes, la question des différentes formes de l'oppression qu'elles subissent. Dans la première partie, les auteures discutent de cette oppression dans le domaine de l'éducation. Dans la seconde partie, les auteures décrivent les relations qu'elles entretiennent avec leurs employeurs et leurs collègues de travail. La troisième partie montre l'importance des transformations qui se produisent dans la vie des femmes,

describes the relations between women and their employers, co-workers, and unions. Part III examines the issue of transforming ourselves at any age, and demonstrates the importance of empowering women across the lifespan. The next section acknowledges that women's oppression exists in domains less concrete than those previously discussed. In Part IV, our authors address the topic of healing the body and the spirit. Ironically, women's caring natures serve both to oppress and liberate women. In Part V, entitled *Caring*, authors provide examples of how the state, the family, and the community all have the potential to reproduce women's oppression and to transform the relations of caring. Part VI presents what we have learned about feminism in Canada is today. Based on our analysis of each paper, we identify the themes emerging from feminist theory and practice. This section is our attempt to portray feminism as it exists "on the ground" across Canada as we approach the close of the twentieth century.

We realize that there are many other "success stories". Recognizing that other stories exist and are yet to be told, we recommend that readers see this collection of success stories as one in progress to be continued...

quel que soit leur âge ou la forme d'oppression subie. Dans la prochaine partie, les auteures discutent de l'oppression des femmes à partir des milieux médical, théologique, religieux et organisationnel. Pour elles, guérir le corps et l'esprit permet la libération des femmes. Ironiquement, la cinquième montre que la prise en charge, par les femmes, des soins apportés à leurs proches, sert à la fois à leur oppression et à leur libération. Elle permet de voir comment l'État, la famille et la communauté contribuent à reproduire certaines formes d'oppression tout en permettant la transformation des relations des femmes dans leurs environnements. La dernière partie du livre présente notre vision du féminisme actuel au Canada. Ici, notre analyse présente les thèmes principaux qui émergent de l'ensemble des textes soumis pour ce livre. C'est donc une occasion de faire le point sur nos théories et nos pratiques et de les consolider, spécialement en cette période où les acquis des femmes sont remis en question.

Les textes présentés dans ce livre ne sont que quelques exemples de réussites accomplies par les féministes canadiennes. Il en reste bien d'autres à raconter. C'est une histoire à suivre...

At the beginning of each section, we refer to Tong's (1989) well-known definition of feminist theory to organize summaries of the

En guise d'introduction de chacune des parties de ce livre, nous empruntons la définition féministe de Tong (1989). Selon elle, la

papers in that section. Feminist theories "attempt to describe women's oppression, to explain its causes, and consequences, and to prescribe strategies for women's liberation" (p. 1). In other words, in our introduction to each section, we review the sites of oppression each author has uncovered, the explanation or theory she has presented, and the outcomes of feminist actions she has identified.

théorie féministe doit permettre de décrire les multiples oppressions vécues par les femmes, en expliquer les causes et les conséquences et proposer des stratégies de libération des femmes. Par conséquent, dans chacune des parties, nous présenterons une brève description des lieux de l'oppression présentés par chacune des auteures, leurs explications théoriques et les actions qu'elles ont mises en place pour effectuer des changements sociaux.

Reference

Tong, R. 1989. *Feminist Thought: A Comprehensive Introduction.* Boulder: Westview Press.

PART I — PARTIE 1
Education — Éducation

Linda Christianson Ruffman, Francine Descarries, and Mary Lynn Stewart come together to identify the power of federal granting agencies in discouraging woman-centered research and scholarship in post-secondary institutions. The Canada Council and later the Social Sciences and Humanities Research Council (SSHRC) failed to acknowledge women until the Royal Commission on the Status of Women and the 1975 United Nations Decade on Women. The steps which led to SSHRC's Women and Work Strategic Grant and the grant's limited success in opening research funding to women are described. This chapter is written from the perspective of the academic activists who initially proposed the grant.

Monique Hébert discute de la place des «maîtresses d'école» durant les années 1922 à 1947 et montre que, malgré la volonté du gouvernement manitobain d'assimiler la population francophone au moyen de l'école et malgré l'illégalité de l'enseignement en français, ces femmes ont assuré la survivance des francophones et ont lutté contre leur assimilation en fonction des frontières auxquelles elles étaient quotidiennement confrontées. Elle ajoute qu'à l'époque ces enseignantes ont été obligées de démissionner lorsqu'elles ont voulu se marier et qu'elles ont abdiqué leur profession pour être au service de leur famille. Géographiquement isolées, les institutrices n'ont guère développé de liens de solidarité ni acquis un sentiment d'appartenance à leur groupe professionnel. Pour Hébert, ces enseignantes sont des modèles de résistance. Et, s'il y a lieu d'approfondir ce concept théorique pour montrer la force tranquille des institutrices de l'époque, elle l'amorce avec autant de ferveur que les femmes qu'elle présente. Leur ferme détermination a poussé ces femmes à porter bien haut le flambeau de leur ethnicité. Leur lutte n'est pas éclatante; elle est plutôt livrée au quotidien et ancrée dans une profonde certitude, celle d'être des Canadiennes-françaises ayant des valeurs culturelles et une mission : inculquer la fierté francophone et solidifier la foi catholique, ce qu'elles ont fait auprès de nombreux enfants et qui se fait toujours. Si le Manitoba francophone contemporain possède des institutions offrant une éducation en français, la situation n'est certainement pas étrangère à leur lutte quotidienne. Ces femmes ont été des courroies indispensables à la survie des écoles, de leur gestion et, surtout, dans la protection des droits linguistiques et religieux des francophones. C'est là que réside la clé du succès des institutrices Franco-Manitobaines.

Barriers to advancement for female university faculty and to inclusion of feminist course content and design are the oppressions cited by Juanita Epp. This article outlines the gradual implementation of post-secondary courses which transform misogynist views of women, the organization of women faculty, and the introduction of Women's Studies as an academic program within one educational institution. The barriers Epp speaks of include heavy work demands which intrude on the conceptualization and implementation of any political change agenda. These demands are made evident to the reader through this academic's personal snapshot of her experience.

Sandra Kirby acquaints readers with the broad context in which Canadian women strive for fitness and achievement in sport. Her examination of sports organizations clarifies how exclusion of women has been established and maintained not just in the university but at every level of participation. As a leader in creating a place for women in Canadian sport, she provides a history of how women athletes have come together to gain greater influence across Canada in creating opportunities for women as athletes, coaches, and sports organizers.

Linda Christiansen-Ruffman, Francine Descarries, and Mary Lynn Stewart

The Unfinished Story:
SSHRC's Strategic Grant Program on
Women and Work

Once Upon a Time...

Once upon a time — what seems like a long time ago but is really only yesterday — women were invisible — theoretically, academically, and politically.[1] From the vantage point of the early 1990s, it is hard to remember — and difficult to imagine — the scholarly world without books, journals, newsletters, or courses that even mentioned women.[2] It is hard to recapture the enthusiasm that greeted Maggie Benston's article on the Political Economy of Women's Liberation[3] and Marylee Stephenson's edited book, Women in Canada, in 1973.[4] It is difficult to describe that taken-for-granted world without women[5] and the sudden "clicks" of recognition at first seeing data on discrimination, perceiving our problems as public issues, and understanding the potential intellectual significance of feminism. During the late 1960s and 1970s, it was exciting to rediscover a thriving women's presence at other historical times and places, but frightening to realize how quickly women's previous struggles and gains had disappeared from our view with hardly a trace.

These were times before strategic grants, even before the Social Sciences and Humanities Research Council (SSHRC), when academic research in the social sciences and humanities was supported through the scholarly programs of the Canada Council.[6] Scholarship was blatantly and unapologetically patricentric, grounded in the experiences of men.[7] For example, women's paid and unpaid work experiences were not seen; they were outside of conceptual frameworks. Researchers conducted surveys of labour force participation that either did not disaggregate for sex or were restricted to male samples. The assumption that work was male permeated research design, data, and conclusions. The invisibility and hence undervaluation of women's work had direct research and policy implications in every field — business, politics, religion, science, and technology.[8] A vicious circle of invisibility, undervaluation, and silence on the subject of women perpetuated itself.

Women at the time were not accepted in the ivory tower — as scholars or theoretical actors. Times began to change as a result of the

7

women's movement in the late 1960s, the rapid expansion of universities, the Royal Commission on the Status of Women, and efforts by Canadian femocrats.[9] Within the context of International Women's Year, 1975, it was risky, but far more legitimate than previously, to participate publicly as women. On behalf of the newly formed Women's Caucus at Saint Mary's and with other women university representatives from Halifax, Linda Christiansen-Ruffman presented a brief to the Canada Council describing the minimal participation rates of women at the Canada Council; discrimination was denied, perhaps not even recognized, by the Chair. In that same year, Lynn McDonald, Susan Clark, and Linda, with contacts around the country, planned a negotiated grant proposal to the Canada Council to produce books on women. The grants officer, however, said that it was premature and that research was needed in the field first. Canada Council did support the national conference held in Halifax in November 1976 entitled "Research on Women: Current Projects and Future Directions." This first major national conference on women's research, also financed by Canada's Employment and Immigration and Secretary of State, mushroomed from a proposed 30 participants to hundreds. Exactly a year later, the Canadian Research Institute for the Advancement of Women (CRIAW) held its first annual conference, and its mandate to promote research by, for, and about women has been instrumental in developing feminist research in Canada. CRIAW conferences have also received some support from Canada Council and its successor, the Social Sciences and Humanities Research Council, but the major granting councils in Canada have a long way to go before fully supporting women's research.

In the Beginning…Initiation of the Women and Work Strategic Grant Program

The 1970s brought a growing awareness in Canada of discrimination against women within academia, of the biases against women in scholarship, and of the need for research by, for, and about women. The CSAA Women's Caucus, one of many status of women organizations, was among those that focused occasionally on the Canada Council and, after 1978, its successor, SSHRC.

"Strategic research" in Canada was initiated in 1978 when the Canadian government granted $10 million of additional funds to the three granting councils for the purpose of carrying out research in areas of national concern; $2 million was allocated to SSHRC. While many CSAA Women's Caucus members, out of concern that political interference would shape the scholarly agenda, outspokenly opposed the new policy-oriented initiative of Strategic Grants, the Caucus and its members also saw potential for a strategic grant focused on women: not only would it increase research on women, but its combined policy and scholarly focus would support new theories and methodologies in Women's Studies and develop feminist praxis.

In identifying strategic themes, the Council consulted "widely" in the research community, including the presidents of all universities, the Canadian Federation for the Humanities, the Social Science Federation of Canada, presidents of all learned societies, and about 75 non-university research institutes and foundations. Because of demographics, few women were actually consulted, but we made our voices heard. From this process, eight broad themes emerged, one of which was Women's Studies. After examining these themes, Council asked the Planning and Evaluation Division to sponsor workshops on four themes, not including Women's Studies. When the Strategic Grants Division was officially created in 1980, it ran programs on three themes: Population Aging, the Human Context of Science and Technology, and Family and the Socialization of Children.

This is only one indicator of the chilly climate for women that characterized SSHRC in its early days. Working within this climate and being pressured by women from outside was Maureen Woodrow, the SSHRC officer who became responsible for the development of *Women and Work*. It was a long planning process that involved a major conference in British Columbia in 1981, then a series of nine regional workshops, and then a meeting of workshop sponsors. In the course of this process, the theme changed from the impact of education on the role of women in the labour force to *Women and the Canadian Labour Force* (the theme of the BC conference), to *Women and the Canadian Economy* (the recommendation of the BC conference), to *Women and Work*. These changed titles were attempts by women and feminists at the time to ensure that the topic was as free as possible of patricentric and androcentric presuppositions and that it did not isolate women's work in the labour force from women's work in the family. Indeed, many feminists were enthusiastic about the potentially innovative research that might be generated by exploring the idea of work from women's experiences and inviting a critical reinterpretation of the concept of work. The successive titles also increasingly favoured multidisciplinary and interdisciplinary collaborative approaches and were seen to allow increasingly for innovative policy and scholarly research. A number of recommendations from the BC conference and the regional workshops were radical at the time although they prefigured later policy initiatives within the Strategic Grant program for interdisciplinary, genuinely collaborative, user-relevant research based on partnerships between academics and non-academics.[11]

The development of the *Women and Work* grant within SSHRC, however, was characterized by caution. At the January 1983 meeting with organizers of regional conferences and SSHRC decision makers, for example, feminist proposals were cast in terms of guidelines for existing strategic themes: those in attendance were strongly supportive of full participation of community-based research groups and private scholars as well as collaboration between university and community based researchers. The minutes report that they recommended that a statement similar to that found in the guidelines for *Family and the Socialization of Children* be used. As part of encouraging interdisciplinarity and fresh approaches to the material of traditional disciplines, scholars in the humanities were to be invited to make proposals by including the paragraph to that effect from another theme's guidelines, *Population Aging*; the 1983 guidelines invited scholars in the humanities to take advantage of the program "through critical studies of history, literature, philosophy, or art." There seemed to be a concerted attempt to avoid any hint of innovative scholarship associated with this theme, to stress how this focus on women would fit in to existing research agendas,[12] and to avoid "rocking the boat." The minutes report that the participants "agreed that Council should adopt a policy of non-sexist research for all of its programs." However, they "ultimately...agreed that it was premature to make a recommendation on the matter at this time."

Despite these cautionary processes, the Women and Work Strategic Grant Program inaugurated in 1983 was consistent with some recommendations from the British Columbia conference and regional workshops. As stated in the 1983–89 Guidelines for the theme:

> The overall objective of the program on *Women and Work* is to foster and encourage research and scholarship which is **non-sexist in language and methodology**...In addition to supporting individual research, the program is designed to encourage the following:
> 1. Cooperation and collaboration of researchers inside or outside the university.
> 2. Projects of a multidisciplinary nature.
> 3. Cooperation and consultation between researchers and organizations which will potentially benefit from the research.
> 4. The compilation, synthesis, and national dissemination of research carried out in different parts of the country.

Despite statements of policy endorsing the humanities, private scholars, and the community, the message about the program was ambiguous. The critical interpretation of the concept of work and its potential for affecting policy envisaged during some of the regional consultations and reflected in the change of name and in the explicit inclusion of the humanities was not encouraged by the concrete list of topics.[13] In fact, humanists read the list as explicitly excluding their concerns. The list disregarded innovative formulations and suggestions from many of the feminist planners, and thereby diminished the theme's analytic potential. Even potentially transformative concepts such as unpaid work were framed in conventional language that did not draw scholars into questions or reflections related to underlying theoretic assumptions, but favoured empirical work within existing (sexist) paradigms. When the Guidelines were revised in 1990 after the Paquet Committee report, they reflected an increasing specificity and focus on work in the paid labour force. The potential for understanding the powerful but unquantifiable "obstacles" created by cultural prohibitions and inhibitions was thereby reduced. The language of "obstacles," "careers," and "contributions" suggested simple problems with simple solutions; it discouraged analysis of systemic biases and intersecting systems of oppression and opportunity.

So What's the Story?

Women and Work had become the longest surviving Strategic Grant Program when in early 1991 Carmen Lambert, first Chair of the Women's Issues Network of the Social Science Federation of Canada, discussed a peer review plan to evaluate this program with senior SSHRC administrators, including Louise Dandurand, and with the Network, representing women from each member professional association. After these discussions, Carmen convinced Linda Christiansen-Ruffman to lead an evaluation team that would include a representative from the Canadian Federation for the Humanities and from Quebec. With Carmen's help, Linda put the team together and then wrote a quick proposal to SSHRC which received a special grant from SSHRC's President, Paule Leduc. The study began in April 1991 and a final report was submitted to SSHRC's Council in April 1992. In 1993, both English and French versions were jointly published as *Women and Work: Feminist Research in Progress* by the Canadian Research Institute for the Advancement of Women (CRIAW), the Social Science Federation of Canada, and the Canadian Federation for the Humanities. One important recommendation for a new theme on Women and Change was implemented.

To better understand the differing assumptions and empirical findings from the sociologists and historians within our team, we developed an analogy of understanding and describing a tomato. One can smell, touch, taste, or look. Each approach gives a different and equally valid sense of the tomato, but each is also incomplete. Slicing the tomato in different ways discloses additional information. Each slice reveals a distinct pattern of seeds and flesh, some with more seeds and some with fewer. It goes almost without saying, as well, that a tomato also looks differently on the vine, in the store, in the salad, or in the spaghetti sauce, and thus its description must be contextualized.

From this point in history, *Women and Work* may be analyzed in many different ways. As with any complex event, various credible stories may be told, depending upon one's framework for analysis.

Women and Work had different faces in different locations. We found, for example, considerable geographic variation in the number of research grant projects funded. Between 1983 and 1991, UQAM with its 21 projects had a high profile as did Laval with 9 projects.[14] The larger anglophone universities — the University of Toronto and the University of British Columbia — each had 8; Queen's University had 6. In contrast, only 11 successful projects came from the Prairies and 8 from the entire Atlantic region.

Besides regional distributions, we also examined the accomplishments of the program and its funded projects. For the purposes of this paper, we have grouped some of our findings under three headings which each give valid characterizations of *Women and Work* from its inception: accomplished success; gains — won and lost; and unaccomplished potential.

Accomplished Success

Women and Work focused research projects and research money toward the study of women and women's experiences. From 1983 to 1991, *Women and Work* awarded 160 research grants,[15] 82 seed grants, 20 research workshop grants, and 3 partnership development grants. Research grants were awarded at an average rate of 18 per year. In 1989, however, the number fell to 9 and in 1990 rose to 26. Over the period studied, $7,736,031 was distributed in the research grant program, $2,099,663 of which was distributed in the 1990 and 1991 competitions.[16] Overall, *Women and Work* supported research projects at an annual average of $859,559, reaching over a million dollars twice (in 1988 and 1990), with a relatively uneven pattern of awards ranging from $642,636 in 1987 to 1.2 million in the following year of 1988 and back to $657,962 in 1989.

Increased Research on Women

The Women and Work grant program itself was extraordinarily successful in increasing research on women. The first year of *Women and Work* resulted in an almost seven-fold increase of projects focused on women or gender within strategic grants and a doubling within SSHRC overall. More specifically, within Strategic Grants, the number of projects focused on women or gender increased from 3 to 53, or from 3.3% to 21.8%, while the overall percentage for all projects within SSHRC increased from 3.8% to 7.5%, (28/729 to 82/1090).

Increased Research by Women

Women and Work was also successful in attracting and supporting women researchers. Within strategic grants, the theme was atypical in that the majority of applicants to all other themes were men. Women were between 2 and 5.4 times more likely to have applied for either strategic research or seed grants under the women and work theme than under other themes: 80.6% of the applicants to *Women and Work* compared to 40% in the *Family and Socialization of Children* and 15% in *Managing the Organization*.[17]

Increased Multidisciplinary/Team Research

Within the objectives of the strategic grant program, *Women and Work* was exceptionally successful. It achieved the organizational objectives of the program both by encouraging team research and multidisciplinary research, and its performance improved over time. Moreover, in both these research areas, *Women and Work* far exceeded the other strategic grant themes. Outstanding performance involving these objectives was empirically found at both the level of the individual research project and the program as a whole.[18]

Importance of a Different Style of Research for Women

Women and Work also had an important and generalized impact on valuing a different style of research that challenged the extant ivory tower mentality. More than scholars in other fields, *Women and Work* researchers saw policy and scholarly objectives, as well as non-sexist research, as interrelated. As the first program within any of the granting councils to focus on women, *Women and Work* also had an important symbolic role in legitimizing research on women. The program assisted in the development of Women's Studies in Canada at a time when there was considerable discrimination against women and women's scholarship within the ranks of academia and in society itself.

    Women and Work symbolically encouraged and financially supported research that would not have been possible at the time in discipline-based committees (and that is still not possible in many of them). It provided financial support for some of the few SSHRC-supported projects in which graduate students participated in research on and about women. Moreover, this program helped Canadian researchers and scholars develop what has rapidly become a dominant field of research and theory in Women's Studies. The program's research results contributed to making a formerly unrecognized segment of Canadian society visible and, in doing so, have valorized women and the multiple forms of work they do.

Gains — Won and Lost

Two major components of *Women and Work* might have been considered achievements — the policy of support for private scholars and the stated objective of non-sexist research. Both had been prominent in the planning stages. Pressure from women within the academy led to the institutionalization of both these policies within *Women and Work* and to some progress more generally within SSHRC. Both initiatives, however, were cancelled shortly before we started research on this evaluative review.

Non-Sexist Research Objective

This strategic grant program on women had an explicit objective of non-sexist research. Generally, the research within *Women and Work* did live up to its non-sexist objective, and, to this extent, the program has made an important contribution to non-sexist scholarship in Canada. From a questionnaire addressed to all researchers who applied to *Women and Work*, we also learned that almost all respondents strongly affirmed the importance of non-sexist research, indicating that they always or almost always conducted their own research in this manner.[19] Nevertheless, the criterion of non-sexist research still had a strong impact within *Women and Work*. Over 30% of the respondents to our questionnaire reported that their research practices were changed in some way by the program's objective of non-sexist research. A number of scholars were enthusiastic about new insights and intellectually invigorated by new realms of scholarship.

Internationally and nationally in comparison with the other granting councils, SSHRC was at the forefront of recognizing the problem of sexist research. The initiation of this strategic area signalled the beginning of SSHRC's attempts to correct the long-term, taken-for-granted sex biases in research.[20] Feminist scholars had lobbied SSHRC to adopt non-sexist policies for all its programs, arguing that sexist and racist biases created bad research and unethical research. Rather than adopt a non-sexist policy, however, SSHRC Council decided to publicize non-sexist research guidelines. They commissioned Margrit Eichler and Jeanne LaPointe to write *On the Treatment of the Sexes in Research* and freely distributed copies to researchers across Canada.

Although some of the discrimination in society and in scholarship which gave rise to non-sexist policies has remained, the utility of and favourable reception to non-sexist policies were not heeded. In 1990, when the objectives of all strategic grants were changed, the objective of non-sexist research could have been added as an overall objective within strategics and, indeed, within SSHRC itself. Instead, the objective of non-sexist research was dropped from *Women and Work*. Its absence gives conflicting signals to potential applicants concerning the mandate of the Council and its commitment to non-sexist values in funding, research, and national public policy.[21]

Support for Private Scholars

The policy of support for private scholars grew out of discussions in Women's Caucuses that recognized the need for support of new Ph.D.s without jobs, many of whom were women, in a time when jobs were scarce. Pressure from women within the academy led to the temporary institutionalization of a policy allowing private scholars to apply directly to SSHRC for funding of research, including stipends.

While the objective of non-sexist research was only implemented within *Women and Work*, the policy of supporting private scholars was implemented across SSHRC programs — and reiterated as an objective at all stages of the development of *Women and Work*. The 1983 guidelines for *Women and Work* explicitly stated that the program was "open to researchers outside the university community as well as to university-based scholars." Council has also made special reference to researchers "beyond the university community" in encouraging multidisciplinary approaches.

Private scholars played a comparatively significant role in *Women and Work*.[22] Between 1979 and 1988, the 22 grants to private scholars within *Women and Work* (10 research, 11 seed, and 1 workshop) comprised more than half the 42 grants made to private scholars in all five strategic grant programs during that period. As SSHRC researcher, Robert Hanson (1989:18) commented, only *Women and Work* at 10% is a success.[23]

The program, although more successful than the others, might have been more generous to private scholars, especially in the area of research grants. If we look at another period from 1983 to 1991 in *Women and Work*, only 12 research projects proposed by 8 private scholars won research grants totalling $703,449. This number represents only 8% of the total percentage of successful applicants. Private scholars were better represented among the holders of seed grants: 11 grants or between 14 and 15% of the total. Of course, this accounted for only a very small amount of the funds expended. In their evaluation of applicants, some university-based scholars were intolerant of the more policy-based research designs submitted by private scholars.

Interestingly, none of the private scholars receiving seed grants reappeared as private scholars among the holders of research grants. However, one or two of the same persons reappeared with university affiliations. This is indicative of the fluidity of status among young scholars in difficult economic times and of the fact that seed grants did support the research of unemployed scholars until they got permanent academic positions. The private scholar policy, as well as the non-sexist research objective, also had a significant generalized impact in shaping the research conducted under the program in important policy-oriented directions. For example, private scholars were likely to be especially supportive of the policy-oriented partnership goals of the Strategic Grant Program. In 1983, the only private scholar to receive a grant also had a formal partnership with the Economic Council of Canada, 1 of only 2 formal partnerships; in 1984, 2 of the 3 successful private scholars arranged the only 2 formal partnerships: 1 with the Canadian Labour Congress and the other with the Vancouver Centennial Bibliographic Project.

Ironically, given the recent decision to eliminate funding for private scholars, the research undertaken by the successful private scholars was important in terms of its subject matter as well as its scholarly production. For instance, private scholars received 1 of only 9 grants awarded for projects focusing on pink-collar work and 1 of only 3 grants for projects on the important subject of the impact of new technology, specifically computerization of clerical work, in this "feminine" sector. In 1986, 1988, and 1990, another private researcher received 3 of only 10 grants given to study unions and unionization.

The tight economic and job situation within universities has forced some researchers into the position of private scholar. If the situation has been hard for all private scholars, it has been particularly difficult for women because of the persistence of systemic, cultural, and structural factors, including lack of affordable daycare and restricted mobility resulting from family obligations that make it more difficult for them to get regular appointments. Nevertheless, in 1991, the private scholars policy was cancelled, partly because it was unique to SSHRC among granting councils and partly as a cost-cutting measure. When challenged about this restrictive, sexist, and elitist policy, senior staff at SSHRC argued that private scholars could easily affiliate with universities as adjunct professors for grant submissions. Factors unique to women such as the chilly climate and resistance of old boys' networks to feminist scholarship, as well as the more significant effect of this policy on female scholars, were ignored in this policy change.

Unaccomplished Potential

In its subject matter and conceptual frameworks, its organization of research and its contribution to Women's Studies, *Women and Work* was not as creative as it might have been. Its feminist potential was never realized and researchers who worked for its development still harbour unaccomplished dreams.

The Subject Matter

Rather than emphasizing conceptual and methodological innovation and developing feminist knowledge, the subject matter of the research in *Women and Work* tended to reproduce the mainstream, male-conceptualized world of work. As demonstrated by the qualitative review of subjects funded during the period from 1983 to 1991, over two-thirds of the projects studied specific occupations.[24] This focus on occupations was consistent with the proposed topic of various kinds of women's work in the guidelines from 1983 to 1989 and the even more particular reference to women's careers and career patterns in the 1990–1991 guidelines.

Not only was the occupational focus on paid work; it also favoured women in traditionally male occupations. Nearly twice as many projects examined women's non-traditional jobs compared to conventionally feminine jobs or occupations (60 versus 34). More research could have been funded on the so-called "caring professions"[25] and on traditional "pink-collar" and service occupations where women are concentrated in the labour force.[26] *Women and Work* missed the opportunity to reassess the social, cultural, economic, and political dimensions of occupations and professions where women have accumulated knowledge and experience. Such women-centered research would have been especially important in adding the standpoint of women's occupations to the scholarly literature.

Researchers planning for *Women and Work* had developed innovative and challenging conceptions of the content of the theme, especially the nature of work, and of the collaborative and community-based ways in which research might be organized in the newly emerging discipline of Women's Studies. These were slow in being picked up because the program and its research agenda were defined in more traditional terms than had been envisaged by feminist planners. In addition, this feminist understanding of the program's potential was not necessarily shared by SSHRC staff, by scholars to whom SSHRC staff sent projects for assessment, or by members on the adjudication committees; they tended to apply standards consistent with their well established disciplines rather than one that was quickly growing, needed to draw on fresh insights, was multidisciplinary, had a policy orientation, and embraced a changing conceptual framework. More innovative and qualitative projects were apt to receive mixed reviews. Moreover, pressures were felt by some scholars and committees to legitimize the newly emerging field according to traditional, "objective scholarly" criteria.

Given the orientation of many research projects to quantitative research and measurement, it is surprising that no projects were geared to the design of non-sexist measurements for use in the Census and in national accounts.[27] Such studies would clearly have been appropriate to the scholarly and policy goals of *Women and Work*. They would have corrected some of the legacy of distortions that remain because sexist concepts formed the basis for scientific measurements in the past.

Despite the explicit interest in Aboriginal and rural women while planning this strategic grant program, minority women were under represented among the funded topics. Only two studies privileged immigrant women (Labelle 1983 and Giles 1991) or First Nation women (Lange 1984 and 1985). Only one privileged the experiences and strategies of women with disabilities in the workplace (Dyck 1991). Bakan's (1991) study of women and citizenship focused on women of colour. Some better way must be found to encourage research on different ethnic, class, racial, and cultural groups so that research does not so clearly replicate the prestige structure of society.

The anticipated policy research for the advancement of women also failed to materialize. We were perplexed by the relative inattention among funded projects to critically important policy issues. Daycare was considered in several successful research grant applications, but formed the core of none. Almost as surprising is the fact that only one successful project focused on sexual harassment (Smith 1990), taxation (Lahey 1986), and pensions (Black 1986).[28] The relative absence of policy studies in important areas was confirmed by another analysis comparing major research themes in funded and non-funded research projects between 1987 and 1991. We found that policy projects were unlikely to be submitted. Of the 13 topics identified, studies of (1) social inequality and (2) social policies, including employment equity programs, accounted for only 17 and 15 projects respectively, for a total of 32 out of the 254 submissions during this time period, less than 4%. Even more startling, however, is their lower acceptance rate. Only 4 of the 17 projects on inequality were approved and only 5 of 15 projects on social policy. In these two topic areas with the clearest focus on policy, 72% of the projects submitted did not receive funding compared with an overall rejection rate of 55%. These data on project themes also confirm the dominant focus on occupations and are another indicator of the way in which the description of topics has limited the scope of

Women and Work. The discovery of such an imbalance in a strategic grants program should stimulate thought about ways of generating and evaluating more innovative and critical projects.

Partnerships

Both the planners and the strategic grant guidelines promoted "partnerships," and we expected to find many partnership projects. We were surprised. Only five formal partnerships can be found among the funded research grant recipients in the first seven years. After the guidelines changed to give more weight to partnerships, the numbers jumped to six in both 1990 and 1991 (over 23% of all the successful recipients in those years). Before 1990, the partners included the Women's Skills Development Corporation in Vancouver, the Canadian Labour Congress, and the Vancouver Centennial Bibliographic Project. After 1990, partners were the Law Society of BC, a Ministry of Social Affairs, a multiple sclerosis clinic, the Canadian Congress for Learning Opportunities for Women, and Hydro Québec.[29]

Partnerships were supposed to encourage policy relevant research outside the university, but the Vancouver based Women's Research Centre experienced SSHRC's unwillingness to support projects based in groups outside the "academy." The Women's Research Centre applied for a national working session on alternatives to job evaluation based pay equity — a subject virtually unexplored in the research grants. Women across the country in women's groups, unions, government, and academic institutions had endorsed the need for such a session, and the Centre was well suited to develop background research, given its previous study and publication on the subject. Still, SSHRC rejected the application because it interpreted the funding guidelines to exclude projects falling within the "existing mandate" of the Centre. While this interpretation was technically correct, the Centre could not afford to mount the conference. The relatively poor financial resources of this potential partner meant that this valuable research was not done; we lost the unique contribution of knowledge only available from the perspective of the community.

The contradictory dimensions of the idea of partnership were a frequent source of discussion during the review process. From many quarters, there was strong support for the concept of collaborative research relationships between academics and women's groups. In such discussions, concern was expressed about the financial component now explicit in the SSHRC guidelines, since most women's groups do not have the financial ability to contribute. Given this criteria, researchers expressed concern that their proposed studies with women's groups might be judged less important than those with well-funded organizations. Some focus groups recommended that SSHRC drop the explicit reference to financial resources and recognize the contribution of groups in terms of their knowledge and experience. Researchers were reluctant to go through the process of developing a working partnership and building expectations and trust unless there was a relatively good chance of receiving funding. As one potential applicant explained:

> I considered working with a group, but… I figured that I had a better chance doing the project alone, despite the formal criteria of partnerships. Everyone knows that the partnership idea is to bring in money. This project would take rather than give to the slim resources of this group.

Those familiar with the incredibly scarce financial resources of women's groups, the busy agendas, and difficult work of such groups, recommended that groups should not have to invest money to pay for their collaboration. Feminist research models promote a non-hierarchical, non-exploitative, egalitarian relationship between researchers and research collaborators, and several current features of the SSHRC guidelines and process were seen to undermine this relationship. Some feminist researchers noted a problem with SSHRC's concept of the ownership of intellectual property, a concept that grants the rights of cultural interpretation and ownership of intellectual property to the researcher. This leads to cultural appropriation and violates the collaborative arrangement necessary for a true partnership. Another problem with the relationship between researchers and women's community members is the imbalance in power relationships and the potential for the time, agenda, and scarce resources of community groups to be exploited by researchers. Historically, this has been a problem with research on marginal and relatively powerless groups, a problem that has contributed to a public suspicion of researchers in some communities. For example, in Labrador and Northern Canada, specific research protocols were developed to protect the needs of local people and prevent exploitation of their resources and culture by outside researchers. One creative solution for this problem would be to allocate funds for the use of community groups to hire the researchers they think they need to address their policy needs. If SSHRC encourages partnerships with disadvantaged groups, it is imperative that there be protection against entrepreneurial researchers infringing on the rights of local communities.

In light of these considerations, we recommended:

> That several types of partnerships henceforth be recognized and that one type be designed for community-initiated projects and community-needs assessments. Community-based partnerships should be designed to acknowledge the

contribution and expertise of community-based partners in the creation of new knowledge and to avoid relationships that drain resources from community-based groups. A special fund for partnerships with community-based groups should be established that would allow researchers to buy the time of community-based staff or volunteers so that they could participate as full members of the research team without negatively affecting the work of the community group.

We also cited the UQAM/Relais-Femmes protocol as an interesting example of collaboration between universities and women's groups. It encourages "action-oriented" research, premised on the assumption that interaction between the parties concerned contributes to the analysis and eventual solution of real socio-economic and cultural problems that preoccupy the participants. Relais-Femmes is an umbrella organization bringing together the majority of women's federations and associations in Québec on the basis of their communication, education, and research needs. It signed a protocol with UQAM in 1982 with the explicit objective of making "certain human and technical university resources, especially in the areas of non-credit instruction, research, and consultation accessible to Relais-femmes and its members." This agreement provides a unique channel through which women's groups gain access to university-based resources, on the one hand, and researchers gain access to the activities of women's groups, on the other.

Innovative Methodologies

As described above, *Women and Work* was more successful than other strategic grant themes and research grant guidelines in developing a collaborative, multidisciplinary team approach to research. Some scholars, however, criticized *Women and Work* for promoting only one research model, a quantitative approach based in the physical sciences.[30] Feminists felt that their methodologies and innovative approaches to knowledge creation were, by and large, discouraged. Some feminist applicants wrote projects in traditional, positivist terms in order to receive funding. This practice led to distortions in feminist knowledge creation, discouraged feminist substantive and methodological innovation, and undermined the feminist planners' vision for this strategic grant program.

The challenge for SSHRC is to acknowledge and foster diversity in its policies and to appreciate fully that real differences exist in research models and paradigms. Policies designed to perpetuate the hegemony of patriarchal knowledge refuse to accept diversity and lead to decisions that allocate resources unwisely and unfairly. Consistent application of decision-making to unequivalent conditions undermines rather than maximizes the skills and interests of researchers working under diverse conditions and within divergent intellectual frameworks. Social sciences and humanities within contemporary Canadian society are too diverse for one model. Yet, within the present context of limited resources, it is all too easy to seek solutions to identified problems by increasing consistency and favouring one model rather than inventing policy and program solutions cognizant of excellence in its diverse forms. For example, although the guidelines foreshadowed an alternative research model promoting knowledge discovery through the interaction of scholars and community partners, assessors favoured standard research proposals aimed at measuring variables and testing hypotheses in the quantitative scholarly tradition, a tradition in which a partner has nothing to contribute except money.

Women's Studies/Feminist Research

Women and Work played an important role in shifting research resources to the study of women and in providing symbolic legitimation for this field of study. Although Women's Studies scholars and feminist researchers were instrumental in the definitional stage, their vision was not taken up by the new program. Throughout the 1980s, while the two grew together, mutually reinforcing each other in many ways,[31] they also grew apart. Innovative projects were not encouraged by guidelines and were actively discouraged by adjudication committees. Well known feminist scholars, including some of the best known researchers in the field of women and work, had their applications rejected. Knowledge of such decisions dampened enthusiasm for the program.

What might have been a supportive relationship between *Women and Work* and Women's Studies does not seem to have worked out in practice. The policy guideline on non-sexist research was dropped rather than expanded. Assessors and members of adjudication committees did not necessarily have knowledge and expertise in Women's Studies/ feminist research. High-quality and innovative studies from the perspective of Women's Studies/feminist research were often rejected because they did not fit the mould; their qualitative objectives and methodologies were not valued by researchers guided by positivist paradigms and assumptions of quantitatively-oriented disciplines.

We were initially surprised by the concerns about SSHRC's reception of feminist scholarship during the consultative part of the Review. Women's Studies scholars reported that they felt that self-censoring was necessary in order to respond appropriately to what they perceived to be Council staff and committee members who preferred traditional disciplines to Women's Studies. The questionnaire confirmed that one-third of the successful women applicants (one-quarter of the sample) considered it prudent to reformulate their research proposal so that their feminist perspective would not be as explicit or evident. This perceived and actual institutionalized threat to the academic freedom of Women's Studies scholars and feminist researchers is an on-going problem.

Women and Work might have been used to contribute to the infrastructural development of Women's Studies in Canada during the 1980s. The program's objectives could have fostered this developmental support; two of the three consistently stated objectives of the Strategic Grants Program were as follows:

- to support areas where the research capacity is currently limited and requires special stimulus for development;
- to improve the capacity for research in Canada through support of the infrastructure for that research.

As well, there were precedents for stimulating special types of research and supporting the infrastructural development of special fields. The first strategic theme on aging did receive special infrastructural support for research centres and infrastructural development. Extra resources and programs supporting infrastructural development were also part of the other Strategic Grant Program established in the same year as *Women and Work*, guidelines for *Managing the Organization in Canada* included a special type of grant, Research Initiatives, that provided up to $75,000 "for projects on any aspect of Management or Administration which do not fit within the provisions of the programs defined, but which fall within the terms of reference of the Council." The lack of needed infrastructural development within Women's Studies was a lost opportunity.[32]

SSHRC did not give resources to Women's Studies nor contribute to its development.[33] Despite widespread support for this emerging field of study,[34] SSHRC has still not even recognized its existence. It was not persuaded by our study to do so. Our recommendation of a Women's Studies Research Committee would have enabled research begun under *Women and Work* to continue its development.[35] It would have prevented the patricentric paradigms of existing disciplines from stunting the growth and distorting the development of this newly emerging field and its innovative methodologies. A separate field of scholarship is needed to counter the strength and power of patriarchal knowledge and to prevent an undermining of research by, for, and about women. We note, for example, the ease with which Women's Studies can become appropriated as Gender Studies and then transposed to produce an androcentric perspective on gendered roles.

The recommendation for a separate body of Women's Studies knowledge is sometimes construed as a segregationist position in opposition to an integrationist position, or mainstreaming that sees the incorporation of a perspective on women as necessary in every discipline. The frequency with which this debate is raised is an indicator of the dominance of the either/or syndrome in contemporary consciousness. The fruitlessness of debating this false dichotomy is clear when we recognize the importance, and interdependence, of both the need for a concentrated and focused field of Women's Studies and the need for this topic and developing perspective to enter all disciplines. Successful incorporation of women into contemporary scholarship requires a field of Women's Studies to create, gradually, a more well rounded understanding of society and to minimize the dominant patricentric approach to all knowledge in this patriarchal world. The minuscule amount of research focused on women needs to be expanded across the broad spectrum of areas and programs.

In this spirit and with this understanding, delegates to the symposium on "Women, Research and Strategies," held October 18 and 19, 1991, were united in presenting a package of interdependent motions. The Review Team joins the executives of the Social Science Federation of Canada and the Canadian Federation for the Humanities in endorsing this set of recommendations:

- that Women's Studies/Études féministes be recognized as a discipline by SSHRC and have a place among the discipline committees;
- that in the Strategic Grants Program a specific theme on women be maintained and defined in order to focus on women's perspectives in the organization and institutionalization of knowledge;
- that all strategic themes include pertinent reference to women;
- that discipline committees recognize and encourage feminist scholarship within the disciplines and that SSHRC monitor these committees for that recognition and encouragement.

It is incumbent upon Women's Studies scholars to work toward these goals and to do the monitoring as well. The failure to implement all but the second of these components, either during the last decade or as a result of our report, points to the unfinished nature of this story.

The End/Beginning of this Unfinished Story

The end of the Women and Work Strategic Grant Program was announced after our report was tabled in Spring 1992. And the end became the beginning of the new strategic grant program, *Women and Change.* The story of *Women and Work* turned out to be only the first chapter in a continuing saga of feminist research and scholarly activity. The future of this unfinished story will be formed in part by the staff and senior management in the major granting council for the social sciences and humanities. Their decisions in naming assessors and forming adjudication committees will shape the story. Decisions by these groups and projects submitted by Canadian researchers will form its new character. Time will tell how its future will be built by feminist academics in Canada and framed by our colleagues within the women's movement around the globe.

Endnotes

1.   The first draft of this paper was written for presentation at the Canadian Sociology and Anthropology Association meetings in Ottawa, June 4, 1993. It is based on research funded by SSHRC and submitted as a Report to SSHRC in April 1992. A slightly modified version of the report has been published by the Social Science Federation of Canada, the Canadian Research Institute for the Advancement of Women, and the Canadian Federation for the Humanities in 1993 in both English and French. The English title is *Women and Work: Feminist Research in Progress.* For further information about this research, please contact Linda Christiansen-Ruffman, Department of Sociology, Saint Mary's University, Halifax, Nova Scotia, B3H 3C3.

2.   It is true that some empirical researchers such as Paul Lazarsfeld insisted that "sex" (or what we would now call "gender") was a basic socio-economic or demographic variable and that it should be included on all questionnaires, but the dominant theoretical paradigms provided no sets of questions or analysis. The few times that male and female roles were examined, they reproduced the sexual stereotypes that helped to maintain patriarchy and women's inferior position in society.

3.   This article was first published in the *Monthly Review*, XXI (New York, September 1969, 13-27.). It was widely circulated in mimeographed form, and in readers (e.g., pages 119-128 of Nona Glazer-Malbin and Helen Youngelson Waehrer (eds.), *Women In a Man-Made World*, Chicago: Rand McNally, 1972). It is also mentioned as such in the opening pages of the Royal Commission on the Status of Women, chaired by Florence Bird and published in 1970.

4.   The first edition was published in 1973 by New Press, Toronto, and the second, revised edition in 1977. The editor was not rewarded by the university system for her pioneer work in academia. In a much publicized case, she was denied tenure by McMaster University, despite strong support from the Canadian Sociology and Anthropology Association and feminist scholars. She left academia.

5.   Most people do not realize the power of the taken-for-granted societal assumptions. In a 1996 book written to celebrate twenty years of the Canadian Research Institute for the Advancement of Women, we have tried to describe the context as well as what it felt like being in different "times."

6.   Support for Canadian research is administered through one of three granting Councils: SSHRC, MRC, and NSERC (Social Sciences and Humanities Research Council, Medical Research Council and National Sciences and Engineering Research Council). Canada Council supports the Arts. While tradition in these councils differs slightly, each is based on a peer-review assessment of research projects, submitted by qualified scholars, almost all of whom have Ph.D.s and hold university positions. The requested funds support specified research costs. Because funds are very limited, the process is highly competitive. It is based on "peer review" and is carried out in the following manner: Researchers submit detailed proposals by annual deadlines through their respective universities. The proposals are sent for evaluation by assessors identified by SSHRC staff for their expertise. The proposal and assessments from at least two scholars are then sent to members of an adjudication committee, also comprised

of "peers" selected by SSHRC staff who meet to decide how the limited budgets will be distributed among the applicants.

7. For a discussion of the patricentric nature of scholarship, see Linda Christiansen-Ruffman, "Inherited Biases Within Feminism: The 'Patricentric Syndrome' and the 'Either/Or Syndrome' in Sociology," in Angela Miles and Geraldine Finn, *Feminism: From Pressure to Politics*, Montreal: Black Rose Press, 123-145, 1989.

8. When women were considered, they were primarily discussed as exceptions or deviants. They were not subjects of research.

9. In response to the Royal Commission and the Women's Movement, women friendly bureaucrats (femocrats) prepared for the United Nations decade on women, which officially began with International Women's Year in 1975. They influenced public policy to achieve official recognition of Canada's need to improve the status of women. Governmental mechanisms were created to work toward that objective (e.g., Secretary of State Women's Program, Advisory Council on the Status of Women, Status of Women Canada), and all departments of government were supposed to be dedicated to this goal. Although there have been many problems with state sponsored status of women's efforts, they have been significant in Canada as well as in Australia where the concept of femocrats was developed by Hester Eisenstein. See her paper "The Australian Femocratic Experiment: A Feminist Case for Bureaucracy," pp. 69-83 in *Feminist Organizations: Harvest of the New Women's Movement*, edited by Patricia Yancey Martin and Myra Marx Ferree, Philadelphia: Temple University Press, 1995. See also *Resources for Feminist Research* 17(3), 1988 for a Canadian commentary.

10. For a history of the CSAA Women's Caucus, see Janice Drakich and Eleanor Maticka-Tyndale, "Feminist Organizing in the Academic Disciplines: The Canadian Sociology and Anthropology Association," in Jeri Wine and Janice Ristock (eds.) *Social Change, Feminist Women and Activism in Canada.* Toronto: James Lorimer, pp. 283-98, 1991 and Eleanor Maticka-Tyndale and Janice Drakich, " Striking a Balance: Women Organizing for Change in the CSAA" in William K. Carroll, Linda Christiansen-Ruffman, Raymond F. Currie and Deborah Harrison (eds.) *Fragile Truths: Twenty-Five Years of Sociology and Anthropology in Canada.* Ottawa: Carleton University Press, 1992.

11. It was seven years later, however, as a result of the Paquet Report and the Focus on Strategics, that these suggestions were more fully translated into program guidelines.

12. The minutes record the following policy concerns about women's equality and interest in specifying that diversity that was also on Council's agenda at the time: "There could be no doubt that the research arising from the theme would need to affect in a meaningful way the formulation of social policy to equalize treatment between the sexes in both the short and long terms. The research would, in addition, need to be empirical in nature and regional in emphasis, there being a need within each region to address the status and problems not only of the urban but also of the rural and native women" (Minutes, Women and Work Program Development, Ottawa, January 24, 1983).

13. The 1983 Guidelines contain the following list of suggested topics: the status of different kinds of paid or unpaid work done by women within the formal or informal economic structure (e.g., barriers to equality of opportunity and to equality of rewards); the structure and process of change in the labour force; the effects of current social security, unemployment insurance, and other work-related policies on women; women in trade unions and other work-based organizations; women and new technologies; and educational choices made by women. This list of topics resembles the earlier ones from the BC conference and regional workshops. When the Guidelines were changed in 1990, a number of specific topics remained such as the structure and process of change in the labour force, the effects of work-related public policy on women, and women in trade unions. However, the guidelines became more focused on occupations, more concrete and less analytic than envisioned in the planning process. The structural and institutional focus of the BC formulation had become

even more individualistic. For example, even under the 1983-89 Guidelines, the topic of "educational choices made by women" put more stress on individual choices than the conference sub-theme of how education mediates women's relationship to the labour force through streaming and policies. In the reformulation, the injunction to consider the impact of structures on individuals had been lost as had the complexity of the social processes. One consequence of this loss was the missed opportunity for the kind of research that humanists do best. Another overlapping consequence of this loss was that the goals of the early planners for truly innovative theorizing and research were not fulfilled.

14. The pre-eminence of these two large Québec universities may reflect greater emphasis on attaining outside funding; it certainly reflects the level of assistance in making applications that is routinely supplied to prospective researchers by the administrations of these universities. But this relatively high degree of success within Québec is certainly also due to the development of multidisciplinary études féministes/women's studies networks and centres. L'IREF at l'UQAM and le GREMF in Laval are well organized multidisciplinary feminist groups that have been important institutional factors in encouraging and facilitating research on this theme. It probably is this same situation that helps account for the fact that 32% of the 160 funded projects were submitted in French.

15. Of the 160 successful applications for research grants, our qualitative review found that 19 of these were, in fact, applications for continuation of funding for previously submitted projects. Although research projects could be supported for up to three years, sometimes applicants asked for only the first phase of a project and other times the committee only awarded one or two years of support. Because of these cases where applicants reapplied for what was essentially the same project, it might be more accurate to think about 141 research projects as having been supported under this granting program over the nine year period.

16. Data furnished to us by the Evaluation and Statistics Division of SSHRC (November 26, 1991) indicate that the total amount awarded over the last two years reached $2,292,410 if network and workshop subventions are included in the calculation.

17. The low participation rates of women in *Managing the Organization in Canada* show that themes do not have to mention men explicitly to be considered by and for men. *Managing the Organization in Canada* supported a higher proportion of male scholars than *Women and Work* did female scholars. This suggests that systemic biases in the organization of knowledge itself still remain to be addressed. (See also Table 3.5 and Figure 2 in Christiansen-Ruffman, Descarries, and Stewart, 1993; *Women and Work: Feminist Research in Progress*, published by the Canadian Research Institute for the Advancement of Women (CRIAW), Social Science Federation of Canada, and Canadian Federation for the Humanities (also in French).)

18. See pp. 78-102 of Christiansen-Ruffman, Descarries, and Stewart, 1993.

19. The review of the applicant files did not generally find a problem with sexist research. Nevertheless, there were some exceptions. One project funded under the program, for example, submitted an article that mentioned receiving SSHRC funding but made no mention of women in the article's summary of findings. Other grant holders were told by assessors and occasionally by committee members to include males in their data set, even though their studies were not intended to be comparative. The insistence on comparing women with men has the consequence of continuing the practice of treating male activities as the norm and not taking women's standpoints and experiences seriously. It continues a sex bias in research and points to the importance of research funded under *Women and Work* and under targeted funding that make women central rather than incidental to all phases of the research.

20. It is not a good idea to force either men or women to study a particular gender if they have no interest in doing so, but it is important to recognize that such decisions

taken together result in bias as in the case of patricentrism (see endnote 7). In a bizarre twist in the late 1980s, a few feminists were accused of bias because they focused only on women. In research, it is important that scholars do not use biased concepts and procedures and do not generalize beyond their empirical base. Scholarship that offers an exclusive focus on women, however, is *not* sexist given the historical trend in scholarly research to assume that only men, and not women, were the only category of person worthy of study. In fact, considerable scholarly attention directed solely at women and their diverse experiences is needed to redress distortions created by the centering of both scholarship and society around men in the past. In fact, to correct the past, some feminist researchers suggested that strategic grants programs should fund only research from the perspective of women and other minority groups for a 25 year period.

21.   Among the dominant ideas that animate Canadian public policy is its continued commitment to equity and fairness. This ideal has yet to be realized fully in part because this idea continually competes with other dominant ideas and values that are central to Canadian public policy such as liberty of the individual. In the scholarly world, some people falsely claim that non-sexist research infringes on academic freedom. Clearly the features of non-sexist research that argue against biased concepts and imprecise inferences are simply good scholarship. As Bruce G. Doern and Richard W. Phidd, (Canadian Public Policy: Ideas, Structure, Process: Toronto, Nelson, 1988, p. 55.) note *"The idea of equity enjoins policy administrators to treat people in equivalent situation equally and to treat people who are not in equivalent situations unequally (that is to be fair and reasonable)"*. The added emphasis is the writers'. The immediately apparent incompatibility between the two injunctions is not necessarily a source of irresolvable conflict. As Phidd and Doern, two of the most highly respected analysts in Canadian public policy note, there is a creative tension here that is consistent in its own way with the competing demands of public policy. The idea of "creative tension" in public policy is discussed by Richard Simeon.

22.   Between 1979 and 1988, *Managing the Organization in Canada* funded no private scholars; *Population Aging* supported only one such project. Both *Family and the Socialization of Children and Education and Work in a Changing Society* awarded approximately 6% of their grants to private scholars while *Women and Work* gave 11.8% of its awards to private scholars.

23.   See Tables A-1 to A-6 and Table 7 of Hanson, 1989. *Human Context of Science and Technology* had 6 awards or 3.5% of its successful applications. The absolute numbers for *Family and The Socialization of Children and Education and Work* were 8 and 5 respectively.

24.   A qualitative review of 157 successful research grant files funded by *Women and Work* found 138 were new or significantly revised projects. The remaining 19 were new applications for second- or third-year support for the same project. Of the 138 research grant files, 94 address specific occupations in the paid labour force.

25.   One workshop was funded in 1985 with a focus on "Women in Women's Work: a study of the work environment of women in the Health Care Field" (Callahan). Applications in the 1992 competition began to address this area. There were 6 projects on nursing and 6 projects on caring in this competition.

26.   As the gender-typed label indicates, these jobs employ more women and are gender-typed as being feminine; yet they were the subject of only nine projects. The topics covered were secretarial careers (Clark 1983); the double load of clerical workers (Hessing 1986); the computerization of clerical work (White 1987); working knowledge and technology in office and housework (Meissner 1988); unions, information technology, and clerical workers (Glenday 1990); the consequences of union activism and leadership among bank workers (Baker 1991); and negotiating gendered jobs, a case study of the Office and Technical Employees Union at B.C.

Hydro (Creese 1991). Given the profound changes occurring in clerical work, the paucity of studies of this ongoing process is disheartening, as is the complete absence of studies on the rapidly changing retail sales sector.

27.   The Canadian Census, prior to 1996, did not take account of work that was unpaid. Unpaid work was not considered important enough to be counted. In 1991, the questionnaire asked: "Last week how many hours did you work (not including volunteer work, housework, home repairs)?" Imagine Terry, whose activities in a week included 14 hours a day raising children, several hours of volunteer work in the community, and time spent painting the garage. However, Terry must answer, "I did no work," meaning merely that she did no paid work of the sort that is socially valued enough to find its way onto a Census questionnaire. The 1991 Census had no place to record unpaid but productive and regular work that contributes to the Canadian economy. In the Census based conception of work, unpaid work simply does not count as work. Occasional and potentially cost saving community work such as shopping for a disabled neighbour, bathing a sick parent, circulating a petition, baking a donation for the school fair in order to raise money for a new computer, answering a questionnaire for town planners, or mediating a disagreement between neighbours so as to avoid resort to the police and courts are all examples of activities that are *not* work, according to standard measures of productive activity. Such activities are therefore not considered important to society. Not taking into account the long hours of unpaid work done by women and ignoring the economic, political, health, and social service consequences of women's unpaid work seriously distorts socio-economic analysis and policy development in Canadian society. (The PEI Ad Hoc Committee on the 1991 Census pointed out the shortcomings, and the example of Terry has been taken from their literature). Unpaid work will be covered in the 1996 census.

28.   Slightly more notice was given to employment equity in the mid 1980s (Agocs 1985; Harvey 1985; Harvey 1988) and to unemployment and UIC (the subject of three studies: Guberman 1983 and Pierson 1984 and 1986). Although almost every study considered women's earnings, after the first two years, it was never the pivotal concern (Cannings 1983 and 1984; Stelcner 1983). Double standards in systems of pay evaluation was the topic of only one research grant project (Foschi 1988), while pay equity was the topic of three such projects in the later years of the program (Warskett 1987; McDermot 1990; Pujol 1990).

29.   Fifteen project summaries mention informal collaborations with women's groups as diverse as the La Leche League, the Women's Press Club, the Women's Engineering Association, the Fédération des Agricultrices du Québec, and the Jewish Women's Business and Professional Club, as well as with unions and women's employment directorates. Collaboration took various forms, from opening up archives, membership lists, and meetings to scholars, to joint projects such as setting up local history exhibits and participatory theatre about issues identified by working women.

30.   This was exacerbated because universities began to equate the amount of grant money with scholarly excellence. In reaction, some scholars argued that such large scale projects were contradictory to important theoretic and scholarly work. They worried about distortions in the research agenda and about the equation of research excellence with criteria adopted from a mature science and from physical and natural sciences. Adopting a natural science model is especially problematic without the financial resources to support such a model, and such a model does not adequately appreciate the importance of creative and critical thinking. This type of argument ignores the real need for supporting a variety of research styles and models. The importance of diversity in research styles and models needs to be stressed.

31.   Although only five research projects were funded to principal investigators in Women's Studies departments, a large majority cited literature from the area of Women's Studies and feminist research in their research proposals. From our

questionnaire, we found that 41% of the sample identified the research they do in the women and work area as being within the field of women's studies.

32. Perhaps the difference between *Women and Work* and these other two fields lies in the fact that both the fields of aging and business were more developed and were already receiving money for policy research from other sources. With strong political support for these areas with allies within SSHRC, and with their existing resources, researchers in these fields were able to mobilize in order to ask for these needed research centres and other infrastructural development. Perhaps researchers in Women's Studies did not feel entitled to ask SSHRC for the needed infrastructural help, and SSHRC did not seize the opportunity to develop the infrastructure necessary to allow the newly emerging discipline of Women's Studies to flourish. For example, suggestions from the British Columbia conference to involve research organizations such as CRIAW, Relais Femmes, and the Vancouver Women's Research Centre were not pursued: there was no concerted effort to support the growth of new research centres within the *Women and Work* framework. Although one research centre at UQAM has been helped considerably by its researchers utilizing *Women and Work*, women's research centres remain resource poor and have not been able to develop the critical mass of scholars and resources necessary for significant long-term growth.

33. During the 1980s, the Canadian Women's Studies Association was established and grew. It received SSHRC funding from a program supporting professional organizations. Funds were used to support participation at executive meetings and at the Learned Societies. This funding, however, was withdrawn in the early 1990s.

34. For example, most universities have Women's Studies courses and programs. The findings of Smith's Commission of Inquiry on Canadian University Education urged continued encouragement for Women's Studies. The granting councils have a pivotal role to play within Canada in pursuing the intent of Smith's recommendation. As part of our research, we found that considerable support for formal recognition of Women's Studies exists within the Canadian scholarly community. Most universities have departments and programs of Women's Studies, and the Aid to Scholarly Publications has recognized this field. Several of the focus groups and organizations such as CRIAW made formal representation to the Review Team concerning the importance of establishing a disciplinary committee in Women's Studies. A number of scholars who have sat on disciplinary adjudication committees in SSHRC have become especially strong advocates for such a committee. At the colloquium held with members from the social sciences, the humanities and the policy-making communities, there was overwhelming support for this resolution. The executives of both the Social Sciences and the Humanities Federations have endorsed it as well.

35. Our analysis of disciplines points to some possibility of research support for some types of women and work research in the disciplinary fields of sociology, psychology, and history. However, it is our view that a large amount of excellent scholarship that has begun under *Women and Work*, especially in the field of women's studies, needs a place to continue to grow. One of our major recommendations, therefore, was for the *establishment of a Women's Studies discipline committee as the timely solution to the continuing need for research on women.*

Monique Hébert

Mais où sont-elles?
Fragments de l'histoire des Franco-Manitobaines de 1916 à 1947[1]

Cet article vise à montrer à quel point les institutrices qui ont travaillé dans les écoles franco-manitobaines de 1916 à 1947 ont été présentes pendant tout le temps qu'a duré l'illégalité de l'enseignement du français, période nommée pertinemment «la traversée du désert» (Blay, 1987 : 59). Le gouvernement manitobain cherchait alors à assimiler la population franco-manitobaine au moyen de l'école. Le mouvement d'assimilation visait, il est vrai, non seulement les francophones, mais aussi tout élément non anglophone (Blay, 1987; Leblanc, 1968; Morton, 1967; Taillefer, 1979).

Nous examinerons d'abord brièvement certaines sources écrites pour vérifier la présence des femmes dans les institutions scolaires. Puis, nous présenterons le nombre d'écoles où elles ont enseigné le français et la religion entre 1922 et 1947, et ce malgré l'interdiction. Ensuite, nous verrons que les femmes viennent en tête de liste dans ces institutions. En plus, certaines constatations seront enrichies par les témoignages de 19 «maîtresses d'école», comme on les appelait à l'époque.

Après avoir vu ces caractéristiques, il faudra déterminer dans quelle mesure il y a eu une féminisation de l'éducation dans la communauté franco-manitobaine. Aucune autre étude avant la nôtre n'a tenté de montrer à quel point les femmes étaient présentes dans ces institutions. Il est donc impossible de déceler une évolution quelconque. Chose certaine, les femmes y sont et, en plus, elles y sont en très grand nombre. Cette réalité persiste pendant toute la période étudiée : non seulement elles composent la majorité du corps enseignant, mais elles sont à la tête des écoles. Voilà donc ce que nous entendons par féminisation : les femmes sont présentes dans une proportion telle qu'on pourrait facilement avancer que l'enseignement, dans sa gestion quotidienne, est une histoire de femmes. Les documents et les témoignages cités viendront prouver cette réalité.

Des rapports instructifs

Les rapports des visiteurs de l'Association d'Éducation des Canadiens Français du Manitoba (AÉCFM) ont été utilisés pour décrire la situation dans le monde de l'éducation entre 1922 et 1942. De plus, ils ont fourni

31

les chiffres qui ont permis d'attester la féminisation de la profession enseignante franco-manitobaine durant cette même période. Les visiteurs des écoles étaient des membres du clergé[2] qui se rendaient chaque année dans les écoles fréquentées par des catholiques et des francophones. Ils avaient une tâche fort simple, celle «de voir à la mise en vigueur du programme, de déterminer le progrès des enfants dans leurs connaissances du français, de stimuler les institutrices et les commissaires moins enthousiastes» (Leblanc, 1968 : 44). Afin d'avoir une liste complète des écoles de la province ayant été visitées, il a fallu consulter les rapports de trois années scolaires consécutives (ASHB, 1922 à 1942). En effet, un visiteur prenait trois ans pour se rendre dans toutes les écoles choisies. L'année 1922 marque le début des visites, soit six ans après l'interdiction gouvernementale d'enseigner le français.

Les rapports des visiteurs fourmillent d'informations sur le milieu de travail des enseignantes : salaire, nationalité des élèves, enthousiasme de la population environnante face à l'enseignement du français, etc. À quoi pouvaient servir ces rapports? Tout d'abord, ils étaient écrits pour l'AÉCFM. Le secrétaire de l'organisme en envoyait à chaque président des cercles paroissiaux, membres de l'AÉCFM. On peut facilement supposer leur utilité en lisant ce qu'écrit le visiteur à Woodridge, le 25 octobre 1927 : «il semble que ce soit la meilleure chose à faire, qu'on devrait tâcher de changer cette récente maîtresse avec le moins d'éclat possible» (ASHB, Paroisse Woodridge, 1927). Les rapports pouvaient donc contribuer au renouvellement ou à la résiliation du contrat, comme le confirme d'ailleurs une enseignante de l'époque : «Quand les commissaires cherchaient une nouvelle maîtresse, ils cherchaient les rapports pour savoir comment j'avais fait ça l'année précédente» (MÉ 1[3]). Il est à noter que le caractère oral des entrevues a été respecté dans la transcription afin de préserver la couleur unique du parler (Hébert, 1994 : 26-27). Pour conserver l'anonymat des informatrices, les lettres MÉ, suivies d'un nombre correspondant à l'ordre chronologique des interviews, ont été utilisées pour les identifier.

Nombre d'écoles

Quelle qu'ait été l'utilisation faite alors par les autorités en place, les rapports des visiteurs sont essentiels aujourd'hui, car ils donnent une image de la population enseignante entre 1922 et 1942. Pour la période de 1922 à 1925, le visiteur dénombre 124 écoles où la majorité des élèves est de nationalité canadienne-française et ce, malgré déjà huit ans d'illégalité[3]. Entre 1930 et 1933, il en compte 143[4]. De 1939 à 1942, le visiteur se rend dans 172 écoles où l'on enseigne le français et la religion[5].

Dans les multiples rapports rédigés entre 1922 et 1942, les mots «directrice» ou «directeur d'école» sont rarement employés. Il est toutefois possible de déduire que, lorsque deux femmes enseignent au même endroit, l'une d'elles est responsable de la bonne marche de l'école. Comme vient le confirmer cette remarque d'une enseignante de l'époque : «C'tait moé la boss, mais on était rien'qu'deux» (MÉ 7).

Institutrices en tête de liste

En compilant les rapports des visiteurs, nous voyons qu'en 1922 les femmes dirigent 92 % des écoles visitées. De ce pourcentage, les communautés religieuses en administrent seulement 22 % et les laïques, 70 % (ASHB, 1922-1923). Vingt ans plus tard, on trouve même une légère augmentation : 94 % des écoles visitées par le responsable de l'AÉCFM sont dirigées par des femmes. La proportion de laïques et de religieuses à la direction demeure presque semblable à celle de 1922 : 68 % contre 24 % (ASHSB, 1941-1942). Les femmes constituent donc la quasi-totalité de la population enseignante. Les chiffres parlent d'eux-mêmes : entre 1922 et 1942, l'éducation française au Manitoba est sans équivoque une histoire de femmes!

Il serait maintenant intéressant de voir dans quelle mesure le personnel enseignant est religieux ou laïc. En 1922, moins de 1 % (0,85 %) des enseignantes sont mariées, alors qu'en 1942, ce nombre est de 6 %. Les femmes célibataires composent 47 % de la population enseignante en 1922 et 40 % en 1942. Nous ne pouvons nous empêcher de noter que l'augmentation de 5 % de femmes mariées coïncide avec une réduction de 7 % du nombre de célibataires. La guerre offre-t-elle de nouvelles possibilités d'emplois aux femmes, qui choisissent alors moins l'enseignement?

En 1922, les religieuses constituent 44 % des enseignantes visitées par le responsable de l'AÉCFM (ASHSB, 1922-1923 et 1941-1942). Pour 1942, les proportions sont inversées : 48 % de religieuses contre 44 % de laïques. Quel que soit leur état civil, un fait demeure : les femmes constituent la vaste majorité du personnel enseignant des écoles françaises puisqu'elles en représentent 91 % en 1922 et 94 % en 1942.

Des maîtresses d'école en chair et en os

Pour redonner la parole aux institutrices de l'époque, nous avons interrogé 19 femmes qui ont enseigné entre 1922 et 1947, période de l'illégalité (Hébert, 1994 : 3-6). Le choix de l'histoire orale a été motivé du fait que ces femmes possédaient un savoir irremplaçable. Vu leur grand âge, c'est-à-dire 72 ans et plus, certaines n'étaient déjà plus en mesure de répondre à nos questions. Sans notre compilation, leurs connaissances uniques auraient été perdues à tout jamais puisque peu d'écrits traitent du rôle des maîtresses d'école pendant la période en question. Grâce aux informations recueillies, les générations futures pourront mieux interpréter le passé. Voici un tableau de l'état civil des 19 maîtresses d'école interrogées.

Tableau 1— État civil des informatrices

État civil	Nombre	Pourcentage
Mariées[6]	13	68 %
Religieuses	5	27 %
Célibataires	1	5 %
Total	**19**	**100 %**

La majorité des institutrices interrogées, soit 13 sur 19, se sont mariées et ont dû démissionner pour ce faire. Elles n'auraient pas pu se marier et poursuivre leur carrière. Pourquoi les commissaires ne le permettaient-ils pas? Selon l'informatrice MÉ 6 : «Fallait faire des enfants, chu'pose. Yap. Tsé dans c'temps-là, fallait n'avoir une vingtaine! (Rires)». Toutefois, ce n'est pas seulement la grossesse qui détermine la cessation de l'emploi, mais bien le mariage lui-même. En effet, dans la mentalité de l'époque, une femme doit arrêter de travailler dès qu'elle décide de se marier.

> Ah oui, j'ai dû démissionner parc'que j'étais pour me marier. Là, j'voulais m'marier en 36, pis dans le temps, y prenaient pas d'femmes mariées. Dès qu'on s'mariait, fallait quitter, même si on était pas enceinte. Fallait donner sa démission en juin, même si on se mariait rien'qu'en décembre, pour leur donner l'opportunité de s'trouver une autre enseignante pour septembre, qu'était pour faire l'année, qu'y disaient (MÉ 11).

En fait, seule l'informatrice MÉ 6 a continué à enseigner après son mariage, mais elle a dû le faire dans les écoles allemandes. À la question «Vous avez eu le droit d'enseigner après vous être mariée?», elle répond : «Ben, j'l'ai pris. J'ai pas d'mandé. J'avais du front. Les Canadiens-Français voulaient pas d'maîtresses mariées». Une seule informatrice est restée célibataire, ce qui lui a permis d'enseigner toute sa vie. En moyenne, les informatrices ont enseigné huit ans avant de se marier. La durée de leur carrière a varié entre deux ans et 15 ans. Comme elles doivent démissionner pour se marier, il est possible de supposer un grand roulement de personnel ainsi qu'une population enseignante jeune.

Âge et renouvellement de la population enseignante

Les femmes interviewées ont commencé leur carrière à 19 ans en moyenne. La plus jeune avait 16 ans lors de son premier jour de travail et la plus âgée, 23 ans et demi. Il est assez difficile de déterminer l'âge des enseignantes de la province à partir des rapports des visiteurs de l'AÉCFM. Il est toutefois possible d'y arriver indirectement au moyen de l'année d'obtention du diplôme qui y figure.

Pour l'année scolaire 1922-1923, 66 % des enseignantes laïques ont obtenu leur diplôme entre 1919 et 1923 (ASHSB, 1922-1924). Donc, en grande majorité, elles sont dans les écoles depuis peu. Si nous prenons pour hypothèse qu'elles ont obtenu leur diplôme à 19 ans, comme c'est le cas des informatrices, elles auraient donc entre 19 et 22 ans. Qu'en est-il pour les deux décennies suivantes? Pendant l'année scolaire de 1932-1933, le pourcentage de femmes ayant obtenu leur diplôme quatre années auparavant est moins élevé que durant la décennie précédente, mais il reste tout de même significatif. En effet, plus de 56 % d'entre elles ont obtenu leur diplôme entre 1928 et 1931. Une fois encore, la population enseignante visitée par le responsable de l'AÉCFM est surtout âgée de 19 à 22 ans. Pour les années scolaires de 1939 à 1942, seulement 42 % des laïques ont obtenu leur diplôme durant les quatre années précédentes et sont âgées de 19 à 22 ans. Puisque 29 % d'entre elles l'ont reçu entre 1930 et 1933, nous pouvons conclure qu'elles sont dans la trentaine pendant ces années (ASHSB, 1939-1942). Ce dernier pourcentage signale une transformation. Ainsi, la proportion des enseignantes âgées de 19 à 22 ans tombe de 66 % (1922-1923) à 56 % (1932-1933), puis à 42 % (1939-1942). Ceci semble indiquer un vieillissement de la population enseignante ou une diminution des mariages chez les jeunes filles francophones. Il est aussi possible que les institutrices en poste aient gardé plus longtemps leur emploi parce qu'il y avait moins de jeunes. Mais tout de même, ceci confirme que les laïques devaient démissionner pour se marier, puisque la population enseignante se renouvelle durant les deux premières décennies et que le nombre de recrues reste très élevé durant la dernière décennie.

En ce qui a trait aux religieuses, il est possible de déterminer leur âge pour l'année 1922-1923 seulement. Après cette date, le visiteur omet, en effet, d'écrire l'année d'obtention de leur diplôme (ASHSB, 1931-1932). En 1922-1923, 51 % des religieuses visitées par le responsable de l'AÉCFM ont obtenu leur diplôme entre 1897 et 1910. Encore une fois, si les religieuses ont obtenu leur diplôme à 19 ans, comme les informatrices, elles auraient entre 29 et 45 ans. Elles sont donc plus âgées que les laïques (ASHSB, 1922-1923). Mais les chiffres cités permettent-ils de conclure à une féminisation de la profession?

Féminisation de la profession pour les francophones

À la lumière des données présentées, nous pouvons discerner la spécificité de la féminisation de l'éducation chez les francophones du Manitoba à l'époque de l'illégalité. La première caractéristique réside dans le fait que les femmes forment la presque totalité de la population enseignante. La deuxième est que l'enseignement n'est pas le but de toute une vie pour les femmes. Ce n'est qu'une étape avant d'assumer le rôle social attendu, c'est-à-dire celui d'épouse et de mère. Comme le suggère la journaliste qui écrivait sous le pseudonyme de Mère-Grand dans *La Liberté*, la fonction première des femmes est l'abnégation pour être au service des hommes et de leur progéniture (Hébert, 1994 : 322-326). Étant donné l'obligation pour les enseignantes de démissionner afin de se marier, le personnel enseignant se renouvelle souvent. Les femmes ont donc peu de chances de développer des liens de solidarité et d'acquérir un sentiment d'appartenance au groupe professionnel.

Ce phénomène, troisième caractéristique de la féminisation de l'éducation au Manitoba, peut aussi s'expliquer par le fait que les institutrices travaillent surtout dans des écoles de campagne, donc isolées les unes des autres. Elles ne se rencontrent que deux fois par année, lors de conventions; elles ont donc peu d'occasions qui permettraient le développement d'un sentiment d'appartenance à la profession. Toutefois, ce sentiment est perceptible par rapport au combat pour la survie. Les conventions, nous apprend l'informatrice MÉ 3, «C'était comme un encouragement pour les professeurs de langue française, de s'réunir ensemble, et puis de parler de nos problèmes, d'entendre des discours qui donn'raient un peu de courage». La solidarité était plus facile chez les religieuses : C'était un avantage le couvent. C'était une équipe d'enseignantes. Quoi qu'on avait pas 50 000 réunions comme aujourd'hui (rires). Mais on avait de beaux partages. Les enfants les plus difficiles qu'avaient des problèmes d'apprentissage, [...] on s'demandait comment est-ce que tu t'y prendrais, toi? etchétéra» (MÉ 18) (Hébert, 1994 : 237-242).

Le Bulletin de la Ligue des Institutrices Catholiques de l'Ouest pourrait peut-être servir à faire éclore ce sentiment, mais il devra être analysé sous cet angle avant que nous puissions en tirer des conclusions. D'ailleurs, à l'époque, les femmes percevaient l'enseignement d'abord et avant tout comme une vocation et non comme une carrière. Comme le disait l'une d'entre elles, qui n'est pas restée dans l'enseignement bien longtemps, «C'est par la force des choses que chus dev'nue maîtresse d'école. C'est un accident d'parcours. [...] J'avais pas trop la vâcâtion» (MÉ 12).

Lors des entrevues, nous n'avons pas perçu chez nos informatrices une conscience face à une certaine pédagogie féminine ou féministe.

Elles sont surtout au service de la communauté pour préserver la langue et la foi. Ceci pourrait être, à notre avis, la quatrième caractéristique de la féminisation de l'enseignement pour les francophones du Manitoba. Comme le résume bien l'informatrice MÉ 17 : «J'voulais dire comme Sainte-Thérèse, elle à disait «Moi, j'veux passer mon ciel à faire du bien sur la terre». Moi, j'disais j'veux passer ma vie à garder l'français dans les écoles». D'ailleurs, ne les exhorte-t-on pas à l'abnégation dans _Le Bulletin de la Ligue des Institutrices Catholiques de l'Ouest_ : «Vous êtes institutrices catholiques, des soldats et comme tout soldat, vous devez être prêtes à vous sacrifier pour la cause que vous défendez» (_Le Bulletin_, 1924 : 36). Et la présidente de la Ligue, Madame Houde, de reprendre la notion de combat : «C'est autour de l'école que s'engage tout d'abord la lutte» (_Le Bulletin_, 1941 : 30).

Les institutrices interrogées n'avaient guère de critiques face à leur rôle, sauf en ce qui a trait à la transmission de la langue et de la culture (Hébert, 1994). À cet égard, la très grande majorité sait pertinemment avoir été une courroie essentielle. Ceci représente la cinquième caractéristique de la féminisation de l'éducation. D'ailleurs, l'informatrice MÉ 16 le résume très bien : «J'ai donné tout mon cœur, toute mon énergie et toute la science du français que je connaissais. Je me suis donnée entièrement à la cause».

Conclusion

À partir des données compilées par les visiteurs de l'AÉCFM, il a été possible de trouver le nombre d'écoles où enseignaient les jeunes filles franco-manitobaines entre 1922 à 1942. Malgré la volonté du gouvernement provincial d'assimiler les francophones, il existait beaucoup d'écoles où l'on enseignait le français et la religion. La féminisation de cette institution qu'est l'éducation se manifeste d'abord par la très grande concentration de femmes : au Manitoba français, elles occupent 92 % des postes en 1922 et 94 % en 1947. Par contre, elles n'enseignent que pendant très peu de temps, ce qui favorise difficilement une prise de conscience en tant que groupe professionnel. Ensuite, nos 19 informatrices ont confirmé l'obligation de démissionner pour se marier. Le travail d'enseignante n'est donc qu'une étape avant d'assumer le rôle premier d'épouse et de mère.

D'autres recherches devront être faites sur le développement de la conscience socioprofessionnelle pour la période après 1950. Pendant les deux décennies suivantes, le gouvernement manitobain imposera en effet la centralisation des écoles rurales, ce qui permettra aux enseignantes d'avoir plus de contacts avec leurs collègues. C'est aussi pendant les années 1950 et 1960 que débute la syndicalisation du personnel enseignant et administratif. Là aussi, les femmes ont été actives. Il faudra toutefois attendre la fin des années 1960 pour assister à une prise de conscience de la part des enseignantes face aux rapports de pouvoir pourtant déjà perceptibles dans les chiffres dès le début du siècle.

En ce qui a trait à la féminisation de cette institution au Manitoba français durant la première moitié du XXe siècle, il faut le répéter, sa plus grande caractéristique concerne la très forte présence des femmes. Individuellement, elles y sont pour un court laps de temps, car les autorités en place ne désirent pas de femmes mariées. Cette réalité persiste pendant toute la période étudiée bien que vers la fin, il y ait une légère hausse des effectifs d'enseignantes mariées. Le roulement de personnel ne favorisera certainement pas l'établissement d'une certaine solidarité entre les femmes qui composent le corps enseignant.

Le but du présent article était de corriger la norme de l'historiographie traditionnelle qui a passé sous silence la présence des femmes dans le milieu de l'éducation. Nous laissons à d'autres la tâche d'analyser l'histoire des 20 dernières années où les femmes ont, croyons-nous, perdu un certain contrôle de l'éducation au quotidien, puisque presque toutes les directions des écoles franco-manitobaines sont actuellement occupées par des hommes. Étant donné la présence massive des femmes dans les écoles à l'époque de l'illégalité, il ne sera désormais plus possible de parler de l'éducation franco-manitobaine sans mentionner leur grand rôle. Elles ont été sans conteste «les grandes gardiennes de la langue et de la foi»[7].

Bibliographie

Archives de la Société Historique de Saint-Boniface (ASHSB), Fonds de l'Association d'Éducation des Canadiens Français du Manitoba (AÉCFM) (1922 à 1942), *Rapports des visiteurs*, boîtes 18 et 19. 1922-1923 : fiches 42/1011, 42/1012; 1923-1924 : fiches 42/1013, 42/1014; 1924-1925 : fiches 42/1015, 42/1016; 1930-1931 : fiches 42/1027, 42/1028; 1931-1932 : fiches 42/1029, 42/1030; 1932-1933 : fiches 42/1031,42/1032; 1939-1940 : fiches 42/1045, 42/1046; 1940-1941 : fiches 42/1047, 42/1048; 1941-1942 : fiches 42/1049, 42/1050; 1942 : fiche 42/1051.

Archives de la Société Historique de Saint-Boniface (ASHSB), Fonds de l'Association d'Éducation des Canadiens Français du Manitoba (AÉCFM) (1927), *Rapports des visiteurs*, Paroisse de Woodridge, 25 octobre 1927, boîte 18, fiche 42/1021.

Blay, Jacqueline (1987), L'article 23, Saint-Boniface, Les éditions du blé.

Chroniques des Missionnaires Oblates du S.C. et de M. I. (Juin 1922), 11e année, vol. VI, no 5.

Hébert, Monique (1994), *Les grandes gardiennes de la langue et de la foi : une histoire des Franco-manitobaines*, 1916-1947, Thèse de doctorat inédite, Winnipeg, Université du Manitoba.

Leblanc, Paul-Émile (1968), *L'enseignement français au Manitoba* (1916-1968), Thèse de maîtrise (histoire), Ottawa, Université d'Ottawa.

Le Bulletin de la Ligue des Institutrices Catholiques de l'Ouest, 1re année, no 2 (Déc. 1924), et 18e année, no 1 (Sept.-oct. 1941), Winnipeg, Maison Saint-André.

Morton, W.L. (1967), *Manitoba, a History*, 2e éd., Toronto, Université de Toronto.

Taillefer, Jean-Marie (1979), *Les Franco-Manitobains et les grandes unités scolaires*, Thèse de maîtrise (histoire), Winnipeg, Université du Manitoba.

Taillefer, Jean-Marie (1988), *Les Franco-Manitobains et l'Éducation, 1870-1970 — une étude quantitative*, Thèse de doctorat inédite, Winnipeg, Université du Manitoba.

Notes

1. Cet article présente quelques conclusions de la thèse de doctorat de l'auteure (Hébert, 1994).

2. La première année, l'abbé Sabourin est le visiteur de l'AÉCFM pendant qu'il est curé à Sifton, selon l'informatrice MÉ 2. Toutefois, selon *les Chroniques des Missionnaires Oblates du S.C. et de M. I.*, il serait plutôt directeur du Petit Séminaire de Saint-Boniface. Voir *Chroniques des Missionnaires Oblates du S.C. et de M. I.* (Juin 1922), 11e année, vol. VI, no 5 : 76.

3. À partir de la liste des écoles qui participaient aux concours de français tenus au printemps par l'AÉCFM et dont les résultats paraissaient dans *La Liberté*, journal de la communauté franco-manitobaine, l'historien Jean-Marie Taillefer dénombre 73 écoles en 1926, alors qu'en 1916, il y en aurait eu 133 (Taillefer, 1988 : 268).

4. Pour la même époque, Taillefer (1988) en dénombre 92 qui ont participé aux concours.

5. Tandis que l'historien Taillefer (1988) en dénombre 106. La différence entre ses chiffres et les miens peut provenir de ce que les écoles où s'enseigne le français ou la religion ne prennent pas toutes part aux concours de l'AÉCFM. De plus, les visiteurs pouvaient se rendre à des endroits où il existait une faible majorité de francophones mais qui étaient surtout habités par des catholiques, comme des Galiciens. Par exemple, l'informatrice MÉ 2 a enseigné dans deux villages, sous les auspices de l'AÉCFM, mais elle n'a jamais participé aux concours, car, dit-elle, «les parents s'intéressaient pas à ça, dans ces coins-là».

6. Informatrices mariées après quelques années d'enseignement.

7. *La Liberté*, 21 mars 1916, cité dans Blay, 1987 : 6.

Juanita Ross Epp

The University's New Clothes:
Morality Tales for Feminists in Modern Academe

Introduction

The original call for papers for this book asked for accounts of success stories in feminizing Canadian institutions. When that request landed on my desk, I thought it must be a joke. There seemed to be too many oxymorons in those phrases: successful feminizing? feminized institutions? I work at a university. Entire books have been devoted to an examination of how the "invisible paradigm of the academic system...marginalize(s) or trivialize(s) the lives of all women...so effectively that we no longer see it, notice its presence, or, most important, name it for the determining force that it is" (Schuster and Van Dyne 1985, 7-8). To a female academic, marginalization is like "bad building syndrome": hard to avoid and dangerous to the health unless fresh air is available elsewhere.

Attempting to "change the air" of an institution is slow work, but the appearance of this call for papers coincided with several inroads that had given me hope. We had, in a victory over red tape and resistance, inaugurated a Master's program in Women's Studies, and received funding for a Centre for Feminist Research. While these were both exciting developments, the clincher for my optimism was the following motion passed in the university Senate:

> Moved that the Senate direct the academic leaders (Chairs, Deans of Faculties, School Directors, Department Heads) to report back to Senate at the February meeting, on their actions in their respective academic units on raising the awareness level of their peer colleagues on the issues concerning continuing Women Canada Scholars and women in science generally.

This seemed like a show of support. Perhaps our institution did have some feminizing stories to tell. It would not hurt to ask. How would I frame the question and to whom would I pose it?

My first problem was in defining the term "feminism." In my own journey, I had passed through several "stages" of feminism which I later found identified in the literature (Schuster and Van Dyne, 1985; Pateman and Gross 1986). I began in "denial," sure that any woman willing to work hard should and would be treated in the same way as her male colleagues. I entered a "consciousness raising" level (Kirschner, Atkinson and Arch 1985, 35) when I allowed myself to notice the dearth of women in public positions and question the history and justification for our exclusion (Schuster and Van Dyne 1985, 16). However, I was still not sure that I wanted to be associated with the feminist movement. My resistance to being an "out" feminist was eventually overcome by a story attributed to Charlotte Whitton. When asked if she was a feminist, she responded with words to this effect: "I don't know what a feminist is, but I do know that whenever I stand up and demand what is rightfully mine, that is what I get called."

Thus I reached the "equity" stage (Gross 1987). Later, I was to recognize the improbability of an equitable solution within inherently inequitable patriarchal structures. I was soon in transition into autonomy: "Struggles for equality...imply an acceptance of given standards and a conformity to their expectations and requirements. Struggles for autonomy, on the other hand, imply the right to reject such standards and create new ones" (Gross 1987, 193).

Herein lay my problem in identifying the feminizing of our institution. Which of these stages of feminism would qualify? Our university's patriarchal structures had obviously not been replaced with those of a new feminist social order, but attempts had been made to accommodate women within the existing order. If feminizing means incremental steps toward justice and equality, perhaps our institution had some feminizing in progress. It was by no means complete or even in sight, but there were some stories to tell.

In Search of the Stories

Lulled into a perhaps false sense of security by that incredible pronouncement from our Senate body, I set out to document the "feminizing" of our institution. First, I went to human resources for a list of female professors so that I could contact potential feminizers.

The complications of this process were indicative of the hierarchical (and some would say patriarchal) structures inherent to universities. Did I want all the women, including sessionals, or just tenure-track professors and term appointees? Without sessionals, 51 of the 255 professors, or 20%, were women. That was lower than the national average, which is 33.8% (McDougall and Hajnal, 1996, 214)! As well, many of the women on the list were filling term appointments and would be sent on their way when the persons they were replacing returned. I hesitated in the research process. How could this institution be called feminized?

However, I sent out my questionnaires. I asked my colleagues to describe individual and combined attempts to make the university more welcoming for women and special programs or additional resources set aside for women. Participants were also asked to describe incidents in which they felt blocked in their attempts at feminizing some part of the institution.

Two months later, I had received two responses. One was from a woman who had made several attempts to gain a senior position. She wished me luck at finding anything feminized about our institution. The second was from a woman who had held a term position for four years before it was made tenure-track. She still retained some optimism. However, that was all — two responses.

The research process was stalled again. Could I report a 4% response rate? I asked non-responders, in informal "interviews" over coffee or in the halls, about the lack of response. There seemed to be several reasons:

1. *Fear of the f-word.* Many did not really know what feminizing might mean and did not like the word. They associated it with "male bashing" and therefore did not want anything to do with it. I was to find, as have others before me, that " resistance…on the part of some faculty ran very deep…the insurmountable intellectual barrier was a profound unwillingness to let go of the idea that culture is defined by inherent biological differences between the sexes" (Schmitz, Dinnerstein and Mairs 1985, 120).

2. *Lack of a sense of involvement or lack of confidence.* Some women felt that they had made some small inroads toward feminizing but not really enough to bother reporting. Others told me that they had did not have anything to do with the "feminizing stuff." They would leave that to those of us who "were really into it and knew what we were doing." There was some question as to who those people might be. People associated with Women's Studies seemed to qualify. Schuster and Van Dyne described a similar situation in another institution. Most faculty members are not engaged in research that focuses on women: further they are often intimidated by the quantity of research that has become available in the last two decades, and because this work is frequently interdisciplinary by nature, they are often unsure how it might relate to their own research and teaching (Schuster and Van Dyne, 1985, 99).

3. *Lack of institutional backing.* Some women were reluctant to answer the questionnaire because they were on term or sessional contracts and did not want to "get involved" in

anything that might influence their employment. In our institution, as in those surveyed by the National Centre for Education Statistics in the United States, the opportunity for tenure is less for the new generation, as a third of the junior academics…are not even in positions where they are eligible for tenure…Women are far more likely to be employed in non-tenure track positions than males (cited in McDougall and Hajnal 1996, 216).

4. *Too busy feminizing.* Many women assured me that they would answer my questionnaire as soon as they could. However, they were on so many committees, had so many students and were so busy lobbying, that they had not had time. This is perhaps the "downside" of an institution attempting feminizing. Many of our university committees have a requirement that at least one member be female. Women, particularly tenure-track women, serve on more governance committees than do their male counterparts because there are so few of them. There is a similar problem associated with academic committees. Half of university students are women and many seek out female faculty to serve as their advisors and on their academic committees. Again, the dearth of women means extra work for those who do exist. The time consumed by the committee process often keeps women from the activities that count toward promotion — the research and publication components of the job.

If this were a story, there would be a multitude of morals. Perhaps the most obvious moral would be this one: "Being a woman does not necessitate being a feminist." Or, perhaps it would be "Women without power must be cautious." I would like to think that it would be this: "Just because no one has time to write it down doesn't mean there is no story." By adopting this moral, I could continue with my "research."

An unexpected bonus of my quest for stories was the identification of fellow female professors. I invited them to a public meeting and we formed a loosely structured group we have dubbed the Women's Caucus. Nearly half of the women faculty members attended the first meeting, and we have continued to meet at intervals for over a year. Sometimes we meet just to talk, but at other times we have formulated strategies to address specific issues, such as female representation on Senate and on promotion and tenure committees. We have also established an "ad hoc" standing committee to support individual women who may be experiencing difficulty within a department or faculty. This is especially important to women in non-traditional fields who may be alone in an otherwise all-male discipline, teaching classes dominated by male students. From members of the women's caucus, I have heard stories that deny optimism about feminizing, but I remain determined to tell what positive stories I can.

The University's New Clothes

The situation in our institution has probably been no different from those in many others. Feminizing is not being conducted through "a top-down model that begins with an administrative directive to make sweeping changes" (Schuster and Van Dyne 1985, 92). Any gains have been the result of a "bottom-up coordination or consortial model" (Schuster and Van Dyne 1985, 92). Although "feminizing" was not a stated goal, the process has been going on in several places simultaneously, often in curious isolation. Moves toward an equitable institution started with threads, individual attempts which added little twists of colour to overwhelmingly masculine fabrics. Then, collaboration on various projects provided patches for the portions of the garment most in need of repair. Eventually, we could hope to create whole items of clothing to replace aging garments.

If we can make any claims of feminizing, it is due to gradual change rather than sudden awareness. In the early 1990s, two things started to happen on our campus: more women and women in general became increasingly intent on doing something about equity. The "old timers," who had been doing the ground work quietly, year after year, were starting to gain institutional support. Six of them were now actually "full professors," which meant they had jumped all the hurdles to the top of the career ladder. However, the proportion, 2% of all faculty, was well below the national average of 9.1% or the American average of 16.2% (McDougall and Hajnal 1996, 215). As well, the fact that 11% of the female faculty were full professors was moot when compared to the 38% of male faculty who were full professors.

In spite of this, the years of chipping away at the collective consciousness were beginning to show. Feminist research was, in some small ways, filtering into mainstream thought. For example, teaching methods and syllabi content, in isolated instances, reflected what Schuster and Van Dyne (1985) have called "a pedagogy of empowerment" (168). Such a pedagogy values students' individual experiences, attempts to "broaden the authority group in the classroom," includes both students and the instructor in the validation process, and fosters collaborative learning and shared responsibility (Schuster and Van Dyne 1985, 168). These processes are often associated with feminist teachers, as evidenced in student evaluation comments criticizing or applauding feminist approaches. One student described the change by comparing it to a class she considered to be lacking in feminizing:

> The format of the (non-feminized) class was the exact opposite of yours. We were lectured to, took notes, had to memorize for the exam, and had no time allowed for discussion. I did learn a lot of content, rules and regulations, but I do not feel that my own thinking grew in any way related to the class content (a graduate student).

The changes are also gradually happening in balancing the numbers of male and female faculty members. However, recent reductions in the number of faculty employed in Canadian institutions, from 27,888 in 1992 to 26,402 in 1994 (McDougall and Hajnal 1996, 213), have countered some of the gains of recent years in terms of equity in hiring practices. Actual counts of males and females hired in recent years show that hiring tends to be balanced rather than skewed in favour of females so the gains have been gradual. Now, in times of restraint, retirees are not being replaced and many faculties have been downsized, so we cannot expect large influxes of female or male faculty.

However, the use of an equity watchdog on tenure and promotion committees (another job for one of the few tenured women) has helped new hirees to overcome barriers that might have kept them in the lower ranks. As more women are promoted, more women have more status and are able to add their voices in administrative places.

Another gradual but important change has been in the recent attention to harassment and exclusion. New harassment and equity policies, combined with renewed societal awareness of individual rights, have contributed to a gradual change in attitudes. The more cynical among us would suggest that the attitudes have not really changed but have gone underground. However, the formal process for pursuing charges of harassment has made people more conscious of the possibility of harassment and more sensitive to the needs of women and minorities. Systemic changes have been small, and slow, but, collectively, they have begun to make a difference.

Of course, the chilly climate (Hall and Sandler 1982) has not suddenly melted away. Each of us has a separate horror story to tell at the women's caucus meetings. The big stories are about women forced out of tenure track positions or fighting to maintain research funds. There are stories of deliberate sabotage by fellow faculty members or of harassment by whole classes of male undergraduates. We also talk about the thousands of small things — a librarian unwilling to stock more of those "feminist" books, jibes in faculty meetings, quiet blocking of individual endeavours, and subtle disregard of women's issues. However, this was to be an article about successes in the feminizing of institutions. The setbacks must be reported at another time. Reminiscent of frogs in boiling water and elephants and ants, the moral of the story is that "every little bit counts." The environment of hope produced by gradual positive changes is the setting for the tales to follow.

Morality Tales for Feminists in Modern Academe

I do not teach in Women's Studies. I am a professor of education who also serves on the Women's Studies Advisory Committee. This committee is a group of volunteers from various faculties throughout the campus who "run" the Women's Studies program. The real work of keeping the program afloat falls to a sociology professor who gets a half-course reduction in her teaching load in exchange for being the program co-ordinator. Although there are some institutions that have an "advisor to the president on women's issues," there is no one person in our institution whose designated duties are full-time in Women's Studies, let alone in "full-time feminizing." I tell you this so you will understand that the "feminizing" at our institution is not an organized or even intentional or verbalized goal. The stories, which follow, tell of attempts at feminizing which happened in tandem with, and often in spite of, the full-time jobs that all of us hold in other disciplines.

The Feminist Pedagogues

When my colleague from biology suggested that we attend a conference entitled "Feminist Pedagogy," neither of us was really sure what feminist pedagogy might be. Unaccustomed to trips into unknown disciplines, we were a little frightened. What if we were to embarrass ourselves by asking uninformed questions?

We need not have worried. At the conference, we quickly came to understand that an important aspect of feminist pedagogy is acceptance of others at various stages of understanding and the support of individuals as learners and risktakers. The focus was on pedagogy rather than on women. Although a video (Concordia University 1992) was used to document the differences in the way women and men are treated in higher education, most of the speakers and workshop leaders focused on alternative methods of teaching and learning aimed at improving understanding and retention for all students (Brookes 1992; Briskin 1990; Sadker and Sadker 1994).

The conference gave us a name for many of the things that we were already doing in our classes — the things that were the most rewarding and the ones that got us into the most trouble. These things had labels like "negotiated curriculum," "affective awareness," "interactive journaling," and "recognition of power differentials." We knew how to do them and the conference enabled us to know what to call them.

We were so excited that during a four hour stopover in an airport on the way home we wrote a paper on the conference to be published in the university's teaching journal. We applied for internal funding to study feminist pedagogy and started a group to examine the literature and discuss the implications for teaching. The conference turned out to be a starting point for affirmation of alternative teaching strategies and a catalyst for forming a support group for professors interested in continuing the experimentation. The moral of the story: "Seek affirmation from like-minded others to sustain change."

The Quest for a Mentor

The literature suggests that mentors are very important to women's career development. When the administration agreed to fund a mentoring project, there appeared to be real movement toward the "feminizing" of our institution. Even the concept of mentoring, however, can be unbalanced by the skewed demographics of women in educational institutions. At the information meeting to launch the program, we had the opportunity to sign up either as a mentor or a mentee. New faculty would then be matched with senior people to be "shown the ropes."

In theory, this was a very good idea. In reality, we were overwhelmed by an ironic problem. The sign-up process produced two disproportionate lists. The list of those wanting mentors far exceeded those willing to be mentors. The three full professors in attendance could not mentor 30 or so people. Even associate professors were rare as most of the women had fewer than five years of university teaching experience. There were also imbalances in disciplines. The new people in need of mentoring were rarely in departments where there were other women. (After all, if they already had one woman, why would they need to hire another one?) As a result, we decided to assign mentors in clusters rather than on a one-to-one basis.

The processes to be used were decided by the people in the individual clusters. At the end of the year, the entire group met again. When we asked people to share things that they thought would be useful to others, both mentors and mentees had good lessons or ideas to share. Some brought experiences in getting published; others had learned about negotiating contracts and applying for research money. We learned a great deal from each other and from our own inexperience. The moral of this story? Perhaps it is in the irony of our plight: "Too few mentors spoil the stew." I prefer, however, that it be this: "Mentoring can be a collective activity."

The Day Women's Studies Became a Department

The title of this tale is a dream yet to be realized. Women's Studies, although not yet a department, has been growing, slowly but surely, since its beginnings in 1991. Legend has it that, in answer to a sudden, overwhelming call, women from all over campus dropped what they were doing (or perhaps brought it with them) and followed the voice to a little room in the basement of the university. In that room, the Women's Studies Advisory Committee was born. Suddenly, women who had never had the opportunity to take Women's Studies courses themselves found themselves managing a Women's Studies program.

The members of the new committee stirred from their positivistic roots with questions on their minds. "Do we really need Women's Studies?" they asked. "Is it only temporary? Will it no longer be necessary when we realize our place in the mainstream?" Deep in their hearts was the real question: "Can we afford to sacrifice our personal gains in our home disciplines by risking public affiliation with Women's Studies?"

In spite of the questions and doubts, the process began. First, a first-year course. Then a second-year one. Add a few "cross-listed" classes from other disciplines and we had an undergraduate minor. It was run by sessionals and term people, which meant that the program had the same lack of security as those teaching in it. We finally got five-sixths of a full tenure-track person in 1994. Actually, it was parts of two people who had appointments in other disciplines, but they were "real" Women's Studies professors; that is, people who had actually studied Women's Studies as a discipline, not people who were qualified to teach it by accident of gender at birth. Still, our work remains undone. Next year, our new Master's level seminar will begin. Perhaps then we will be able to start the slow process of applying for departmental status.

The moral of this story? Each year, as we scrounge for dollars in hard times, woo the dean for resources, and beg for another sessional stipend, we feel that the process is too slow, too demanding. Looking back, however, it has only been five years and we have come a long way. Perhaps we should be making sure we celebrate our successes. The moral is "Small incremental successes can lead to institutional change."

The Amazing Birth of a Research Centre

Nobody else knows exactly where it came from, but I can tell you the secret of the Centre for Feminist Research. You see, it began in a magic paper that floated into my mailbox one September day. It was a notice of a research grant that could be used for several purposes, one of which was the establishment of a research centre. The Women's Studies Advisory Committee was a multidisciplinary group; we had sometimes talked about setting up a centre. This grant opportunity seemed an answer to our dreams. We took that piece of paper and performed a spell over it, using a word processor and a bottle of wine and behold — a research centre was conceived.

Research centres, however, are a bit like elephants. It takes a long time for them to give birth. In fact, that first spell appeared to be a miscarriage. When the research monies were eventually awarded, there was none for our research centre. Our rejection letter did include an encouraging note advising us to try another source. We tried that source, but their funding was cut before our proposal came up for review. It was beginning to look as if our time spent writing proposals had been wasted.

Fortunately, our plight came to the attention of a sorceress who happened to be the dean of graduate studies. She summoned us to her office. "A Centre for Feminist Research?" she asked. "Why didn't you say something before? This is simple. All you have to do is sit in a circle and rewrite this research proposal yet again. Then you close your eyes and wait."

We hurried away to try the magic spell. Sure enough, less than a year later, the first research money came in. You see, the trick was that we had to already be a centre in order to become eligible for funding. So we applied for the grant as if the centre were already operational. The granting agency was then willing to fund projects conducted out of it. The magic of this centre is in its location. It is not a room or a place; it is a centerless centre that lives on paper and in our hearts. The moral of this story is: "There is more than one way to start a research centre: sometimes inventiveness wins the research grant game."

The Disappearing Female Students

The disappearance was first noticed in the student services department. Each year since 1988, the Canada Scholars Program had been supporting equal numbers of male and female students. These were students in the "hard" sciences; that is, in disciplines such as engineering, chemistry, math, physics, and so forth. In order to renew their scholarships from year to year, students were required to maintain an 80% average. The male students had a fairly high renewal rate, but the female students rarely lasted past the first year. What was happening to these female students?

Student services called in the ace sleuthing team from the Women's Studies committee. We were becoming familiar with the literature on female student retention, including Hall and Sandler's (1982) work on "chilly climate." We invited female Canada Scholars to a series of focus-group meetings. These groups were so successful they have continued in the form of support groups, but that is another story.

The women students claimed that, at first, they were treated no differently from male students. As we talked, however, they remembered the incidents, the comments about how they were dressed, the sexual innuendo in jokes, the times when they were made to feel unwelcome or stupid or when they noticed that male students got breaks that they did not. They recognized that sometimes they had trouble finding classmates to help them or to study with them and that there did seem to be a male culture in most of their classes. Even so, they felt that they were usually not treated any differently from the male students. They were using whatever tactics were necessary to sustain themselves, but a combination of social pressures, academic demands, lack of interest, and/or too many extracurricular activities was gradually driving them out of the program.

We also arranged for focus-group meetings with the professors in the targeted programs. One person showed up at each meeting. The first blamed the high schools for inferior products and the second suggested that the girls' entrance marks were inferior to boys' so they shouldn't expect to do as well. One wanted a list of Canada Scholars so he could make sure that they got the extra help. We brought this idea back to the women students in the focus groups. They were horrified. They did not want any special attention. They already got enough exposure as isolated females in male-dominated classes.

Our study was then taken to the university Senate in the form of a report. We made some recommendations, suggesting, among other things, that female students get more attention, that they be provided with tutoring and support groups; we also slipped in a suggestion that faculty members could benefit from some professional development on the issue.

When the report was brought to Senate there was some discussion, but no real decisions were made. We thought it had gone the way of so many other reports before it. The next time the Senate met, however, a man, one whom we never expected to pay any attention to women's issues, was there with the motion I quoted at the beginning of this article. It was seconded by another man whom we had supposed to be similarly disinterested, and it was passed.

Before you resign from your job and head for our "feminized" institution, you should finish reading this story. Although the passing of this motion sounds like a powerful pronouncement of commitment to equity, you probably know that shows of support cannot necessarily be taken at face value. In this case, the motion was passed only because it was late and most of the Senate had gone home; some say it was made in order for one department to point out the failings of another. In any case, it did pass, so we began to prepare for the fallout.

Our immediate concern was to get ready for the flood of requests we expected as each department would come to beg for our services in the consciousness raising that was about to begin. Would we have the time and resources to meet the demand? We called on the Gender Issues Centre (established in 1991 and supported by the student union). They provided a list of resources (including the film from Concordia). The package was soon ready and so were we.

Strangely, no requests came. Time went by. The package was available, so we sent one to each department head. We can only assume that the package was enough. None of us was ever invited to do a workshop. No one called to ask about the resources. The February Senate meeting came and went, and nothing was said.

This is a good news/bad news story. The good news is that we are all becoming more aware of the needs of female students. The bad news is that being aware of the needs does little toward meeting them. The moral of the story? Perhaps it is "Resolutions of public governing bodies do not necessarily mean change or commitment." An alternate moral would be "Preach to the converted; you never know who might be listening."

This may not be a "feminizing" story. Perhaps it would have happened this way even if the characters had been all men or all women. I have heard it said that intrigue is a part of academic life regardless of gender. This is the story of how a man attempts to "divide and conquer" two women and almost succeeds.

The story begins when two women are both eligible for promotion at the same time. It is not as if there are only so many promotions to go around. Any number of assistant professors can become associate professors, and any number of associate professors can become full professors. So there is no need for blocking others to promote self. However, the promotion process requires that candidates make their CVs available to all other faculty members and that all others have a right to vote on any individual's promotion. The vote and accompanying supporting or detracting comments are presented to the promotion committee which makes the ultimate decision. The process becomes very intense and personal, although it is supposed to focus on academic credentials. There are also secret little games that begin when the candidates submit their "documentation." In this case, the games became quite bizarre. One of the women actually found the following note in her mailbox: "Someone that you consider both a friend and a colleague is neither."

It was a nasty time. There were accusations that a journal article that one of the women had listed as "refereed" was not really refereed. There were rumours that that rumour had been started by the other woman up for promotion. There were suspicions that the first woman had tried to block the second woman in her bid for an administrative position. Soon the two women were avoiding contact. They were detouring to avoid each other in the hall and rallying their supporters in two separate camps.

There are not enough women in our university to support separate camps so eventually one of the women decided she had had enough. She marched into the other woman's office for a showdown. The story could be embellished here if I were to tell you that the secretaries gathered at the door to listen, but I suspect that would be overly dramatic.

Inside the office, the standoff was short lived. Once the cards were on the table, it immediately became apparent that neither woman had done what the other thought she had done. In fact, by comparing notes, they were able to identify the true culprit as a man who had very cleverly planted the seeds of mistrust and suspicion that had driven these two women into separate rages. They had done exactly what he had wanted. Each had believed his innuendo and had blamed and sabotaged the other. When they cut communications with each other, there was no way for them to become aware of his manipulation. They could have gone on hurting each other every chance they got for the rest of their careers had they not talked about it. I am not sure what they did to get even; perhaps they did nothing. I do know they left early that day to plan their next move over a glass of wine. By the way, they both got their promotions.

The moral of this story hardly needs to be pointed out. If you think another woman has wronged you, confront her and get the facts. We do not have to all be friends, but we must keep our integrity as colleagues. There are enough others out there undermining women. They need no help from us.

The Good Idea

Sometimes I would get lonely. I would look up from my work and realize that it was time to hurry home to my children. Another day had gone by, another week had disappeared, and I had not been in touch with my friends and colleagues. There were people that I had planned to lunch with, but we were all too busy that we were each grabbing sandwiches in our separate offices as we juggled classes, research, meetings, and home responsibilities.

I looked at my calendar and saw that there was a gap between classes on Tuesday around lunch time so I sent the word out to all the women I knew. I said that there would be a group of women having lunch at a specific restaurant on any given Tuesday. I did not know who else would be there but they were all invited.

I went to the restaurant that first Tuesday and waited. Five people arrived. During the following weeks, there were usually five or six of us. Different people came each time and sometimes we had as many as ten at the table. Once, I did dine alone, so now I check with a few others until I find at least one other person planning to go. No one needs to feel compelled to come; there is no one to phone if you need to cancel. The restaurant gets irritated because the first one there cannot say exactly how many will eventually join her, but it always works out. Sometimes there are a few empty chairs and sometimes we have to pull up a few extras.

We do not always talk about women's issues, but we often do. Individuals bring their teaching dilemmas and their research concerns. In fact, most of the stories I have told you today I heard (or told) in that restaurant. This story has no moral. It is just the sharing of an idea that has been very rewarding.

The Moral of the Story

On first glance, our university would appear to be an inclusive place. Our institution is advertised as an equal opportunity employer and there is an equity policy in place. We have a Women's Studies program at both the undergraduate and graduate levels, a Feminist Research Centre, an excellent harassment policy, a gender issues centre, a gay and lesbian centre, and the requirement that there be an equity advisor on all promotion and tenure committees. While it would seem that there are great things happening, these are baby steps in the "feminizing" process.

If we accept as feminizing the process of paying attention to justice issues, the university has made a start. However, vital as these things are, their existence may mask other underlying issues at other levels of feminizing. Although the university has done many things to make sure that policies and practices are affirming, the stated policies cannot prevent individualized patriarchy. Unless these policies are understood, accepted, and enforced, they do nothing to change individual actions. Their existence does not prevent professors from marginalizing female students, from omitting the "female content," or from placing higher value on traditional androcentric structures. This is not to say that inclusive policies are not important. Difficult as they are to implement and impossible as they are to enforce, they are necessary foundations for change. However, policy is sometimes propaganda. Policies can make institutions appear to be "feminized" when they are not. The issues do not go away because someone addressed them in a policy manual.

Attention to policy issues and interpretation of policy may deflect energy from the more transformative aspects of "feminizing" as "an ethics, a methodology, a more complex way of thinking about, thus more responsibly acting upon, the conditions of human life" (Rich 1979, 213). At our institution, we have learned to play the academic games, creatively if necessary. We have learned to mentor in a collective way. We now understand that, if we are lacking wise women, we must combine our lesser wisdoms. We have learned to nourish our networks, with food and wine where possible, and always with passion and laughter. We have learned that it is not all bad to continually preach to the converted; we can never tell when others might be listening. We have learned to put women in high places and to continue to support them once they are there, taking our battles to another level. We have learned to value the female students who are where our future lies. Is this, though, the use of feminism as what Rich (1979) called a "frivolous label" (213)? This is not Rich's "feminist evolution…leading to radical change" (Rich 1979, 213).

Perhaps the most important thing we have learned is the vital role of continued communication and support among women. The support of others makes the difference between a devastating blow and an incentive to carry on. This support leads to creative responses, to challenges and problems, to responses that would not be conceived of or dared by an individual. Mentoring, supporting students, transforming programs, applying for research grants, enlightening colleagues, and understanding adversity are all best done in a supportive group context. If Rich's feminism "rooted in the conviction that all women's lives are important; that the lives of men cannot be understood by burying the lives of women" (213) is ever to happen, it must be done by working in concert.

The things that we have done, the small gains that we have accomplished, are important (if minute) steps toward change. They represent a step toward an inclusive community of professors, administrators, staff, and students. A feminized institution would encourage women and men to cooperate for the growth of all people in all aspects of the educational process. It would also hear the voices of the traditionally disenfranchised and value diversity. It would "make visible the full meaning of women's experience, [and] reinterpret knowledge in terms of that experience" (Rich 1979, 213). This requires more than attention to demands for equitable treatment. It would involve a rethinking of the meaning of knowledge and education. That, however, is another story.

References

Briskin, L. 1990. *Feminist Pedagogy: Teaching and Learning Liberation.* York University: Social Science Division.

Brooks, A. L. 1992. *Feminist Pedagogy: An Autobiographical Approach.* Halifax, N.S.: Fernwood.

Concordia University. 1990. *Inequity in the Classroom.* (Video). Montréal: Concordia University.

Gross, E. 1987. "Conclusion: What is Feminist Theory?" *Feminist Challenges: Social and Political Theory*, eds. C. Pateman and E. Gross. Boston: Northeastern University Press.

Hall, R. and B. Sandler. 1987. *The Classroom Climate: A Chilly One for Women?* Washington, D.C.: Association of American Colleges.

Kirschner, S., J.M. Atkinson and E. Arch. 1985. "Reassessing Coeducation." *Women's Place in the Academy: Transforming the Liberal Arts Curriculum*, eds. M. R. Schuster and S.R. Van Dyne. Totowa, NJ: Rowman and Allanheld.

Lather, P. 1992. *Getting Smart.* New York: Routledge.

Lewis, M. 1993. *Without A Word: Teaching Beyond Women's Silence.* New York: Routledge.

Luke, C. 1992. *Feminisms and Critical Pedagogy.* New York: Routledge.

Martin, J.R. 1993. *Changing the Educational Landscape.* New York: Routledge.

McDougall, M. and V. Hajnal. 1996. "Gender Equity in Education: Taking our Temperature in 1996." *Advancing the Agenda of Inclusive Education: Proceedings of the CASWE Summer Institute*, eds. C. Harris and N. Depledge. St. Catharines, Ontario: Brock University.

Pateman, C. and E. Gross. 1986. *Feminist Challenges: Social and Political Theory.* Boston: Northeastern University Press.

Rich, A. 1979. *On Lies, Secrets and Silence: Selected Prose 1966-1978.* New York: Norton.

Sadker, M. and D. Sadker. 1993. *Failing at Fairness: How America's Schools Cheat Girls.* Charles Scribner's Sons.

Schuster, M. R. and S. R. Van Dyne. 1985. *Women's Place in the Academy: Transforming the Liberal Arts Curriculum.* Totowa, NJ: Rowman and Allanheld.

Schmitz, B., M. Dinnerstein and N. Mairs. 1985. "Initiating a Curriculum Integration Project: Lessons from the Campus and the Region. Advancing the Agenda of Inclusive Education: Proceedings of the CASWE Summer Institute." Women's Place in the Academy: Transforming the Liberal Arts Curriculum, eds. M.R. Schuster and S.R. Van Dyne. Totowa, NJ: Rowman and Allanheld.

Stibbs, A. 1992. *Like a Fish Needs a Bicycle.* London: Bloomsbury.

Stone, Linda. 1994. *The Education Feminism Reader.* New York: Routledge.

Taylor, S. 1989. "Empowering Girls and Young Women: The Challenge of the Gender-Inclusive Curriculum." *Journal of Curriculum Studies* 21, 5: 441-456.

Sandra Kirby

Gender Equity in the Canadian Sport Council: The New Voice for the Sport Community

> Equity is an issue of democracy. Changes to improve equity and access must involve those affected in significant ways. (Gerd Engman, Sweden)

> Equity is an issue of quality; excellence in sport cannot occur without equity. (Marion Lay, Canada)

Introduction: Readiness for Action

This paper is about the formation of the Canadian Sport Council (CSC) in response to pressure from the Canadian sport community and the public to create a value based, equitable, drug-free sport system. Opportunity to create a more gender equitable system presented itself when the whole "amateur" sport system was thrown into an intense self-examination by the positive drug test of sprinter Ben Johnson at the 1988 Seoul Olympic Games and the ensuing Dubin Inquiry. A broad consultation process occurred over three years, concluding with the establishment of the CSC.

When opportunity knocked, women and other marginalized groups in sport were well prepared and conversant with the equity issues. They vigorously sought representation at all levels of decision-making during the creation and implementation of the CSC. As a direct result of their readiness, gender equity was identified as a key value of a quality sport system.

Sporting women have been active participants and competitors in Canadian sport for more than a century. Gender equity was one of the key issues initially raised at the 1974 first national conference on women and sport. However, a real opportunity to create a gender equitable system did not present itself until "amateur" sport found itself under a magnifying glass shortly after Ben Johnson's infamous positive drug test result at the Seoul Olympic Games in 1988.

Prior to 1988, sport in Canada was not noted for its access or gender equity successes. The majority of women probably have stories to tell about their experiences with organized sport either in school or in community participation, which reflect poorly on the ability of sport to respond to and meet the needs of its female participants. Many

Canadian sport sociologists have written extensively about the discriminations which occur within such a "capital p" patriarchal institution.[1] Their critiques have generally been from outside organized sport...looking in. What this paper addresses is from the inside out, the author being one of several women active in the formation of the CSC.[2]

The process by which the CSC was formed is presented in chronological order and an analogy to building blocks is used to show how the interaction of events and people produced a gender equitable organization. The keys to success in feminizing the Canadian sport structure include the early setting of feminist goals, the networking among women and some men within the system, and the readiness by feminists to move quickly and efficiently when the opportunity to change sport arose.

First, a little about how sport is organized and the nature of the changes which have recently occurred. Fitness and Amateur Sport Canada was established in 1961 to do the following:

- provide leadership, policy direction, and financial assistance for the development of Canadian sport at the national and international level; and
- support the highest possible levels of achievement by Canada in international sport (Fitness and Amateur Sport Act, 1961).[3]

Although this mandate applies to both women and men, it would be difficult to tell by looking at the administrative and team development structures within various sport organizations. Sport has been remarkably successful for a selected population, so much so that, for the majority of males, it is remembered as one of their best childhood experiences. For the majority of girls and women, sport has not been nearly so positive an experience.

Currently, women are underrepresented at all levels of sport in Canada. For example, although we comprise 52% of the population, we represent approximately one-third of the registered participants in sport. Women are also significantly underrepresented in coaching, especially at the high-performance levels. At the 1990 Commonwealth Games, Canada had 43 male coaches and 3 female coaches in sports, although about one-third of the team was composed of female athletes.[4] Such a small number of women coaches presents few role models for girls and discourages female athletes from coaching. At that time, all federal, provincial, and territorial ministers responsible for sport were men. With one exception (New Brunswick), the same was true for senior deputy ministerial positions.

Sportswomen, feminists included, have been actively seeking change in the Canadian sport system since early 1974 when the first national conference on women and sport was held.[5] A second conference concerning girls and women in sport was held in March 1980.[6] Some of the recommendations of these conferences were carried out, but many were not.

Twenty years after the founding of Fitness and Amateur Sport Canada, and, as a direct result of those conferences, the Canadian Association for the Advancement of Women and Sport (CAAWS) was founded in 1981 to "promote, develop, and advocate a feminist perspective on women and sport."[7] Initially, CAAWS was an advocacy group outside of sport governance and delivery systems. CAAWS now rents space alongside other sport organizations at CSFAC[8] and receives some operational funding from government.

As Lorraine Code notes, "Patriarchal societies are those in which men have more power than women, readier access than women to that which is valued in society, and in consequence, are in control over many, if not most aspects of women's lives."[9] This describes the majority of sport organizations, and, hence, the institution of sport. CAAWS has struggled to change this and its identity as a feminist organization-moving from liberal to radical and back to liberal as the need for action dictated. Along the way, CAAWS has developed a reputation as a successful advocacy group. It has produced numerous written documents[10] and worked towards increasing the representation of women and sport.

The Beginnings of Institutional Change: The First Four Building Blocks

The first building block is the development of a human rights context for sport, a necessary condition for feminist action in sport. Canada has a reputation as a liberal nation; in particular, the adoption of the Canadian Constitution in 1981, enshrined in the *Canadian Charter of Rights and Freedoms*, guaranteed certain basic rights to all Canadians. Of special significance to sport were the anti-discrimination and equality provisions of the Charter "which refer to governmental actions and laws which make clear that sex equality is not a privilege to be conferred or withdrawn at will, but rather a state that should exist."[11]

A second building block was set in place when the federal government released the *Sport Canada Policy on Women and Sport*,[12] which stated that

> Sport Canada's goal with respect to women in sport is as follows: *To attain equality for women in sport.*
>
> Equality implies that women at all levels of the sport system should have equal opportunity to participate. Equality is

not necessarily meant to imply that women wish to participate in the same activities as men but rather to indicate that activities of their choice should be provided and administered in a fair and unbiased environment. At all levels of the sport system, equal opportunities must exist for women and men to compete, coach, officiate, or administer sport. (1986, 14)

Now, Canadian sport needed to find a way to use the policy to come into line with the spirit of the Canadian constitution. CAAWS was extensively referred to in this government document and its members were elated at the government's commitment, albeit at the policy level, to gender equality. Sport Canada, for whom the document was prepared, was a government organization which at that time reported to the Federal Minister of Sport.[13]

However, having a policy and acting on that policy are two different things. Once Sport Canada had *the policy*, its Women's Program[14] gained a somewhat greater profile in the sport community and the nature of research commissioned by Sport Canada[15] changed noticeably to include more issues of women and girls. However, there was little noticeable impact of *the policy* on the way in which the various government supported sport organizations actually functioned.

The dominant emphases in sport remained unchanged, those of maintaining a working bureaucracy with some clear lines of authority, decision-making, accountability, and producing athletes on an annual and quadrennial basis (Olympic years marking the end of each quadrennial). Despite the sport policy, the ratio of female to male athletes on national teams was 1:2; of coaches 1:9.[16]

In 1988, Canada held the first international conference on drug use in sport and gained a reputation internationally as a leader in the drug-free sport movement. At the Seoul Olympics later that year, Ben Johnson's urine was found to have abnormally high levels of testosterone indicating the presence of the anabolic steroid, stanozolol.

The Canadian government responded to the mounting public pressure to "clean up sport" with building block number three, the *Dubin Commission*, to study amateur sport and recommend change. The Report of the Dubin Commission was released in late 1989 and challenged both sport organizations[17] and government to make significant changes in how sport was run. This meant looking at fundamental issues: ethics and values, equity and access, collective voice for the sport community, accountability, and government involvement in sport.

Shortly thereafter, government people, volunteers, and staff of the national sport community met in Ottawa at the Sport Forum (later called Sport Forum I), building block four. Here, in an effort to address the specific issue of drug-free sport, participants realized that organized sport was unable to respond to the changing needs of modern society. In the *Task Force 2000* report (April 1991), representatives called for a Sport Forum II. They wanted a broader, more representative meeting of the sport community to create a more democratic and responsive sport system. Lorraine Greaves[18] noted that, as organizations endeavour to increase their participation and positive public profile, they must become increasingly critical of their internal processes. Similarly, participants in the Sport Forum process were aware of the need for change and most welcomed the opportunity to completely re-evaluate sport.

It is important to note that CAAWS was not invited to Sport Forum I. Throughout the 1980s, the relationship between CAAWS and Sport Canada's Women's Program had been an awkward one, partly because CAAWS called itself an organization that was openly and "blatantly feminist." At that time, CAAWS was positioned outside of sport, and, although it worked diligently to bring gender equity to the government and various sport organizations, it was clearly not considered part of the sport community by the funders of the Sport Forum process.

Moving Quickly and Efficiently: More Building Blocks, More Interaction

Increased federal government involvement in sport was reflected in the increased size of Sport Canada[19] and of the national sport organizations. One of the outcomes of this was the increasingly complex relationship between government bureaucracy and sport governance by paid and volunteer workers from the national sport organizations. In May 1991, Sport Canada took a strong leadership stand on gender equity by appointing Marion Lay as Manager of the Women's Program, Sport Canada, providing building block five. Lay was a medallist in the 1968 Olympic Games and a high profile advocate for women and sport. Lay resigned as Coordinator of CAAWS, moved "inside" government as the Women's Program Manager, and took with her the CAAWS, feminist agenda as the blueprint for change. As a result, a strong feminist voice from government began working collaboratively with national sport organizations and with CAAWS. Sport Canada and sport organizations quickly began to make dramatic changes.

Sport Forum II, building block six, was held in October 1991. Lay ensured that four CAAWS representatives were present and CAAWS functioned as an equal among the Sport Forum representatives. All CAAWS representatives were long-standing members and active advocates in their various communities. At Sport Forum II, participants representing the majority of national sport organizations, multisport organizations, athletes, and special interest groups together reviewed, discussed, modified, and reached consensus on a) a new collective vision for sport in Canada, b) strategic directions for this vision, and c) a possible collective mechanism for sport. In this exceptionally well-facilitated meeting,[20] Judy Kent ensured that every delegate had ample opportunity to express views on the vision, mechanisms, and action.[21] Familiar with the aims of CAAWS, Kent and others encouraged participation of women in the discussions and ensured that the debates were held in a climate of respect and good will. A spirit of solidarity was actually palpable at the Sport Forum, as all members of the sport community were encouraged to wear "big hats"; that is, to give priority to the big picture of what was good for sport in Canada. This was no mean achievement, given the long history of competitiveness and territoriality among sport organizations.

The impact of CAAWS' presence at Sport Forum II was noticeable, particularly in the strength and visibility of outcome statements on equity, accessibility, and responsibility. For example, the *Vision for Sport in Canada* contains four critical points:

- Sport is accessible and available to all persons in Canada;
- Sport is based on and reflects fundamental values and ethics, including *equity, collaboration, safety, and enjoyment*;
- Sport is participant-oriented and athlete-centred, and relies on quality coaching and support services;
- Sport has a responsibility for promoting values and ethics;
- Sport Forum II delegates also called for a re-evaluation of the sport recognition policy, a policy which gave Olympic sports greater access to resources than non-Olympic sports. Since women's sport had fewer Olympic opportunities than men's sport, this marked a potential advance for women. Also, sport organizations agreed to address equity and access policies and goals. Encouragingly, consensus and collective leadership figured prominently in the discussion about self-governance.

Finally, delegates were unanimous in calling for a collective mechanism for the organization and administration of sport:

> Such a mechanism would for example, establish a national forum for debate on sport issues and identify emerging issues. Since *equity* and in particular, *gender equity* are critical to the advancement of women and sport and physical activity, CAAWS is optimistic about the impact on women of such a collective mechanism for sport.[22]

By the end of Sport Forum II, CAAWS had shifted identities from that of an advocacy group outside of sport to an accepted organization with legitimate concerns within the sport community. CAAWS positioned itself as a resource that the sport community needed.

Building block seven, *Sport: The Way Ahead*, was released in April 1992. The federal government had been very much in control of sport budgeting and policy,[23] but this long-awaited Parliamentary Committee report called upon government to take a more "hands off" approach to sport to allow increased private control over what had been defined as a public responsibility of government only 31 years earlier. *Sport: The Way Ahead* signalled an attitudinal change by government, dramatically reducing its role in sport delivery.[24]

Building block eight? In May 1992, eleven women were selected for the International Professional Development Program tour (IPDP),[25] and travelled to the United Kingdom, Norway, and Sweden to speak with women active in changing national sport systems. They met with sport and human rights advocates, politicians, media, government representatives, researchers, athletes, community centre programmers, and coaches.[26] The results of the tour were many and varied. For example, Swedish sport advocates had concluded that a gender balance must be at a minimum 60% to 40% participation on gender lines. The rationale was that if women were 10% of a committee, they had a presence; 20% meant they did a lot of the work; at 30% men would congratulate the women on their visibility and at the same time subtly warn men on the committee that the women were getting too strong; and at 40% women started to have real impact on decision making. In Norway, the tour participants learned that women brought a women's perspective to sport, that *being women* was the qualification they brought to their position. The tour returned to Canada with a collective voice and a stronger, clearer vision for sport including the knowledge that Canada would be called upon to play a significant and international leadership role in sport and equity issues.

Sport Forum III, the final building block nine, fell into place. The forum met in early October 1992 and CAAWS and IPDP participants were present. This meeting included representatives from most of the National Sport Organizations (e.g., Basketball Canada, Rowing Canada) and multi-sport and service organizations (e.g., Canadian Commonwealth Games Society), government, athletes, coaches, researchers, and interested people from the sport community. The purpose of Sport Forum III was to finalize the structure and processes created by earlier Sport Forums and to give definition to a new collective voice for sport.

The author's role during Sport Forum III was to be a member of the writing group, a group which facilitated decision making in the meeting. Imagine a very large room holding 34 tables of 8 persons.

Judy Kent, the facilitator, had overheads summarizing the decisions made at Sport Forums I and II and the decisions remaining for Sport Forum III. After discussion on a group of options, Kent would have the assembly raise a green card if they agreed with an option or a red card if they did not. On points where there was near unanimity, she considered that consensus was reached and the group would then move on to the next set of decisions. If consensus was not reached, the writing group would retire to prepare newly worded options. These would then be brought back to the assembly for red and green carding.

The assembly struggled with the equity concerns. How would an organization get gender balance if an *odd* number of representatives was to be selected for future Forums? What if there currently were no women in a sport? For example, one man stood up to say that he felt totally overwhelmed and pushed into accepting gender equity because of pressure from a special interest group. A woman stood up to say she wanted to be selected only because she was the best person for the position, not because she was a woman. Another woman suggested that the fact she was a woman qualified her to bring a woman's perspective into her organization and to the assembly. Another man suggested that participants were all very clever people and could figure out how to make their organizations more gender equitable. He further suggested that not having the particular solutions "at the tip of our tongues should not stop us from supporting the equity resolutions." Evident throughout the discussions were the strong reasoned voices of CAAWS, IPDP tour participants, men who understood the need for equity and, in particular, gender equity, and, for the first time in a collective way, Canadian national level athletes.

At the end of Sport Forum III, this is what was accomplished:

- a new organization temporarily called the Coalition was formed to be the collective voice for sport in Canada and composed of all organizations at the national level of sport plus organizations of provincial sport groups which will meet yearly;
- each member group can send four representatives to the annual assembly.[27] There must be gender balance in the delegation (50% female and 50% male) and one of the four representatives must be an athlete. First Nations people are invited to send one delegate from each of the provinces and territories in addition to four representatives of member groups; and
- a smaller management group will be composed of four executive and five members at large. Gender balance requirements must be met (no more than 60% on any one sex) for the management group and for any committees or delegations the management group organizes.[28]

For the first time in the history of Canadian sport, gender equity is built into a structure endorsed by all its members. Participants then settled on a phase-in period to enable organizations to meet equity requirements gradually. All felt that something enormously important had been achieved: a commitment by the sport community to create a different and more equitable sport system.

After Sport Forum III, CAAWS decided not to do a news release because some members thought it would be "flaunting success." It was not the success of CAAWS that would have been flaunted, but the success of the sport community's "moving into the 20th century, and not a moment too late."[29] It was Sport Canada Women's Program who released the notice to the public. Could it be that it is difficult for women to advertize or announce their successes?

In December, Tom MacIllfactrick and the author, the co-chairs of the original writing group from the Sport Forums, were invited to the Federal, Provincial, Territorial Strategic Planning Sport Committee (FPTSPSC). The task was to work with the federal Assistant Deputy Minister of Sport and his provincial counterparts to bring the provinces and territories in line with a coordinated sport planning structure for the future. Equity, and, in particular, gender equity[30] was a major part of that work:

- Under the equity and access banner are many marginalized groups seeking redress from inequitable situations in sport. A group may be considered marginalized if they have low participation rates, status, and/or visibility within the sport system. Groups traditionally disadvantaged in the public arena include women and minority groups such as those from racial or ethnic minorities, Aboriginal peoples, and people living with disabilities. As these groups and individuals within them seek to participate more fully in sport, sport is changing for the better.

- Women form the largest "marginalized" group in sport. Despite being the majority of Canadians (52% of the population), women are considered a minority in governance and policy formation, participation in the full range of opportunities, and the promotion of sport. In essence, women participate as a minority group in a sport system designed by men. As well, women's achievement in sport is largely measured against standards set by men. Gender equity is the principle and practice of fair and equitable allocation of resources and opportunities to both females and males. Gender equity is synonymous with fairness, justice, equality, and reasonableness. To be equitable means to be fair and to appear to be fair.

- Other minority groups within Canadian sport include visible minority and immigrant groups, ethnic groups, aboriginal persons, persons living with disability, and seniors. In a society where there are historically advantaged groups which receive continuous systemic reinforcement, equity programs are being developed to eliminate the barriers to full participation for disadvantaged groups.
- The quality of participation for some may be limited by language, economic disadvantage, or regional location. To achieve equity and access, all barriers to full participation must be addressed.[31]

Conclusion

Women have made significant steps forward inside the institution of sport. Change has resulted from the culmination of some 20 years of efforts made by a variety of people, mostly women, with both liberal and radical strategies for change, working together almost companionably side by side. Changes to the sport system and the ramifications of those changes for sport organizations would not have occurred unless significant energy had already gone into the development of a general awareness of gender as an issue.

For women in sport, the oppressive social structures are sometimes difficult to see. As Marilyn Frye has noted, when one is in a cage, it is difficult to realize that each wire of the cage is a form of oppression and that it is only by stepping back to contemplate the entire structure that we can see the interconnections and mutually reinforcing practices which make us feel trapped.[32] It is through education and seeking to understand our own experience and the experiences of others that the oppression becomes visible, and we can see that sport does not have to remain an "intractable structure" based on discriminations of race, class, sex, ability, and age.

CAAWS has maintained a two-pronged approach to facilitating change, education, and advocacy. It was gratifying to see that many who came to the microphones for Sport Forum II and III were members of or had volunteered with CAAWS in the past. Further, the women who went on the IPDP tour had an overall view of the nature of oppression. They were able to speak clearly and strongly about their view of a gender equitable sport system. Since the formation of the CSC, CAAWS has emerged as an international leader on issues such as sexual harassment, body image, and disordered eating in sport.

The Women's Program, Sport Canada, continues to develop policies and programs for more equitable sport. Sport organizations know they cannot survive as gender inequitable organizations, and Sport Canada has shown leadership in assisting them to change.

The coalition building, both among women and between women and men, was key to bringing about change. Gender equity agreements would not have been passed by the Sport Forums without courageous presentations made by, for example, persons with disabilities, athletes' rights representatives, and Aboriginal Canadians, who fully supported equity in all its forms and resisted attempts by the assembled body to divide the groups (e.g., gender equity against all other equity issues).

Finally, there remains the question of success. In "feminizing" the sport institutions in Canada, a number of issues have arisen which qualify "success." First, there is the issue of liberalism. As CAAWS helped sport people to become more aware and conscious of sexism in themselves and in their organizations, it was increasingly seen as a multi-service organization to help the sport community to become more gender equitable rather than as a "radical advocacy group." CAAWS moved from a radical to a liberal stand. How then will CAAWS protect itself from co-optation?

Second, in moving the sport community beyond tokenism (e.g., for gender and for athlete representation), CAAWS and other advocates made themselves vulnerable to a backlash from those who are in positions of authority with strong resistance to change. Safilios-Rothschild (1974) identified such shifts in policy without shifts in leadership as a lethal combination for resisting change.[33] Favourable public opinion about the changes taking place in sport and increased access by currently marginalized groups are key to maintaining positive momentum.

Third, while commitments have been made within the formal political process, the politics of private interaction have not been addressed. The changes that have been brought about are through policy and organizational change in relation to policy. How then are individual interactions between women and men and between gender equitable and non-gender equitable organizations going to take place? Signs are that, although behaviours may be changing, resistance to gender equity that exists on an attitudinal level alters more slowly.

Fourth, many of the women involved in these changes are not feminists; nor, as Naomi Black[34] noted, "do they identify their efforts as likely to expand women's autonomy." By what means can all women be supported in their efforts to bring about change?

Women in sport face many challenges in the future. This quotation from the late Audre Lorde points us clearly in the right direction:

> We must root out internalized patterns of oppression within ourselves if we are to move beyond the most superficial aspects of social change.[35]

Endnotes

1.   See, for example, the writings of Suzanne Laberge, Nancy Theberge, and Helen Lenskyj.

2.   I have been working for more than thirteen years on issues concerning girls, women, and sport. For the first time, I feel something of great significance for equity and access has happened in this country and feminists made it happen! We have been successful in creating a major breakthrough for the participation of women in the sport community. In many ways, I never thought that this would be possible in my lifetime.

3.   Bill C-131.1961. The Fitness and Amateur Sport Act.

4.   Kirby, S.L. and A. LeRougetel, *Games Analysis*, Canadian Association for the Advancement of Women and Sport. 1, 2, May, 1993.

5.   National Conference of Women and Sport, Government of Canada, Toronto, 1974.

6.   The second national conference was The Female Athlete Conference co-sponsored by the Institute for Human Performance at Simon Fraser University and the federal government. Popma, Anne (Ed.). 1980. *The Female Athlete: Proceedings of a National Conference.* Vancouver, BC: Simon Fraser University.

7.   Personal notes from the founding meeting held in Hamilton, Ontario.

8.   Canadian Sport and Fitness Administration Centre.

9.   Lorraine Code. 1980. "Feminist Theory" in Burt, S., Code, L. and L. Dorney. *Changing Patterns: Women in Canada.* McClelland and Stewart: 15 - 50.

10. Titles include *Games Analysis, On the Move Handbook, Adolescent Women, Women in International Sport: Advancing Gender Equity, Making and Informed Decision about Girls' Participation on Boys' Teams, Harassment in Sport-A Guide to Policies, Procedures and Resources, Toward Gender Equity for Women in Sport-A Handbook for National Sport Organizations.*

11. *Sport Canada Policy on Women in Sport,* Fitness and Amateur Sport, Minister of State, 1986: 6.

12. Ibid.

13. This was later altered when the new Liberal government created a 'super ministry' of Heritage and sport lost its minister and thus its direct access to the government.

14. Diane Palmason was Manager of the Women's Program during the late 1980s and left the post in mid-1990.

15. For example, the Hall. A., Slack, T. and D. Cullen report on Women and Administration in sport was produced in 1990 as a direct result of Sport Canada funding.

16. Kirby, S.L. and A.J. LeRougetel. (1992). *Games Analysis,* CAAWS occasional papers, Ottawa.

17. Sport organizations at the national level include organizations such as Judo Canada and Basketball Canada (National Sport Organizations or NSOs). Also, multi-service organizations such as the Sport Information Retrieval Centre (SIRC) and the Sport Federation of Canada (SFC) and multi-sport organizations such as the Commonwealth Games Society and the Canadian Federation of Sport Organizations for the Disabled (CFSOD) are included. With some exceptions, the sport organizations are housed at the Canadian Federation Sport Administration Centre in Gloucester, outside Ottawa.

18. Lorraine Greaves. 1991. "Reorganizing the National Action Committee on the Status of 1986-1988," in J. Wine and J. Ristock. *Women and Social Change: Feminist Activism in Canada.* James Lorimer and Co.: 101-116.

19. Sport Canada grew from 30 in 1970 to 121 in 1984 (Canada, DNHW, 1971-72, 1984-85) in Macintosh, D. (1988). "The Federal Government and Voluntary Sport

Associations." In J. Harvey and H. Cantelon. (1988). *Not Just a Game: Essays in Canadian Sport Sociology*, University of Ottawa Press: Ottawa: 121-140.

20. Judy Kent, Kent Consulting, Ottawa.

21. My particular task that weekend was to represent CAAWS and I volunteered to be on the team which drafted the Sport Forum mission statement, goals, and objectives.

22. S. Kirby, CAAWS Action Bulletin, November, 1991.

23. Government control of budgets (and hence organizations) was largely a question of the degree of dependence various sport organizations had on federal government financing. An organization such as Figure Skating Canada had considerable financial independence because of its ability to fundraise and its high media profile while Rowing Canada had considerable financial dependence because of the expense of organizing the sport and its limited ability to attract financial sponsors.

24. Success for Fitness and Amateur Sport Canada (the government) is still largely marked by the number of medals athletes won at the various multi-sport games (Commonwealth, Olympic, and Pan American Games specifically).

25. The International Professional Development Tour was co-sponsored by the Sport Canada — Women's Program, The International Relations Program of Sport Canada, and the Canadian Sport and Fitness Administration Centre. The eleven women travelling, mostly at their own expense, were Phyllis Berck (Ont.), Jennifer Brenning (Ont.), Peggy Gallant (N.S.), Sandi Kirby (Man.), Danelle Laidlaw (B.C.), Marion Lay (Ont.), Vicki Luke (Alta.), Marg McGregor (Ont.), Rose Mercier (Ont.), Toby Rabinovitz (Ont.), and Sheila Robertson (Ont.).

26. See the International Professional Development Report, The R. Tait MacKenzie Leadership Institute, Ottawa, 1992.

27. On the issue of equity, organizations representing Aboriginal Canadians had been particularly vocal. Since the organizational representation for Aboriginal Canadians was well developed, the Forum participants decided that an affirmative action step was necessary to enable Aboriginal Canadians to be "at future forums." Vocal too were those representing those with disabilities. Since sport organizations for the disabled already existed, equity measures for sport benefited these organizations. Disabled athletes also gained additional and very direct access to future forums through the "athlete representative" requirement.

28. Personal notes, Sport Forum III, October, 1992.

29. Ibid.

30. Personal notes from the FPTSPSC. Equity is defined as *the principle and practice of allocation of resources, programs and decision-making, fairly to all.* Access is defined as *the principle and practice of providing opportunities to participate fully and of changing sport to accommodate the changing needs of all its participants.*

31. From my notes of the FPTSPSC document prepared on Equity and Access by myself and Sue Neill, Strategic Planning, Sport Canada.

32. Marilyn Frye. 1983. *The Politics of Reality*. Trumansburg, New York: The Crossing Press.

33. Constantina Safilios-Rothschild. 1974. *Women and Social Policy*. Prentice-Hall.

34. Naomi Black. 1989. *Social Feminism*. Cornell University Press.

35. Audre Lorde. 1984. *Sister Outsider*. New York: The Crossing Press: 122.

PART II — PARTIE II
Women at Work — Femmes et travail

Linda Briskin's article addresses the topic of women and unions within economic parameters. She notes events from as early as 1981, and informs us about unions and feminist leaders across Canada. Exclusion from male-dominated executive boards and educational courses has been central to oppression of women in unions, particularly at national levels. In spite of the introduction of affirmative action policy, Briskin recognizes that complex patterns of structural discrimination continue. A feminist leader in labour studies, she emphasizes the importance of mutual support among union women at the local level in achieving goals important for working women.

Parsons and Goggins focus their article on the formation of a women's caucus within a university-based union of female and male educators on time-limited contracts. Since the female members are of diverse ages, races, sexual orientations, and bodily conditions, the sources of their oppression are complex. Based on their experiences as doctoral candidates and women's caucus organizers, these authors locate the oppression of female members in the social relations of educational work and unions. They argue from personal and academic knowledge that male thinking by union executives and memberships can only be transformed by politically aware women who share both their burdens and their strengths.

Même si les principes et les valeurs qui définissent les coopératives sont la prise en charge personnelle et mutuelle — la démocratie, l'égalité, l'équité et la solidarité — il n'en reste pas moins que les femmes ont senti le besoin de créer leurs propres coopératives afin de contrecarrer les effets du sexisme et de la discrimination dans le domaine du travail. Or, lorsque les femmes tentent de développer de nouvelles structures fondées sur des principes féministes, de nouvelles formes d'oppression s'ajoutent : celles des instances gouvernementales ou des autres institutions qui reconnaissent difficilement les principes démocratiques et économiques que la féminisation présuppose. Bouchard et Cholette offrent un exemple de théorisation des pratiques de gestion d'une coopérative de femmes francophones. Selon elles, la féminisation est une voie essentielle pour assurer le développement et l'épanouissement de nos communautés de femmes et de notre société. Les acquis des femmes étant encore très fragiles, les auteures pressent les femmes qui travaillent dans les institutions traditionnelles de mener, de l'intérieur, la lutte à la féminisation. Finalement, ces auteures soulignent que la féminisation des structures dans lesquelles elles travaillent entraîne un partage des pouvoirs, offre un environnement de travail flexible, tend à l'inclusion de personnes ayant moins de privilèges et favorise l'autonomie des femmes.

Linda Briskin

Feminisms, Feminization, and Democratization in Canadian Unions

Introduction

In a 1981 assessment of the situation of women in Canadian unions, Charlotte Gray concluded that the main achievement of the previous five years of union activity was a shift in attitudes.[1] In 1996, extensive evidence suggested that the organizing of union women has had a dramatic impact on the structures, policies, practices, and climate of the union movement — a transformation that goes well beyond the elusive change in attitudes. The 1994 Policy Statement "Confronting the Mean Society" (Canadian Labour Congress [CLC]) underscores the significance of these changes:

> Equality seeking groups have strengthened our movement, bringing new ideas and perspectives into the practice of unionism. The diversity that is now present in our unions has not divided the labour movement: on the contrary, it has energized us and brought many more committed people into our activist cadre. (#8)

Notwithstanding, women unionists continue to face significant barriers to participation. In fact, most of the literature on women and unions has focused on these barriers (for example, Braithwaite and Byrne 1995; Cuneo 1993; CLC 1990; Chaison and Andiappan 1989.) This article, however, concentrates on successes. It documents and evaluates strategies of union women in four key areas: representation, leadership, separate organizing, and redefinition of union issues. The conclusion reflects on some general issues about feminisms, feminization, and democratization that emerge from this discussion of union women's organizing. In a time when so many equity gains are under attack from economic and state restructuring as well as right-wing ideologies, the victories of union women provide some strategic optimism and act as important reminders of the possibilities for exercising agency.

Representation

Not surprisingly, concerns about representation, which have been central to women's organizing in all institutional contexts, have been a major focus in Canadian unions. For over ten years, many key Canadian unions and federations have had affirmative action policies that designate or add seats on leadership bodies for women in attempts to address their underrepresentation in top elected positions. In 1983, the Ontario Federation of Labour (OFL) broke new ground in Canada by amending its constitution to create five "affirmative action" positions on its executive board. The leadership role played by the Women's Committee of the OFL was crucial to winning this first affirmative action policy. The Committee organized a grassroots campaign and promoted an analysis linking employment equity in the workplace with affirmative action in the unions.[2]

As a result of this successful initiative, women unionists across the country promoted affirmative action seats. In 1984, the CLC adopted a constitutional change calling for a minimum of six female vice-presidents. Subsequently, many large labour federations and unions across the country did the same. Undoubtedly, affirmative action strategies have increased women's participation in top leadership positions in unions:

> Of the ninety-five executive seats held by women in these organizations, fully thirty-nine of them (41 percent) are affirmative action positions. Without them, the representation of women on these labour central executives would fall from 28 to 18 percent. (White 1993, 105)[3]

These high profile positions give visibility to women in leadership positions, challenge stereotypes, and provide role models. Since some of these women are committed to addressing the specific concerns of women as workers and unionists, the visibility of these issues has also increased. Penni Richmond from the CLC Women's and Human Rights Department reports that the presence of "outsiders" on the CLC Executive has

> changed the issues raised, changed who gets to hear what we talk about, and changed rank and file perception of who has power; in fact, it has put the discussion of power itself on the agenda.[4]

Increased awareness of issues of representation and power has had spin-off effects in other areas: employment equity for union staff; affirmative action seats for visible minorities and gays and lesbians; equity representation in education courses; and improvements in gender distribution in local leadership. Since affirmative action policies have often benefited white, able-bodied, heterosexual women to the exclusion of others, it is encouraging that, in at least some areas, the representation of minority women and members of other equity-seeking groups is on the agenda. Some examples include the following. In the OFL, by 1989, "women filled 4 of the 9 program staff positions (1 a visible minority), and 7 of the 11 field staff positions (1 a visible minority)" (Cuneo 1993, 128). In 1992, the CLC added 2 seats for visible minorities to its Executive Board; around the same time, the Public Service Alliance of Canada (PSAC) added equity seats to its Human Rights Committee for racial minorities, aboriginals, people with disabilities, and lesbians and gays (Hunt 1996, 21). In February of 1995, PSAC signed an employment equity plan with its staff unions to target recruitment and selection of equity group members (designated in employment equity legislation: women, people with disabilities, aboriginal peoples, visible minorities). The Alliance also ensures equity representation in its education courses.[5] Since union education is one of the stepping stones to union leadership, increasing inclusivity in union education may improve representation in the future.

Although women have always been better represented at the local level,[6] concern with representation has been trickling down through the union movement, and the leaderships of some male-dominated unions are proactively encouraging the participation of women and other underrepresented groups on local executives. For example, in 1991, Leo Gerard, then Director of District 6, the Ontario Region of the United Steelworkers of America (USWA), encouraged local presidents to keep in mind that

> the makeup of our Local Union Executives should reflect the membership of the local as well as the community in which the local exists. I, therefore, ask that... you consider encouraging women, people of colour, the disabled, etc., to run for executive positions.

Increasing the numbers of women in leadership positions is important, and affirmative action positions do represent a significant turning point for union women; nonetheless, some cautionary notes are worth sounding. Women who fill designated affirmative action positions, often chosen or elected through a special process, can face considerable resistance. Their credibility may be challenged and their ability to fill their mandates hampered by their association with affirmative action. They may encounter systematic exclusion from information networks and from formal and informal decision making processes. They may also experience ghettoization to narrowly-defined "women's issues" and become the object of feminist, lesbian, and red-baiting (Briskin 1990).

To some union activists, the focus on affirmative action seats sidelined more substantive demands for equality: "Many female activists saw affirmative action for exactly what it was, an admission of defeat in their bid for equal treatment within the labour movement" (Bail 1985, 9).

Penni Richmond (CLC) concurred with the substance of Bail's assessment: "The measures were not designed to actually change the arrangement of power."[7] Moreover, a few high profile women leaders can make it appear, mistakenly, that great strides toward "women's liberation" have been made. This misconception can weaken the drive to more proactive and substantive solutions to women's marginality in unions. It is certainly easier to appoint/elect a few women as vice-presidents than to challenge the deeply rooted male domination of union structures, strategies, and ideologies.

A narrow focus on changing the gender profile of leadership does not recognize the limits of a strategy of numerical representation based on biological sex. There is no guarantee that a woman, by virtue of her sex, will have progressive political views on women's issues. This reality has raised the question of whether representational strategies should be linked to a feminist perspective rather than a biological fact.

To some researchers and union activists, the focus on top leadership makes more invisible local and informal leadership by women, thereby exacerbating women's low status in unions and reproducing traditional patterns of organization and male domination. This is explored in the next section, which examines some structural (rather than representational) strategies that women have used to transform the institutional reality of unions.

When we consider the broad picture, we find that, despite some gains in numerical representation, despite a growing consciousness that women are prepared and competent to take on leadership positions, and despite the development of creative strategies to encourage this participation, women continue to be seriously underrepresented. This suggests that leadership patterns reflect deeply embedded patterns of structural discrimination and that increasing women's profile in leadership will require complex and multifaceted strategies that go well beyond a focus on numbers.

Leadership, Process, and Participation

Out of women's organizing in unions, and in response to male-dominated and hierarchical union practices, a new approach to leadership and alternative ways of working can be identified which emphasize process, accountability, and constituency building: participation rather than representation.[8] This politic supports the decentralization of power traditionally associated with leadership positions and provides "members opportunities to develop their own power and the self-reliance required to effect democratic changes in the union" (Edelson 1987, 6). In practice, this often means that women leaders encourage leadership development among women (Needleman 1988). For example, one of the major tasks of equal opportunity officers in many Canadian unions is to support and encourage the self-organization of rank-and-file women so that they can "speak" for themselves.

This view of leadership is reflected in the practices of female union staff. Based on their extensive experiences as union staff, Jane Stinson and Penni Richmond (1993) contrast the work styles of male and female representatives. In the dominant male model, the staff act as authority figures, experts, and "white knights" who charge in to rescue weak locals. In contrast, women staff tend to promote a participatory approach whose aim is to develop the confidence and skills of members. These ways of working draw on "expertise," but also recognize that experience and everyday knowledge are forms of that expertise.

This politic of leadership moves toward greater democracy and accountability, emphasizing a strong and active link between leadership and constituency. For example, in response to what was seen as a top-down and male-dominated mechanism for selecting women to fill affirmative action positions in the CLC, women in the Alberta Federation of Labour (AFL) won the right for the women's caucus to elect the women who would stand for these positions (Cuneo 1993). These new practices also provide a foundation for re-valuing "women's ways" of working and the local work and informal leadership of women. Traditionally, women have been better represented in local leadership positions and have often wanted to work at the local level. The tendency to undervalue local work and see it primarily as a stepping stone to higher positions (see, for example, Elkiss 1994; Melcher et al. 1992) reinforces the individualism of personal success stories and the hierarchical practices associated with male-dominated and bureaucratic unions. The focus on affirmative action for top leadership positions, along with the focus on expertise in staff positions, makes less visible the leadership contributions of elected women at the local level, the commitment of local women activists to union transformation, and the informal leadership provided by rank-and-file women.

Research suggests that women often play a critical role in informal leadership positions. In his study of women activists in Canadian unions, Carl Cuneo (1993) disaggregates leadership and formal elected positions, thereby making informal rank-and-file leadership activities visible. He concludes that "activist rank-and-file leaders...are women; they are more likely than men to be unpaid for what they do, and engage in temporary, voluntary activities" (118). This politic of leadership also emphasizes process, sharing work collectively, and consensus decision making. For example, Ann Marie Wierzbicki (Canada Employment and Immigration Union [CEIU-PSAC]) recalls sharing the duties of strike captain: "Officially there was just one strike captain, but unofficially we shared the responsibilities" (Little 1989, 12). In another example, Local 7 of the Canadian Union of Educational Workers [CUEW: now part of CUPE] experimented with rotating the position of chief negotiator:

> This gave everyone a chance to face management head on. I would never have run for the position of chief negotiator but when it was shared I became familiar with important adversarial skills which then encouraged me to run for chief steward. (Jacquie Buncel quoted in Little 1989, 13)[9]

In 1995, PSAC instituted an innovative employment equity plan for union staff. On every staffing action longer than three months, a joint decision is made about whether the position will be posted as a preferential hiring. Joanne Ursino, the Employment Equity Officer, characterized the process of developing the plan as a "model of consensus decision-making" through joint committee work.[10]

Many of these innovations around decision making and leadership practices are informed by the organizing strategies of the grassroots women's movement. In that context, what is often referred to as "feminist process" has been the source of strength but also of problems (Ristock 1991; Briskin 1990; Adamson, Briskin and McPhail 1988). In the women's movement, feminist process is often situated in a non-institutional setting where the focus on political goals is difficult to sustain, and the desire and potential to create a haven from the "world out there" is stronger.

The daily reality of the workplace and the union seem to minimize some of the problems. The unions provide an institutional structure and a resource base; that is, the workplace as a common reference point. The informal and formal skills encouraged through feminist process are directly and immediately applicable to work and union situations.

Notwithstanding, when assumptions about process do not take account of the diversity of cultural and class experiences, women's committees and "women's" ways of working can be made less accessible to women who are not white or middle-class. For example, what constitutes a safe environment for some women may be experienced as dangerous by others; interpersonal practices which emphasize sharing experiences may be more comfortable in some cultural contexts than in others. Further, the time commitment necessary to make "process" work can easily exclude women who work full-time, face a double (triple) day, are single parents, and so forth.

Separate Organizing

Separate organizing takes a variety of forms within the union movement: informal women's networks or caucuses; formal, sometimes elected, provincial or national women's committees; women only educational conferences; women's locals of mixed unions or women's auxiliaries; and women only unions such as the Federation of Women Teachers Associations of Ontario (FWTAO). Separate organizing is increasingly supported by union resources and facilitated by equal opportunity coordinators, newsletters, and women's bureaus. In examining "separate organizing," it is useful to distinguish between separatism as a *goal* — an end in itself, and separate organizing as a *strategy* — a means to an end (Briskin 1993a, 91). It is also important to recognize that separate organizing is not segregation, either imposed or chosen, but rather a strategic response to differences in power.

Such structures, especially women's caucuses and committees, were generated by women unionists, originally on the margins of traditional union organization (Field 1983; Little 1989). By highlighting the specificity of women's concerns as workers and unionists, these committees mobilized women in large numbers. They have provided a supportive context from which women can do union work, and modeled alternative and often more inclusive ways of working. Evidence suggests their efficacy in promoting women leaders and women's rights (Trebilcock, 1991). For example, Barbara Nichols-Heppner (1984) concludes that, in public sector unions in Quebec, establishing women's committees was a more effective strategy than seeking greater electoral representation, and that such committees "evoke more organizational responsiveness from unions" and are "the strongest determinant of the negotiation of collective agreement provisions favourable to women unionists" (294).[11]

More than 20 years of women's committees and caucuses in the unions have not led to a decline in such organizing among women. Evidence also suggests a growing acceptance and legitimation of separate organizing — at least in the public discourse of unions — and increasing institutionalization and formalization of structures to facilitate it: constitutional clauses to incorporate women's committees (for example, the constitution of the Canadian Auto Workers (CAW) mandates women's committees at all levels of the union); policy statements to address women's concerns, allocation of staff and financial resources, etc. (Boehm 1991). Peggy Nash, a CLC Vice-President and a staff member with Canadian Auto Workers (CAW), a male-dominated union mostly organizing industrial workplaces where "women have to get along with the guys to do anything," commented:

It used to be the kiss of death to be involved in the women's committees in terms of other involvement in the union. Most women activists don't feel this way now. There is a growing sense that 'sisterhood' in the union is a good thing, that organizing separately is a good thing, and that fighting to include women of colour, and lesbians strengthens the women's movement inside the union.[12]

Women's separate organizing in the unions has provided a strategic foundation for responding to issues around race and racism as well as sexual orientation and homophobia. First, it has provided a *venue* where issues of concern to minority workers were first raised and continue to be raised:

Issues of race or disability or gay/lesbianism were often first raised within women's committees or women's conferences because these forums were more accepting of the problems and more prepared to deal with them. One exception is the women's committee of the Quebec Federation of Labour, which opposes the introduction or handling of these issues in the women's committee, and does not agree with the position taken by many women's committees in English Canada. (White 1993, 232)

Notwithstanding, the efforts by women of colour to raise issues of racism inside women's committees and inside unions have not always been welcomed (Leah 1989 and 1993). Evidence suggests, however, some union responsiveness to the pressure of women of colour. Changes in union educational programs, new policy statements, and the commitment of resources indicate the development of a discourse of race privilege among white women, a growing sensitivity to the needs of minority groups of women in Canada, and the facilitation of dialogue about these issues.

Second, women's separate organizing has provided an important precedent; increasingly, women and men of colour, lesbians and gay men, and Native peoples are organizing "separately" inside the union movement, often through Human Rights Committees, Pink Triangle Committees, and Aboriginal Circles. Separate organizing also provides the basis for different constituencies to come together from positions of strength; for example, consider the links established between health and safety committees and women's committees (Messing and Mergler 1993), and the convergence of human rights and women's issues (Leah 1993).[13]

Women's separate organizing challenges not only men's power but also the organizational practices of unions. Historically, unions have been male dominated. Yet, perhaps more significant than the numerical domination of men has been the domination of an organizational model based on bureaucratic, hierarchical, overly competitive, and often undemocratic practices. Men's power, privilege, and leadership, then, combine with traditional organizational forms to exclude and disadvantage women. It may or may not be useful to label these organizational approaches as "masculine," but they do often co-exist with numerical domination by men and exclusionary practices such as sexual harassment. Since women's separate organizing simultaneously contests the gender relations of power and organizational structures and practices, it is experienced by men as a serious challenge.

Since separate organizing is about gender *and* about organization, organizing "separately" is not itself enough to guarantee success; the location of the separate organizing in the structural web of the institution is critical. The success of women's separate organizing in unions depends upon maintaining a balance between the degree of autonomy from the structures and practices of the labour movement, on the one hand, and the degree of integration into those structures, on the other. Too little integration and the separate organizing is marginalized; too much integration and the radical edge is necessarily softened. Relatively successful integration produces the level of legitimacy necessary to ensure access to adequate resources. Sufficient autonomy provides the foundation for a strong voice about women's concerns and the context for building alliances between union women and the community-based women's movement.[14]

Despite the incontrovertible evidence of the success of separate organizing and the significance of "women's" ways of working to a re-visioned union movement, ambivalence continues.[15] First, there is a serious concern, supported by extensive feminist research, that focusing on "women" as a group can make invisible the diversity among women based on class, race, sexual orientation, and ability, and thus privilege the experiences and needs of white middle-class women.

The second concern relates to the biological essentialism that can emerge in discussions of "women's" ways of working and separate organizing. Biological essentialism is

> that set of assertions... designed to demonstrate that there
> is a 'female nature'... It assumes a psychology and emotional
> temper peculiar to women... a set of preoccupations [and,
> I might add, occupations] appropriate, by nature. (Kramarae
> and Treichler 1985, 142)

Talking about "women's" ways of working, then, can reproduce common stereotypes about women: they are more nurturing, relational, and emotional, by nature. *Recognizing the realities of gender-specific experience and discrimination,* however, need not invoke biological essentialism.

A non-essentialist approach begins from the position that women's experiences are socially constituted. It recognizes that women enter unions differently from men because of their workplace locations and their household/family responsibilities; that women's work bridges the public and the private, and that each has an impact on the other; and that the pervasive violence women experience in both public and private spaces influences workplace and family experience as well as women's political strategies. It is not surprising, then — and it need have nothing to do with biological natures — that women identify different issues as salient, and organize and resist in distinct ways.

The experience of the Service, Office, and Retail Workers Union of Canada (SORWUC) provides an excellent example. SORWUC was an explicitly feminist union which, in the 1970s, took on the enormous task of organizing bank workers in Canada (Bank Book Collective 1979; Lennon 1980; Warskett 1988; Baker 1991). It focused on the banks as a sector of women's low-wage work that had been virtually ignored by the trade union movement. SORWUC felt that women had to organize women because women had respect for the work of women; because women organized differently with more participatory decision making strategies and with a recognition of the limits placed on women workers by the double day; and because women focused on different issues such as pay equity, childcare, and sexual harassment. SORWUC was able to organize many bank branches where others had failed.[16] Their success was related to the recognition of gender-specific concerns and methods of organizing, such recognition highlighting the structural and ideological discrimination of women.

No doubt, there is a danger that the practices of separate organizing and claims about "women's" ways of working can be mobilized in support of a right wing agenda which uses biology as a justification to enforce women's "special" responsibilities for children and caring and to exclude them from the public sphere. This means that discussions of gender specificity must not be framed by essentialist arguments, but by a recognition of the socially constructed nature of experience and of structural power imbalances.

Redefining Union Issues and the
Collective Bargaining Agenda

Over the last two decades, women unionists have successfully pressured unions to take up the issues of childcare, abortion, sexual harassment, pay equity, affirmative action, employment equity, and so forth. Around each of these issues, union men and union hierarchies have questioned the legitimacy of unions addressing such issues. With each victory (expressed in policy statements, expansion in the collective bargaining agenda, changes to political focus), the boundaries of what constitutes a legitimate union issue have shifted, the understanding of what is seen to be relevant to the workplace has altered, and the support for a more social and political analysis of the role of unions has increased.

A dramatic case in point is the increasing union involvement, often with explicit and active support from top leadership, in the broad issues around violence against women. These campaigns go well beyond a focus on employer harassment or even co-worker harassment, and many have successfully integrated race issues. For example, the Canadian Auto Workers (CAW) sponsored a women's conference on the issue of violence against women in August 1991 and again in 1992, passed a resolution committing the CAW to the goal of creating "zero tolerance level of sexist treatment of women," and did a mass distribution of posters and buttons with the slogan "Violence: Break the Silence." To mark December 6, a national day of remembrance and action on the issue of violence in commemoration of those women who died in the Montreal massacre in 1989, the CAW urged its locals to conduct educationals, participate in local events around December 6, and support their local shelters and rape crisis centres through fundraising and volunteer work.[17]

The transformation in the union agenda to address women's concerns has set the stage for three other shifts: gendering union issues, recognizing diversity ramifications, and understanding the impact of family-workplace connections. Gendering issues has meant a subtle move from an identification of a women's platform of concerns to a recognition of the gender implications in all issues. This is evident in recent discussions on free trade, on economic restructuring, on seniority, on health and safety, and on telework.

The family-workplace nexus has been recognized in union support for childcare and in the provision of childcare at union meetings. The CAW, responsible for some of the most innovative gains in collective bargaining, has linked issues of family, workplace, and violence. In a recent contract with Chrysler, the following clause was negotiated:

> The parties recognize that women sometimes face situations of violence or abuse in their personal life that may affect their attendance or performance at work. The parties agree that when there is adequate verification from a recognized professional..., a woman who is in an abusive or violent personal situation will not be subjected to discipline without giving full consideration to the facts in the case...

At the same time that the significance of gender is examined, issues are increasingly scrutinized for their impact on diverse groups of women. Education, policy development, and negotiations around harassment acknowledge the specific forms of harassment experienced by women of colour. Discussions of family benefits more often reject traditional definitions of "family" that exclude gay and lesbian couples:

> Many of us assume that our collective agreements apply equally to all members. They do not. Our lesbian sisters, gay brothers, bi-sexuals in same sex spousal relationship and their families are denied access to the basic rights that heterosexual members take for granted. (PSAC Policy on Sexual Orientation, 1994)

These shifts in the understanding of what constitutes a union issue, as well as the increase in gender visibility and specificity, have had impacts on the collective bargaining agenda. The most recent national assessment of the gains made by women through collective bargaining in Canada concludes that there is now

> widespread consensus within the Canadian labour movement that unions need to escalate their efforts towards labour market equality, safe and harassment-free work environments, and policies and practices to make it easier for women to balance more effectively their work and family life. (Kumar 1993, 207)[18]

Feminisms, Feminization, and Democracy

This conclusion considers the contribution of feminisms and feminization to union democratization, which I would argue is a critical thrust of union women's organizing. In a generic way, feminisms challenge gender-based inequity and, as such, can highlight the common problems women face. Given the complex diversity of class, race, ethnicity, ability, and sexual orientation operating in most union contexts, however, this trajectory toward gender commonality can be strategically mobilizing or fragmenting. Moreover, not one but a multiplicity of feminisms struggle for place within the union movement as elsewhere, bringing different approaches to prioritizing union issues, expanding women's participation in leadership positions, developing new process mechanisms, and organizing with the community outside the labour movement. To this complexity, any study of feminisms in the unions must be sensitive.

Not surprisingly, the self-identification as feminist and the labelling of organizing practices, strategies, or solutions as feminist remain quite contested inside unions:

> When I first ran for a national position in the trade union movement...I said 'I'm a trade unionist and a feminist and I think the words are synonymous.' I was advised by a number of labour leaders not to say that — that I would be seen as only concerned about the women's side of the trade union movement. What concerned me was that I had to say it at all — that I had to say that trade unionists and feminists were synonymous. Because I had assumed in my trade union life that it was... that the principles of feminism and the principles of trade unionism and social democracy were all the same. (Nancy Riche 1991)[19]

Penni Richmond, from the CLC Women's and Human Rights Department Bureau, has a similar view:

> It used to be that few women would identify themselves as feminists; now there is a very significant group but still there is an ambivalent relation to feminism and a discomfort labelling oneself a feminist. The problem is that when feminist women organize openly and militantly, other women sometimes feel they are being criticized and support men.[20]

Caution, then, is needed in labelling the practices of union women organizing as "feminist," given that women militants in the unions might not understand their movement or their militancy in this way (see also Sugiman 1993 and Coulter 1993). This paper has prevaricated around such labelling in order to respect the struggles around feminism inside the union movement and to avoid a reification of feminist practices. For example, the discussion on ways of working begs the question of whether characterizing the new politic of leadership and process as "feminist" is appropriate. Although I have in the past so labelled it (1990), I am increasingly uncertain about the relevance, accuracy, or meaning of such naming, given a more fluid understanding of feminism and a move away from abstract criteria; a recognition of the multiplicity of feminisms that produce different leadership styles, practices, and politics; and the fact that women unionists themselves do not, by and large, use this language. Such labelling might limit rather than open a debate about the relationship of feminism to new organizational practices. At the same time, there is no doubt that the ideologies, strategies, and, indeed, the resistances outlined in this paper would be familiar to any feminist activist.[21]

I suggest, then, that it is both more appropriate and accurate to study *women's* organizing in unions rather than *feminist* organizing. Such an approach allows the relationship between women's organizing and feminisms as ideologies, as strategies, as analyses, as organizing practices, as visionary alternatives, and as complex self-identifications and identities to be examined. Feminisms emerge, then, not as abstract criteria or boundary markers against which union women's organizing is assessed, but as a fluid, contextually located set of meanings and practices. Feminism is a site of struggle, a moment of resistance, an organizing tool; it helps produce communities of interest and patterns of exclusion.

Notwithstanding these concerns, it is noteworthy that Jane Stinson and Penni Richmond (1993), both long time union staffers, argue that the feminist project in unions is directly related to the future health of the labour movement, and that a feminist approach to unionism, based on more participatory and inclusive decision making, is needed for unions to grapple successfully with the challenges ahead. Additionally, a 1990 CLC discussion paper, *Empowering Union Women*, speaks directly to the issue of feminism: "We need to develop a more woman-centred union perspective, a feminist perspective; one which will become part of the dominant outlook of the trade union movement" (23).

At the same time that I suggest caution in how we talk about feminisms in the unions, evidence suggests the increasing significance of gender in the complex web of work and unions. We see the feminization of labour (more part-time, low-paid service jobs), the feminization of the workforce (more women workers), the feminization of unions (with increasing numbers of women members) and, indeed, the feminization of militancy (with growing numbers of women activists) (Briskin and McDermott 1993b).[22]

Distinguishing between feminisms and feminizing helps us to see the contribution of each to women's calls for more democracy in the unions. Feminization, which transforms the gender profile in unions, precipitates calls for equitable representation of women. Feminist analyses which take account of gender-specific realities and challenge the organizational practices of unions and their culture inevitably push the discussion of democracy beyond representation.

Moreover, feminisms provide the tools for a gender-specific analysis of democracy that takes account of multiple diversities. The challenge to make gender realities visible has undermined the notion of a generic worker with a homogeneous and self-evident set of interests and laid the basis for legitimating the multiplicity of experiences based on class, race, ethnicity, age, ability, and sexual orientation.

Increasing women's representation in elected leadership positions is not sufficient to engender democracy in the unions or elsewhere. In fact, the causal relationship may be the reverse. For representational strategies to be successful, they must be deeply embedded in larger processes of democratizing organizational practices and union culture. In a study of public-sector unions in Quebec, Barbara Nichols-Heppner (1984, 270) found that "an increase in the level of democracy practised in union internal government will foster greater election of women as presidents and officers of union locals." Throughout women's initiatives on representation, leadership practices, separate organizing, and redefining union issues are calls for a substantively different form of democracy — for structures of participation and inclusivity rather than simply representation. Furthermore, there is a strong connection between democratic, participatory processes within the labour movement, and the militancy needed to face employer intransigence. For example, in her analysis of the roots of militancy of the United Nurses of Alberta (UNA), Rebecca Coulter (1993) isolates the highly democratic and participatory collective bargaining process within the UNA as the catalyst for nurses' militancy and a key element in explaining both the solidarity of the membership and their willingness to strike.

What women unionists have learned is that democracy is not an abstraction, nor is it gender-neutral; that is, since women and men have unequal access to political and economic power and to union power, they do not experience democracy, or the lack thereof, in the same way. Gendering democracy, then, speaks not only to making the internal practices of unions more democratic and welcoming, but also to making them more accessible by taking account of childcare and domestic responsibilities. It means ensuring that the bargaining agenda reflects the needs of women workers and promoting organizational structures such as women's committees that encourage the participation of women. Gendering democracy is inherently linked to rank-and-file empowerment.

Not surprisingly, resistance to the organizing of women and other marginalized groups by both patriarchal and bureaucratic union interests continues. It is also not surprising that there is a convergence of demands by rank-and-file unionists for more democracy, and by union women struggling for more voice. Dierdre Gallagher, a long time feminist activist in the union movement currently on staff at the Public Service Alliance of Canada (PSAC), makes this link:

> There is still an unwillingness…and a real fear of sharing power with women. In some ways, it is a fear of democracy itself, because women's push within the labour movement has represented a demand for a more democratic union. These people who fear democracy, fear women. (1987, 354)

Some of the resistance to women's organizing inside unions, then, is resistance to the implicit challenge to entrenched leaderships:

> Women activists face two kinds of resistance in the union movement. One is resistance to us as women, a reflection of patriarchal norms and values implicit in part of every institution in capitalist society. We expect this kind of resistance. The other form of resistance is not a particular resistance to us as women. It is a resistance to our militancy: to our challenge to the leadership, to our demand that the union movement take up issues outside the narrow framework of business unionism and that it operate with more democratic and accountable structures. (Briskin 1983, 268)

Gendering democracy is a way of actualizing the principles of equality, solidarity, justice, and fairness which are such a deeply ingrained part of union ideology, if not its practice. The struggle for new forms of democracy within the union movement is critical: it will be the key to gaining and maintaining women's access to, and voice within, the labour movement; it will empower women to stand firm when confronting their employers; and it will help provide a vision for a new kind of unionism.

References

Adamson, Nancy, Linda Briskin and Margaret McPhail. 1988. *Feminist Organizing for Change*. Toronto: Oxford.

Bail, Marg. 1985. "Getting the Girls to the Top." *Canadian Dimension* 19, 4, 8-9.

Baker, Patricia. 1991. "Some Unions Are More Equal Than Others: A Response to Rosemary Warskett's 'Bank Worker Unionization and the Law'." *Studies in Political Economy* 34, Spring, 219-233.

Bank Book Collective. 1979. *An Account to Settle*. Vancouver: Press Gang.

Boehm, Marina. 1991. *Who Makes the Decisions? Women's Participation in Canadian Unions*. School of Industrial Relations Research Essay, Series No. 35. Industrial Relations Centre: Queen's University.

Braithwaite, Mary and Catherine Byrne. 1995. *Women in Decision-Making in Trade Unions*. Brussels: European Trade Union Confederation.

Briskin, Linda. 1977. *Gendering Union Democracy: A Swedish-Canadian Comparison*. Working Paper Series #13. Centre for Research on Work and Society: York University.

Briskin, Linda. 1994. "Equity and Economic Restructuring in the Canadian Labour Movement." *Economic and Industrial Democracy* 15, 1, 89-112.

Briskin, Linda and Patricia McDermott (eds.). 1993. *Women Challenging Unions: Feminism, Democracy and Militancy*. Toronto: University of Toronto Press.

Briskin, Linda. 1993a. "Union Women and Separate Organizing." *Women Challenging Unions: Feminism, Democracy and Militancy*, eds. Linda Briskin and Patricia McDermott, Ed. Toronto: University of Toronto Press. 89-108.

Briskin, Linda and Patricia McDermott. 1993. "The Feminist Challenge to the Unions." *Women Challenging Unions: Feminism, Democracy and Militancy*, eds. Linda Briskin and Patricia McDermott, Ed. Toronto: University of Toronto Press. 3-19.

Briskin, Linda. 1990. "Women, Unions and Leadership." *Canadian Dimension* 24, Jan-Feb, 38-41.

Briskin, Linda.1983. "Women's Challenge to Organized Labour." *Union Sisters: Women in the Labour Movement,* eds. Linda Briskin and Lynda Yanz. Toronto: Women's Press. 259-271.

Canadian Labour Congress.1990. *Empowering Union Women: Toward the Year 2000.*

Chaison, Gary and P. Andiappan. 1989. "An Analysis of the Barriers to Women Becoming Local Union Officers." *Journal of Labour Research* 10, 2, 149-162.

Colgan, Fiona and Sue Ledwith.1994. *Women's Trade Union Activism: A Creative Force for Change and Renewal within the Trade Union Movement?* Paper presented at the Annual Conference of Work, Employment and Society..

Coulter, Rebecca.1993. "Alberta Nurses and the 'Illegal' Strike of 1988." *Women Challenging Unions: Feminism, Democracy and Militancy,* eds. Linda Briskin and Patricia McDermott. Toronto: University of Toronto Press. 44-61.

Crain, Marion. 1994. "Gender and Union Organizing." *Industrial and Labour Relations Review* 47, 2, 227-248.

Cuneo, Carl. 1993. "Trade Union Leadership: Sexism and Affirmative Action." *Women Challenging Unions: Feminism, Democracy and Militancy,* eds. Linda Briskin and Patricia McDermott. Toronto: University of Toronto Press.109-136.

Edelson, Miriam. 1987. *Challenging Unions: Feminist Process and Democracy in the Labour Movement.* Ottawa, Canadian Research Institute for the Advancement of Women (CRIAW).

Elkiss, Helen. 1994. "Training Women for Union Office: Breaking the Glass Ceiling." *Labour Studies Journal* 19, 2 (Summer), 25-42.

Field, Debbie. 1983. "The Dilemma Facing Women's Committees." *Union Sisters: Women in the Labour Movement,* eds. Linda Briskin and Lynda Yanz. Toronto: Women's Press. 293-303.

Gallagher, Deirdre.1987. "Affirmative Action." *Working People and Hard Times,* eds. Robert Argue, Charlene Gannage and D. W. Livingstone. Toronto: Garamond Press. 348-355.

Gray, Charlotte. 1981. "What Will Unions do for Women in the 80s?" *Chatelaine* (May).

Hunt, Gerald. 1996. *Sexual Orientation and the Canadian Labour Movement.* Unpublished paper, Nipissing University.

Kramarae, Cheris and Paula Treichler.1985. *A Feminist Dictionary.* Boston: Pandora Press.

Kumar, Pradeep. 1993. "Collective Bargaining and Women's Workplace Concerns." *Women Challenging Unions: Feminism, Democracy and Militancy,* eds. Linda Briskin and Patricia McDermott. Toronto: University of Toronto Press. 207-230.

Leah, Ronnie. 1989. "Linking the Struggles: Racism, Feminism and the Union Movement." *Race, Class, Gender: Bonds and Barriers.* Socialist Studies, A Canadian Annual, No.5, 166-195.

Leah, Ronnie. 1993. "Black Women Speak Out: Racism and Unions." *Women Challenging Unions: Feminism, Democracy and Militancy,* eds. Linda Briskin and Patricia McDermott. Toronto: University of Toronto Press. 151-171.

Lennon, Elizabeth J. Shilton. 1980. "Organizing the Unorganized: Unionization in the Chartered Banks of Canada." *Osgoode Hall Law Journal* 18, 2, 177-237.

Little, Margaret. 1989. "Women and Unions: Movement Make Over." *Our Times* (December), 12-14.

Melcher, Dale, Jennifer Eichstedt, Shelley Eriksen and Dan Clawson. 1992. "Women's Participation in Local Union Leadership: The Massachusetts Experience." *Industrial and Labor Relations Review* 45, 2 (January), 267-280.

Messing, Karen and Donna Mergler.1993. "Unions and Women's Occupational Health in Quebec." *Women Challenging Unions: Feminism, Democracy and Militancy,* eds. Linda Briskin and Patricia McDermott. Toronto: University of Toronto Press. 266-283.

Needleman, Ruth. 1988. "Women Workers: A Force for Rebuilding Unionism." *Labor Research Review* 11 (Spring), 1-13.

Nichols-Heppner, Barbara. 1984. *Women in Public Sector Unions in Quebec: Organizing for Equality*. Unpublished Phd Thesis, McGill University.

Pocock, Barbara. 1995. "Gender and Activism in Australian Unions." *Journal of Industrial Relations* 37 (Sept), 377-400.

Ristock, Janice. 1991. "Feminist Collectives." *Women and Social Change*, eds. Jeri Wine and Janice Ristock. Toronto: Lorimer. 41-55.

Stinson, Jane and Penni Richmond. 1993. "Women Working for Unions: Female Staff and the Politics of Transformation." *Women Challenging Unions: Feminism, Democracy and Militancy*, eds. Linda Briskin and Patricia McDermott. Toronto: University of Toronto Press. 137-156.

Sugiman, Pamela. 1993b. "Unionism and Feminism in the Canadian Auto Workers Union, 1961-1992." *Women Challenging Unions: Feminism, Democracy and Militancy*, eds. Linda Briskin and Patricia McDermott. Toronto: University of Toronto Press. 172-188.

Trebilcock, Anne. 1991. "Strategies for Strengthening Women's Participation in Trade Union Leadership." *International Labour Review* 130, 4, 407-426.

Warskett, Rosemary. 1988. "Bank Worker Unionization and the Law." *Studies in Political Economy* 25 (Spring), 41-73.

White, Julie. 1993. *Sisters and Solidarity: Women and Unions in Canada*. Toronto: Thompson Educational Publishing.

Endnotes

1. This article draws freely on other articles I have written on women and unions. See especially Briskin 1997, 1994, 1993a, and 1990.

2. In 1982, the OFL Women's Committee drafted a discussion paper on affirmative action, entitled "Our Fair Share." The 1992 OFL Convention adopted a policy statement on affirmative action, "a clear mandate for the OFL to embark on a major campaign both for mandatory affirmative action legislation and the promotion of women within union ranks." In 1983, the OFL sponsored an Ontario wide series of public forums on affirmative action 'which raised awareness of the size of the problem of discrimination faced by women in the workforce.' The forums resulted in over 170 submissions. At the 1983 OFL convention, the OFL amended its constitution to create five affirmative actions positions on its executive board. In 1984, the OFL published "Making up the Difference" which summarized the findings of the public hearings. The brief made over 40 recommendations to the government for legislative and other action to create some measure of equality for women. Summary and quotations from "Affirmative Action: How We got Started" #1 in a pamphlet series on *Organizing for Affirmative Action*, produced by the Women's Committee of the Ontario Federation of Labour, nd. For more information, see Cuneo (1993).

3. White (1993: 99) reports that women constituted 18% of executive seats in 1980 and 9% in 1970.

4. Telephone Interview, 12 Oct 1994.

5. Correspondence, Joanne Labine, PSAC, 1995.

6. For example, a 1989 QFL found that "at the local level women had reached or exceeded proportional representation in executive positions; on average, women accounted for thirty percent or more of them. While recording secretary or secretary-treasurer were the most common positions for women on the local union executive, women were found as president or vice-president in over one-third of the local unions who responded" (CLC 1990, 10-11).

7.   Telephone interview, 12 Oct 1994.

8.   This discussion is excerpted from Briskin, 1990 which deals exclusively with women, unions, and leadership; it was based largely on a transcript of a workshop on Women, Unions, and Leadership held at the Workers and Communities Conference (York University, Ontario, 1989) which brought together about 60 women militants and leaders.

9.   In May 1988, CUEW formalized this collective process at the national leadership level in a structure which called for two co-chairs (one of whom must be a woman) and rotation of responsibilities.

10.   Telephone interview, 6 June 1995.

11.   In *Women and Decision Making in Trade Unions*, an extensive study done for the European Trade Union Confederation [ETUC], Mary Braithwaite and Catherine Byrne (1995, 2-3) draw the following conclusions: "The great majority of national confederations have a women's or equality committee, generally dealing with gender equality issues only and reporting to the executive committee. Most are open to women and men. Those confederations with markedly low levels of female representation within the confederation structures have no such committee, suggesting that women's or equality committees are a necessary part of achieving better female representation...More than half of the 31 national confederations have a women's or equality department, and there appears to be a correlation between the existence of such a department and higher levels of female representation in confederation structures and decision making positions. Those confederations with no women's or equality department have low levels of representation of women in key decision making areas...Less than half of national confederations organize a women's congress or conference, but again there appears to be a strong correlation between the existence of a regular women's congress or conference and higher levels of female representation in decision making positions and structures."

12.   Interview, 9 Sept 1994.

13.   At the same time, Penni Richmond of the CLC Women's Bureau notes that the self-organization of these communities of interest is beginning to raise the question of "how these groups will work together, and heal some of the artificial split: since, for example, half of gays and lesbians are women, and some persons with disabilities are visible minorities, etc." Telephone interview, 20 Oct 1994.

14.   See Briskin, 1993a in which I compare the conditions of separate organizing in SORWUC and FWTAO.

15.   See, for example, the 1992 and 1994 Reports of the Women's Rights Committee to the Convention of the British Columbia Federation of Labour [BCFL].

16.   From an interview with Jean Rands, a founding member of SORWUC conducted on 7 May 1991. See also Crain, 1994.

17.   From a letter to all Local presidents, secretaries, women's committees from Peggy Nash, Assistant to the President, CAW (30 October 1991).

18.   Despite significant changes in the collective bargaining agenda, Kumar (1993, 224) concludes that the record of negotiated successes has been disappointing. For an analysis of this lack of success, see Briskin, 1996.

19.   Executive Vice-President of the Canadian Labour Congress (CLC), in a speech to the 1991 Annual General Meeting of the National Action Committee on the Status of Women (NAC). Transcribed from the tape provided by NAC.

20.   Telephone interview, 20 Oct 1994.

21.   In a provocative preliminary study of women union activists in two unions in Britain, Colgan and Ledwith (1994, 18) find that, although only about 25% self-identified as feminists, "there appears to be a remarkable consensus among feminists and non-feminists about what is needed to be done for women in their unions.

Regardless of self-perception, trade union women's primary attitudes seemed to be in agreement with what can be labeled feminist principles and strategies." What this suggests is that a feminist analysis can co-exist with a rejection of a feminist self-identification.

22.   In an Australian study, Barbara Pocock (1989, 387) found that the feminization of the workplace was one of the predictors of activism among women unionists.

Intersecting Multiple Sites of Marginalization: The Work of Feminizing Within an Educational Workers' Union

The politic of separate organizing recognizes that the problems women face in unions are a result of structural and ideological discrimination, and that women must organise collectively — bringing to this process their own gender-specific knowledge — in order to effect institutional change. (Briskin 1993, 97)

Starla Goggins

I am a Black woman of West African and American cultural heritage. Having witnessed firsthand the Detroit riots of the late 1960s, my politics have been greatly influenced by the efforts of those involved in the Civil Rights Movement. This history, in conjunction with my own experiences of racism within Canada, give me the particular perspective which I bring to my activist work.

Marianne Parsons

I am a white woman from Nova Scotia. Having been raised in a region of economic disparity and in a large family with a strong commitment to grassroots community activism, I became politically aware of social inequity and injustice at a very early age. My politics find voice in my activism.

Joining Our Perspectives and Taking Action

We share a twelve-year history of teaching part-time within the university. From 1989 to the present, we have been politically active within part-time educational workers' collectives at several Canadian universities, located in southern Ontario and Nova Scotia. In this article, we focus on our activist work as co-chairs of a women's caucus (1991-1993) within a Toronto-based union local serving part-time educational workers. Through self-reflection, discussions with other caucus members, and a review of documents, events, and literature in this area, we provide a critical account of our experience of feminist organizing, locating it within the broader context of part-time university teaching within Canada.[1] Specifically, we examine the strategies and methods of resistance

93

we employed as a feminist collective in our struggle to politicize and address issues of race, gender, class, and disability as part of the process of feminizing union policies and practices. It is important to emphasize, however, that the efforts of countless women and men over the years secured this separate sphere for women, and that our story is only one of many in a rich history of feminist organizing within this union.[2]

For the purposes of this paper, "feminizing" is defined as the active process of effecting social change within institutions through the recognition and inclusion of women's multiple and diverse experiences of marginalization. We argue that, by revealing the intersections between and within marginalized groups, the women's caucus within this union provided the "woman space" wherein systemic discrimination could be addressed, and strategies for social change developed and implemented. Without a politic which recognizes and includes diversity, union "solidarity" becomes a vehicle through which the rights and privileges of the powerful are reproduced and maintained.

Our story is one of empowerment, of personal transformation and institutional change. By documenting these experiences within a feminist framework — one that links personal narrative to feminist activism and social change — we continue the work of providing testimony to the history of the feminist movement. In the words of Bell Hooks

> we must have more written work and oral testimony documenting ways barriers are broken down, coalitions formed, and solidarity shared. It is this evidence that will renew our hope and provide strategies and direction for future feminist movement.... If a revitalised feminist movement is to have a transformative impact on women, then creating a context where we can engage in open critical dialogue with one another, where we can debate and discuss without fear of emotional collapse, *where we can hear and know one another in the difference and complexities of our experience,* is essential. Collective feminist movement cannot go forward if this step is never taken. When we create this woman space where we can value difference and complexity, sisterhood based on political solidarity will emerge (1994, 110, own emphasis).

Locating Ourselves as Part-time Educational Workers

We were employed as teaching assistants and members of a part-time educational workers' union at a large Toronto university.[3] Our union local served part-time faculty, teaching assistants, and graduate assistants. The union membership included approximately 1800 workers, with

94

an equal proportion of women and men (Ornstein, Sandilands and Teiman 1992). As co-chairs of a women's caucus within this union, our relationship to each other as feminists activists provided the framework within which we worked together for change. As with any political strategy employed to affect social change, the work of "feminizing" is context bound. In order to understand the strategies employed by the women's caucus, it is necessary to locate part-time university teaching within the broader historical context of economic restructuring within the university.

Historically, massive changes within the Canadian post-secondary educational system in the post WWII era effected change in the academic labour market. Briefly, a dramatic increase in student enrolment (initiated by returning war veterans) facilitated the expansion of post-secondary institutions (Rajagopal and Farr 1989). Many students pursued graduate studies and new faculty were hired. In the 1970s, government funding to universities "levelled or declined...and both government and corporate leaders...called for economic measures to reduce duplication and produce 'more scholar for the dollar'..." (Rajagopal and Farr 1989, 269). To fill the labour gap in the most economically feasible manner, universities increasingly hired employees on a contractually limited or part-time basis. This growth in part-time teaching has led to the development of a tiered system within the academic labour market, separating privileged, full-time, tenured academics from marginalized, part-time, non-tenured academics (Rosenblum and Rosenblum 1994; Rajagopal and Farr 1992; Rajagopal and Farr 1989; Warme and Lundy 1986).[4]

Part-time faculty generally receive low pay and work in unsatisfactory conditions:

> the majority experience working conditions that to some
> extent resemble the conditions of low-skilled labour... akin
> to industrial 'homework' in terms of isolation, low pay for
> long hours of effort...the characteristics generally identified
> with sweatshop work (Sharff and Lessinger 1994, 6).

Part-timers have little or no political voice in university and departmental governance (Gappa 1987) and teach the lower level, larger courses, and the "off-hour, off-campus, and summer school..." courses (Rosenblum and Rosenblum 1990,153). There is virtually no opportunity for advancement or job security within this part-time labour market. Part-time workers are typically the "last hired" (after teaching assignments have been allocated to full-time faculty) and the "first fired" in times of economic restraint and retrenchment: "As a cost-efficient, highly skilled workforce, part-timers have become an integral part of academe not in spite of their low cost, but because of it" (Rajagopal and

Farr 1992, 318). While individual departments may vary in their attempts to better accommodate these workers, it is not surprising that part-time university teachers are referred to as "the new working class" (Jackson and Clark 1987); "the underclass" (Committee G 1992); "second-class educators" (Thompson 1992); and "gypsy scholars" (Rajagopal and Farr 1989).[5]

This economic restructuring within universities provides management with a group of disposable workers who have little bargaining power and virtually no job security (Rajagopal and Farr 1992). We argue that, for marginalized groups within this labour market, racism, sexism, and other forms of systemic prejudice place historically disadvantaged groups in the centre of equity backlash: "This backlash is a conscious attempt to protect the privileged position of white males in a period of economic decline and assault on union rights, making it increasingly difficult to gain broader support for equity measures" (Creese 1995,146).

Other than a few studies which examine women part-time faculty, there is little research examining the location of other equity groups (Aboriginal Peoples, visible minorities, and persons with disabilities) within the academic labour market. Given women's predominance in the part-time labour market (Armstrong and Armstrong 1994), it is not surprising that compared to men who dominate the full-time academic labour market, women are disproportionately employed as part-time faculty (Edwards 1994; Rajagopal and Farr 1992; Simeone 1987; Warme and Lundy 1986; Kantrowitz 1981), and are particularly vulnerable to remaining within the part-time pool for the duration of their academic careers (Rosenblum and Rosenblum, 1994). A Quebec study found part-time women faculty to be more "dependent upon the university for a major share of their income" than their male counterparts, for whom the majority (76%) enjoy "regular full-time non-university employment" (Rajagopal and Farr 1992, 327).

At the university which employed our union membership, full-time and part-time faculty positions were rare among Aboriginal Peoples, visible minorities, and persons with disabilities who comprised less than 1%, 6.5%, and 3.9% of full-time faculty, respectively (Ornstein, Sandilands, and Teiman 1992). The corresponding figures for part-time faculty are less than 1%, 9.0%, and 3.1%. (Ornstein, Sandilands, and Teiman 1992). Himani Bannerji contextualizes the relationship between disenfranchised groups and the university (as a site of racist, sexist, and class oppression) and discusses the effect it has had on her career as a part-time university teacher:

> From 1974 to 1989, I was a temporary, contractual, part-time, piece-work teacher of part-time students... In the last

year, I have, at this late stage in my life, finally found favour in the eye of the establishment and become an assistant, non-tenured (but possible) professor. Once, a long time ago, I was a tenured faculty in India- from 1965 to 1969. I came to Canada on leave from my job — it took twenty years to find myself comparable employment. (1991, 72)

The intersection of race and gender serves to doubly disadvantage women of colour in the academic labour market (Ornstein, Sandilands, and Teiman 1992). The prioritization of one issue (for example, gender) can lead to the invisibility of these interconnections, and negate the individual experiences of marginalization (Belkhir 1995). We argue that the only way to raise consciousness around these issues and work toward change is to reveal the intersections between and within marginalized groups. Feminizing within this broader politic is very difficult, particularly within mainstream institutional structures.

Feminizing Within the Mainstream

Mainstream union and feminist ideologies, politics, and practices fail in their ability to provide an adequate framework within which to locate and address the concerns of marginalized groups (Leah 1993). Historically, unions in Canada served as a microcosm, replicating larger societal forms of discrimination by actively excluding visible minorities and women from union membership (White 1993). The social construction of "work" and "worker" within traditional trade unionist discourse conceptualized workers as white, able-bodied, skilled crafts men, thereby negating the work performed by women, ethnic/racial minorities, people with disabilities, and immigrants (Modibo 1995; White 1993).

Mainstream feminists, while advocating economic, political, and social equity with men, do not always recognize diversity in their efforts to eradicate systemic discrimination for women (Hooks 1989). The withdrawal of several middle-class, predominantly white women's groups from NAC (National Action Committee on the Status of Women) in the mid 1990s is a prime example of the non-inclusive nature of mainstream feminism. With Sunera Thobani (an activist within the Southeast Asian community and then chair of NAC), and the development of an executive board with members from various marginalized groups, many women's groups maintain that NAC no longer responds to the needs of "all" women. An interesting paradox, to say the least.

In her interviews with three Black women unionists, Ronnie Leah reveals the barriers and opposition encountered by Black women in their struggles to integrate issues of race and racism within the mainstream women's movement:

> Throughout the interviews there were numerous references to Black women being 'disillusioned' with the mainstream, largely white women's movement and there emerged a common perception that there was little support from white women activists for either individual women of colour or for the issue of racism... 'Progressive women have to recognize that there is a struggle. And it's a women's struggle; racism is a women's struggle.' (1993, 168)

As a women's caucus, we were particularly strident in our efforts to address issues of racism in our organizing efforts. It takes considerable effort to confront issues of systemic discrimination within a union setting. Unlike other bodies on the executive and those within the larger structures of the union, we had to struggle to keep our space and make our voice heard.

Mainstream Resistance/Caucus Struggle

The need for a separate sphere for women to define issues for themselves and work together for change is often challenged within unions (Briskin 1994, 1993). One year prior to our appointment as co-chairs, a small group of union members refused to pay their union dues on the basis of the existence of an exclusive women's caucus within the union. The person who spearheaded this initiative argued that unless men were allowed membership in the women's caucus, the budget and voting rights of the caucus should be discontinued and the caucus disbanded. It was only through solidarity with women and men union members who supported women's caucus initiatives that members of the women's caucus we were able to successfully defend their right to remain a "woman only" space.

Our experience as members of the executive board of the union served to reinforce our commitment to separate organizing for women. This antagonistic political climate created many tensions for us as feminists working for change within the system. The following examples provide insight into the ways in which "male model" process and mainstream politics served to marginalize our participation within the executive.

An initial example of minimizing women's power occurred following our first women's caucus meeting as co-chairs (February 1991). The outgoing chair argued that the duties of the chair warranted an increase in honorarium. The chair of the women's caucus is responsible for ensuring the representation of women at the caucus, executive, and national levels, and on twelve committees within our local. We had a two-tiered system of honoraria ($350.00 and $600.00 per month), whereby certain executive positions received the lower honorarium (e.g., Secretary), and other positions received the higher honorarium (e.g., Chair of the Local).

When we proposed the increase and rationale to the executive, we were faced with two opposing points of contention:

1) that all union positions should have equal honoraria in the spirit of "solidarity"; and

2) that the exclusion of men from women's caucus membership meant that the work of the women's caucus could not be recognized within the larger framework of the union, and therefore did not warrant the higher honorarium.

The first argument was quickly dropped, as various members of the executive were quick to point out that the duties attached to certain positions required much more work and were deserving of the higher honorarium. With regard to the second argument, the majority of executive members maintained their view. Since the women's caucus was exclusionary and, therefore, did not serve the interests of the union as a whole, the work of the caucus was considered to be significantly less onerous and less deserving than other executive posts. Our motion to receive the higher honorarium was defeated by the executive.

The next step was to bring the issue to the general membership (the highest governing body within the union) for consideration. At the next general membership meeting, the women's caucus argued that our position served the membership at large in representing equity aims, which required a high level of skill and dedication. We also argued that our efforts in addressing job security, stewardship within departments, tuition increases, and accessible childcare on campus affected many of our members — not "just" women. After considerable debate, our motion to receive the higher honorarium was passed by the general membership.

It was months before we began to receive our full honorarium on time, as the staff representative and treasurer kept forgetting that the honorarium had been increased. On several occasions, we had to re-submit copies of the minutes from the general membership meeting to both of these men as "proof" that our motion had been passed. It is important to emphasize that our ability to organize effectively was due in large part to the existence of an operating budget for the caucus and honoraria for the position of chair, and the fact that the chair of the caucus was a member of the executive with full voting rights.

Racism was a second form of oppression faced by women's caucus representatives. Starla was the first woman of colour to hold the position of chair (in our case, co-chair) of the women's caucus. Attending executive meetings became one of the most difficult duties of our position as women's caucus co-chairs. Raising issues that addressed the existence of systemic racism and sexism within the union was often met with open hostility by several members of the executive. Labelled "dictators of the politically correct," we often felt harassed and isolated during these meetings, both as union activists and as feminists working for change within an institution. For Starla, the situation was particularly difficult as "...a woman of colour can be singled out for harassment around race as well as gender, thereby reinforcing and intensifying feelings of isolation from her male as well as her white female co-workers". (Leah 1993, 158)

The high value placed on a masculine "presentation of self" during executive meetings was a third form of oppression. Men were expected to speak with authority, and state their case in an assertive manner. However, speaking with an authoritative voice was totally unacceptable for women members. As exemplified in her own experience, Judy Darcy (president of the Canadian Union of Public Employees) articulates these double standards:

> It is not easy for a woman to be labelled shrill and strident and even hysterical for speaking forcefully on a convention floor when her brothers, who say exactly the same thing and bellow as if they ate megaphones for breakfast, are heartily congratulated for their fire and brimstone speeches. (Darcy 1985, cited in White 1993, 138)

It was also unacceptable for women to demonstrate any emotionality, as this would be interpreted as weakness:

> It is not easy to be told by a higher up male trade union official, as I was quite a few years ago, that when I cried a little in a very emotional strike meeting which I was chairing, when we were voting to go back to work under wage controls, that I was not displaying 'leadership qualities' and also to be told that 'you have to be tough to be a union leader you know.' (Darcy 1985, cited in White 1993, 138)

Even those executive members who agreed with our politics and strategies sometimes failed to support us when caucus concerns were being debated. During informal discussions, these members admitted to feeling very stressed and ultimately silenced by the ever present adversarial "male model" group dynamic. We would spend time debriefing after every executive meeting, consulting with caucus members as to how best to address caucus concerns within the union, and supporting other executive members who were being marginalized.

The manner in which parliamentary procedures were applied constituted a fourth method of silencing us. We arrived as executive members with a working knowledge of this process, unaware of the ways in which rules of order and other formal rules of process could be used (and improperly invoked) to silence members. When we spoke, we were constantly interrupted and/or ignored. Issues raised by the women's caucus were placed at the bottom of the agenda, so that the executive could attend to the "real" business of the union first. Given the fact that our input was often unwelcome, on a number of occasions (usually at the end of a five hour meeting), we were resolved to decline to give a report from the women's caucus, and instead conduct our work and strategize for change within the women's caucus.

Caucus decision-making operated within a "consensus model," where formal parliamentary rules of order were abandoned in favour of a more accessible, open style of communication. As consensus had to be reached in order to act on initiatives brought to the caucus, concerted efforts were made by caucus members to invite the viewpoints of all women present. While at times a difficult process, by using this method, the women's caucus was able to provide a space where women could voice their concerns.

Jacquie Buncel (1990) discusses the need for feminist activists both to organize separately (in women only spaces) and to work within mainstream institutional structures when organizing for change. She refers to these strategies as "disengaging" and "mainstreaming." Drawing on the work of Adamson, Briskin, and McPhail (1988), Buncel articulates the problems associated with choosing one strategy over the other:

> If feminists operate solely out of a mainstreaming politics, they can become submerged within the existing social institutions and thereby lose their critical analysis of the status quo... feminists who rely solely on a disengagement strategy run the risk of becoming marginalized. If feminists separate themselves completely from social institutions, they become removed from the lives of the majority of women and are unable to count on their support in creating a mass movement for social change. (Buncel 1990, 8-9)

In the following discussion, we share the strategies and methods of resistance the women's caucus employed as part of the process of feminizing within the union. As these examples reveal, it was necessary for the caucus to employ both strategies of disengaging and main-streaming in order to effect change. By detailing these activities, we provide a framework and context to the process of feminist organizing for change.

Strategies for Inclusion/Methods of Resistance

In an effort to address the concerns of marginalized groups, members of the women's caucus focused their energies in three main areas:
1) recruiting new members and ensuring caucus membership and gender parity on the executive and all union committees (internal and external);
2) networking with the broader activist community within the union (including other locals and the national), the university, and allied groups outside of the university; and
3) proposing changes to the collective agreement.

Recruitment/Committee Membership

Women's caucus members encouraged women within our local to become actively involved within the caucus. This included sign-up sheets during fall registration for graduate studies, mailing information packages to all women union members of our local, encouraging union stewards to solicit members in their departments, recruiting members at general membership meetings, establishing phone trees to contact new members and maintain links with existing members, and ensuring that the caucus was a vital and visible part of any public outreach or media event in which the union was involved. As a result, women's caucus membership tripled to over 200 members in two years. It is important to emphasize that the wisdom and efforts of past chairs and caucus members provided a strong, viable, feminist collective with a core group of seasoned activists. Without this firm foundation, it would have been virtually impossible for the caucus to realize this success.

Regarding committee membership, all union committees had women's caucus representatives who would keep the caucus informed of any important union business. Almost all of the work performed by members of the caucus was performed on a volunteer basis. Some of this work included proposal writing for bargaining, membership on the bargaining team, the development of employment equity language, the disbursement of funds to members in need, and various other activities, including raising awareness of caucus goals and initiatives within the broader university community.

Being active on these committees gave many women's caucus members the experience, skills, and courage they needed to vie for an executive position. Union activism can, very often, have the effect of raising consciousness and empowering women to meet their potential as leaders and change makers within their union (Baker 1993; Buncel 1990). We lobbied women within our local to run for positions on the executive, and supported pro-feminist male candidates. Women's participation in leadership positions within their union (and the labour movement as a whole) is essential if unions are to successfully address the concerns of women workers (Cuneo 1993).

Networking

Networking is a crucial element of union activism. Through attendance at national women's committee meetings, national educational forums, and national conventions, we met regularly with women from sister locals to discuss common concerns. As the only local (out of twelve locals) with a budget and executive voting rights for a women's caucus, we shared information regarding our caucus structure and history in an effort to support those women who wanted to establish feminist collectives formally within their union locals.

We also maintained ties with national women's organizations and other political organizations (international student collectives, women's collectives, graduate and undergraduate student networks, progressive left organizations, and lobby groups) outside the union. The women's caucus sent two delegates to the National Action Committee on the Status of Women Conference every year. Caucus proposals for the conference focused on women and education, and, most importantly, the need to support access to higher education for women from marginalized groups. We lobbied for changes within the NAC executive board, focusing on the need for the Board to be more diverse in its membership.

Through these networking strategies, the women's caucus was able to gain support for our union local during both the process of negotiations and at other times when the caucus was organizing for change both inside and outside of the union (for example, during lobbying efforts to change discriminatory provincial legislation, when supporting other workers during a strike, and so forth).

Changes to the Collective Agreement

The main focus of union activity and the place where union practice becomes formally entrenched in policy and organizational structures is through the collective bargaining process:

> The attainment of the goals of a group of workers... depends on their political influence with the union. Because of the low participation of women in the negotiating process it is not surprising that, in many workplaces, women's issues are still the first to be dropped at the bargaining table. (Kumar 1993, 209)

The women's caucus has been instrumental in prioritizing issues for bargaining and ensuring that the concerns of marginalized groups be represented within the collective agreement. Past chairs and caucus members successfully lobbied and bargained for part-time daycare on campus, sex and gender harassment language, maternity leave provisions, and language on race and ethnic relations.

During our time as co-chairs, the women's caucus was actively involved in prioritizing health and safety issues for bargaining. The attack of a woman maintenance worker at knife point in a secluded basement area of the university politicized the issue of safety and security for women on campus. She managed to pull the fire alarm (and probably saved her own life) as that was her only means of emergency contact. A caucus member was commissioned by the executive to devise, distribute, and compile the results of a survey concerning the health and safety of our union members. This led to the formulation of proposals for bargaining, and ultimately to changes in the collective agreement; for example, the provision of telephones in secluded basement offices and near laboratories.

Accessibility for persons with disabilities was also raised in the health and safety survey and resulted in changes to the collective agreement. We gained language in the collective agreement providing physically disabled members with the option of classroom re-assignment in the instance that the classroom was far removed from their office and/or difficult to get to. Also, a fund for the distribution of assistive devices which support teachers in their work (e.g., scooters, adaptive computer screens, and other resources) was proposed by the women's caucus and successfully bargained.

In our networking with the African Students' Association, we were sensitized to the plight of international graduate students, many of whom were union members. By legislation, they were restricted to employment within the university. The overwhelming majority of those who were able to obtain employment wound up working for low wages as domestic labourers cleaning toilets and student residences during the summer months. The women's caucus proposed that priority be given to visa students in the allocation of summer teaching assistantships, teaching positions which were rarely given to visa students. The bargaining team was successful in gaining language on this issue in the collective agreement.

Through the work of the women's caucus in proposal development for bargaining and the participation of women's caucus members on the bargaining team, the caucus was successful in its efforts to organize for change within the institutional structures of the union, and thereby create a safer, more equitable work environment for union members. However, the process of bringing bargaining issues to the general membership and broader university community for consideration and support and working through these issues at the executive level was difficult within the negotiations process. The following account examines our struggle as a union executive to produce and disseminate information on key bargaining issues that included the experiences of marginalized groups within our union.

The Poster

At an executive meeting (during contract negotiations), a finished proof of a poster was revealed to executive members. This poster was intended to bring the local (and allied groups) together in support of the bargaining process in preparation for the possibility of a strike. Neither of us recalls being consulted about the nature or content of the poster, and we were quite concerned that, having been commissioned and completed, it was ready for printing. In order to appreciate our response to the poster fully, it is necessary to describe its visual presentation.

Starla recalls the poster vividly. The background pictorial was of a jagged cliff overhanging a river which contained large sharp rocks jutting upward. On the top of the cliff stood three white pot-bellied men, wearing suits and carrying briefcases (marked "administration"). The man near the edge of the cliff had his foot raised in a kicking position. Hanging off the side of the cliff, holding on to a breaking tree branch with one arm, was a caricature of a Black person (kinky short hair, large lips, bare feet, a ripped shirt, and ragged pants) with a footprint on the person's buttocks and the words "teaching assistant" printed on the person's back. Hanging off the ankle of this person was a white woman with "student" printed on her back. At the bottom of the cliff floating in the river was a slogan referring to better access to education.

Upon seeing the poster, we immediately called "caucus" in order to discuss it privately. Our first reaction to the poster was that it appeared to be depicting the lynching of a Black man. (We were surprised to find out later that the figure was intended to be a Black woman). We objected to the fact that the poster relied on stereotypical notions of Black people, both in terms of the physical appearance of this person and her social location as that of victim. Our key concern was how the poster *could be* interpreted by union members and other groups within the university community. As women's caucus co-chairs, we had an obligation to members of our community that our union local address issues of race and racism in a sensitive manner. We fully recognized that the poster was intended to portray diversity. However, intentionality is of little significance in the final analysis if *the effect* of distributing the poster is the creation of racist antagonisms within the university community. As articulated by George Sefa Dei, "racist practices *do not require intentionality...* such practices are deemed racist *in terms of their effects.*" (1995,13, own emphasis)

We made a decision to argue against the distribution of this poster. We informed executive members that, by endorsing this poster, we risked losing the support and trust of allied groups on campus; this could negatively affect our bargaining efforts and our reputation. Given the high level of racist tension and conflict within our community — the recent media coverage of the beating of Rodney King, rioting within the Toronto downtown core, and the intrusion of the white supremacist group, Heritage Front, on campus — our union local could have inadvertently contributed to an already volatile situation by using the poster.

In addition to the issues of race and racism, we were very concerned about the possible ramifications for our local of distributing a poster which was overtly violent and portrayed our relationship with the administration of the university as inherently adversarial. The poster relied on traditional, male, trade-unionist notions of worker struggle — the "fat cat" capitalist stereotype of management beating down the suffering, struggling worker. We argued that it was time to be more creative and think of different (less violent) visual ways to depict our struggle as workers, ways more representative of who we are as a collective of university educators. Our critical insights were not well received by other executive members.

Starla was immediately verbally attacked by those defending the merits of the poster. She was forced to remind executive members of the systemic nature of racism within Canada (historically and currently) and our need to consider cautiously how this poster might be interpreted. If both of us were offended by the poster, perhaps other people would also be offended. Nonetheless, many executive members failed to see how the poster could (even remotely) be considered racist by any person or group. Several executive members denied the possibility that racism existed within our union. The motion to continue with the poster was only defeated when we insisted that the names be recorded in the minutes as to how each executive member voted. We were not going to be associated with this poster should the executive decide to distribute it.

Given our concerns with the poster, several executive members insisted that we address the "problem" directly by suggesting ideas for another poster. Marianne suggested a quilt motif to represent diversity and solidarity, rather than realistic visuals of people which typically rely on stereotypes. Several male executive members commented that we needed a "hard hitting" poster; the quilt idea was too feminine. We ended the discussion at this point and agreed that the caucus would become involved in developing a new poster.

The caucus developed several posters depicting various bargaining issues: employment equity; wage increases; safety and security on campus; access to education; and tuition increases. The quilt motif was used to represent employment equity and access to education. The posters were so well received that the national head office of the union used them to represent these issues on a union-wide basis.

By confronting the issue of racism and working within the caucus to find a solution, we (as a caucus) were not only successful in addressing the immediate need of publicizing and seeking support for bargaining issues; we were also successful in confirming "the power of solidarity and sisterhood" (Hooks 1994, 108).

Final Word

The women's caucus forum provided a space for women part-time educational workers to voice their concerns and participate in the decision-making processes of their union. Through the implementation of various strategies and methods of resistance, we as a caucus made a conscious effort to avoid the adoption of mainstream models for organizing, models that often reproduce and maintain existing relations of oppression. We were a feminist collective that focused on addressing the intersections of multiple sites of marginalization — race, gender, class, and disability.

As co-chairs with voting rights on the executive, we effectively brought issues of concern raised by marginalized groups within our union to the executive and general membership for consideration; through these efforts, we were successful in opening dialogue on sensitive issues of systemic discrimination. Our success in feminizing union policies and practices and providing a more equitable workplace for union members was won through the persistence and hard work of activists from within the union and larger university community. This network provided the support base the women's caucus needed to meet the challenge of effecting positive change for marginalized groups within the union.

Marianne is currently active within part-time faculty collectives in Nova Scotia; she is conducting research examining the career patterns of part-time university faculty, focusing on gender differences in the context of economic restructuring within the university.

Starla continues her activist work on race and gender within the broader Toronto community. She is also conducting research examining the rapidly decreasing availability of land for subsistence farming in West Africa and the effects of this change on women farmers and their families.

References

Armstrong, Pat and Hugh Armstrong. 1994. *The Double Ghetto: Canadian Women and Their Segregated Work.* Toronto: McClelland and Stewart Inc.

Baker, Patricia. 1993. "Reflections on Life Stories: Women's Bank Union Activism." *Women Challenging Unions,* eds. Linda Briskin and Patricia McDermott. Toronto: University of Toronto Press. 62-86.

Bannerji, Himani. 1991. "But Who Speaks for Us? Experience and Agency in Conventional Feminist Paradigms." *Unsettling Relations: the University as a Site of Feminist Struggles,* eds. Himani Bannerji, Linda Carty, Kari Dehli, Susan Heald, and Kate McKenna. Toronto: Women's Press. 67-107.

Belkhir, Jean. 1995. "Integrative Anti-Classism: Race, Gender and Class." *Race, Gender and Class* 2, 3 (Spring), 143-166.

Breslauer, Helen J.1985. "Women in the Professoriate — the Case of Multiple Disadvantage." *The Professoriate — Occupation in Crisis,* eds. Higher Education Group. Toronto: Ontario Institute for Studies in Education. 82-104.

Briskin, Linda. 1994. "Equity and Economic Restructuring in the Canadian Labour Movement." *Economic and Industrial Democracy* 15, 1 (February), 89-112.

Briskin, Linda.1993. "Union Women and Separate Organizing." Women Challenging Unions, eds. Linda Briskin and Particia McDermott. Toronto: University of Toronto Press. 89-108.

Buncel, Jacquie. 1990. *Walking the Socialist Feminist Tight-rope: Feminist Education and Organizing in the Canadian Union of Educational Workers.* Unpublished Master's Thesis. Department of Adult Education. Ontario Institute for Studies in Education.

Committee G. 1992. "On the Status of Non-Tenure Track Faculty." *Academe* 78, 6 (Nov./ Dec.), 39-49.

Creese, Gillian. 1995. "Gender Equity or Masculine Privilege? Union Strategies and Economic Restructuring in a White Collar Union." *The Canadian Journal of Sociology* 20, 2 (Spring), 143-166.

Cuneo, Carl J. 1993. "Trade Union Leadership: Sexism and Affirmative Action." *Women Challenging Unions,* eds. Linda Briskin and Patricia McDermott. Toronto: University of Toronto Press. 109-136.

Dei, George J. Sefa. 1995. "Integrative Anti-Racism: Intersection of Race, Class, and Gender." *Race, Gender and Class* 2, 3 (Spring), 11-30.

Edwards, Mary G. 1994. "The Decline of the American Professoriate, 1970-1990." *Anthropology of Work Review* XV, 1 (Spring), 21-28.

Gappa, Judith M. 1987. "The Stress Producing Working Conditions of Part-Time Faculty." *New Directions for Teaching and Learning,* 29 (Spring), 33-42.

Hooks, Bell. 1989. *Talking Back.* Boston, MA: Southend Press.

Jackson, Pamela Irving and Roger Clark. 1987. "Collective Bargaining and Faculty Compensation: Faculty as a New Working Class." *Sociology of Education* 60 (Oct.), 242-256.

Kantrowitz, J. 1981. "Paying Your Dues, Part-time." *Rocking the Boat: Academic Women and Academic Processes,* eds Gloria DeSole and Lenore Hoffman. New York: The Modern Languages Association of America. 15-36.

Kumar, Pradeep. 1993. "Collective Bargaining and Women's Workplace Concerns." In Linda Briskin and Patricia McDermott (eds.). *Women Challenging Unions.* Toronto: University of Toronto Press. 207-230.

Leah, Ronnie. 1993. "Black Women Speak Out: Racism and Unions." *Women Challenging Unions,* eds. Linda Briskin and Patricia McDermott. Toronto: University of Toronto Press. 157-171.

Modibo, Najja N. 1995. "Immigrant Women's Participation in Toronto Union Locals." *Race, Gender and Class* 2, 3 (Spring), 83-103.

Ornstein, Michael, Kate Sandilands, and Gill Teiman. 1992. *Equity Counts: The 1990 Employment Equity Census.* Toronto: York University.

Rajagopal, Indhu and William D. Farr. 1992. "Hidden Academics: the Part-time Faculty in Canada." *Higher Education* 24, 3, 317-331.

Rajagopal, Indhu and William D. Farr. 1989. "The Political Economy of Part-time Academic Work in Canada." *Higher Education* 18, 3, 267-285.

Rosenblum, Gerald and Barbara Rubin Rosenblum. 1990. "Segmented Labor Markets in Institutions of Higher Learning." *Sociology of Education* 63 (July), 151-164.

Rosenblum, Gerald and Barbara Rubin Rosenblum. 1994. "Academic Labour Markets: Perspectives from Ontario." *The Canadian Journal of Higher Education* XXIV, 1, 48-71.

Sharff, Jagna Wojcika and Johanna Lessinger. 1994. "The Academic Sweatshop: Changes in the Capitalist Infrastructure and the Part-time Academic." *Anthropology of Work Review* XV, 1 (Spring), 2-11.

Simeone, A. 1987. *Academic Women: Working Toward Equality.* South Hadley, Mass.: Bergen and Garvey, Publishers, Inc.

Thompson, Karen. 1992. "Recognizing Mutual Interests." *Academe* 78, 6 (Nov./Dec).

Warme, Barbara and Katherina Lundy. 1986. "Part-time Faculty: Institutional Needs and Career Dilemmas." *Work in the Canadian Context: Continuity Despite Change*, eds. Katherina Lundy and Barbara Warme. Toronto: Butterworths.

White, Julie. 1993. *Sisters and Solidarity: Women and Unions in Canada.* Toronto: Thompson Educational Publishing Inc.

Endnotes

1. Many thanks to those past chairs and members of the women's caucus who provided us with information and valuable insights during the course of writing this paper. We thank the reviewers for their insightful suggestions which were instrumental in making the paper a much better organized piece. We thank Karen Blackford for encouraging us to share our story. Marianne would like to thank the faculty and staff in the Department of Social Science and Practice at the University College of Cape Breton (especially Dr. Constance deRoche and Ms. Carolanne Sheppard) for their valuable insights and encouragement during the writing of the first draft of this paper.

2. The dedication and hard work of many feminist activists at various points in time made the caucus what it is-a separate sphere within which women can voice their concerns and work toward change. When we talk about the caucus, we are including all of these women. However, we want to make it clear that the analyses and views we espouse in this paper are our own, and do not necessarily reflect the views of all the women involved with the caucus over the years.

3. The job descriptions of teaching assistants vary greatly among universities. It is important to emphasize that as teaching assistants we were very involved in every aspect of the teaching process, from grading and exam construction to tutorial instruction and lecturing. Many professors consider teaching assistants to be part of a "teaching team," as the work provided by teaching assistants is heavily relied upon, especially by instructors in large classes.

4. Universities vary in their categorization of full-time and part-time faculty. In our discussion, we lump together tenure-track and tenured faculty as full-time workers/faculty, and non-tenure track, contractually limited appointments as part-time workers/faculty. Rajagopal and Farr (1992) discuss the difficulty in the categorization of part-time faculty in Canada, emphasizing that the lack of data on part-time faculty makes it very difficult to define them (as a group): "The variety is astounding, and astoundingly imprecise." (Rajagopal and Farr, 1992: 321) It is

beyond the scope of this paper to delve into this discussion in any detail; therefore, we have chosen to define part-time faculty in the most simplistic and straightforward way — non-tenure track, contractually limited teaching appointments.

5. We were the only local (out of twelve locals) with a budget and executive voting rights for a women's caucus. The position of chair of the women's caucus is selected by women members of the local at a caucus meeting.

Lyne Bouchard et Chantal Cholette

La création de nos propres institutions : une voie à emprunter

Cet article relate notre expérience de gestion féministe qui est en constante évolution depuis 14 ans[1]. Nous y discutons, tout particulièrement, de la question de la création d'institutions féministes. Les concepts et les critères de féminisation que nous présentons sont le fruit d'un processus de théorisation des pratiques de *La coopérative Convergence*. Cet exercice, que nous avons nommé «Peau neuve», nous a permis de réfléchir sur nos pratiques, de raffiner notre analyse et de positionner notre expérience de gestion féministe dans un cadre théorique. Cette démarche de théorisation a marqué un point tournant dans l'évolution de la coopérative puisqu'elle nous a amenées à confirmer ses valeurs tout en nommant certaines prémisses tenues pour acquis. Le fait que les membres se soient impliquées dans ce processus, en y consacrant plus d'un an de réflexion et de discussion, illustre son importance.

Les pratiques de *La coopérative Convergence* et les concepts qui en découlent ont été façonnés à l'image du bagage expérienciel des femmes qui sont ou ont été membres de la coopérative. Issues de différents milieux et munies d'expérience et de formation diversifiées, chacune des membres a contribué à modeler une entreprise unique, empreinte de valeurs féministes, coopératives et collectivistes.

Après avoir cherché en vain des modèles, nous sommes venues à la conclusion que les pratiques de gestion de la coopérative sont uniques. Pour établir une entreprise à notre image, nous avons accepté de prendre le «beau risque» d'innover. Ce chemin, parcouru à tâtons, nous semble parfois truffé de mines. À d'autres occasions, nous y faisons de grandes découvertes. Nous avons souvent regretté, et regrettons toujours, l'absence de modèles de coopératives féministes, car il est à la fois ardu et gratifiant d'être des précurseures dans un domaine. De plus, s'il est actuellement facile de trouver des renseignements écrits sur la gestion au féminin, il est très difficile de mettre la main sur des travaux traitant de la gestion féministe.

Cet article s'inscrit dans l'approche de la pédagogie féministe (Solar, 1992b). Nous utilisons notre expérience comme source de savoir dans le but de démystifier nos pratiques. En adoptant cette approche, nous souhaitons contribuer à la multiplication d'institutions féministes ou, à tout le moins, à la transformation d'institutions pour qu'elles s'ouvrent à l'inclusion graduelle de principes et de pratiques de gestion féministe.

Dans cet article, nous énoncerons d'abord certains concepts qui serviront de guide à notre analyse au sujet de la création d'institutions ou d'entreprises féministes et qui peuvent également s'appliquer à la féminisation des institutions. Puis, nous présenterons, sous forme de témoignage-réflexion, l'expérience de *La coopérative Convergence* et de son modèle de gestion comme exemple d'institution féministe. Nous discuterons ensuite des stratégies qui favorisent, le cas échéant, la féminisation des institutions canadiennes. Enfin, notre conclusion portera sur l'application des critères de féminisation aux institutions.

Critères de féminisation

Quatre critères sont à la base de la gestion féministe des institutions. Et ces critères prennent leurs racines dans les pratiques de *La coopérative Convergence*. Ce sont l'absence de hiérarchie, la flexibilité, l'inclusion et l'autonomie. Ils s'appliquent tant à la structure qu'à la gestion d'un groupe comme le nôtre. Nous aborderons donc ces quatre critères à la lumière de ces deux dimensions.

Mais avant d'aller plus loin, nous tenons à faire une mise en garde. Notre expérience nous a fait prendre conscience que même si les critères que nous énonçons servent de fondement à la gestion féministe, ils ne doivent pas être perçus ni traités comme des absolus. Nous savons que les idéaux sont difficiles à mettre en place et cela constitue peut-être l'un des plus grands obstacles qui se posent à la féminisation des institutions.

Absence de hiérarchie

La structure d'une institution, d'une entreprise ou d'un regroupement définit ce que cette organisation veut «être». Notre structure est le reflet de notre identité et de notre fonctionnement à l'intérieur de la coopérative mais elle permet aussi de préciser l'image que nous voulons donner à l'extérieur de la coopérative. La structure est au fondement de nos façons d'agir, de notre orientation et de notre mode de fonctionnement (la gestion). Dans la société actuelle, il est évident que les structures et les modes de gestion patriarcaux et traditionnels dominent et ils sont souvent fermés, voire vertement opposés à la féminisation, comme d'ailleurs à toutes autres formes de changement. Ces structures reposent sur une idéologie traditionnelle qui conçoit l'humanité comme étant divisée en deux clans distincts : celui des «dominants» dans lequel se trouvent les mâles producteurs et celui des «dominées», où se trouvent les femmes reproductrices (St-Jean, 1983 : 138). Cette ségrégation des pouvoirs entre dominants et dominées se reproduit grâce aux structures hiérarchiques en place. À l'opposé de ces structures, où les pouvoirs sont le monopole d'une personne ou d'un groupuscule, la féminisation des institutions adopte le principe d'un partage du pouvoir et l'applique à ses modes de fonctionnement.

Toutefois, il est difficile d'amener les instances gouvernementales à reconnaître les principes démocratiques et économiques alternatifs que suppose la féminisation des institutions et à légitimer ce type de fonctionnement. Toutes les lois sur l'incorporation, qu'elles soient de juridiction fédérale ou provinciale, imposent une structure décisionnelle et administrative de type hiérarchique. Par conséquent, de nombreux groupes communautaires se sont résignés à nommer des personnes postiches à la présidence, au secrétariat et à la trésorerie, dans l'unique but de satisfaire aux exigences légales qui refusent d'emblée de reconnaître la légitimité d'une structure marquée par l'absence de hiérarchie.

Nous croyons que l'absence de hiérarchie dans la structure d'une institution est la pierre angulaire de toute féminisation des institutions. Elle implique du coup un second principe, celui de l'acceptation des leaderships individuels propres à favoriser le partage des responsabilités entre les membres d'une équipe et à leur permettre de se relayer dans l'exercice de leurs tâches. Les effets d'un tel principe sont nombreux : valorisation des ressources humaines, remise en cause des notions de détentrice ou de détenteur exclusif de savoirs, reconnaissance des forces et des limites de chaque membre. Chacun de ces éléments contribue à l'efficience de notre gestion. L'exemple du parti des femmes en Islande est une belle illustration de ce qui précède. À la fin des années 80, ce parti formait l'opposition officielle au gouvernement. Une des caractéristiques non traditionnelles du parti des femmes était l'alternance des critiques se voyant confiés la responsabilité d'un dossier. Ainsi, plusieurs femmes partageaient les dossiers et pouvaient défendre les positions du parti. Cette pratique d'alternance a eu des avantages stratégiques importants puisque les membres du gouvernement étaient plus souvent qu'autrement désarçonnés par cette pratique, ne sachant à quels adversaires ils auraient à faire face lors de la période de questions ou du travail en comité.

Paradoxalement, l'absence totale de hiérarchie semble pratiquement impossible à atteindre tant dans les structures gouvernementales et institutionnelles, qu'au sein des grandes ou des petites entreprises. Comme nous l'avons déjà mentionné, l'idéal, ici comme dans d'autres sphères d'activités, est difficile à atteindre. Cependant, nous croyons qu'il est possible de tendre vers l'adoption de pratiques qui ne sont pas conformistes, afin d'amoindrir l'impact d'un déséquilibre dans l'allocation des pouvoirs. La diminution des échelons hiérarchiques, la non-subordination des unes aux autres, les politiques et pratiques qui favorisent l'appropriation des pouvoirs individuels et collectifs sur la vie de travail sont autant de moyens qui permettent d'atténuer les répercussions qu'entraîne l'iniquité en milieu de travail. Les femmes évoluant dans des lieux de travail qui ont adopté de telles pratiques ne sont pas de simples employées mais plutôt des travailleuses, gestionnaires et militantes.

Flexibilité

Le second critère de féminisation a trait au degré de flexibilité dont fait preuve une institution. On peut penser à plusieurs exemples de flexibilité dont les heures de travail adaptées aux besoins des individus, les charges de travail qui respectent la réalité des travailleuses et les méthodes de travail qui peuvent être transformées au fur et à mesure qu'évoluent les circonstances. Tous ces éléments, qui témoignent des structures politiques et des pratiques d'une gestion flexible, assurent un mouvement constant au sein de l'organisation.

Le concept de flexibilité permet d'augmenter la qualité de vie au travail. La créativité, la marge de manoeuvre dans les méthodes de travail, la maîtrise des mécanismes internes dictant le rythme du travail (heures d'ouverture du bureau, fréquence et durée des rencontres d'équipe, moments de répit, accès à la formation professionnelle, etc.) contribuent à rendre l'entreprise plus flexible tout en mettant en valeur l'importance de coopérer afin d'assurer une saine gestion.

La flexibilité dans les tâches oblige chaque membre d'une équipe à être perpétuellement à l'affût des transformations qui s'opèrent tant à l'intérieur du groupe que dans l'environnement extérieur. Elle permet d'éviter que certaines personnes s'incrustent dans des routines de travail. Cela dit, pour que la flexibilité ne cesse d'être un atout, il est essentiel de bien documenter toutes les transformations afin de mieux transmettre les savoirs acquis. Plus que de simples procès-verbaux qui satisfassent les exigences légales de toute organisation ou corporation, ces exercices sont une occasion unique de cultiver la mémoire collective.

Inclusion

Pour bâtir une structure inclusive, nous devons également tenir compte du fait que les structures traditionnelles, y compris de nombreuses structures dites «féminines», sont empreintes des valeurs d'une culture dominante blanche, mâle, nord-américaine et de classe moyenne. Il est donc important de prendre conscience des fondements sociaux et historiques de l'inégalité entre les origines ethniques, les sexes, les cultures et les classes sociales. Or, une étape essentielle dans la compréhension de la domination est de reconnaître les privilèges rattachés à ce système inégal. Ce faisant, on peut alors travailler, sur une base individuelle ou

114

collective, à renverser la vapeur de cette influence pernicieuse en spécifiant clairement le type d'accueil désiré et en transformant les structures pour que l'inclusion ne soit pas seulement la formulation de grands principes, mais qu'elle se traduise en une pratique efficace. En ce sens, la gestion inclusive peut être l'occasion d'un échange continu de formation informelle entre les membres ou encore, celle de la mise en place d'un programme d'embauche favorisant l'accès aux personnes moins privilégiées.

Autonomie

La structure d'une institution est féminisée lorsqu'elle tend à promouvoir l'autonomie. Une structure s'appuyant sur des principes d'autonomie crée des espaces formels et informels de prise de décision. Ainsi, la pratique de l'autonomie dans la gestion peut correspondre à la création d'équipes de travail qui fonctionnent sans aucune forme d'ingérence. Cela demande à l'institution d'établir clairement ses principes et ses pratiques de fonctionnement de base et, inversement, aux membres de l'équipe, de préciser leurs objectifs personnels sans la moindre confusion. De plus, l'autonomie ne s'acquiert pas sans une bonne dose de confiance réciproque entre les membres de l'équipe. Cette ouverture à l'autonomie de l'autre amène facilement les femmes à développer, tant sur le plan personnel que professionnel, des pratiques de formation informelle, essentielles à la construction et au renforcement de la confiance des femmes.

Exemple de féminisation : *La coopérative Convergence*

La coopérative Convergence est une entreprise de consultation francophone cogérée. Elle offre ses services[2] dans les deux langues officielles du pays et est composée exclusivement de femmes.

Si l'entreprise existe depuis 1984, trois femmes ont entrepris, dès 1988, sa transformation en coopérative de travail, laquelle s'est conclue par son incorporation officielle en 1991. Les objectifs de la coopérative sont les suivants :

1) favoriser l'accès au travail rémunéré pour les femmes par l'entremise d'une coopérative de travail francophone cogérée par les coopératrices, offrant des services et des produits égalitaires et non stéréotypés à travers le Canada, dans une optique de changement social;

2) favoriser le mouvement coopératif en faisant sa promotion dans différents milieux. La vision globale de la coopérative est de créer un milieu de travail propice au partage des ressources et des avoirs[3].

Regardons de plus près les rouages internes et publics de la coopérative afin de comprendre en quoi elle est un vibrant exemple de féminisation d'une institution. Nous décrirons l'entreprise en suivant les quatre critères de base mentionnés plus haut.

Absence de hiérarchie et autonomie

En tant que féministes, nous préconisons la création de structures non hiérarchiques qui visent une répartition équitable des pouvoirs et des avoirs. À *La coopérative Convergence*, l'absence de hiérarchie est définie selon la membriété, les mécanismes décisionnels et la distribution des biens.

La coopérative est incorporée auprès du gouvernement fédéral. Elle est donc soumise à la *Loi canadienne sur les associations coopératives*. Cette loi stipule que l'entreprise doit compter un minimum de sept membres. Afin de se conformer à cette loi, nous avons invité quatre femmes supplémentaires à devenir membres de la coopérative. Elles ont donc acheté une part sociale de la coopérative et se sont engagées à participer au développement de la coopérative. Toutefois, nous étions conscientes que la coopérative ne pourrait pas générer du travail de manière soutenue pour les sept femmes. C'est pourquoi nous avons contracté une entente avec les quatre dernières coopératrices dans laquelle nous reconnaissons leur pouvoir décisionnel dans les grandes orientations de la coopérative, mais où nous précisons que l'entreprise n'est pas tenue de leur assurer un travail. Ces quatre femmes, que l'on peut appeler des membres «périphériques», ont été choisies en fonction de deux critères. Premièrement, elles détenaient déjà un emploi à temps plein et, deuxièmement, elles souhaitaient éventuellement s'intégrer activement au sein de la coopérative.

Ainsi, en réalité, les trois coopératrices originales se partagent en ce moment les responsabilités associées à la gestion interne et peuvent être rémunérées à partir des contrats de services passés par la coopérative. Pour elles, le travail de gestion regroupe les tâches administratives de toute entreprise, soit le développement, le fonctionnement et l'évaluation aux niveaux structurel et opérationnel. La production de services, c'est le travail qu'elles effectuent avec les groupes clients.

Sur une base occasionnelle, la coopérative embauche aussi des associées lorsqu'un contrat exige une expertise particulière ou pour nous permettre de respecter des échéanciers serrés. Ainsi, nous retenons les services d'une dizaine d'associées par année.

Mécanismes décisionnels

Dans la pratique, les membres de la coopérative ont un pouvoir décisionnel égal. En effet, toutes participent, si elles le désirent, aux discussions et aux décisions portant sur les orientations de l'entreprise et toutes sont également imputables à l'égard des exigences légales. Les décisions sont prises de façon consensuelle. Finalement, soulignons que toutes les membres ont les mêmes privilèges et les mêmes pouvoirs décisionnels puisque dans une coopérative, c'est la part sociale qui détermine le droit de vote et non le montant de capital investi.

Puisque trois membres assurent le bon fonctionnement de *La coopérative Convergence* au quotidien, c'est à elles qu'on confie les responsabilités décisionnelles associées à la gestion interne et externe. Ces membres sont les signataires officielles des contrats de services et chacune est responsable d'une partie de la gestion et de la coordination des équipes de production.

Certains de nos mécanismes formels de prise de décision sont semblables à ceux des corporations ayant une structure traditionnelle, alors que d'autres s'en démarquent clairement. Par exemple, la *Loi canadienne sur les associations coopératives* requiert la tenue d'une assemblée générale des membres une fois par an. Pourtant, à *La coopérative Convergence*, nous avons décidé de tenir annuellement deux assemblées générales, car elles constituent des moments de réflexion privilégiés et permettent un contact plus fréquent avec l'ensemble des membres.

Par ailleurs, c'est au quotidien que l'on peut clairement faire la distinction entre les pratiques traditionnelles et non traditionnelles. Ce ne sont pas les cadres formels de prise de décision qui diffèrent mais plutôt le processus décisionnel qui s'y déploie ainsi que la latitude que nous nous accordons entre nous. D'entrée de jeu, il est important de préciser que notre processus décisionnel se veut souple, efficace et inclusif. En termes pratiques, cela signifie que chaque membre peut proposer, à tout moment, de nouvelles approches ou méthodes de travail. Les coopératrices peuvent alors prendre une décision éclairée quant à leur mise en oeuvre. Cela confère au groupe une emprise directe sur les résultats escomptés dans la gestion et la production d'un service. C'est aussi le groupe qui définit le type et le degré de souplesse de la coopérative. Les mécanismes informels et consensuels de prise de décision ont une grande importance dans le travail de production. Dans la mesure où les travailleuses respectent les principes de la coopérative, c'est-à-dire la notion de travail égalitaire et le respect des personnes pour ce qu'elles sont et non en fonction de leur titre, de leur ethnie, de leur sexe, de leur race, de leur langue, de leur orientation sexuelle, de leur capacité intellectuelle ou physique, les équipes de travail demeurent autonomes.

Distribution des avoirs et responsabilités financières

La répartition des contrats de services entre les coopératrices s'établit selon les habiletés et la disponibilité de chacune ou, occasionnellement, selon la demande d'un groupe client. Les tarifs professionnels peuvent varier d'un contrat à l'autre selon les ressources des groupes clients. Cependant, une fois que le taux horaire d'un contrat est établi avec le groupe client, toutes les coopératrices qui y sont assignées reçoivent le même tarif indépendamment du type de travail effectué. Toutes les membres et les associées qui obtiennent un contrat par l'entremise de la coopérative versent 25 % de leurs honoraires professionnels au budget de fonctionnement. À la fin d'un exercice financier, s'il y a un surplus financier, la somme peut être répartie, en totalité ou non, aux membres selon leur apport à l'entreprise, réinvestie dans la coopérative sous forme d'achat d'équipement ou placée dans un fond de réserve. Ici encore, la décision est prise de façon concensuelle par les coopératrices.

Flexibilité

Un autre aspect qui unit et caractérise les membres de la coopérative est notre approche et nos valeurs entrepreneuriales. En effet, les coopératrices :

- misent sur la qualité du service et la satisfaction de la clientèle[4];
- valorisent la flexibilité pendant la réalisation d'un contrat afin d'assurer l'atteinte des objectifs; et
- visent le maintien d'une entreprise qui octroie un revenu convenable aux coopératrices.

Dans une entreprise comme la nôtre, plutôt que de chercher à maximiser les profits, nous visons la création d'emploi pour un groupe de femmes, ce qui teinte définitivement les services, les relations de travail et les produits différents offerts à la clientèle.

À *La coopérative Convergence*, la flexibilité se manifeste, entre autres, par la détermination de l'équipe d'accorder les meilleures conditions de travail possibles aux coopératrices. Si les modalités définissant ces conditions varient à tous les six mois ou d'année en année, l'objectif demeure le même. Par le passé, cela s'est traduit en termes concrets par une diminution des voyages d'affaires, par une diminution des heures de travail, par l'augmentation du temps consacré au militantisme et à l'engagement social, par l'investissement énergique dans des contrats de création et, finalement, par la possibilité de travailler davantage à partir de son domicile. Ces quelques exemples permettent d'entrevoir comment la coopérative a adopté le principe de la flexibilité au quotidien.

Inclusion

Les membres de la coopérative travaillent activement à éliminer les stéréotypes en questionnant les préjugés véhiculés à l'égard de certaines personnes, bien que cela ne soit pas toujours évident. Malgré tout, nous y tenons, puisque c'est un peu notre raison d'être. C'est pourquoi nous avons pris l'initiative de concevoir et de créer un atelier assorti d'outils pédagogiques et didactiques sur l'oppression des francophones vivant en milieu minoritaire, et cela bien avant que cette demande soit à la mode. De plus, lorsqu'un groupe client nous invite à réaliser un travail portant sur une clientèle spécifique, nous cherchons systématiquement à embaucher des personnes qui appartiennent à cette communauté. Par exemple, nous embaucherons des jeunes femmes si nous faisons un contrat pour un organisme jeunesse, ou des femmes autochtones pour offrir une formation en habiletés parentales à un groupe autochtone, etc.

Engagement

Les membres de la coopérative s'engagent personnellement et bénévolement dans des groupes qui oeuvrent pour le changement social. On estime d'ailleurs que le quart du travail de production est fait bénévolement. La coopérative juge essentielle d'inscrire sa volonté de transformation globale des rapports de sexe dans une action précise et réelle.

Par exemple, comme entité collective, la coopérative est membre de la Table féministe francophone de concertation provinciale de l'Ontario (TFFCPO) et y participe activement depuis sa fondation en 1992[5].

Développement de stratégies

Dans une coopérative comme la nôtre, le développement de stratégies doit inévitablement tenir compte du contexte. Dans les institutions qui aspirent à une féminisation absolue, le contexte diffère grandement des autres institutions. Ce choc des cultures institutionnelles fera que les critères de féminisation seront plus ou moins contraints par les pratiques en vigueur dans l'environnement immédiat.

La création d'institutions dans le secteur privé, comme *La coopérative Convergence* ou certains groupes de femmes du secteur communautaire, témoigne de la féminisation grandissante de nos institutions. Toutefois, la structuration et la gestion de nos institutions féminisées prennent parfois l'allure d'un long voyage tortueux où nous avons l'impression d'avoir égaré l'itinéraire. Les modèles qui pourraient être si utiles pour alimenter notre réflexion et guider nos actions se font rarissimes. Pourtant, de nombreuses femmes persistent dans leur lutte pour inventer des espaces empreints de nouvelles croyances et façons de faire. Des collectives remplacent maintenant des conseils d'administration. La présidente, la vice-présidente, la secrétaire et la trésorière sont devenues des porte-parole et des responsables de dossiers. La direction générale cède sa place à la coordination ou aux comités de gestion.

En apparence, les différents conseils consultatifs provinciaux et le défunt Conseil consultatif canadien sur le statut de la femme[6] (CCCSF) peuvent constituer des modèles à suivre en matière de féminisation des institutions. Par contre, ces institutions sont structurées selon un modèle gouvernemental et elles sont soumises à une philosophie fondamentalement patriarcale et hiérarchique. Elles sont structurées selon des principes dominants imposés par les minorités masculine, blanche et anglophone[7]. Chaque conseil est dirigé par un petit groupe de personnes qui ont pour tâche de prendre les décisions en suivant un processus et un cadre rigides et lents.

Ce qui fait le propre de la féminisation des institutions est l'accent mis sur le processus. Habituellement, la clarification du projet et des valeurs occupe une place de choix au sein d'un milieu féminisé. L'institution traditionnelle accordera plus d'importance aux résultats à court terme. Si les deux approches ont leurs mérites, sans vouloir faire l'apologie de la féminisation, nous croyons que les résultats à court terme doivent s'inscrire dans un projet de société pour qu'ils soient véritablement utiles.

À notre avis, la création d'institutions qui nous ressemblent est une voie essentielle pour assurer le plein développement et l'épanouissement de nos communautés de femmes et de notre société. Elles offrent le ressourcement et l'énergie nécessaires afin de parvenir à l'équité. Les acquis demeurent cependant très fragiles[8]. Les mentalités ne changent pas rapidement. La liste complète des iniquités qui touchent les femmes et les autres groupes exclus de notre société contemporaine est trop longue pour en faire l'énumération ici. Pourtant, certaines d'entre elles méritent d'être soulignées pour les rendre plus visibles :

- la violence continue à terroriser les femmes et les filles... Une enquête de Statistique Canada révèle que la moitié (51 %) des Canadiennes a subi au moins un acte de violence physique ou sexuelle depuis l'âge de 16 ans et près de 60 % des femmes qui ont été agressées sexuellement ont été la cible d'un tel acte plus d'une fois (Statistique Canada, 1993);
- le travail obligatoire porte atteinte aux droits fondamentaux des femmes pauvres de l'Ontario. Le travail obligatoire (*workfare*) affectera les conditions de vie des femmes de nombreuses façons et pourrait avoir pour conséquence l'élimination de postes permanents, la diminution de la sécurité d'emploi, l'élimination ou la diminution des avantages sociaux à plus ou moins brève échéance, l'instauration d'un système de travaux forcés et la baisse de l'ensemble des revenus d'emploi. Cette réforme prive les personnes de la possibilité de choisir leur emploi en brimant leur liberté

d'association; elle crée des emplois sans possibilité d'avancement professionnel; elle rend légitime le double emploi des femmes comme travailleuses et mères; elle augmente l'ostracisme à l'égard des bénéficiaires de l'aide sociale; elle rend les femmes plus vulnérables à la violence en limitant leur accès à des ressources financières et ainsi les contraignent possiblement à rester plus longtemps sous l'emprise tyrannique d'un conjoint violent (Côté, 1996 : 11);

• les lois de l'immigration se moquent impunément des droits et du bien-être des nouvelles arrivantes. Les femmes immigrantes ont de la difficulté à obtenir le statut de réfugiée politique lorsqu'elles tentent de fuir une situation de violence à caractère sexuel. On leur impose des taxes élevées lors d'une demande d'immigration. Le système de parrainage est élaboré de telle sorte que pour obtenir son statut de résidente permanente, une femme immigrante doit se placer en situation de dépendance à l'égard de son parrain pendant une période de dix ans. Si le parrain est le mari, on imagine aisément la vulnérabilité des femmes aux abus de pouvoir et à la violence conjugale du mari. Par ailleurs, les femmes immigrantes parrainées par un employeur demeurent sous sa tutelle pour deux ans et leur statut d'immigration dépend de l'évaluation de l'employeur. Les politiques actuelles d'immigration ont pour effet de perpétuer le racisme puisqu'elles sont fondées sur l'idée que les immigrantes abusent du système et qu'il est nécessaire de mettre en place des contrôles stricts pour éviter de telles situations (Côté, 1996 : 12).

Les femmes qui travaillent dans le contexte des institutions traditionnelles doivent mener la lutte de la féminisation de l'intérieur et, pour ce faire, emprunter des stratégies d'infiltration. Les diverses stratégies possibles peuvent s'inspirer des principes de base suivants : la prise de parole, la participation active, la culture de la mémoire et la prise de pouvoir[9].

Les femmes doivent prendre la parole. Cette parole aura davantage d'impact si elle s'articule dans un langage inclusif, car on ne saura trop souligner l'importance de se nommer et de se faire nommer. Combien d'entre nous ignorons l'ampleur de la violence faite aux filles et aux femmes parce que ce sujet était jusqu'à tout récemment considéré comme honteux? Combien d'entre nous méconnaissons la réalité lesbienne et sommes encore remplies de préjugés et de stéréotypes à leur endroit? Combien d'entre nous associons aux lesbiennes la sempiternelle image des «amazones» ou des «grandes folles» télédiffusée à chaque célébration annuelle de fierté gaie? Trop souvent, les femmes sont demeurées muettes pour se protéger de la violence, de la haine, du jugement et du rejet. En faisant éclater le mur du silence, les femmes manifestent leur droit d'exister, de vivre et d'être respectées.

Seule une implication dans nos communautés nous permettra d'être présentes aux différents paliers et aux divers moments de la prise de décisions. Pour favoriser une participation active, il est essentiel de créer des espaces propices à la formation continue qui offrent la possibilité d'un véritable épanouissement. La participation active devient impossible sans la coopération et la solidarité.

La mémoire collective de l'histoire des femmes et de leur apport au développement de notre société est courte. Nos institutions doivent donc participer à la construction de cette mémoire et diffuser les connaissances acquises. Les femmes doivent reconnaître et faire reconnaître leurs expériences qui s'élaborent à partir de leurs connaissances, mais aussi de leurs intuitions et de leurs émotions. La prise de pouvoir commence par le partage des lieux de pouvoir afin de contrer la domination. Cette démystification du pouvoir peut s'accomplir surtout par la valorisation de l'expérience comme source de savoir. Les savoirs féminins ou féministes peuvent se transmettre par des outils de réflexion simples et vulgarisés ou, tout simplement, en créant un espace propice à l'apprentissage[10]. Les femmes se doivent de transmettre les savoirs qui seront utiles aux autres femmes et qui font référence à leur vécu.

La féminisation des institutions canadiennes se concrétisera si les femmes développent une analyse des diverses formes d'oppression dans la société et si elles s'investissent dans la lutte pour y mettre fin. Plusieurs personnes vivent quotidiennement de multiples oppressions. Il faut être des alliées inconditionnelles dans les luttes, car pour contrer toutes les formes d'oppression, nous devons mutuellement nous appuyer. Les femmes peuvent rassembler une multitude de groupes pour qu'ils partagent et qu'ils actualisent une vision commune des problématiques. Ensemble, nous pourrons élaborer des stratégies qui nous permettront de féminiser les institutions, guidées en cela, par les principes d'équité et de respect de nos diverses réalités.

Conclusion

La solidarité à tous les niveaux demeure la condition essentielle du succès de la féminisation, qu'il s'agisse de la création de nos propres institutions ou de l'infiltration dans des institutions traditionnelles. Nous croyons que chaque femme ou les groupes de femmes s'adaptent à leur contexte de travail et choisissent d'intervenir pour féminiser les institutions. Nos succès sont modelés à la faveur de nos milieux et du contexte de la situation.

Par contre, nous devons être conscientes de notre socialisation, car elle crée plusieurs embûches à la mise en place des critères de féminisation. «Une multiplicité de facteurs intervient dans la dynamique conduisant à la féminisation d'un secteur donné : ceux-ci vont des éléments d'ordre structurel aux représentations sociales et aux mentalités» (Collin, 1992 : 39).

La féminisation est l'expression d'une volonté de transformation globale des rapports entre les sexes. Cette transformation demandera du temps. Plusieurs moyens peuvent être utilisés pour accélérer le processus. Parmi ceux-ci, l'engagement des individus et des individues ainsi que des institutions est, à nos yeux, le moyen de prédilection qui favorisera le processus de féminisation et le projet d'une transformation globale.

Mais, attention, l'engagement est un fort beau principe qui peut être perçu et mis en pratique de manière fort différente. L'institution ou l'entreprise traditionnelle peut développer un volet d'engagement social dans le seul but d'en tirer des bénéfices financiers ou de redorer son blason corporatif auprès d'une population convoitée ou jugée hostile. Ainsi, il est fréquent de voir de grandes corporations épouser des causes sociales en créant des fondations chargées de distribuer des dons aux personnes et groupes sociaux ou qui subventionnent des activités en donnant l'impression que l'entreprise agit en bon citoyen corporatif, responsable et désintéressé. Cependant, on ne peut s'empêcher de froncer les sourcils et de douter des bonnes intentions de ces fondations lorsque certains de leurs bénéficiaires travaillent de pied ferme à réparer les pots cassés que laisse l'entreprise sur son passage. Quelques exemples suffiront pour illustrer nos propos.

- Que penser d'une entreprise de fabrication de boissons alcoolisées qui subventionne des activités ou des groupes qui luttent pour mettre fin à la dépendance à l'alcool?
- Que penser de la compagnie pharmaceutique fabriquant des produits anticonceptionnels testés sur les femmes de pays en voie de développement qui verse de l'argent à des projets prônant la justice sociale ou des recherches sur le cancer du sein et de l'utérus?
- Que penser de l'industrie du tabac qui investit des sommes astronomiques dans les grands événements sportifs?
- Que penser des corporations de loterie qui offrent une ligne téléphonique d'aide et de soutien sans frais aux joueurs compulsifs?
- Que penser d'une association francophone provinciale qui achète un espace publicitaire dans une publication communautaire lors d'un événement spécial, mais qui, l'occasion venue, refuse d'appuyer activement les revendications

politiques d'un ou de plusieurs groupes de sa communauté sous prétexte qu'elles ne correspondent pas à l'un de leurs dossiers prioritaires?

L'institution féminisée s'engage socialement parce qu'elle a endossé le principe d'autonomie et qu'elle lie le changement individuel au changement social en préconisant l'engagement social et politique à long terme. L'institution féminisée met ainsi sa pensée et ses ressources au service d'une lutte, d'un projet parce qu'elle croit que la coopération, l'entraide, la collaboration et la concertation lui permettent de contribuer au développement durable de sa communauté. Donc, contrairement au milieu traditionnel qui s'engage parce qu'il veut paraître (phénomène éphémère), l'institution féminisée s'investit dans le but d'être (épanouissement durable).

Il va de soi que toutes les initiatives de croissance et d'épanouissement comportent leur part de risques dont ceux de rencontrer des obstacles ou de commettre des erreurs. En relevant le défi de la féminisation, nous tenons pour acquis qu'il y aura inévitablement quelques problèmes et que ceux-ci seront inhérents à un processus d'apprentissage sain. Nous avons donc également besoin de parler de nos erreurs de parcours et de les documenter pour que d'autres femmes puissent en bénéficier. L'adage «mille fois sur le métier, remettez votre ouvrage» indique bien que c'est à force de persévérance que nous éveillerons les consciences et ouvrirons les esprits et, qui sait, peut-être parviendrons-nous à changer le monde.

Bibliographie

Collin, Johanne (1992), «Les femmes dans la profession pharmaceutique au Québec : rupture ou continuité?», *Recherches féministes*, vol. 5, no 2, 31-56.

Côté, Andrée (1996), *Les Franco-Ontariennes et les droits à l'égalité garantis à l'article 15 de la Charte canadienne des droits et libertés, Rapport de consultation*, Ottawa, Table féministe francophone de concertation provinciale de l'Ontario (TFFCPO).

Solar, Claudie (1992a), *Apport de la pédagogie féministe*, Ottawa, Université d'Ottawa.

Solar, Claudie (1992b), «Dentelle de pédagogies féministes», *Revue canadienne de l'éducation*, vol. 17, no 3, 264-285.

Statistique Canada (1993), «L'enquête sur la violence faite envers les femmes», *Le Quotidien*, Ottawa, no catalogue 11-001F.

St-Jean, Armande (1983), *Pour en finir avec le patriarcat*, Montréal, Les éditions Primeur.

Notes

1. Nous tenons à remercier Marie-Luce Garceau de l'Université Laurentienne de nous avoir donné l'occasion de participer à ce livre. Nous voulons aussi rendre hommage à la mémoire de Lorraine Gauthier qui avait commenté la première ébauche de ce texte.

2. Nos services de recherche comprennent des études de besoins, des recherches qualitatives, des évaluations de programmes et de services; les services offerts en formation sont, entre autres, la création d'outils de formation et le design de programmes de formation; nous offrons également des services de développement organisationnel, de planification stratégique et d'animation de groupes.

3. Cette vision est diamétralement opposée aux institutions traditionnelles où on constate une ségrégation des femmes sur le marché de l'emploi qui fait qu'elles sont cantonnées majoritairement dans des positions structurellement inférieures. Le milieu du travail traditionnel établit une différentiation hiérarchique très claire entre les hommes et les femmes. Cette frontière est parsemée de femmes-alibis qui stagnent lorsqu'elles atteignent le «plafond de verre» et de femmes qui occupent des postes d'exécutantes qualifiés de «ghettos féminins», et donc sous-payés.

4. On nous invite fréquemment à préparer une offre de services suite à la recommandation d'un groupe client antérieur. Nous avons donc compris très tôt l'importance de fidéliser nos groupes clients.

5. La Table féministe francophone de concertation provinciale de l'Ontario est une tribune dont le mandat principal est la concertation entre groupes et l'action politique.

6. Le Conseil consultatif canadien sur le statut de la femme a été aboli le 1er avril 1995.

7. Exception faite du Conseil du statut de la femme du Québec, où l'aspect linguistique de la structure est, dans ce cas aussi, le reflet de sa société dominante.

8. On peut penser à l'abolition du CCCSF en avril 1995.

9. Nous nous inspirons de la grille élaborée par Claudie Solar (1992a).

10. Il faut donc réduire les modes de compétition et mettre en place des modes de coopération et d'entraide.

PART III — PARTIE III
Reinventing Ourselves at Any Age —
Réinventons nos vies

Describing the locus of oppression for young Girl Guides of Canada, Patricia Whitney identifies some of the historic male-centered and eurocentric principles which underpin the Scouting movement. She also points out the domination of white middle-class girls, especially in the early Canadian Guiding movement. Consciousness-raising among Girl Guide leadership and an openness in seeking the views of the Guides themselves resulted in important symbolic changes to the Girl Guide Law and the Promise. As a scholar in Women's Studies and a former Girl Guide leader, Whitney also sees an increased appreciation for ethnic and racial diversity within the Guiding movement.

Jane Gordon's description of an innovative dance school in Nova Scotia acquaints us with women's oppression in the world of Canadian art. The main problems for young girls in traditional dance school organizations are the potential for low self-esteem, anorexia nervosa, and a worldview narrowly circumscribed by dance practice regimes. Dance professionals in such locations rarely acknowledge the work or the ideas of volunteers, many of whom are mothers of students. When Canadian girls become adult dancers, they, along with other professional artists, are then oppressed economically by wages lower than those in most other occupations. As the mother of a young dancer in Nova Scotia, this feminist sociologist sees a need for research into the positive effects on girls who participate in community-organized dance schools.

Marie-Luce Garceau montre que les femmes, tout comme les Franco-Ontariennes, âgées de 45 à 64 ans sont ignorées du monde de la recherche. Doublement minoritaires dans leur province parce que femmes et francophones, un groupe d'entre elles se sont réunies pour faire une recherche-action afin de sortir de l'ombre et de dénoncer les conditions difficiles dans lesquelles elles vivent. Au cœur de cette recherche-action, réside la notion d'empowerment, entendue comme étant un processus d'apprentissage et une démarche de transformation individuelle et collective indispensable à l'avènement de changements sociaux pour améliorer les conditions de vie des femmes. Or, ce que Garceau développe, c'est que les Franco-Ontariennes qui ont participé à cette recherche-action se sont prises en charge et qu'elles ont développé une vision sociale et une volonté d'action afin de transformer la situation.

Patricia Whitney

Girl Guides of Canada:
The Feminist Promise in the "Promise and Law"

Introduction

If woman came from Adam's rib, as the Bible claims, so the Girl Guides came forth from the Boy Scouts. The analogy is apt, given the "Muscular Christianity" that imbues the foundations of both the Guides and the Scouts. This particular form of Christian practice saw Victorian men living "by God's blessing 'a strong, daring, sporting wild man-of-the-woods' life" while preaching "a healthful and manly Christianity, one which does not exalt the feminine virtues to the exclusion of the masculine," as the Reverend Charles Kingsley wrote in *His Letters and Memories of His Life* (1877) (Houghton 1964, 204).

The Boy Scouts were founded by just such a Muscular Christian, Sir Robert Baden-Powell (1857-1941), the "hero of Mafeking," later to be styled Lord Baden-Powell of Gilwell and known to Boy Scouts as "B-P" or "The Founder." Baden-Powell set out his philosophy in *Scouting for Boys: A Handbook for Instruction in Good Citizenship Through Woodcraft*, the original edition of which appeared in 1908 after his return from the Boer War (1899-1902). This manual admonishes boys and leaders to think of the Movement, as it came to be known, as "a school of citizenship through woodcraft" where boys would learn "to live, not merely how to make a living" (*Scouting* 4). Baden-Powell further writes that "the aim of the Scout training is to replace Self with service, to make the lads individually efficient, morally and physically, with the object of using that efficiency for the service of the community" (*Scouting* 4). These character-building aims were to be achieved whenever possible in the open air, rousing, Baden-Powell writes, the "vast reserve of loyal patriotism and Christian spirit lying dormant in our nation to-day" (*Scouting* 5). Boys were to aspire to a vigorous manliness and to learn the medieval code of knightly chivalry, emulate the deeds of St. George who slew the dragon, and be particularly polite to and considerate of "respectable" women.

In his later writings, such as *Rovering to Success: A Guide for Young Manhood* (1922), Baden-Powell again counsels his readers never to forget "the chivalry due to women" and to heed "the development of the manly and protective attitude to the other sex" (101). Baden-Powell suggests that the boy look to the stag, the "Monarch of the Glen," sketched after the portrait by Landseer, and model his behaviour accordingly: "He is the king of the herd.... He is of a type of courage, strength, and virile beauty...And he takes his responsibilities, ready at all times-and able-to protect his hinds and fawns against all aggressors" (*Rovering* 101-2).

Although his view of women was highly romanticized and intensely patriarchal, Baden-Powell's advice on health, diet, and exercise seem generally enlightened, if class-bound. A dark shadow is cast, however, by his racism and his discussion of women not as persons, but as objects to be chosen wisely or foolishly by young men. Africans, for example, are "Swazi savages entranced by the London omnibus": "They were so taken with its brilliant colours and the idea of its being entirely for joy-riding!" (*Rovering* 119). In a similarly condescending tone, Baden-Powell states: "There are women and there are dolls" (*Rovering* 121). Wives are to be "pure and clean" women, both virtuous and malleable; Baden-Powell writes that "women's character shapes itself according as it is led by their man" (*Rovering* 127).

Throughout the chapter on "Women" in *Rovering to Success*, Baden-Powell, while advising his readers — all of whom are assumed to be male, white, Christian, and heterosexual — to show women utmost respect, reinforces the position of women as mere adjuncts to men. For example, man's duty to present himself to his wife as "clean and strong and chivalrous" is necessary in order to fulfil his duty to "God in carrying on the race on the best lines" (121). Semen is presented as a sacred substance. Life is passed from father to son, with woman's role scarcely acknowledged: "The germ from which you were made was passed down by your father just as he came down from the germ of his father before him...So it is a sacred trust handed down to you through your father and his fathers from the Creator — The Great Father of us all" (*Rovering* 105).

For Baden-Powell then, the woman is the mere vessel in this triumphalist framing of life as derived from and perpetrated by the male, who is himself the image of the Creator, the Ultimate Father. This model is, in the words of feminist theologian Rosemary Radford Ruether, "the doctrine of patriarchy as the normative order of history" (1993, 80). In the philosophy of Thomas Aquinas, woman is "defective and misbegotten in her individual nature," yet still essential owing to her role as birth giver; nonetheless, for Aquinas, "for any form of spiritual help, man is better served by a companion of the same sex than by woman" (Ruether 1993, 96).

I am not suggesting that Baden-Powell knew of Aquinas, although as the son of an Oxford professor-priest it is likely. Rather he was advocating a Christian way of life that revered "pure" women, particularly mothers (women who had, obviously, fulfilled their procreative role), while establishing and maintaining an organization in Boy Scouting that, like the Church and the institutions of the State, forbade women's participation in any meaningful way while asserting men's superiority. If the man was to be the "Monarch of the Glen" as well as Bishop of the Church and Prime Minister of the State, woman was to be, in the words of Coventry Patmore's, *The Angel in the House*, she who is "most excellent of all," she who must be praised "as Maid and Wife," and, before whose "affecting majesty," all men must bend the knee. Such is the position, stifling for the middle-class women assigned to it, and simply ludicrous for the millions of working-class and destitute women in the British Isles that underlies Baden-Powell's assumptions and writings.

Baden-Powell had come to adulthood in the Victorian age, but by the time Scouting was getting under way in England in 1907, the old Queen was dead and new ideas were beginning to ferment. For example, in 1905, Emmeline Pankhurst (1858-1928) organized the Women's Social and Political Union and took up the struggle for women's suffrage in Britain. So, perhaps it is not surprising that girls were casting an eye at Baden-Powell's Scouting Movement, misogynist as it was, and wondering if it held anything for them.

The Crystal Palace

The first Boy Scout Rally was held at the Crystal Palace in London in September 1909. Among the eleven thousand boys and men parading before Sir Robert Baden-Powell were many girls wearing the broad-brimmed Boy Scout hat and homemade uniforms. In fact, there were "already six thousand girls registered as Boy Scouts" by this time (Rosenthal 1984, 11). The girls had hidden their gender by registering under their surnames and initials.

Not wanting a female presence in Scouting, Baden-Powell turned to his sister, Agnes, and asked her to take on organizing the girls. This she did (although the girls feared they would lose all the adventure of Scouting in this new organization) and the Girl Guides were born. In fact, parents were apprehensive that their daughters would be engaged in unseemly pursuits in Guiding. To Baden-Powell's credit, he wrote in 1918: "Now I shall be told that I am trying to make girls into tomboys. Not a bit of it — quite the opposite; but girls don't want to be dolls, they have ambitions beyond that, and also men do not desire to have dolls as their wives — they want comrades" (Robinson 1984, 2). Baden-Powell was still harping on what was best for the male ("they want comrades"), but, nonetheless, girls and women did get their own organization — and they were ready to make the most of it.

Agnes Baden-Powell and the Girl Guides

Agnes Baden-Powell was a remarkable woman who spoke six languages and played four musical instruments (Crocker 1990, 17). Her book, *The Handbook for Girl Guides or How Girls Can Help Build the Empire* [1912], became the first manual of Guiding. In it, she writes that the aim of the Girl Guides is "to get girls to learn how to be women — self-helpful, happy, prosperous, and capable of keeping good homes and of bringing up good children" (vii). She visualizes this training for "all classes" in society but particularly sees Guiding as "a grand field for national work [for] young women who have had a better upbringing" (vii). These advantaged women are to provide leadership to "the girls of the factories and of the alleys of our great cities, who, after they leave school have no restraining influence, and who, nevertheless, may be the mothers, and should be the character trainers, of the future men of this nation" (vii). Thus women's responsibilities were to be the mothers of the nation and indeed the mothers of the British Empire. Robert Baden-Powell, who collaborated with his sister in writing *The Handbook*, was fond of quoting Lloyd George to the effect that "You cannot maintain an A-1 Empire on C-3 men" (Rosenthal 1990, 3). Girl Guides were to become the mothers of those necessary "A-1" men.

Agnes wanted her girls to grow in "womanliness," a state marked by sweetness and tenderness but also by courage. Girls, but particularly those who live in "one of the British Dominions," must be particularly resourceful, able to milk cows, cut firewood, and indeed "defend yourself for your life" (*The Handbook* 24). Above all else, however, the plucky, competent, and able Girl Guide is to be a mother, bringing up her children to be "good, hardworking, honourable, and useful citizens for our great British Empire.... Britain has been made great by her great men, and these great men were made great by their mothers" (*The Handbook* 24).

A marked characteristic of the Guiding movement was, and remains, an emphasis on fitness and competence in nature. In *The Handbook*, Agnes Baden-Powell writes that Guides must "be accustomed to living in the open: they have to know how to put up tents or huts for themselves; how to lay and light a fire on the ground; how to kill, cut up, and cook their food; how to tie logs together to make bridges, and rafts; how to find their way by night as well as by day in a strange country, and so on" (1912, 27). A Guide was to be trained to lift manhole covers in an emergency to allow sewer gases to escape and to turn a barn or school into a hospital; she was to assist her parents in creating a serene home. Above all, she was to be brave and intensely patriotic. The model Guide presented was an honourable girl, fit in body and mind, courageous and strong, resourceful, and compassionate. Certainly, her

132

destiny was to bear and raise the next generation of the Empire; nonetheless, she was more than a brood mare for imperialism; she was a woman who would "*know* the right thing to do at the right moment, and [be] willing to do it" (*The Handbook* 38).

It is almost impossible to realize today just how unusual the Guiding program was in its beginnings. The Victorian ideal had been the pale faced, delicate woman who eschewed exercise and strove to suggest gentility in all her behaviours. Moreover, this "concept of the Victorian woman was not necessarily reserved for upper-class women; even working-class women who had to work hard each day were still expected to maintain a mythical gentility" (Henderson *et al.* 1989, 22).

Fitness, the Empire, and Social Control

In *Sporting Females: Critical Issues in the History and Sociology of Women's Sports*, Jennifer Hargreaves writes that "Physical education became an integral feature in the curriculum in increasing numbers of elite girls' schools from the middle of the nineteenth century" (1994, 63). Girls from wealthy as well as merely economically comfortable homes were playing field hockey, tennis and cricket; doing gymnastics; and riding horses. Girls, like boys, were to be trained for empire building, the 1890s being "the height of the era when notions of empire-building were an entrenched part of British ruling-class ideology" (Hargreaves 1994, 67).

Hargreaves writes, however, that "throughout the nineteenth century there was no equivalent form of physical activity in schools for working-class girls" (1994, 68). Military style drilling was introduced for working-class boys as "an effective device to inculcate 'mechanical obedience,' viewed as necessary to provide an industrial and paramilitary training for workers and soldiers" (Hargreaves 1994, 69).

The equivalent means of social control for girls was Swedish gymnastics, introduced to the London schools in 1879 (Hargreaves 1994, 69). Agnes Baden-Powell recommends this system of fitness to the Guides in *The Handbook*: "Swedish or ju-jitsu exercises every morning and evening [are] a grand thing for keeping you fit" (1912, 33).

The Swedish system received legitimacy through the support of ruling-class figures, but the hidden reality was that the Swedish system was a means of social control which had an ideologically subordinating function: it was no accident that Swedish gymnastics, rather than freer, more spontaneous forms of movement, became the accepted from of exercise for working-class girls…(Hargreaves 1994, 72).

With its emphasis on fitness-Guiding was early defined as a "jolly game played in the out-of-doors" — and its opportunities for women of the "better classes" to "guide" girls of the lower orders, it seems reasonable to position the early Guiding movement not only within the project of empire-building, but also within the influence of "useful" leisure (the Victorians and Edwardians, with their reverence for the Protestant work ethic, could justify leisure only if it served to refresh one for labour) and sport for women. That said, it is of considerable interest that Guiding was radically committed to those "freer, more spontaneous forms of movement" for girls and women, albeit within a fixed set of class assumptions. Compare, for example, Agnes Baden-Powell's emphasis on health, physical strength, and outdoor adventure in *The Handbook*, published in 1912, with the advice in *The Journal of the American Medical Association* in 1925, which "implied that young girls in this 'age of feminine freedom' were overdoing athletics" and thus having "a harmful effect on the all-important role of motherhood" (Henderson *et al.* 1989, 23).

The early days of Girl Guiding provided middle-class women with forms of "leisure" outside the home. As Hargreaves has pointed out, "youth work was a socially acceptable extension of the traditional female role" wherein women could "escape from the confines of domesticity without undermining their prior duty to home and family" (1994, 110). Certainly, there was a class-based agenda here, and indeed it can be argued that such voluntary work was "part of a conscious attempt to control working-class free time and collective group behaviour" (Hargreaves 1994, 110); nonetheless, such "practical recreation," to use Henderson's term, gave middle-class women an opportunity to socialize and to assume leadership roles within their communities. This model of female interaction remains a feature of adult women's involvement in Girl Guiding today.

Among the groups organized to provide a healthful and disciplined environment where bourgeois values could be imparted to the working classes were the Church of England working girls' clubs, the Girls' Friendly Society, the YWCA, and the Girl Guides: "Almost all these 'socio-religious' organizations included some form of sport or physical activity...chosen for their 'improving' qualities" (Hargreaves 1994, 111). The Girl Guides Association in Britain may be seen, then, as providing the opportunity for the upper social classes to determine the leisure practices of working-class (and other) girls; develop the female body for childbearing; provide "suitable" social interaction for middle-class women interested in philanthropic youth work; and support of the goal to "Help Build the Empire."

Guiding in Canada

This enthusiasm for social improvement and control and for the project of empire building was also embraced in Canada. In 1912, Lady (Mary)

Pellatt was named Chief Commissioner of the Girl Guides in this country; in 1916, she hosted the second Annual (Canadian) Girl Guide Rally at her home, Casa Loma, in Toronto. In the secretary's report of 1 April 1917, Guide Companies were recorded as organized in Day and Sunday Schools, the YWCA, the Girls' Friendly Society (Social and Factories), while Senior Guides to be trained as officers were organized among undergraduates at the University of Toronto. Thus, we see in Canada a continuation of the model of girls and women from the higher social classes developed for leadership of working-class women and girls.

While Guiding developed in Canada in ways that were unique (for example, a girl did not need to be a British Subject to become a Guide in this country), and "newcomers were allowed to use their own language at meetings and were encouraged to carry their National Flag at enrolment ceremonies along with the Union Jack" (Lax, 13), the culture of Canadian Guiding was absorbed from the "Mother Country" with scant criticism or reflection. Canadian Guiding remained a creature of British colonialism, even as it surpassed Britain in program innovation and cultural and ethnic inclusivity.

The Promise and Law

An essential component of Guiding is the Promise and Law. These consist of a pledge and a code of conduct. The original Guide Law, as set out in Agnes Baden-Powell's *The Handbook for Girl Guides or How Girls Can Help Build the Empire* states:

- A Guide's honour is to be trusted. A Guide is loyal.
- A Guide's duty is to be useful and to help others.
- A Guide is a friend to all, and a sister to every other Guide, no matter to what social class the other belongs.
- A Guide is courteous.
- A Guide keeps herself pure in thoughts, words, and deeds.
- A Guide is a friend to animals.
- A Guide obeys orders.
- A Guide smiles and sings (under all circumstances).
- A Guide is thrifty.

The original promise reads: "On my honour, I promise that I will do my best: To do my duty to God and the King (or God and my country for those outside the Empire); To help other people at all times; To obey the Guide Law" (*Constitution and By-Laws*).

Although there were minor adjustments over the years, the Promise and Law remained basically true to this 1910 wording, save the excision of "no matter to what social class the other belongs" and a reordering of the laws.

Project of Renewal

In March of 1991, I was approached by Joan Howell, Chief Commissioner of Girl Guides of Canada/Guides du Canada, to begin looking at the Promise and Law with an eye to making them more contemporary in both thought and language. The project of empire building was long dead; the rigid social class stratification of Guiding's early days was obsolete if not downright offensive; Canada was recognizing herself as a multi-cultural and multi-faith (or no-faith) society; and we were twenty-five years into the contemporary women's movement.

Believing, as I do, in the unique capacity of the Canadian women's movement to be welcoming to the efforts of first wave women's organizations to renew themselves within feminist principles, I accepted the challenge. For the next two years, a committee of women volunteers from across Canada devoted countless hours to the design of a consultative process that would allow girls and women from every province and from all ethnicities to participate in focus groups, complete questionnaires, discuss, debate, write letters — and above all, be heard. Our objective in consulting our members was to establish and maintain feminist process in this project as we undertook the renewal of the Promise and Law. The result has been, I believe, a re-forming of the principles of the Girl Guides of Canada.

Making the Model

Since the incorporation of the Canadian Council of the Girl Guides Association in 1917 by an act of the Canadian parliament, Guiding had grown by 1991 to a national organization of women and girls numbering about 275,000. It is common knowledge that the demographic profile of the country has altered radically during those years. Canada is characterized by more people of colour, many more immigrants from the southern hemisphere, an overall weakening of the majoritarian influence of Anglo-Celtic culture, the independence movement in Quebec, a sharp decline in the authority of the mainline Christian denominations, and second and third waves of the women's movement.

It was clear that if Canadian Guiding were not to disappear in the next century, then Girl Guides of Canada (GGC) had to examine its roots and revise its rules. First steps were taken at the National Council meeting held in Toronto in June 1991. Members of Council, including the Chief Commissioner and her deputies, National Directors, Provincial Commissioners, elected members, and members of the senior paid staff participated in discussion groups on the Promise and Law.

136

Overwhelmingly, these women agreed that the Promise and Law were "too authoritarian," that obedience had to be removed from the Law, that both the term "God" and the term "Queen" should be examined (Canadian Guides in 1991 were still promising to do their "duty to God [and] the Queen"). In addition, Council members stated that concern for the environment and the enhancement of girls' self-esteem were essential components of a Promise and Law for the twenty-first century.

Subsequent to the June 1991 National Council discussions on the Promise and Law, the members of the National Communication Services Group, including women from Newfoundland, Quebec, Ontario, Manitoba, British Columbia, and Nova Scotia, developed a questionnaire designed to elicit opinions from girls and women across Canada. This questionnaire was tested by the 200 participants at the GGC National Conference held in Toronto in January 1992. Minor adjustments were made to the instrument following the Conference. The Service Group then developed a Promise and Law Renewal Kit which included an open letter from the Chief Commissioner, "Facilitator's Notes for Conducting Focus Groups," and ten copies of the questionnaire, "Looking at the Promise and Law." We also produced a simple ten-minute video which explained how to organize and conduct a focus group.

In May 1992, Promise and Law Renewal Kits were sent to all National Council members and to every Division, Area and Provincial Commissioners across Canada and to Companies and Packs on Foreign Soil (Canadian Guiding units overseas). In June, the National Council met in Corner Brook, Newfoundland, and participated in Promise and Law focus groups.

In addition, each Provincial Commissioner was sent twelve "flagged" Kits to be distributed to target groups such as teachers (non-Guiding women), parents, units with Guiders and girls with disabilities, women and girls of colour, older women, Aboriginal girls and women, and religious groups, as well as Guiding committees at every level of the organization. Some provinces chose to integrate the Promise and Law focus groups into trainings or events (for example, about 150 women and teenaged girls participated in a Promise and Law weekend at Doe Lake Camp in Ontario in October 1992 as did Canadian Guiders in Germany).

All completed questionnaires were submitted for tabulation by December 1992; the final report of the Promise and Law consultation was submitted to me as National Director of Communications and Chairwoman of the Communication Services Group in January 1993. The results of this "snapshot" of our membership indicated that some

10,000 girls and women, either as individuals or as participants in focus groups, had taken part in this key step in the Promise and Law Renewal Process.

Working with these data, the discussion notes from the June 1991 National Council, and our knowledge of and experience with girls and adolescent women, the Service Group set about drafting a renewed Promise and Law. An important document in this process was the Promise and Law section of the 1992 WAGGGS *Programme Pack* (WAGGGS refers to the London-based World Association of Girl Guides and Girl Scouts, the coordinating body of the 129 Girl Guiding and Girl Scouting countries in the world). The WAGGGS document was timely for our purposes in affirming the role of Guiding as an organization dedicated to "the advancement of girls and young women" and celebrating difference within the world "sisterhood" of Guiding.

In drafting the renewed Promise and Law, we sought to stress beliefs and values over behaviours, stating the following:

> If a girl is taught to develop a spiritual centre in her character and to respect herself and others she is on the right track to developing behaviours that will increase her self-confidence, enabling her personal vision to grow outwards from her own small self to her unit [Guide Company], her community, and to the world sisterhood of Guiding. (Whitney 1993)

In May 1993, two draft options for a renewed Promise and Law were presented to National Council in Toronto for discussion. These options, essentially alike, differed in whether to use the word "law" or the word "challenge" for the Guide Law.

These options were widely distributed to girls and women across Canada during the spring and summer of 1993. In July, GGC hosted 3000 girls and women from some 30 countries at an international camp held over a period of ten days near Guelph, Ontario. This gathering presented GGC with an ideal opportunity to seek additional feedback from Canadian young women as well as from international adolescent women. Sally Steers, Allison Whitney, and I conducted focus groups with about 50 of these young women, whom we found to be overwhelmingly in favour of renewal of the Promise and Law. In this, they reflected the results of the 1992 national consultation which indicated that almost 95% of participants wanted a change to the Promise and Law.

By the fall of 1993, many women and girls from across Canada had taken the opportunity to write to GGC with their views on the Promise and Law options that had been circulating throughout the country. All these letters were read and key issues identified before the Communication Services Group met in mid-October 1993. This, then, was the final opportunity for this committee to prepare a proposed Promise and Law, incorporating the results of over two years of research, for presentation to National Council for vote in November 1993.

The document presented to National Council in November was a compromise. As might be expected in an organization rooted in the first wave, some members were reluctant to see any change, and some few were adamantly anti-feminist and seemed to perceive, rightly, that the process of renewal of the Promise and Law would change Canadian Guiding significantly.

It would be quite wrong to suggest that the Promise and Law Renewal process was a survey. Rather, it was an attempt to involve as many women and girls as possible in a national "dialogue" about the fundamental code of GGC. The members of National Council who were called upon to vote did not reflect the face of Canadian Guiding. There were no "out" lesbians nor First Nations nor poor women. There were some young women, some women of colour, and some women with visible disabilities, but the majority were middle-class and upper middle-class women, from Christian, white, able bodied, and heterosexual situations. While precise demographic information is sketchy, these women were a fair representation of GGC, although the tendency was to higher income and education level than the "average Guider."

The proposal presented to and approved unanimously by the National Council of Girl Guides of Canada-Guides du Canada was as follows:

Promise:
- I promise to do my best.
- To be true to myself, my God/faith* and Canada.
- I will help others and accept the Guiding Law.

* Choose either the word *God* or the word *faith* according to your personal convictions.

Law: the Guiding Law challenges me to:
- be honest and trustworthy,
- use my resources wisely,
- respect myself and others,
- recognize and use my talents and abilities,
- protect our common environment,
- live with courage and strength,
- share in the sisterhood of Guiding.

This renewed Promise and Law, while abiding by WAGGGS regulations that all Guides must make a promise that includes patriotism, acknowledgement of a spiritual quest, and service to others, nonetheless, goes a significant way toward a more inclusive and woman-centred Promise and Law. We were striving for a Promise and Law that would affirm self-respect for every girl and woman (the Promise and Law were designed to be accessible to the girl of nine years, the developing adolescent, and the mature woman). We were determined to honour the deeply felt religious beliefs of many members and yet be open to those girls and women engaged in a spiritual quest; to maintain the tradition of service to girls and women between 5 and 85, and yet state this idea simply as "I will help others" rather than in the words of the "old" Promise which spoke of helping "other people at all times" — not a useful notion for girls and women too often socialized to servitude.

The new Law is designed to maximize a girl's potential and to help her respect and believe in herself as a person, as well as in her talents and abilities. The new Law acknowledges the need for all girls and women to protect and nurture the Earth, our mother, and to use our resources — time, energy, intellect, and insight — for our own good and for humanity's welfare. The girl and woman are challenged to "live with courage and strength" in an echo of Agnes Baden-Powell's exhortations to the Guides of 85 years ago, and in the certainty that today's woman and tomorrow's woman had need to be prepared for a massive struggle to achieve and secure dignity and equality.

The new Law ends in sisterhood, surely a much disputed term in a time of identity politics when the "sisterhood is powerful" slogans of a generation ago ring hollow. Yet, this Law, "share in the sisterhood of Guiding," was very much welcomed. This is sisterhood with our eyes open. This is a sisterhood that is struggling with strong anti-racist policies and practices. This is a sisterhood that is, very late in the day to be sure, finally beginning to acknowledge the essential role that lesbian women play in Canadian Guiding. This is a sisterhood that, in spite of the gross horrors of inequality and racism and the erasing of the dignity of difference in western society, still happens among women and girls across Canada every week of the year as they meet in school gyms, churches, synagogues, and temples to learn to be stronger, more competent women. It is a model of women taking girls by the hand and saying "come and grow into your potential as a woman."

It would be incorrect to argue that the Promise and Law Renewal process has transformed Girl Guides of Canada into a fully feminist organization. It has not. The procedure has, however, introduced feminist process in a way and to a degree that has subverted the male, military model that prevailed heretofore.

I would argue that GGC is now better equipped to re-form itself into an inclusive pro-feminist organization, one which provides a single-sex environment that values diversity and valorizes the girl-child as strong, independent, and cooperative. The renewed Promise and Law were accepted by Girl Guides of Canada/Guides du Canada in a unanimous vote held at National Council in November 1993. Subsequently, the Constitutions Committee and the World Committee of WAGGGS gave approval in the spring of 1994, in time for the proclamation of the renewed Promise and Law at the Annual Meeting of Canadian Guiding held in Saskatoon, Saskatchewan, on June 11, 1994. There is no looking back now, as Girl Guides in Canada face the future as part of the Canadian women's movement.

References

Baden-Powell, Agnes. 1912. *The Handbook for Girl Guides or How Girls Can Help Build the Empire*. In Collaboration with Lt.-Gen. Sir Robert Baden-Powell, K.C.B., etc. London: Thomas Nelson and Sons.

Baden-Powell, Robert. 1912. *Rovering to Success: A Guide for Young Manhood*. London: Herbert Jenkins. 1922 rpt.

Baden-Powell, Robert. n.d. *Scouting for Boys: A Handbook for Instruction in Good Citizenship Through Woodcraft*. Scout Brotherhood Edition. National Council: Boy Scouts of Canada.

Crocker, Dorothy. 1990. *All About Us: A Story of the Girl Guides in Canada 1910-1989*. Toronto: Girl Guides of Canada-Guides du Canada.

Hargreaves, Jennifer. 1994. *Sporting Females: Critical Issues in the History and Sociology of Women's Sports*. London: Routledge.

Henderson, Karla et al. 1989. *A Leisure of One's Own: A Feminist Perspective on Women's Leisure*. State College, Pennsylvania: Venture.

Houghton, Walter E. 1964. *The Victorian Frame of Mind 1830-1870*. New Haven: Yale UP. 1957 rpt.

Lax, Joan. n.d. *Window on a Changing World: The Girl Guides of Canada*, The First Fifty Years, 1910-1960. Unpublished paper.

Patmore, Coventry. 1993. "The Angel in the House." *The Norton Anthology of English Literature*. Ed. M.H. Abrams. 6th ed. vol. 2. New York: Norton.

Robinson, Marita. 1984. *Celebration: 75 Years of Challenge and Change: A Portrait of the Girl Guides of Canada-Guides du Canada*. Toronto: Grosvenor House.

Rosenthal, Michael. 1984. *The Character Factory: Baden-Powell and the Origins of the Boy Scout Movement*. New York: Pantheon Books.

Ruether, Rosemary Radford. 1993. *Sexism and God-Talk: Toward a Feminist Theology*. Boston: Beacon.

Whitney, Patricia. 1993. "Rationale: Option #1 and #2, Promise and Law Renewal," National Council, 26-29.

World Association of Girl Guides and Girl Scouts. 1990. *Constitution and By-Laws of the World Association of Girl Guides and Girl Scouts*. London: WAGGGS.

World Association of Girl Guides and Girl Scouts. 1990. *WAGGGS Programme Pack: Promise and Law*. London: WAGGGS.

Endnote

1. Thanks. The renewal of the Promise and Law was made possible through the extraordinary work of many Guiding women, most especially my volunteer colleagues Marjorie Gerrard, Daphne Young, Michelle Chisholm, Sally Steers, Gaby Levesque, and our staff associates Barbara Crocker and Marika Munshaw — a wonderful group of women who have feminist process in their souls.

Jane Gordon

Dancing the Road to Success:
Metro Dance and Women

To most people, dance is a feminine art because women are the majority of performers. However, dance as a performance art has its own gender-based hierarchies. In contrast, the dance group I studied is run largely by and for women and girls, and has been successful and effective in maintaining a structure which is inclusive, non-hierarchical, and appreciative of work done by women, both paid and unpaid. It has sustained these patterns through the twenty-odd years of its existence and through its expansion from a small, informal group of dancers to a large educational and cultural body in its community. It is also a strong and positive environment for the women and girls who work and study there.

The appeal of dance, particularly ballet, to females is evident in the number of girls who begin dance lessons. The ballerina typifies the grace, fluid movement, and elegant beauty that is, for many, the ideal image of dance. Dance training socializes girls to achieve culturally appropriate feminine traits such as grace, poise, and elegance. Ballerinas and ballet shoes are two gender-specific images commonly seen on jewellery, clothes, and other artifacts targeted at young girls. Popular art such as posters shows leaping ballerinas with commentary on overcoming obstacles and striving for perfection. From Hallowe'en costumes to birthday party paraphernalia, dance is almost always visually female and oriented toward girls.

Dance education is also almost exclusively undertaken by girls. That is evident in the enrolment at the dance school studied, where over 98 percent of the pupils listed in the program for the 1994 annual production were girls. For parents, dance classes may allow girls the benefits of physical activity without the roughness or danger of sports. Adult women are more likely to have had exposure to dance as children than did men. The link between youthful exposure and adult participation and interest in cultural expression is a common theme of cultural advocacy groups, whether in dance, music, or theatre. It is also used by sports organizations.

What is the relationship between these images of dance as a feminized performing art and the reality of dance for women? The answers which are available provide a complex and mixed picture.

Women are heavily involved in dance in two specific ways. They are the majority of dancers and the majority of the audience for dance performances (Dagg 1986; Frederico 1974; Hanna 1988; Kleeh-Tolley 1986; Ryser 1964; Sutherland 1976). Girls and women are over represented as students in dance classes, no matter what dance specialty. Women also outnumber men in most professional companies. In Canada, women have been heavily involved in the creation of dance companies and professional training schools of dance (Dagg 1986, 106). They have founded, chaired, and staffed most university dance departments. They have likely founded and run many of the small dance schools at which so much non-professional dance education takes place.

Comparisons of men and women professional dancers show marked differences. Statistics Canada's 1991 census reports 1555 individuals in the occupational category that combined dancers and choreographers, slightly down from 1986 figures. Of these, 285 worked full-time all year round. The mean income for dancers and choreographers with full-time work was $32,489. There were 65 full-time males with an average income of $34,954 and 225 women with an annual income of $31,805 (Statistics Canada 1993, 14-15). In Nova Scotia, the home province of Metro Dance, the 1991 census enumerated only 10 individuals classified as professional dancers or choreographers, down from the1986 census (Statistics Canada 1993, 70).

Women dancers do well in comparison to other performing artists, receiving half of the individual Canada Council grants: "Dance is the only discipline in the arts in which women fare financially as well as men and in which more women than men are able to find work" (Dagg 1986,109). Women dominate ballet more than other forms of dance (Dagg 1986; Hanna 1988). However, dance has a gender-related prestige hierarchy. As Hanna says:

> Like theatre and symphony, dance is to some degree occupationally differentiated and sex segregated separating the performers, choreographers/composers, and directors/managers — the nondancing positions being more powerful and male-dominant. Women have less mobility across these career segments than men (Hanna 1988,121).

In addition, while dance is the most feminized of the art forms, it is also the poorest paid, not unlike other female-dominated occupations. *Funding of the Arts in Canada* (1986) uses census data to provide a comparison of dancers with other artists in Canada.

Table 1 — Artists and Income

	Average Income	% Average Income
Total labour force income	14,700	
Musicians	10,300	70
Painters, sculptors, vis.	9,300	63
Actors	12,600	86
Dancers	9,100	62

(Funding of the Arts in Canada 1986, 46)

Metro Dance: An Introduction

This research was done at a community-based dance group in an urban area in eastern Canada. I have been involved with Metro Dance for over ten years, as a parent, a participant in classes, a volunteer, and a researcher. The data used in this paper comes from a survey I conducted jointly with Metro Dance, supplemented with interviews of key informants, content analysis of written material, and participant observation. Metro Dance has used the findings in public relations and corporate fundraising. Findings and analysis have been shared with members of the Metro Dance staff.

Metro Dance was founded as a dance cooperative over 20 years ago. It has maintained a three-fold commitment to dance: recreational dance programs for children, pre-professional dance training for young people, and dance training and opportunities for adults. More recently, its activities have expanded to include sponsorship of a repertory company of advanced-level dancers.

Metro Dance is the largest institution for dance education in its region. It makes a substantial contribution to the cultural life of the region as well as an economic contribution to its home community. Over the years, the number of students enrolled has multiplied, and the number and variety of classes of dance disciplines have increased. Programs run virtually year round and regular offerings are enriched by special summer programs with guest teachers.

Successful Feminizing

The definition of success at feminizing institutions used in this paper is my own, developed from my work at Metro Dance, but it is applicable elsewhere. I measure success through multiple criteria which include organizational culture, organizational constituency, support for women's culture, and work, whether paid or unpaid. These will emerge from the description of the organization and its operations. The group I studied does not define itself as a feminist group. It does, however, act in and through ways which reflect feminist- and women-centred values.

The Culture of Metro Dance

Metro Dance began as an informal cooperative among area dancers, some affiliated with a local university. Many had studied and danced in urban centres in North America and Europe. The original objectives were to provide dancers with an opportunity to perform, expand opportunities for professional dance training, and support a professional company in the province. The development of dance education was soon added.

The first collective activities were workshops, which provided an opportunity for networking, dance training, and professional development. This led to the formation of a dance company in the late 1970s. During its two years of existence, it developed an extensive repertoire, performed in various locales in its home province, and danced in both Toronto and Montreal. It was supported by national and provincial arts funding agencies and the private sector. The original dance company folded for other reasons, but its existence had demonstrated the viability of local and national support and audience interest.

In turning its concentration to dance education, Metro Dance intended to create a core of professionally skilled but locally trained dancers who could sustain a regional dance company. Early experience confirmed there were area students with the ability and commitment to dance who could be taught to an appropriate level. Education was not just for potential professionals; it also consisted of recreational opportunities for interested youngsters, teens, and adults, and has created a local audience for professional performers.

Women were the majority of the founders of Metro Dance. They did not necessarily define themselves as feminists; however, instinctively, they operated in ways identified as feminist. They were committed to collaborative work and consensus in decision-making. Membership was open and decisions were made by all members.

A permanent organization emerged for practical reasons connected with obtaining studio space. Originally, events took place in donated space and were planned around its availability. These arrangements became increasingly difficult as the number and regularity of activities increased. The dancers wanted their own quarters. However, incorporation under provincial legislation was necessary to undertake the financial and legal responsibilities of acquiring space.

The co-op became the formal organization known as Metro Dance; its goal was to sustain the original objectives and operating styles. A managerial board of volunteers was created for formal governance and

Metro Dance became an employer. By the early 1980s, it employed two management staff, one for administration and one for artistic direction, along with a teaching staff. Their responsibilities included charting direction, developing instructional programs, financial planning, and melding an ad hoc group of individuals into a viable and stable organization.

As Metro Dance grew, most of those involved continued to be women. Decision-making continued to involve consultation and consensus, even as the number of individuals and the extent of activities increased. One characteristic of the organization since its founding has been a strong volunteer component. From the members of the Board on down, use and appreciation of volunteers was a fundamental theme of the organizers. Metro Dance continues as a member based co-operative, run with a combination of volunteer directors and paid staff. However, the hierarchy that these terms might suggest does not exist. The organization and its members are flexible.

The administrative responsibility for Metro Dance lies in a Board of Directors, which operates through a series of task-oriented committees and meetings of the whole. Each of the Board and its committees meet approximately once a month. An annual meeting, open to all members, elects new Board members, receives committee reports, and accepts a budget. The day-to-day business of Metro Dance is managed by an executive director, who is the chief administrator of the organization. There is frequent interaction between the executive director and the President, who is also Chair of the Board.

The staff at Metro Dance is divided into two groups by function. The administrative staff includes the Executive Director, the Registrar, the Volunteer Coordinator, the Office Manager, an Administrative Assistant, and a newly appointed Public Relations and Development Coordinator. Teachers and teaching support staff form the artistic staff, who have primary responsibility for the instructional and performance dimensions of Metro Dance. Regular teachers have on-going responsibility for some aspect of the program. The core or regular staff is augmented by others, paid on an hourly basis, who teach additional classes or fill in.

Regular and frequent staff meetings deal with business. There are joint staff meetings for all, and separate ones for administrative and artistic staff. The organization is small, and the full complement of appropriate staff participates in relevant business. For example, hiring members of artistic staff involves all core teachers and the Executive Director. The entire administrative staff participated when a new administrative assistant was required. Board or committee members are also involved.

Divisions are by major dance discipline (ballet, jazz, modern, and theatre) and program (pre-professional program, company of advanced students). Teachers work collaboratively on scheduling, curriculum, pedagogy, and hiring. This collaborative thrust also includes accompanists who support various dance disciplines.

Women comprise the majority of the paid employees of Metro Dance. The regular Executive Director, a woman, is currently on leave and her position is being filled by a male term replacement. All the other members of the administrative staff are women except the office manager. At present, all teachers, except one, both core and non-core, are women; the male instructor and a woman partner teach ballroom and Latin dance. Guest teachers, often male, are brought in for summer courses to strengthen and complement areas of dance expertise at Metro Dance. Four of the six accompanists are men. Although individuals have specific jobs, boundaries are fluid and adaptability is essential.

The current Board consists of six men and seven women. The President is male; the past-president and two vice-presidents female. Over the last decade, the gender composition of the Board has shifted from being overwhelmingly female to a more equal gender distribution. The Executive Director has commented that masculinization of the Board happened as a result of the search for individuals with influential connections to corporations and government. This was necessary as Metro Dance worked to raise money to replace declining arts grants. Men with a Metro Dance connection and political or corporate ties were invited to join the Board. It has been suggested that the increased presence of men has changed the climate of the Board and its deliberations.

Over the years, there has also been an increase in the involvement of commercial enterprises, through the donation of either gifts or services, and these are acknowledged as "volunteer donations." These are more visible as sponsorships of special events than in the daily routines at Metro Dance. However, the impending relocation of Metro Dance studios will require additional fundraising and may shift the balance between the grassroots orientation (much volunteer labour power, many people, modest expenditures of time and resources) of previous efforts and more professionalized fundraising. Like other arts groups, Metro Dance must move beyond government funding and small-scale fundraising into the world of corporate sponsorship. The presence of a growing number of men on the Board and corporate sponsorship have not yet had a visible effect on the social relationships within Metro Dance.

Metro Dance is primarily about its students. Children begin in recreational programs, continue there, or move into the pre-professional program known as the ITP (intensive training program). They then may become performers and join the local company, or even become teachers. Adults join for dance or fitness classes and may participate for equally long periods.

Students of all ages consider themselves as part of Metro Dance. This is evident in social relationships and use of space. In particular, ITP teenagers dance four or five days a week and use the studios to suit their needs. School homework is done in the hallways, the change rooms, the reception area, and, occasionally, on the stairs leading up to the school. Girls giggle, snack, study, and stretch in the regulation outfits of different dance mediums, wearing sweatshirts, tee shirts, leg-warmers, and other individual touches. They treat Metro Dance space as theirs, indicating ownership and territoriality rights.

The relationship between dance students, particularly those in ITP, and the office staff and teachers is casual and relaxed. Everyone is on a first name basis, and the office staff know the students. Adults mentor, support, and encourage youngsters, and provide joking and practical comments on everyday ups and downs. There is a strong but intangible sense of community among Metro Dance participants, particularly ITP students. Although the atmosphere is informal, there are clear boundaries between students and teachers. Teachers are not guardians and protect their own privacy and space. The teachers' rooms at Metro Dance are off limits to all students, and socializing is restricted to events like the parties which follow productions. Adults may establish personal relationships with teachers, but on a one-to-one basis only.

The presence of boundaries, however, does not indicate hierarchies. Teachers, students, and volunteers all work cooperatively on Metro Dance events and activities. Neither age nor status defines who can perform tasks, only skills and effort. Staff also show respect for the outside responsibilities of adult students.

A fourth category of individuals involved with Metro Dance includes its volunteers, welcomed as part of the Metro Dance community. They are recognized and acknowledged regularly and appear both comfortable with the informal social relationships at Metro Dance and at home in its physical space. Volunteers frequently have a long, if episodic, relationship with Metro Dance, during which time they may have occupied roles at Metro Dance as volunteers, parents dance or fitness-class students, and audience members.

The intention of Metro Dance was to create an opportunity for those committed to dance to have an opportunity to participate. In this, it has been successful. Metro Dance has continued to be run in an open, inclusive, and participatory manner while growing in size and formalizing its organizational structure. Its commitment to consensus and cooperation is evident in its internal activities and external relationships. As well, it continues to be run largely by women.

The People of Metro Dance

Although Metro Dance was originally founded by and for adult dancers, most of those who now participate in its activities are youngsters; most of its students have not yet completed high school. There are also classes for adults. Metro Dance sees itself as a launching ground for young dancers, not as a permanent home.

The majority of those who participate in Metro Dance's dance classes and programs are women who vary from youngsters of 4 who begin in Creative Movement classes, to adults, some in their 40s and 50s who are the backbone of the fitness classes. This reflects both the overwhelming presence of women in dance and the feminized nature of dance as a performance art.

This overwhelming female presence can be seen in Metro Dance's public performances. There were 532 dancers whose gender was evident from their names in the most recent children's showcase. Of these, 516 were female (or 97%), and 16 were male (or 3%). The percentages for the ITP were 98.2% female and 1.8% male, and, for the recreational classes, 96.1% female and 3.9% male.

The number of boys is greatest at the lower levels, although there were no more than two boys in any one class at the last annual children's showcase. In the teen classes, there are no males. Men participate in adult dance and fitness classes, although they are still a small minority except in the ballroom-dance class. The program for the April 1994 adult jazz presentation lists 44 women, 14 men, and 3 individuals whose names are not identifiably male or female. Of the 58 adults identifiable by gender, 76% are women and 24% men. The percentage of male adult participants is higher than that of male children, but is still considerably lower than that of adult women.

There is a consistent effort to make the environment a positive one for the girls and women who study at Metro Dance. All staff members, especially teachers, are concerned with the whole development of students. Individuals are not held to a single standard of achievement. This is evident in the handling of three specific areas: body size and image, future dance orientation, and self-esteem.

The popular physical image of the female dancer is of a slender, almost emaciated body. Grace and agility are most essential attributes. Gelsey Kirkland, among others, comments about her constant struggle to stay within the weight limits required for her dance career.

Although the majority of Metro Dance teachers are slender, not all are. Students see variation in build, weight, and height among their teachers. Nor do teachers try to camouflage pregnancy. In recent years, there have been four children born to three different core staff teachers, and another is currently pregnant. Pregnancy and its physical effects have been visible to and shared with dance students.

In addition to what they see in their teachers, Metro Dance students in the ITP also see variations in body type among their fellow pupils. Teachers monitor the health and growth of ITP youngsters over the years and discuss any concerns at teachers' meetings and in conferences with students.

Survey comments from the ITP parents reflect children's positive experiences in matters related to physical appearance and/or health. Only 3 of 54 responses were concerned about matters of body type, health, or illness. Two were somewhat critical of Metro Dance. One of these perceived passivity on weight matters, saying that the association needed to be more candid and responsive to peer pressure among girls. Another was particularly disturbed about her daughter's experiences with body stereotypes. A third parent praised the association for its understanding of children's illnesses.

Just as Metro Dance teachers do not demand conformity to one body type, they also recognize different capabilities for dance. Although the ITP is defined as a pre-professional dance program, both teachers and students know that not many students will be dancers. Teachers provide positive and realistic feedback and advice to students through term reports and a year-end conference with ITP pupils and parents. These conferences praise achievement and discuss commitment and objectives for the future. Students are encouraged to think realistically about their own abilities and interests. Students are encouraged to develop and follow interests, both inside and outside of dance. ITP pupils who leave the program for recreational courses continue to be welcomed by their peers and teachers.

ITP youngsters learn early that they will not all succeed as dancers. They have friends who have not been successful in entering the program. Annual auditions for The Nutcracker and the performance company result in disappointment for many. Teachers are careful not to use success in competitive auditions as the main evaluations of students. Girls are encouraged in their strengths. Creativity, originality, effort, perseverance, and leadership skills are praised. Students are encouraged to feel proud of their achievements. Teachers regularly tell about some of their own dance-related disappointments to help students understand performance work.

The non-teaching staff share the teachers' commitment to developing the entire student. Talents and activities of dance students are evident in the posted excuses for absences: rehearsals for school drama and music activities, sports competitions, school trips, family trips, band trips, music festivals, babysitting or other jobs, and projects or school work. ITP youngsters see themselves as having a variety of interests. Four-fifths chose "putting time and energy outside of school on dance, but with other interests" as a self-description.

Although teachers avoid competition between pupils, it is a part of the culture. Not everyone succeeds at auditions. Grades on ballet exams are compared. Some girls drop out of the ITP program. Competition is present in other aspects of their lives for all youngsters, who handle it in their school and social lives as well as in dance. At Metro Dance, young women find individual encouragement, sensitivity, and support from their teachers. In this dimension of their lives, they experience positive messages, if not always success.

Parents of ITP students see multiple benefits of participation in Metro Dance programs since Metro Dance is the context in which desirable adult qualities are learned. The benefits described by 54 parents (out of a possible 103) who responded to the questionnaire are described in the table below:

Table 2 — Benefits of Dance Training

Responses	Number	% Parents
Good healthy physical exercise	49	91
Disciplined work toward goal	48	89
Acquire grace, poise	46	85
Encourages maturity, responsibility	43	80
Productively occupied	42	78
Self-confidence, self-esteem	41	76
Good health through fitness	40	74
Friendships	37	69
Performance opportunities	37	69
Pre-professional training, skills	37	69
Mastery of a body of work	37	69
Organization, time management	33	61
Other	4	7

Parents rank pre-professional dance training low. The survey data indicates that parents of ITP students are ambivalent about "a career" in dance for their daughters. Just over half said they would encourage a child to have a dance career if interested. Over ninety percent anticipated that their child would attend university immediately following high-school graduation. They support a child in dance training emotionally and financially as well as through their own time commitment for other benefits. Parents also report sacrificing other aspects of family life to the dance commitment of one child.

The ITP students themselves (85 respondents out of 103) see their experiences as valuable, regardless of vocational objectives. They ranked their most important reasons for participating in the ITP as follows:

Table 3 — Most Important Reason for Dance Training

Rank	Reason	Number of Respondents	% of Respondents
1	Part of my life	28	23
2	Form of self-expression	22	18
3	New skills	16	13
4	Chance to perform	15	12
5	Dance career preparation	11	9
6	Personal growth	9	7
7	Like teachers	7	6
8	Friends in program	5	4
9.5	Dance with others	4	3
9.5	Other	4	3

The value of dance training extends beyond interest in being a dancer. Less than one-third of the ITP students mentioned a career in dance or choreography as an ambition. They mention careers in other performing arts; a variety of professional jobs, including architecture, the law, and psychology; and non-professional jobs.

Both dance students and their parents believe that Metro Dance provides a positive and supportive environment. Youngsters learn discipline, self-confidence, time management, and new skills in an environment in which their role models and mentors are women. Students see teachers as models of independent, competent, career women to whom work is an important and defining part of their lives. The relationship between teachers and students allows young women to find mentors in life skills as much as in dance.

Metro Dance as a Community Resource

Metro Dance is part of a larger dance and cultural community. These ties are important for artistic, creative, and advocacy collaboration. Professional relationships are augmented by personal ties and friendships.

Wall space at Metro Dance is covered with announcements of upcoming performances by local artists in dance, mime, theatre, and music. The groups featured vary enormously and represent experimental and mainstream performances. Over the years, the majority of local artists whose performances are publicized at Metro Dance have been women. A large proportion of local dance audiences have some connection to Metro Dance.

Metro Dance often co-sponsors visits by touring groups including prestigious national companies in varied dance mediums. Metro Dance is a focal point for dissemination of information about dance performances as over one hundred interested individuals visit its studios daily. The presence of Metro Dance provides evidence to touring companies of the local interest in dance. Metro Dance also uses visiting companies and tours to augment its program. Studio and rehearsal space is available to visiting dancers, and members of these companies offer workshops and master classes for students and teachers. Lacking the richness of cultural resources in major urban areas, smaller centres particularly value these visitors.

Metro Dance sustains the local dance community through employment of dancers as teachers, an important resource for many and an asset in terms of exposure. Metro Dance teachers also perform locally and enrich the regional cultural scene, as well as contribute professional skills and expertise to other amateur and professional cultural activities. Metro Dance teachers work with local high-schools in annual productions, including musicals with extensive dance components. They also participate as directors, choreographers, and/or performers in university and professional productions.

Teachers are active in the provincial dance association where they have taken significant responsibilities to sustain dance, including sharing resources and opportunities for dance education and professional development opportunities for teachers.

Finally, Metro Dance and other cultural groups work collaboratively on local and national policy issues and funding for the performing arts. Province wide organizations meet regularly for strategy sessions. Metro Dance is actively involved in an advocacy organization for the arts in public discussion as well as lobbying funding bodies and government. Arts coalitions have also sponsored joint fundraising events.

The Volunteer: Organization Resource and Treasure

One of the distinctive characteristics of Metro Dance is its use of volunteers. This developed for financial reasons and the episodic need for extraordinary amounts of labour power. However, the use of volunteers creates community in a variety of ways.

Metro Dance has been able to minimize the number of permanent administrative positions required through its use of volunteer labour. Funds are budgeted for a volunteer coordinator who carries responsibility for the recruitment, organization, and acknowledgement of the significant numbers of well-intentioned helpers. The strong volunteer dimension also provides an opportunity for parental involvement. This has increased parents' knowledge and contact with Metro Dance, allowed parents to support youngsters' activities, and sustained the commitment of the individual families to dance lessons and Metro Dance. Finally, this involvement of volunteers has brought Metro Dance a continuous stream of energetic, creative, and committed people who have contributed to its positive and broadly based profile.

Parents of both recreational and ITP students were surveyed about volunteer involvement. Data is skewed toward ITP parents because they have a long-term involvement with Metro Dance. Parent volunteers understand the value of the work they do for Metro Dance, and the mutuality of appreciation of volunteer work sustains participation. Parents of the ITP students repeat themes in describing the reasons they volunteer. These include an understanding of the importance of volunteers to arts and cultural organizations, particularly for fundraising; showing support for their child; enjoyment of the activity; and setting examples of civic or social responsibility.

Metro Dance is meticulous about its acknowledgement of volunteer labour. Individuals are mentioned by name in the association's newsletters and special events programs on a regular basis. Cards of appreciation are sent out at Christmas. Metro Dance finds innovative ways to recognize volunteer work. For example, volunteers received an invitation to the opening of a new studio, commemorative fridge magnets to celebrate the organization's 20th anniversary, and acknowledgement on a massive "thank you" poster covering a significant portion of the entry staircase.

Metro Dance regularly makes the work of its volunteers visible. This situation is unlike organizations who acknowledge volunteer contributions only occasionally, anonymously, or by use of exemplars. Metro Dance acknowledges each and every volunteer, from the volunteer Association president to the person involved in a telephone tree. Metro Dance does not differentiate between the amount of time volunteers commit or the skill level or expertise they share. It accepts each and every volunteer as having made a contribution to its activities. It treats individual volunteers in ways that are congruent with the value of their work for the organization.

Volunteer commitment is sustained through communication with Metro Dance. Complete information, often written, is available about each task. If individuals volunteer for event weeks or more beforehand, Metro Dance uses another volunteer to remind them as the time approaches. Volunteers thus feel informed about the responsibility they have undertaken.

Metro Dance also incorporates its volunteer workers as part of the 'community' at Metro Dance. Volunteers work regularly with teachers and staff on an equal basis, and there is an extensive range of tasks available for diverse interests, abilities, and skills. Volunteers are needed at different times of the day, the week, or the year, or volunteers can be given tasks which can be done according to their own schedules. Most of the volunteers at Metro Dance are women. Written records from 1990 to the present, including newsletters and annual show programs, verify this. The gender breakdown of volunteers is described below.

Table 4 — Volunteer Contributions by Gender

	Total	Number Female	Percent Female	Number Male	Percent Male
Newsletter	529	369	69.8	160	30.2
Performance	488	438	89.8	50	10.2
Total	**1017**	**807**	**79.4**	**210**	**20.6**

That women do the largest part of the volunteer work at Metro Dance is evident from these figures. However, it is also important to note that men do a significant portion of the volunteer work as well, although the amount varies from activity to activity. Since women's volunteer work has not generally been acknowledged, it is all the more significant that it is recognized in a setting run by women. It is clear that the environment is one where women feel comfortable. The repetition of names from year to year is something one notices in looking at the acknowledgements.

Gender and Dance: Some Reconsiderations

Dancers and dance students all face enormous pressures about their appearance, particularly in regard to weight. In this regard, male and female dancers are alike. The demands of dance as a profession are not healthful for either sex. The demands of company directors, choreographers, partners, and audiences can also contribute to unhealthful and dangerous practices in weight control. While there is public appreciation of the aesthetics of dance, audiences are ignorant of the cost involved to individual dancers. The harm is not restricted to one gender; instead, it negatively affects both women and men. This is part of the larger context for which Metro Dance trains students.

Conclusion: Success

I have described a number of dimensions of the functioning of Metro Dance to demonstrate why I think it has been effective at maintaining the values and principles of its founding mothers. These illustrate why I think Metro Dance is an example of successful feminizing. Let me summarize these using four specific themes: organizational culture, organizational constituency, fostering women's culture, and valuing women's work.

Metro Dance has been a viable organization for over twenty years, during which time it has grown enormously. At the same time, the organizational culture of Metro Dance reflects its original core values of cooperation, governance by consensus, and respect for the individual. It has been successful in institutionalizing and maintaining these core feminist values and operational styles even as it has grown in size.

Metro Dance creates a sense of community rather than hierarchy among people with different roles in the organization. It welcomes participation by people who care about its purposes, and involves them in its work.

The people who study at Metro Dance are largely women and girls, although it is not closed to men, Metro Dance is effective at providing a caring and supportive environment for its students. Although dance is competitive, even at this level, Metro Dance values all of its community. It encourages all students to appreciate or value their own abilities and uniqueness.

Although women are well represented in dance, this occurs more often as performer than in the other dimensions of hierarchy described by Hanna. Still, Metro Dance celebrates and supports women's multi-dimensional involvement in dance. It trains, teaches, and encourages women students in all of the dance disciplines. It supports and encourages women as performers in all of these disciplines. It offers teaching as a regular source of employment and income in juxtaposition with the uncertainties of a performing career outside the mainstream of professional dance. Finally, it sustains and furthers women in administrative roles in dance organizations, as choreographers, as directors, and as managers in other aspects of dance production.

Metro Dance supports women in their traditional roles and facilitates their involvement in other dimensions of dance. It is the non-performance aspects of dance that allow individuals to follow careers paths within dance. Careers in dance which are broader than just performance allow more flexibility and longevity. For women, in particular, diversity of career opportunities allows for reproductive choices which are more problematic for performers.

Metro Dance also reaches out and works cooperatively with others on issues of common concern to cultural organizations and performers.

Finally, Metro Dance makes visible both the work volunteers do and the importance of this work to its activities. Appreciation for each and every one of its volunteers is significant especially when most of its volunteers are women. It is also one dimension of my description of Metro Dance as a success story in feminization.

Metro Dance is effective and successful precisely because it has brought core values of cooperation, respect, and appreciation to bear on its activities. Although the description of itself as 'feminist' might not fit with all members' classification of their own or the organization's style, it is only the name that might make them feel uncomfortable. Only Metro Dance's principles are feminist — not its self-description or identification.

References

Dagg, Anne Innis. 1986. *The 50% Solution: Why Should Women Pay for Men's Culture?* Waterloo, Ont.: Otter Press.

Frederico, Ronald C. 1974. "Recruitment, Training and Performance: The Case of Ballet." *Varieties of Work Experience.* Phyllis L. Stewart and Muriel G. Cantor, eds. New York: Schenkman Publishing Company, Inc.

Fisher, Jennifer. 1993. "Women in Ballet." *Step TEXT 2,* 3, 8-11.

Forsyth, Sondra (Enos) and Pauline M. Kolenda. 1970. "Competition, Cooperation, and Group Cohesion in the Ballet Company." *The Sociology of Art and Literature.* Milton C. Abrecht, James H. Barnett and Mason Griff, eds. London: Gerald Duckworth and Co., Ltd.

Funding of the Arts in Canada to the Year 2000. 1986. Ottawa, Government of Canada: Minister of Supply and Services.

Hanna, Judith Lynne. 1988. *Dance, Sex and Gender.* Chicago: University of Chicago Press.

Ingram, Anne. 1978. "Dance and Sport." *International Review of Sport Sociology* 13, 1, 85-97.

Kirkland, Gelsey with Greg Lawrence. 1986. *Dancing on my Grave.* Garden City, NY: Doubleday.

Kleeh-Tolley, Karen. 1986. "An Investigation into Aspects of the Process of Becoming a Professional Performing Artist: The Case of Symphony Musicians and Ballet Dancers." (Doctoral dissertation, Kent State University, 1988). *Dissertation Abstracts International,* 49, 3163A.

Peto, Michael and Alexander Bland. 1963. *The Dancer's World.* London: Collins.

Ryser, Carol Pierson. 1964. "The Student Dancer." *The Arts in Society.* Robert N. Wilson, ed. Englewood Cliffs, N. J.: Prentice-Hall, Inc.

Schuster, J. Mark Davidson. 1985. *Supporting the Arts: An International Comparative Study.* Washington, D. C.: National Endowment for the Arts.

Statistics Canada. 1993. Catalogue 93-327. Ottawa.

Statistics Canada. 1993. Catalogue 93-332. Ottawa.

The Status of the Artist. 1986. Ottawa: Government of Canada.

Sutherland, David Earl. 1976. "Ballet as a Career." *Society* 14, 1, 40-45.

Endnote

1.   The survey questionnaire varied somewhat from group to group and was directed
      to students in the Intensive Training Program (ITP) at Metro Dance, to their
      parents, to former students in the ITP or its predecessor, to parents of recreational
      dance students, and to adults in dance and fitness programs. The number of adults
      in recreational programs and the number of youngsters vary from term to term,
      unlike the ITP numbers. There is also overlap between categories. I, for example,
      am the parent of an ITP student and a participant in the adult recreation program.
      The numbers are presented in the table below:

Group	Number	# Returned	Percent Returned
ITP student	103	85	82.5
ITP parents	103	54	52.4
Former ITP students	60	11	18.3
Recreational adults	218	57	26.1

Marie-Luce Garceau

Place aux actrices sociales!
Les Franco-Ontariennes de 45 à 64 ans

En Ontario français comme ailleurs, nombreuses sont les féministes qui ont montré l'androcentrisme de la recherche dans l'ensemble des disciplines. Assimilées à tout prix dans un savoir qualifié d'objectif et de général, les femmes se sont opposées à des traditions scientifiques qui les empêchent de s'ancrer dans de nouveaux modes de lecture et d'interprétation du réel. Constatant le peu de place qu'on leur accorde, les femmes de l'Ontario français s'insurgent contre l'engendrement d'un savoir masculin qui oublie leur existence.

Depuis le milieu des années 1980, les travaux scientifiques des chercheures, tout comme l'action soutenue des intervenantes féministes et des organismes revendiquant l'égalité et l'équité des femmes, contribuent au redressement de cette situation (Garceau, 1995). Les femmes se donnent une voix et des voies pour se sortir de l'invisibilité, voire de l'indifférence dans laquelle elles ont été plongées. Les féministes multiplient, par leurs propres pratiques, les regards, les lieux de réflexion et d'intervention, et montrent qu'il n'est plus possible de penser le monde sans leur présence. Au moment où les questions et les connaissances féministes s'accumulent, les femmes de l'Ontario français font connaître et reconnaître comme légitime leur propre regard sur l'histoire, sur leurs histoires.

C'est dans ce contexte qu'est né le projet de recherche-action sur la qualité de vie des Franco-Ontariennes de 45 à 64 ans de la Fédération des femmes canadiennes-françaises de l'Ontario[1] (FFCFO). En 1989, dans la foulée du mouvement des femmes de l'Ontario français, et tout particulièrement dans cette volonté de la part des femmes de faire la lumière sur les conditions de vie des Franco-Ontariennes, la FFCFO a entrepris une vaste enquête de type recherche-action. Confinées à l'univers domestique et à leur rôle de mère, les Franco-Ontariennes de 45 à 64 ans étaient demeurées invisibles trop longtemps.

En m'appuyant sur cet exemple, je présenterai l'origine de cette recherche-action. Je discuterai brièvement des raisons qui ont poussé la FFCFO et surtout le comité de recherche-action à adopter un point de vue féministe pour procéder à l'enquête. Par la suite, à l'aide de la méthodologie utilisée dans le projet, je montrerai les principales phases du projet. On verra alors comment le comité a procédé afin de dépasser l'engendrement d'un savoir fondé sur un petit groupe pour l'étendre à l'ensemble de la population des femmes de 45 à 64 ans de l'Ontario français. Finalement, la recherche-action, telle qu'elle a été vécue par les membres du comité, est une démarche d'*empowerment*, c'est-à-dire de transformation des conditions individuelles et sociales. En ce sens, je présenterai ces transformations parce qu'elles montrent, tout comme la méthodologie empruntée et les résultats de l'enquête, la réussite de ce projet.

Origine du projet de la FFCFO

La FFCFO recrute la plupart de ses membres parmi les Franco-Ontariennes de 45 ans et plus. En Ontario français, la FFCFO est l'une des plus importantes organisations représentant les femmes de cette tranche d'âge. C'est pour ces raisons qu'il est important de souligner qu'à l'origine du projet de recherche-action correspondent deux objectifs principaux pour les membres de la FFCFO. D'abord, il s'agit de rendre visibles les conditions de vie des femmes âgées de plus de 45 ans et, deuxièmement, d'obtenir une reconnaissance sociale et économique en leur nom.

Pour ce faire, la FFCFO a adopté d'emblée un parti pris en faveur des femmes et du changement social (Dagenais, 1994) et, par extension, s'est engagée dans le projet avec une orientation féministe. Pour la FFCFO, cette prise de position marque un tournant idéologique que l'on peut retracer en faisant l'histoire de cette association. Ce retour historique permettra de contextualiser l'ensemble des activités du comité de recherche-action durant les trois ans qu'a duré le projet. La plupart des femmes qui ont œuvré dans ce projet étant membres de cette association, elles ont donc participé à ce virage idéologique et leurs actions s'inscrivent dans la continuité de l'histoire de la FFCF puis de la FFCFO.

Quelques bribes d'histoire

Fondée en 1914, l'association, alors appelée la Fédération des femmes canadiennes-françaises (FFCF), fut l'une des principales organisations bénévoles féminines de l'Ontario français. Bien qu'ayant ses principales assises en Ontario, la FFCF avait atteint, durant la période 1946 à 1975, une envergure nationale puisque son organisation avait étendu ses ramifications au Québec, au Nouveau-Brunswick et en Saskatchewan. Son histoire permet d'éclairer certains pans du développement de l'action bénévole féminine, des luttes des femmes et des divers courants du féminisme qui l'ont traversée.

Dans cette histoire, il est possible de distinguer deux grandes périodes significatives dans le développement de la FFCF. La première période s'étend de la Première Guerre mondiale aux années 1975. Les bénévoles de la FFCF s'occupent alors principalement d'œuvres caritatives et religieuses. Leur bénévolat est teinté d'une orientation traditionnelle, empreinte de valeurs religieuses et de féminisme maternel, comme le précise Brunet (1992)[2].

> Le féminisme maternel caractérise le début du siècle et les femmes justifient leur intrusion dans les sphères d'activités traditionnellement masculines en soutenant que leurs activités et les qualités qui les rendent si précieuses au foyer peuvent profiter à l'ensemble de la société. (212-213).

La FFCF et ses membres ne questionnent pas les stéréotypes concernant les rôles dévolus aux femmes et aux hommes. L'association valorise la notion de complémentarité entre les sexes au détriment de celles de l'équité et de l'égalité. Cette complémentarité sanctionne l'image des femmes en tant qu'épouses, mères, éducatrices, servantes de la paroisse et gardiennes de la langue française ainsi que de la culture et de la patrie canadiennes-françaises. Ainsi, selon les exigences du moment, l'organisme privilégie l'action, tantôt dans les œuvres caritatives et les revendications sociales ayant trait au mieux-être des femmes dans une perspective d'extension de leur rôle maternel, tantôt dans le travail patriotique de la défense de la nation canadienne-française.

La seconde période de l'histoire de la FFCF s'étend de 1975 jusqu'à aujourd'hui et représente un tournant important pour l'association. Suite à la Commission d'enquête sur le statut de la femme au Canada (Commission Bird) et à la création de conseils consultatifs sur la situation de la femme, la FFCF prend un virage et oriente ses interventions vers les questions touchant l'égalité des femmes. Dans un mémoire soumis à la Commission Bird, la FFCF formule des propositions sur l'égalité des chances des femmes en matière d'éducation, d'impôts, de droits civils, de santé et de droits politiques (Desjardins, 1991).

Comment expliquer un tel retournement dans l'orientation de l'organisme? En 1975, le féminisme maternel, qui avait orienté jusqu'alors l'association et ses activités bénévoles, ne répondait plus aux aspirations de certains groupes de la FFCF. L'expansion provinciale et nationale de la FFCF, accomplie durant la période de 1946 à 1975, avait suscité de nombreux espoirs parmi les groupes de femmes de toutes les provinces. Elles prenaient conscience de leur poids politique. De plus, une enquête interne sur l'organisation révélait un vieillissement de ses membres, une difficulté de recruter de nouveaux membres, un besoin pressant de pouvoir offrir de l'information et de la formation aux femmes francophones et, enfin, la nécessité pour la FFCF d'élargir ses champs d'intérêts (Desjardins, 1991). Bref, on a vu poindre au sein de cette organisation un courant prônant un féminisme égalitaire. Cette lutte interne a conduit au schisme de 1985 quand la FFCF se scinde en deux groupes, dont l'un reprend à son compte l'idée de la mise sur pied d'un réseau national de femmes de langue française.

Ainsi, en 1985, la Fédération nationale des femmes canadiennes-françaises (FNFCF) voit le jour. Ce nouvel organisme qui chapeaute des associations militantes tant nationales que provinciales, adopte une orientation nettement féministe et cherche activement, par ses revendications, une plus grande visibilité au plan politique. Par ailleurs, après une période de deux ans de réflexion et de nombreuses tergiversations quant à sa survie, on assiste en 1987 à la création d'un palier provincial connu sous le nom de Fédération des femmes canadiennes-françaises de l'Ontario (FFCFO), lequel regroupe divers groupes locaux de cette province. Cette association provinciale tente alors de concilier l'inconciliable.

Tout en désirant attirer de plus jeunes femmes et ainsi renouveler ses membres, elle favorise un engagement politique timide, ce qui nuit considérablement à l'effort d'intégration de jeunes femmes plus militantes ou aux vues politiques bien arrêtées. Force est d'admettre que la FFCFO représente actuellement les femmes plus âgées et que celles-ci forment la majeure partie de ses membres. Par ailleurs, pour les membres de la FFCFO, l'idéologie traditionnelle et le féminisme maternel demeurent toujours une conviction bien enracinée, malgré une ouverture certaine vers un féminisme égalitaire. Ainsi, au sein même de l'association, on assiste à un perpétuel tiraillement entre ces deux courants de pensée. Par exemple, les dossiers défendus par la FFCFO répondent au nouveau mandat qu'elle s'est donné lors de sa création, soit d'agir en tant qu'organisme de sensibilisation auprès des femmes et de susciter tout changement permettant de favoriser l'expansion de la culture et de la langue françaises, de promouvoir l'égalité pour les femmes et d'édifier une société plus juste (FFCFO, 1994)[3].

Un tel mandat tend à indiquer une adhésion au courant du féminisme égalitaire. De plus, le palier provincial affirme davantage sa présence au sein du mouvement des femmes, en épousant la cause et les revendications en faveur de l'autonomie et de l'égalité des femmes et en supportant les revendications et les luttes d'autres groupes de femmes ou groupes féministes. Par contre, les membres des organisations locales affichent leur présence de façon plus traditionnelle comme femmes et francophones au sein d'associations locales et paroissiales et continuent à œuvrer au mieux-être des personnes démunies et aux œuvres caritatives.

C'est au cœur de ce tiraillement qu'est né le projet de recherche-action. Comme le palier provincial de la FFCFO et son conseil d'administration devaient mettre en œuvre ce nouveau mandat, ils se sont donnés comme objectif d'initier et de coordonner des actions collectives pour améliorer la qualité et les conditions de vie des femmes francophones de la province. Plus particulièrement, le palier provincial a retenu l'idée lancée par ses membres, lors de son assemblée générale de 1987 : faire un portrait de la situation globale des femmes de 45 ans et plus de l'Ontario français afin, d'abord, de la connaître, puis de contribuer à son amélioration.

Phases du projet

Pour passer de l'idée à la réalisation d'un tel projet, la FFCFO a embauché une coordonnatrice. Suite à des discussions avec divers groupes féminins et organismes subventionnels, la FFCFO a choisi de privilégier le modèle de la recherche-action. N'étant pas familière avec cet axe de recherche, la FFCFO s'est adjoint les services d'une chercheure et d'un chercheur universitaires, parce que ces personnes possédaient l'expertise nécessaire pour assurer que l'enquête offrirait des données empiriques solides sur les femmes de cette tranche d'âge. Ces trois personnes formaient le comité des chercheures.

Parallèlement, suite à un appel lancé par le palier provincial auprès des groupes locaux de la FFCFO, quatorze femmes, appartenant pour la plupart à ce groupe d'âge, éprouvant un vif intérêt pour l'amélioration des conditions de vie des femmes et ayant une bonne connaissance de leur milieu, se sont engagées, pour une période de trois ans. Elles formaient le comité de recherche-action. Les comité des chercheures et de recherche-action étant en place, toutes se sont alors mises au travail afin d'établir les grandes orientations du projet de recherche-action.

Toutes ces femmes d'expériences et de trajectoires inestimables de vie témoignent de multiples réalités. Ainsi, dès la première rencontre, les femmes du comité de recherche-action ayant, pour la plupart, entre 45 à 64 ans, ont choisi de se servir d'elles-mêmes, de leurs expériences personnelles, de leurs connaissances des femmes de cette tranche d'âge fournies par leur implication dans leur milieu, pour construire le cadre de la recherche et le questionnaire qui a servi à la cueillette des données auprès d'un échantillon à l'échelle provinciale.

Ce choix de méthode de travail a orienté les trois phases du projet qui a débuté à l'automne 1989 pour se terminer au printemps 1992.

Phase I : formation et élaboration des objectifs

La première phase correspond à deux objectifs principaux : la formation à la recherche et l'élaboration des objectifs de la recherche.

Formation à la recherche

Les femmes du comité de recherche-action n'ayant que peu de connaissances en matière de recherche ou de recherche-action, elles se sont d'abord initiées au processus de recherche et à la technique du sondage. Il a donc fallu que les chercheures prennent le temps nécessaire pour leur expliquer ce processus afin que la recherche-action ait réellement un caractère collectif, c'est-à-dire que le projet, dans toutes ses phases, se déroule sous leur contrôle et qu'il soit effectué en collaboration avec toutes les personnes concernées. Il s'agissait donc d'expliquer clairement les conditions de réalisation d'une recherche afin que le comité de recherche-action comprenne bien l'ampleur du travail à venir.

Le processus d'initiation à la recherche étant lourd, simultanément, une firme de constultantes a été embauchée par la FFCFO afin de procéder à la recherche documentaire et de données statistiques sur les Franco-Ontariennes de 45 à 64 ans[4]. Les résultats de cette recension ont été soumis au comité de recherche-action afin qu'elles puissent développer un cadre théorique minimal pour la recherche. En fait, ils ont surtout permis au comité de se rendre compte que si l'on pouvait dénombrer statistiquement les femmes de l'Ontario français ou connaître leur profession et certaines de leurs conditions de travail, on ne savait rien des autres aspects de leur vie. Les femmes du comité de recherche-action ont ainsi vite compris qu'elles devaient construire la majeure partie de leur canevas de recherche pour procéder à une telle enquête.

Même si en recherche-action le cadre théorique, la problématique, les objectifs et les hypothèses doivent être définis à partir du vécu et des connaissances des personnes qui en font partie, cette méthode a présenté certaines limites dans le projet. De façon générale, ces étapes demandent aux habitués de la recherche un investissement en terme de temps, un accès à des documents spécialisés et, dans le cas qui nous préoccupe, un survol théorique qui dépasse les cadres de la francophonie ontarienne. Or, pour le comité de recherche-action, il s'agissait d'une première recherche et le temps a été consacré davantage à la formation aux techniques de recherche. En outre, comme certaines régions souffrent d'un manque flagrant de bibliothèques spécialisées, les femmes du comité avaient un accès très restreint à ce matériel. Par conséquent, pour ne pas réduire la portée du cadre théorique, j'ai été chargée de cette tâche par le comité de recherche-action. En ce sens, l'une de mes tâches a été d'aider à formuler et à analyser les problèmes que le comité désirait étudier. Cependant, comme la recherche-action est un projet collectif, je ne me suis pas située, tout comme d'ailleurs les autres membres du comité des chercheures, dans un rapport d'extériorité au comité de recherche-action. Au contraire, au même titre que les autres femmes, nous étions toutes participantes au processus de recherche-action. Toutefois, j'ai ici agit en complémentarité avec le comité de recherche-action pour répondre au besoin collectif et j'ai dû partager, voire restituer mon savoir et mon savoir-faire pour le bénéfice du groupe[5].

Élaboration des objectifs de la recherche

En recherche-action, contrairement à la démarche classique, l'objet est construit par les personnes qui font partie de la démarche. Ceci a pour objectif de favoriser une élaboration théorique tout en contribuant à la recherche de solutions aux problèmes à l'étude. Par ailleurs, la recherche-action étant une œuvre collective, on abolit ainsi la relation sujets/objets entre les chercheures et ceux que l'on appelle traditionnellement les «objets de la recherche» (les participants) (Pâquet-Deehy et Rinfret-Raynor, 1987; Chambaud et al., 1986; Lamoureux et al., 1984). L'abolition du rapport sujets/objets, où se joue d'ailleurs tout le travail de recherche-action, repose sur l'idée de supériorité du vécu des sujets ainsi que sur leurs capacités de construire conceptuellement et de produire un changement social. Dans cette démarche, leurs perceptions, leurs expériences et leurs vécus sont ainsi privilégiés par rapport au savoir d'un ou d'une chercheure.

Dans le projet, le vécu des sujets a été largement mis à profit, tout particulièrement dans la première phase du projet. Ainsi, parallèlement à la formation à la recherche, les discussions du comité de recherche-action ont porté sur les principales aires de la vie des femmes qui devaient être objets de l'enquête. C'est à partir d'exercices individuels et de groupe et à partir des échanges et des discussions concernant leur vie et celles de leurs amies ou de leurs connaissances que les femmes du comité de recherche-action ont choisi les principales aires de la vie des Franco-Ontariennes de 45 à 64 ans sur lesquelles elles voulaient se pencher. Hormis les renseignements généraux usuels, elles voulaient connaître les conditions de vie et les besoins des femmes en matière de logement, de travail, de revenus, d'administration du budget, d'études, de langue, de religion, d'activités sociales, de bénévolat, de santé et de violence conjugale et familiale.

Mais, regardons comment les femmes du comité ont procédé pour faire quelques-uns de leurs choix. Et si cette formulation des domaines peut ressembler à une longue liste d'épicerie tellement les aires couvertes sont vastes, elle constitue une simple réaction à l'inexistence des femmes dans toutes ces aires.

Place aux sujets!

Dans les écrits concernant les francophones de l'Ontario, des conditions de vie des Franco-Ontariennes de 45 à 64 ans on ne fait guère mention.

Leurs histoires et leurs vies ont été méticuleusement maintenues dans un silence qui persiste aujourd'hui, comme en fait foi la recension de documents de recherche et de statistiques effectuée en début de projet. Dans la mesure où le comité de recherche-action faisait face à une absence de connaissance sur les femmes de cette tranche d'âge, cela a légitimé le recours à une approche fondée sur la reconnaissance du sujet porteur d'une histoire spécifique. Cela montre comment les femmes du comité de recherche-action se sont posées en sujet du savoir et comment elles ont déconstruit les fondements de leur exclusion et de leur marginalisation pour permettre l'émergence de leurs réalités.

Le Doeuff (1989) soutient que le creuset du savoir est dans l'expérience des femmes. Transposé au projet, il s'agit de la réalité de l'expérience qui n'est autre que celle qui est vécue par le sujet, entendu ici comme étant chacune des femmes du comité. Le fait de disséquer le privé permet alors d'explorer et de construire un pan de la réalité sociale, intersubjective (Le Doeuff, 1989) et transsubjective. Dans cette construction, il devient alors impossible de dissocier l'expérience de la théorie, le soi individuel du soi collectif. Alors que l'expérience individuelle permet de reconnaître les limites imposées à chacune des femmes et leur oppression en tant que femmes, cette expérience individuelle ne suffit pas pour développer un discours. Il faut donc parvenir à s'en extraire et à s'en abstraire, puis chercher à l'intégrer dans un discours qui se situerait à un second niveau d'analyse.

Dans le projet, il importait donc, en premier lieu, de connaître la situation à partir des expériences et des connaissances que les membres du comité de recherche-action ont de cette population, dont elles font d'ailleurs partie, afin de pouvoir, dans un second temps, bâtir avec elles, à partir de leurs connaissances, les outils qui permettraient de procéder au rassemblement de l'information auprès d'une population beaucoup plus vaste des Franco-Ontariennes de 45 à 64 ans.

C'est au sein même de la démarche de recherche-action, dans la première phase du projet, que se situe le premier niveau. D'abord, les femmes du comité ont délimité, de façon générale, les aires de vie devant être à l'étude. Et cette délimitation des aires est le reflet de ce qui préoccupe les femmes du comité dans leur quotidien. En fait, tout s'est joué comme si elles faisaient leur autoportrait et celui des membres de la FFCFO.

Pourquoi les femmes du comité se sont-elles préoccupées du bénévolat? C'est d'abord parce que celui-ci est le reflet de leur propre investissement dans ce domaine. Mais c'est aussi parce qu'elles souhaitent sortir le bénévolat de l'invisibilité et pour que les instances politiques, publiques ou éducatives reconnaissent officiellement les connaissances et les acquis issus de leurs pratiques bénévoles. De même, pourquoi s'arrêter à l'étude de la santé si ce n'est parce que les femmes du comité, étant vieillissantes elles-mêmes, sont préoccupées par leur propre état de santé et par les incapacités qu'entraîne le vieillissement.

Les écrits sur le travail féminin et les données statistiques traitent bien des écarts des réalités des hommes et des femmes, des Franco-Ontariens et des Franco-Ontariennes, voire des femmes entre elles. Ils supportent, du moins en partie, les perceptions des femmes du comité. Comme la composante économique a été un des axes importants que les membres du comité ont choisis, elles ont indiqué plusieurs pistes de recherche à explorer. À partir de leurs différentes formes d'insertion au marché du travail (temps plein, temps partiel, travail autonome) ou d'exclusion du marché du travail (retraite, chômage, travail au foyer), elles se sont interrogées par rapport aux écarts économiques entre elles et leur conjoint à partir des concepts de dépendance et d'autonomie économique. La difficile articulation entre travail et famille s'est posée en termes d'insertion prioritaire des femmes dans la famille dans un contexte sociohistorique lié à leurs conditions de femmes de 45 ans et plus. Quant à leur autoportrait ou celui de leurs amies proches comme travailleuses, elles se sont vite rendu compte qu'elles n'occupaient pas, pour la majorité, un emploi leur permettant de faire une carrière mais des emplois traditionnels, faiblement rémunérés et non syndiqués. En bout de piste, leurs itinéraires de vie sont marqués par leur assignation traditionnelle dans la famille.

Les pistes fondées sur le vécu des femmes du comité sont à l'origine du questionnement sur les femmes et l'éducation. Cette orientation est d'autant plus importante que cette problématique n'avait jamais été étudiée pour la population des femmes de 45 à 64 ans. Au sein même du comité, elles se définissaient comme apprenantes mais personne n'avait reconnu leurs acquis issus d'une kyrielle d'expériences au cours de leur vie. C'est là un premier constat. Le second, c'est qu'elles ont tôt fait de souligner comment leur socialisation au sein de leur famille, leur niveau d'éducation et leur assignation au rôle domestique les avaient empêchées de faire ce dont elles avaient rêvé ou d'occuper un emploi qui leur aurait permis d'être autonomes financièrement et de se sentir socialement valorisées. Le troisième constat est qu'elles ne se voyaient pas nécessairement capables de retourner aux études. Tous ces constats ont permis aux femmes de réfléchir d'une façon plus large afin d'approfondir les différents aspects liés à l'éducation des femmes de 45 à 64 ans : socialisation, sexisme, aspirations, obstacles, conséquences de la sous-scolarisation et pauvreté.

Force est de constater que la violence conjugale et familiale, malgré son ampleur, a semé le doute au sein du comité. Devions-nous en traiter? Après une première hésitation, les femmes du comité ayant eu tendance à la reléguer au domaine de la vie privée, se sont souvenues de leurs amies qui ne pouvaient s'extraire du milieu violent faute d'argent ou, de celles qui, en quittant le foyer violent, ont vécu des situations lamentables en raison du grand nombre d'années passées au foyer, d'une scolarité insuffisante et du manque d'expérience professionnelle, bref de leur bataille pour survivre. Toutes ces réflexions du groupe, non pas sur lui-même, mais sur une problématique extérieure à lui, l'a amené à discuter du lien entre la violence contre les femmes et la socialisation, la dépendance économique, la santé ou le niveau d'éducation, etc.

C'est par le même procédé de prise de conscience que nous avons élucidé les autres aires de vie de la recherche : activités sociales, logement, administration des biens, incapacités physiques, comportements linguistiques, religion, rapports familiaux.

Malgré les difficultés rattachées à ce procédé, dont une période de formation intense à la recherche, l'implication de chacune des membres du comité de recherche-action a été une expérience précieuse. Chacune, à partir de sa réalité, montre les conflits sociaux qui traversent sa réalité. Comme il s'agit de réalités multiples qui reflètent l'expérience de chacune dans son milieu d'ancrage, les femmes présentes ont pris conscience de leurs conditions de vie et de leur invisibilité. Finalement, ces femmes ont signifié leur détermination de poursuivre le projet compte tenu de ce qu'elles venaient de découvrir et de l'importance accrue de combler une lacune maintenant inconcevable pour elles, celle du manque de données. Au fur et à mesure que se développait le projet, son importance devenait encore plus évidente et le désir des participantes d'aider d'autres femmes a pris une plus grande ampleur.

Phase II : questionnaire et cueillette de données

La seconde phase de la recherche-action se divise en plusieurs volets : construction du questionnaire, tests, planification de l'échantillonnage, cueillette de données dans les régions désignées et analyse des données (Garceau, 1995).

Construction du questionnaire

Fortes de leurs discussions sur leurs conditions de vie, les femmes avec qui cette recherche-action s'est développée ont voulu transposer ces conditions dans un questionnaire pouvant servir à rejoindre un échantillon représentatif des Franco-Ontariennes de 45 à 64 ans. Le choix d'un questionnaire s'est avéré l'instrument privilégié parce qu'il répondait aux objectifs de recherche du comité de recherche-action, soit :

- de systématiser et de normaliser les interventions;
- de procéder à la description et à la quantification des observations grâce à un instrument normalisé;

- de comparer les observations quantifiées; et
- de généraliser les résultats, car le questionnaire devait être soumis à un échantillon représentatif de la population étudiée.

Au départ, le comité s'est inspiré de certaines études effectuées auprès de femmes dans des groupes d'âge semblables afin d'y puiser certaines ressources (Therrien et Coulombe-Joly, 1984; Babineau, 1989). Puis, chacune des membres du comité a choisi une aire de vie qu'elle a travaillée (individuellement ou avec un groupe de sa communauté) afin de mettre sur papier toutes les questions qu'elle croyait pertinentes concernant cette aire de vie. Mon rôle de chercheure a ensuite été de colliger toutes ces informations pour en faire le tri, d'assurer une rigueur méthodologique et de soumettre une première version du questionnaire au comité pour discussion. C'est ainsi que sur une période allant de 1989 à 1990, quatre versions du questionnaire ont été élaborées puis testées selon deux modes que nous nommons l'approche de l'intérieur et l'approche de l'extérieur.

Pour la première, il s'agissait que les femmes du comité de recherche-action répondent à leur propre questionnaire en signalant les lacunes, les préjugés, les erreurs, les difficultés, les changements à apporter, etc. Cela leur a permis de se le réapproprier, car il était passé auparavant entre les mains du comité des chercheures. La dernière version a été l'objet de l'approche de l'extérieur. Autrement dit, chacune des membres du comité de recherche-action a soumis le questionnaire à un petit nombre de femmes de sa région, selon les modalités de l'échantillonnage. Cela a permis à chacune de déceler les dernières lacunes présentes dans le questionnaire et de se préparer à la cueillette des données qu'elles devaient effectuer par la suite. Par ailleurs, fortes de leurs nouvelles compétences et connaissances, ce sont les membres du comité de recherche-action qui ont formé les équipes régionales de bénévoles afin que soit assurée la distribution des questionnaires.

Cueillette des données

Afin de procéder à la cueillette des données, toutes se sont d'abord penchées sur la façon dont il fallait procéder. Le choix s'est posé sur la formation, dans chacune des régions respectives des membres du comité, d'un groupe de bénévoles dont la tâche serait de faire les appels téléphoniques ou les rencontres de groupes de femmes nécessaires, puis de distribuer et de recueillir les questionnaires. Les femmes de ces groupes régionaux ont ainsi reçu une formation afin d'avoir une bonne connaissance du projet, du contenu du questionnaire et des consignes à suivre afin de normaliser la cueillette des données. Au total, 113 femmes ont été formées et les membres du comité de recherche-action étaient, quant à elles, responsables de la cueillette des données dans chacune de leurs communautés.

L'évaluation de cette activité est très positive tant pour les bénévoles des régions que pour les membres du comité[6]. Quant aux bénévoles des différentes régions, elles ont souligné que la formation reçue avait été essentielle afin d'entreprendre la cueillette des données de façon méthodique. De plus, malgré certaines craintes, elles ont apprécié les contacts humains avec les femmes chez qui elles se sont rendues une première fois pour leur donner en mains propres le questionnaire, puis une seconde fois pour le reprendre. Elles se sont senties valorisées. Bon nombre d'entre elles ont indiqué que ce fut là une occasion unique de réfléchir et de discuter de la situation des Franco-Ontariennes de 45 à 64 ans[7]. Quant aux membres du comité de recherche-action, elles ont créé de nouveaux liens avec les groupes et la communauté des femmes de leur région qui, à long terme, peuvent s'avérer fort utiles à la FFCFO en tant que collaboratrices pouvant potentiellement appuyer l'action le temps venu. De plus, elles ont fait valoir, à leur tour, leurs qualités d'animatrices, d'organisatrices, car ce sont elles qui ont organisé une partie de la formation, fait la publicité pour le projet et assuré le suivi et le soutien auprès des bénévoles. Cette phase, débutée en octobre 1990, s'est terminée en décembre de la même année. Dès lors, le comité des chercheures a débuté la dernière étape de la phase II et a procédé à la compilation des informations quantitatives recueillies à l'aide du questionnaire[8].

Phase III : analyse et plan d'action

La troisième et dernière phase du projet a porté principalement sur l'analyse des résultats du sondage et sur le plan d'action à mettre en place.

Analyse des résultats

En recherche-action, les actrices et les chercheures doivent participer collectivement à la discussion des résultats de la recherche et à leur analyse. De cette façon, le milieu se réapproprie réellement l'analyse et les résultats en vue de mener les actions voulues et visant un changement effectif au niveau des groupes concernés (Dubost, 1987).

Dans le projet de recherche-action, il a été impossible au comité de recherche-action d'étudier et d'analyser à fond l'ensemble du matériel à sa disposition. Entre la fin de la collecte des données (février 1991) et l'obligation de présenter un document propre à nourrir la réflexion de l'assemblée générale de la FFCFO (mai 1991), le manque de temps a contraint à prendre le plus court chemin. Se sentant pressé, le comité a donc demandé au comité des chercheures de rédiger un document analysant les principales données sur les Franco-Ontariennes de 45 à 64 ans afin que ce rapport soit étudié par l'assemblée générale et que l'on puisse établir un plan d'action[9].

Mise en place du plan d'action de la FFCFO

Les membres du comité de recherche-action n'ayant pas participé à l'analyse des données et à la rédaction du rapport, elles devaient se réapproprier à tout prix son contenu et prendre connaissance du matériel qu'elles considéraient important pour la préparation de cette assemblée afin de le présenter à l'ensemble des membres de la FFCFO.

Ainsi, suite à une période de formation en animation des groupes offerte par le comité des chercheures, les membres du comité de recherche-action ont étudié collectivement les résultats afin de les transmettre à l'ensemble des membres de la FFCFO, sous forme d'ateliers thématiques qu'elles ont animés lors de l'assemblée générale. De ces ateliers sont ressorties plusieurs recommandations et pistes d'action en vue d'assurer la prise en charge et la continuité du projet dans sa composante action.

On peut donc dire que si un des objectifs de la recherche-action est que le milieu se réapproprie réellement le processus, l'analyse et les résultats en vue de mener les actions visant un changement au niveau des groupes concernés, le projet de la FFCFO a été une réussite aux yeux des membres du comité de recherche-action comme de celui des chercheures. De plus, comme ce projet a emprunté à la démarche classique les méthodes exigées pour assurer la rigueur scientifique et la généralisation des résultats, la FFCFO possède maintenant des données solides sur les conditions de vie des Franco-Ontariennes de 45 à 64 ans.

Et les transformations...

De façon générale, la recherche-action est une intervention, entendue comme une action qui vise la transformation de la réalité sociale, individuelle et collective. La recherche-action est construite en fonction à la fois d'un changement individuel et d'un changement social pouvant aller de l'adaptation au changement social radical. Il s'agit d'une expérience de vie dans laquelle s'engagent les personnes et dont elles espèrent tirer, à terme, des enseignements pour leur propre compte et pour agir socialement (Barbier, 1975; Goyette et Lessard-Hébert, 1987; Dubost, 1987).

Nous pouvons aussi considérer la recherche-action comme une démarche d'*empowerment*, c'est-à-dire de prise de pouvoir et de contrôle sur la réalité, car la recherche-action et l'*empowerment* sont, au même titre, des instruments de progrès social destinés à rééquilibrer les pouvoirs au profit des personnes qui en sont démunies (Le Bossé, 1996). Les Franco-Ontariennes de 45 à 64 ans ayant été pendant longtemps confinées à l'espace domestique et ayant été privées de l'accès aux pouvoirs social, économique, politique ou culturel, ces conditions permettent de les considérer comme faisant partie de l'une de ces catégories sociales. Toutefois, on remarque qu'à l'heure actuelle, la réalité de nombreuses d'entre elles est encore marquée par un manque de pouvoir, tout particulièrement lorsque les femmes sont affectées par des incapacités physiques liées à leur âge ou lorsqu'elles vivent dans des conditions économiques précaires. Ainsi, alors que, dans une démarche d'*empowerment*, la transformation personnelle est un élément indispensable au changement collectif (ce dernier étant l'objectif à atteindre), en recherche-action, le changement individuel et le changement social vont de pair. Il se produit alors un glissement entre les apprentissages d'une personne et la façon dont elle les utilisera afin de produire un changement social.

À partir du projet de recherche-action de la FFCFO, nous pouvons voir certaines des transformations qui ont eu lieu à différents niveaux ayant des influences et interagissant les uns sur les autres. Ces transformations, nous les constatons au sein même des différents systèmes en place : les répondantes elles-mêmes, les bénévoles des régions, le comité de recherche-action, le comité des chercheures, l'organisme et au niveau social, de telle façon qu'une transformation dans l'un affecte les autres[10].

Transformations individuelles et collectives

Dans la recherche-action, l'une des transformations importantes est liée à la formation individuelle et collective que les membres du comité ont reçue en matière de recherche. Comme la plupart des femmes n'avaient jamais fait de recherche, elles se sont initiées à toutes les étapes de ce processus. La formation combinait à la fois un mode de production autonome (apprentissage et réflexion personnelle) et un mode de production hétéronome (recevoir une formation de la part des chercheures). La réflexion et l'apprentissage personnel ont été indispensables à la réalisation, par les membres du comité de recherche-action, d'activités autonomes, comme l'appréciation et la détermination des aires de vie devant être analysées, l'élaboration de questions et l'ordonnancement du questionnaire, la cueillette de données, l'analyse des résultats, etc. La discussion et le partage ont permis d'établir dans ces domaines de solides consensus. Par ailleurs, la formation fournie par la chercheure s'est toujours déroulée de façon à ce que ses interventions ne viennent pas nuire ou faire obstacle aux capacités d'initiative des femmes du comité en ce qui a trait à la prise en charge du projet et à leur participation à l'élaboration d'un nouveau savoir. Certes, la création d'un équilibre entre ces deux modes de production est davantage un idéal que la réalité, mais peu s'en faut pour dire que notre projet de recherche-action a su maintenir une parfaite harmonie entre ces modes dans toutes les phases du projet.

Cela étant dit, au fur et à mesure que progressaient les diverses étapes de la recherche, les membres du comité de recherche-action ont découvert ou redécouvert certaines ressources personnelles qu'elles possédaient et qu'elles ont davantage affirmées ou mises à contribution. Conscientes de leur manque de connaissances du processus de recherche, elles ont indiqué, à une question inaugurale portant sur leur apport éventuel au projet, une volonté ferme d'apprendre. Elles se sont engagées collectivement dans un processus exigeant à tous les niveaux. Elles ont acquis, nous disent-elles, une plus grande confiance en soi et une meilleure compréhension du processus de recherche, une discipline et une rigueur dans la perception et la compréhension des problèmes, etc.[11] Ces compétences acquises leur font dire que ces nouvelles connaissances leur permettent d'accepter avec plus de confiance qu'avant de nouvelles responsabilités sociales. Certaines ont déjà su les transposer dans leur engagement social en acceptant des postes de responsabilité au sein d'autres organismes ou en organisant d'autres activités. Individuellement, le projet a permis à plusieurs de développer ou de raffermir leur détermination face à l'importance de continuer à lutter collectivement pour améliorer les conditions de vie des femmes. La formation, plus particulièrement en animation de groupe, leur a aussi permis d'acquérir une plus grande confiance en leur qualité de leadership dans leur communauté. Qui dit changement, dit action et l'*empowerment* évoque chez les participantes un ensemble d'actions précises qu'elles ont entreprises à la fois individuellement et collectivement durant ou à la suite de la recherche.

C'est en participant à la formation au processus de recherche, à la discussion permanente sur leurs conditions de vie et sur les résultats de l'enquête provinciale sur les femmes de 45 à 64 ans que les membres du comité de recherche-action ont pu transformer leur connaissance subjective (leur propre situation) en connaissance objective (la situation des Franco-Ontariennes). Cette transformation s'est effectuée à partir d'un processus de prise de conscience profondément enraciné dans l'action qui a mené les femmes du comité à voir comment leurs problèmes individuels ont un caractère systémique. Ce passage d'une vision individuelle à une vision collective a engendré, chez les femmes du comité, une volonté d'action sociale plus large.

Finalement, au début du projet, la majorité des femmes qui ont fait partie du comité de recherche-action ne se définissaient pas comme féministes. Même convaincues de l'importance de droits égaux pour les deux sexes, elles ne se seraient pas affirmées publiquement comme telles.

Pour la plupart, il semble qu'elles ne se soient ni réellement senties concernées, ni impliquées. Au contraire, l'image que la plupart d'entre elles avait du féminisme ne correspondait nullement à leur raison d'être. Pourtant, du début à la fin du projet, la plupart des femmes du comité sont passées d'un «je ne suis pas féministe» à «je peux dire maintenant que je suis féministe». Cette transformation est liée au fait qu'elles ont pris le temps d'identifier les problèmes (les leurs et ceux des autres femmes), et aussi de comprendre et d'analyser les conditions de vie des femmes. Elles ont ainsi développé une pensée critique à cet égard. Elles ne voient plus la situation des femmes comme étant de l'ordre du privé mais de l'ordre public. Conséquemment, elles ne se sentent plus aussi démunies qu'auparavant. Au contraire, elles sont en mesure de répondre, à leur mesure et collectivement, à une partie de ces besoins.

Transformations au sein de la FFCFO

Les transformations individuelles et collectives qui ont eu lieu au sein des membres du comité de recherche-action, couplées aux résultats de l'enquête sur la qualité de vie des Franco-Ontariennes de 45 à 64 ans, ont affecté la FFCFO dans son fonctionnement. En effet, la recherche étant terminée, l'organisme devait alors se concentrer au niveau de l'action, ce qui a obligé la FFCFO à délaisser une orientation plutôt traditionnelle pour s'engager résolument dans le courant du féminisme égalitaire.

Les résultats de la recherche ont permis à la FFCFO de faire plusieurs représentations auprès d'instances gouvernementales qui se penchent sur la situation des femmes. Sachant que la violence conjugale et familiale est un problème crucial chez les femmes de 45 à 64 ans, la FFCFO a produit un guide d'animation et une vidéo sur la violence conjugale qui a été présentée dans toutes les régions de la province (FFCFO, 1994). Connaissant mieux le dénuement économique des femmes de cette tranche d'âge, l'organisme travaille actuellement à un projet de développement économique pour les femmes[12]. De plus, la FFCFO collabore avec plusieurs autres groupes de femmes sur différents dossiers dont les objectifs sont liés à l'amélioration des conditions de vie des femmes et à la transformation des structures de domination existantes[13]. Et, bien sûr, rien de tout cela n'aurait été possible sans les solides partenariats que la FFCFO a construits avec les organismes subventionnaires.

Conclusion

Le projet de recherche-action de la FFCFO s'est avéré fructueux à maints égards. Parce qu'il a cumulé plusieurs caractéristiques du processus de recherche-action — élaboration d'objectifs communs, expérience réelle, caractère collectif, communication bi-directionnelle, complémentarité entre participantes et chercheures, intégration des actrices et évaluation continue — et que le comité s'est assuré de répondre aux exigences de toute démarche scientifique, la FFCFO a en main un portrait provincial sur les Franco-Ontariennes de 45 à 64 ans.

Par ailleurs, la recherche-action, tout comme le rapport et les actions qui en découlent, répondent bien au double mandat actuel de la FFCFO, soit la sensibilisation et la promotion de l'égalité pour les femmes et l'expansion de la francophonie. La FFCFO met à l'avant-scène la francophonie des femmes de 45 à 64 ans.

Cette démarche de longue haleine entreprise par la FFCFO et par le comité de recherche-action permet de voir les pas de géantes que les femmes ont faits. De la prise de conscience, en passant par l'analyse des problèmes systémiques vécus par les Franco-Ontariennes de 45 à 64 ans, aux actions entreprises suite aux résultats, parfois douloureux, concernant les conditions de vie de ces femmes, tout cela montre la volonté, la ferveur qui a animé les femmes dans leur lutte contre les iniquités sociales. Certes, il reste beaucoup à faire et elles en sont toutes conscientes. Nous ne changerons pas un système comme le nôtre en si peu de temps.

Finalement, si dans sa version contemporaine, «le féminisme ne se propose rien de moins que d'ouvrir à chaque femme prise individuellement les voies d'expression de son autonomie» (De Sève, 1994 : 25), ce que chaque femme du comité de recherche-action a réalisé c'est qu'il fallait d'abord prendre conscience de soi, de ses aspirations et de ses possibilités afin de déboucher sur une action politique collective. C'est peut-être dans cette direction que la FFCFO devra davantage investir dans l'avenir, car l'organisme est un outil essentiel du changement social.

Bibliographie

Babineau, C. (1989), *Étude sur la situation financière des femmes francophones âgées de 50 à 65 ans et habitant la région Sud-est du Nouveau-Brunswick*, Moncton, Université de Moncton.

Barbier, R. (1975), «Implication, animation et recherche-action dans les sciences humaines», *Connexions*, no 13, 103-123.

Blais, A. (1992), «Le sondage», dans *Recherche sociale. De la problématique à la collecte des données*, 2e éd., sous la dir. de B. Gauthier, 361-398, Sillery, Québec, Presses de l'Université du Québec.

Brunet, L. (1992), *Almanda Walker-Marchand 1968-1949, Une féministe franco-ontarienne de la première heure*, Ottawa, les Éditions l'Interligne.

Chambaud, L., R. Mayer et G. Richard (1986), «La recherche-action en santé communautaire, en travail social et en éducation : une nouvelle pratique ou un alibi pour les professionnels?», *Service social*, vol. 35, nos 1 et 2, 158-187.

Dagenais, H. (1994), «Méthodologie féministe pour les femmes et le développement : concepts, contextes et pratiques», dans *L'égalité devant soi : sexes, rapports sociaux et développement international*, sous la dir. de M. F. Labrecque, 258-290, Ottawa, Centre de recherches pour le développement international.

De Sève, M. (1994), «Femmes, action politique et identité», *Cahiers de recherche sociologique*, no 23, 25-38.

Desjardins, M. (1991), Les femmes et la diaspora canadienne-française. *Brève histoire de la FNFCF de 1914 à 1991*, Ottawa, Fédération nationale des femmes canadiennes-françaises.

Dubost, J. (1987), *L'intervention sociologique*, Paris, Presses universitaires de France.

Fédération des femmes canadiennes-françaises de l'Ontario (FFCFO) (1994), *La violence démasquée*, bande vidéo, Sudbury, FFCFO.

Garceau, M. L. (1995), *Franco-Ontariennes de 45 à 64 ans : analyse de leurs conditions de vie*, Thèse de doctorat non publiée, Montréal, Université du Québec à Montréal.

Garceau, M. L., D. Dennie, B. Tremblay-Matte et M. Charron (1992), *«Cessons de penser que l'amour va tout vaincre!» La situation des femmes francophones de 45 à 64 ans qui vivent en Ontario. Rapport final*, Sudbury, Fédération des femmes canadiennes-françaises de l'Ontario.

Goyette, G. et M. Lessard-Hébert (1987), *La recherche-action : ses fonctions, ses fondements et son instrumentation*, Sillery, Québec, Presses de l'Université du Québec.

Lamoureux, H., R. Mayer et J. Panet-Raymond (1984), *L'intervention communautaire*, Montréal, Éditions Saint-Martin.

Le Bossé, Y. (1996), «Empowerment et pratiques sociales : illustration d'une utopie prise au sérieux», *Nouvelles pratiques sociales*, vol. 9, no 1, 127-146.

Le Doeuff, M. (1989), *L'étude et le rouet*, Paris, Éditions du Seuil.

Mayer, R. et F. Ouellet (1991), *Méthodologie de recherche pour les intervenants sociaux*, Boucherville, Gaëtan Morin, éditeur.

Pâquet-Deehy, A. et M. Rinfret-Raynor (1987), «Le vécu des intervenantes dans une formation en intervention féministe auprès des femmes violentées», dans *Agir contre la violence. Une option féministe à l'intervention auprès des femmes battues*, sous la dir. de G. Larouche, 479-498, Montréal, Éditions La Pleine Lune.

Therrien, R. et L. Coulombe-Joly (1984), *Rapport de l'AFÉAS sur la situation des femmes au foyer*, Montréal, Boréal Express.

Notes

1. La Fédération des femmes canadiennes-françaises de l'Ontario, fondée en 1918, est un organisme provincial divisé en différentes zones disséminées à la grandeur de la province. Elle est formée de membres dont la majorité est âgée de plus de 45 ans.

2. En 1954, l'objectif de la FFCF est de conserver intacts et inviolables la foi robuste, le parler ancestral et les mœurs saines de nos foyers catholiques et canadiens-français tandis qu'en 1975, la FFCF énonce les objectifs suivants : promouvoir la culture française; conserver la foi catholique; contribuer à l'épanouissement intégral et intégré de la femme, au point de vue intellectuel, culturel, spirituel, moral et physique; stimuler la participation de la femme au bien total de la société, en tenant compte de sa féminité, dans les domaines de l'éducation, de l'action sociale et familiale, économique, culturelle et spirituelle (Brunet, 1992).

3. Ce nouveau mandat a été adopté le 8 novembre 1987 dans le cadre d'une assemblée générale extraordinaire réunissant 150 membres des diverses régions de l'Ontario (FFCFO, 1993, *Statuts et règlements*. Sudbury).

4. Il s'agit de *La coopérative Convergence* à Ottawa.

5. Dans l'économie générale du projet, nous n'aurions pu faire autrement. Toutefois, lors du processus d'évaluation, les membres du comité ont souligné leur appréciation du travail des chercheures, notamment celui de l'encadrement du projet et celui de la communication ouverte entre les chercheures et le comité de recherche-action (Garceau, 1995 : 216).

6. L'évaluation étant une caractéristique de la recherche-action, elle a rythmé la démarche du projet de la FFCFO. Dans ce projet, des évaluations ont été effectuées après chacune des rencontres et après les phases I et II du projet. Ces évaluations portaient principalement sur les conditions structurelles du déroulement du projet. Les propos ici tenus sont issus de l'analyse des évaluations des participantes.

7. Les questionnaires étaient placés dans une enveloppe scellée par la répondante. Cette enveloppe était ensuite remise à la bénévole. Au total, 917 questionnaires valides ont été utilisés afin de faire l'analyse des conditions de vie des Franco-Ontariennes de 45 à 64 ans (Garceau, 1995).

8. Il s'agit principalement de l'élaboration de la banque de données, de l'entrée des données et de l'analyse préliminaire des données qui ont été présentées lors de l'assemblée générale de la FFCFO, en mai 1991 (Garceau et al., 1992).

9. Les résultats de cette recherche ont été publiés dans Garceau *et al.* (1992). Une analyse beaucoup plus approfondie des résultats a aussi été effectuée par Garceau (1995). Ce document présente à la fois un cadre théorique et les résultats de cette enquête, tout particulièrement en ce qui a trait au travail, à l'éducation, au bénévolat et à la violence conjugale et familiale.

10. Ce n'est donc qu'après coup ou pendant le projet que les participants peuvent effectuer une analyse des transformations encourues. Le bilan du projet de recherche-action de la FFCFO a été effectué en rétrospective à partir d'un questionnaire concernant l'expérience de la recherche-action. Les sujets abordés dans le questionnaire touchent la motivation, les avantages et désavantages de la recherche-action, les partenariats, les rencontres, l'organisation, la communication et le processus décisionnel, le fonctionnement, le contenu, la participation et les apprentissages. Le bilan intitulé *Pleins feux sur la recherche-action : un bilan des partenaires* a fait l'objet d'une conférence qui a été présentée par Darquise Deschamps et Marie-Luce Garceau, lors du colloque «Visibles et Partenaires : pratiques et recherches féministes en milieu minoritaire» qui s'est tenu à Sudbury en mai 1997.

11. Les propos des participantes sont tirés de l'évaluation de la phase II du projet et d'un bilan du projet de recherche-action de la FFCFO effectué par Darquise Deschamps et Marie-Luce Garceau et dont les résultats ont été présentés lors d'une conférence à Sudbury en mai 1997.

12. Dans l'ensemble de la population, les données de l'enquête montrent que 46,4 % des femmes seules ont un revenu de moins de 15 000 $ par année et que 62,2 % des femmes mariées ont le même revenu (Garceau, 1995 : 384).

13. La FFCFO collabore actuellement avec la Table féministe francophone de concertation provinciale de l'Ontario (dossiers politiques), le Collectif des femmes francophones du Nord de l'Ontario (dossiers régionaux), le Centre Victoria pour femmes (victimes d'agression à caractère sexuel) et plusieurs autres organismes.

Susan Hare and Laura Day Corbiere

Aboriginal Women's Economic Renewal: A Project of Re-inventing Strengths from the Past

I live, but I will not live forever.
Mysterious moon, you only remain,
Powerful sun, you alone remain,
Wonderful earth, you remain forever.[1]

Aboriginal women in First Nation communities in Canada are faced with a legal foundation not of their making. They must also survive with economic possibilities which were not developed with Aboriginal women in mind.

This paper will describe practical methods that allow Aboriginal women to succeed in economic development. A thorough background of the historical oppression and legal limitations imposed on Aboriginal women — and the nature and outcomes of these limitations — will explain that others besides Aboriginal people are responsible for their deprivation. This review will also explain why economic renewal must be based on the cultural and historical strengths of Aboriginal women. This paper emerges from the experience of women in a First Nation community or "Indian reserve" in rural northern Ontario with a band membership of approximately 1 000 people.

M'chigeeng Kwe'uk and Economic Development

The Ojibwe women of M'Chigeeng First Nation are involved in a community-based economic program developed and designed by and for Aboriginal women. The design of the economic program emerged from a community conference which focused on Aboriginal women's economic needs. This design includes small, home-based self-employment ventures supported by the foundation of Ojibwe cultural teachings. The program is a pilot project to build an enabling environment for long-term success for its Aboriginal women participants. This pilot project is being delivered in a First Nation community by Aboriginal women from the same First Nation.

The target group of the pilot project is made up of Aboriginal women who face numerous barriers and obstacles to training and employment. The majority are women caught in the cycle of generational dependency on social programs and services. Their classroom has been confined to the perimeters of the community. There has also been little exposure to structured learning and to experiences that would impact on the thinking conditioned by the environment or on conventional thinking. In their home community, this target group of Aboriginal women is in its element.

Pilot Project Priorities

The pilot project has three priorities. The first is development of the individual. The second is regaining and retaining a sense of belonging within the Ojibwe community culture. The third priority is encouragement of and support for the learning journey towards the creation of self-sustaining self-employment. These three priorities are based on the complexity of needs in the lives of Aboriginal women today.

Priority 1: Development of the Individual

Personal and professional development extends beyond the delivery of knowledge, skills, and experience. Delivery includes a learning environment conducive to support of change in attitude, behaviour, thinking process, and lifestyle. The participants have opportunity to practise their newfound or enhanced knowledge, skills, and experiences before venturing beyond the comfortable perimeters of the home community. Participants must endeavour to be comfortable in all situations so that they will be ready to take new risks. Two excellent examples are "A" and "M" who are both young mothers. "A" has four children and "M" has three children. "A" and "M" accompanied a staff person to Toronto, a place which both have previously visited, for training. They flew on an airplane for the first time and participated in workshops which included company presidents, executive directors, project managers, and business co-ordinators. "A" volunteered to participate in a media conference, a decision which was a significant risk for her. Both "A" and "M," through the pilot project, have developed a comfort zone which has allowed them to take risks in other areas as well. While documentation of this type of success is difficult to measure, it is but important to recognize.

Priority 2: Retaining Ojibwe Community Culture

As indicated, the pilot project revolves around being able to regain and retain a sense of belonging to the Ojibwe community culture. The participants learn first that caring about their community is vital for themselves and for that community. An enabling environment is not one that depends upon individual empowerment; instead, it stems from the culture. The Ojibwe culture offers the foundation for continued development of the Ojibwe language, a rich spirituality involving universal truths, a true understanding of democracy and civil and collective rights, a fine craftsmanship unlike any other, a unique artistic sense of the world, resource conservation principles which give dignity to all life, and an overall respect for humanity. These cultural foundations are the inspiration and bedrock of the participants' long-term plans.

To accomplish this second priority, participants are encouraged to lead and take part in community activities as volunteers. Volunteerism provides an opportunity to experience the other side of social and cultural programs and services. It is very rare to hear a participant say "I don't care," which is a prevalent statement and attitude found in oppressed communities. Documentation of this type of success, again, is difficult to measure, but important to recognize.

Priority 3: Towards Self-Sustaining Self-Employment

The third priority, which is encouragement and support in the continuing journey towards self-sustaining self-employment, is the final goal of the pilot project. When participants first enter the project, they anticipate that their first step to self-employment begins with making a product or providing a service. They soon realize that these are expectations of immediate gratification. The experiences of the Aboriginal women who designed and developed this initiative demonstrate that this pilot project does not work like other training projects, and it should not. After all, Aboriginal women must make their way through a foreign economy. The Ojibwe women who designed the project understood that the program must be based on the individual's being able to become self-reliant within the context of her Ojibwe experience. The focus of the project, therefore, is one of sustainability, rather than start-up. Sustainability is the beam of support which ensures that an enabling environment has a sturdy foundation on which to build. A sustainable form of income for a participant may, for example, be a combination of fine bead work combined with a community catering business; or, it may be a small bakery combined with a community taxi service. The result is adaptability based on a foundation of Ojibwe culture.

The development of the community-based economic plan by and for Ojibwe women involves adaptation of traditional roles as keepers of the culture so that the culture will survive within the changes of modern times. This is because it is Ojibwe women who breathe the air for the lives they carry within them. Their responsibility goes unchanged from one generation to the next for the nurturing of a healthy people.

The Imposition of the Values of Patriarchy and Foreign Religions on Ojibwe Society

Ojibwe women, as part of a tribal society, played an important role in the maintenance of the society in which they lived. Ojibwe women, or "Kwe'uk," were important as bearers of children, as wives and grandmothers, and as an integral parts of the economic machine which characterized their society. Ojibwe women also shared equally in the responsibilities of the Midewewin Society or Lodge, which was the spiritual, or religious, structure for Ojibwe society. Both Ojibwe women and men held positions as spiritual "heads" of the Lodge. Ojibwe women were also the physicians of their society, since the practical daily needs of medicine for their families fell to the women. Ojibwe women played an important role in berry-gathering, drying fish, and curing animals for seasonal use, a role that wielded organizational power within the societal structure. Ojibwe women, especially young girls, took part in the hunting of small game, and this activity often provided them with a spirit of independence and personal pride. The activities of Ojibwe society afforded many opportunities for mutual support among women in the tribe. Leadership was a responsibility given to certain persons by the people; it was not something which was sought so that a male or female person would be in a leadership position. While Ojibwe men did most of the big-game hunting and protective activities such as defending territory, there are likewise stories about Ojibwe women as good hunters and warriors.

The advent of the French and later the English fur trade in Canada provided a new role for Ojibwe women — that of political and economic connection. Relationships between French traders and Ojibwe women brought opportunities for the French trader to access the women's tribe. As well, it provided the Ojibwe woman with a new and different kind of influence that lasted for several decades. However, alliances between English traders and Ojibwe women were not easy for English men were quick to denigrate their Ojibwe spouses if an Englishwoman became available. [2]

How the Legal System Affects Aboriginal Women

"Indian women" (the term "Indian" is used only because it is a legal term under the *Indian Act*) have been treated differently from men in terms of Indian status, treaty rights, and band membership. This situation as occurred most stringently since 1951. An early piece of legislation which directly defined who an "Indian", enacted in 1850, defined Indians to be the following:

- All persons of Indian blood, reputed to belong to the particular Body or Tribe of Indians interested in such lands, and their descendants;
- All persons intermarried with any such Indians and residing amongst them, and the descendants of all such persons;
- All persons residing among such Indians, whose parents on either side were or are Indians of such Body or Tribe, or entitled to be considered as such; and
- All persons adopted in infancy by any such Indians, and residing in the Village or upon the lands of such Tribe or Body of Indians, and their descendants.[3]

People of non-Indian blood could also be considered Indians. In 1851, all women could become "Indians" if they were lawfully married to "Indians."[4]

As early as 1857, the practice of enfranchising male and female Indians began. This practice included a loss of one's Indian status for such reasons as becoming a lawyer or doctor, obtaining a university degree, or being out of the country for too long.[5]

"Enfranchising" means to "invest with municipal rights, especially the right to vote, to release from bondage."[6] Ironically for Aboriginal people, it was also a divesting of rights and Aboriginal culture. In 1880, the enfranchisement of Indian women began with the provision that "[any] Indian woman marrying any other than an Indian or a non-treaty Indian shall cease to be an Indian in any respect within the meaning of this Act...except for treaty annuities."[7] Thus, Indian women began to lose their Indian status but were able to keep their treaty rights until the treaty provision was deleted from the *Indian Act* amendments in 1951. In 1985, what is now commonly known to Aboriginal people as Bill C-31 was passed into law, and Aboriginal women who had lost their status were reinstated as persons with Indian status. However, in First Nations which had developed a Band Membership Code before June 28, 1987, children of the reinstated women had to apply for band membership. The struggle for reinstatement by Indian women was monumental. Many Aboriginal communities were divided and some remain so even today. Women have sometimes brought their non-Indian mates with them to their Aboriginal communities. Although Indian men have had the right throughout history to bring non-Indian women mates to their communities, Aboriginal women are largely resented for bringing their non-Indian mates to live with them in these same communities.

The First Nations have not been provided with adequate financial resources; as well, they have properly been denied recognition of their rights to land. They have insufficient resources to plan for and to accept an influx to First Nation's communities. Again, this situation has caused problems not of Aboriginal communities' own making. Therefore, many First Nation communities must deal with an influx of people who are not used to the "ways" of First Nation culture in the context of an inadequate infrastructure. This mixture adds to a societal condition where the highest unemployment rates in Canada exist (in most First Nation communities, the rate is 60-85%). Social conditions resulting from the effects of colonialism, including the residential school damage, are part of daily life.

Indians' real and personal property on the reserve have been protected from seizure. Historically, the Royal Proclamation of 1763[8] was enacted partially to stop settlers from buying land from Indians and/or defrauding them of it. Thus, unless the Crown purchased territory from Indians through a public "treaty" process, Indian lands remained in Indian hands.

In 1876, legislation provided that "[no] person shall take any security or otherwise obtain any lien or charge, whether by mortgage, judgement or otherwise, upon real or personal property of any Indian or non-treaty Indian within Canada...."[9]

These provisions remain in the present *Indian Act* with slightly different wording. While effect of this provision in First Nation communities is protection of First Nations' land base (not without problems), the provision has also been an obstacle for accessing loans for businesses on reserve. Banks and lending institutions are reluctant to provide loans of any substantial amount, knowing that land pledged to secure loan(s) is questionable collateral. This has similarly been an obstacle for financing of homes. However, many First Nations, along with the Minister of Indian Affairs, have dealt partially with this issue through the issuance of ministerial guarantees which provide a guarantee to an outside lender. The problem with this system is that every Indian in that First Nation is placed at risk. The system, in effect, guarantees that the loan of the individual Indian, in the event of default, is repaid with Band funds.

As far back as 1857, laws such as the "Act to encourage the gradual Civilization of the Indian Tribes in this Province and to Amend the Laws Restricting Indians" [10] specifically stated as their purpose the following: "to facilitate the acquisition of property and of the rights accompanying it, by such Individual Members of the said Tribes as shall be found to desire such encouragement and to have deserved it:...Of course those Individual Members of the Tribes were Indians of the "male sex" [s.III supra].

Although the provisions of the *Indian Act* from 1869 specified that "he or she" may be issued a "location ticket" (lots on reserves), the practice was that most of the "tickets" were issued in the name of the male; this practice continues to this day. The decision about whom the "tickets" would be issued was made by Indian Agents, European males whose patriarchal values favoured male ownership. Many Ojibwe women — including elders — lived on Indian reserve lots with their husbands and children. Upon a husband's death, such a woman might have discovered that her property had been willed by the deceased husband to someone else. The strict interpretation of legislation regarding the "possession of lands in a reserve"[11] does not allow for any legal claims by "Indian" women in such situations, no matter the injustice of the situation. Therefore, ownership of property on a reserve rests primarily with men. When property ownership is shared with a woman, her ownership rights are uncertain. Hence, if a woman wishes to construct a building for a business or a home, she is forced to purchase scarce land or to request Chief and Council for usage of "common lands."

Many an Aboriginal woman has discovered the uncertainty of property ownership through family breakdown when her spouse ordered her and their children out of the home. In these cases, the Certificate of Possession was in the name of the husband-and the law supported this action (Derrickson v. Derrickson [1986] 1 S.C.R. 285, [1986] 3 W.W.R. 193, 1 B.C.L.R.(2d) 273, 50 R.F.L. (2d) 337, 26 D.L.R. (4th) 175, [1986] 2 C.N.L.R. 45, 65 N.R.278).

1937...

We have come a long way since 1937 when the duties and responsibilities of Indian Agents' wives included teaching Ojibwe women domestic skills such as housecleaning, cooking, and sewing. Such instruction was an attempt to condition Ojibwe women to be like the white women of the era. The schools to which Ojibwe women were forced to send their children taught and emphasized the same domestic skills.

This assimilation process extended to the organization of Aboriginal communities. These communities were fashioned by legislation in order that the resultant communities would be like white communities; that is, to be farming communities. Aboriginal people were governed from Ottawa through Indian agents, and they were wards of the government. In other words, they were, treated like children. Aboriginal people, for a time, required permission from the Indian agents to leave the reserve or to move to another reserve; Indian agents controlled most aspects of life on a reserve.

In addition, the churches imposed foreign religions on Aboriginal people. Clergy of these foreign churches discouraged Aboriginal spiritual and cultural practices, going to great lengths to discourage entertainment, such as dances, they thought was unsavory. For example, the clergy planted stories in Aboriginal communities about creatures with hooded capes who would punish sinners who attended dances. The churches, like the government, believed that they knew what was best for Aboriginal people; their vision for Aboriginal people, however, was based on a European lifestyle.

The economic base of reserve communities had been and continued to be barter and trade as more settlers located near Aboriginal communities. Aboriginal women picked berries to sell, baked bread, made Aboriginal crafts, cleaned homes, worked as cooks in tourist camps, and provided laundry services. Aboriginal women, like non-Aboriginal women, were expected to learn nothing more than efficiency in domestic skills in preparation for the day when they would marry and have children.

This time period did not encourage Aboriginal women, or women in general, to have aspirations or dreams beyond marriage. Aboriginal women were forced to adapt to life imposed upon them; they had no choice. The Aboriginal lifestyle had been and continued to be displaced by other beliefs and values. For example, the Aboriginal culture was forced underground for many years. Aboriginal children were beaten for speaking their Aboriginal language in residential schools and in many on-reserve day schools: "I'd always see my mother cry...I was afraid of life and asked myself what will it be like when I'm grown up?"[12]

Chiefs and Councils eventually replaced Indian agents as the agents of the federal government. Gradually, Chiefs and Councils assumed more and more authority and fiduciary responsibility from the federal government. This situation has led successive Ministers of Indian Affairs to predict the demise of the bureaucracy of this department. Along with newly assumed authorities and responsibilities came the control of Band Councils over almost all aspects of their band members' lives. Unfortunately, the result has been conditioned dependency that was and is still reinforced by the *Indian Act.*

Time, endurance, and patience are great teachers and the Aboriginal activists of the 1960s broke new ground in affecting government policies regarding "Indians." Aboriginal people garnered the attention of the news media. Aboriginal people everywhere, it seemed, had new awareness. Exposure to media including television and radio made Aboriginal women aware of the larger world, including the women's movement. Aboriginal women, having a different history from non-Aboriginal women, undertook a different path towards human rights and self-respect. An important reflection to keep in mind about this journey is the misunderstanding that lack of visibility necessarily means that nothing is happening: "It is assumed by many that very little remains of traditional Indian ideology and philosophy because the traditional Indian lifestyle is no longer in evidence; that is, we don't live in teepees anymore."[13]

Unique Measures of Success for Aboriginal Women's Renewal

The measure of success for Ojibwe women who participate in the M'Chigeeng Kwe'uk and the economic renewal project will, of necessity, differ from the measures which might be used in evaluating other women's economic projects outcomes. Significantly, a review of history and culture indicates how such a measure must be different from that which is applied in non-Aboriginal society. Success for Ojibwe women in the project is measured by what an individual can contribute to the community and how "good" that individual can become while she walks this path called earth.

The Nature and Outcome of Legal Limitations

The first legal limitation that Aboriginal women face is denial of their First Nations membership rights. The Aboriginal women's movement continually addresses this limitation.

Lack of property ownership is a second problem that is likewise is being addressed gradually. As economic success is achieved, rental properties can be purchased. Women's collective economic ventures mean increased strength for Aboriginal women.

The third legal limitation is seizure of property by banks and the resulting loan vacuum. This is currently addressed on an incremental basis through organized lending circles: Aboriginal business development corporation loans and larger Reserve-Trust companies that guarantee collateral for outside lenders.

These issues have been identified and addressed creatively by the women in the M'Chigeeng Pilot Project. The solutions to these issues are important benchmarks of success in defining alternate routes to access property and to build credit lines.

Conclusion

Regardless of the legal limits imposed upon Aboriginal women by other societies, it is critical to remember the Aboriginal women who have gone, in the period of one generation, from quill-box makers to million-dollar entrepreneurs. This has been done by building on Ojibwe cultural values, which have, in turn, provided impetus for adaptability and stability.

Endnotes

1. Allen, Paula Gunn. 1986. "The Sacred Hoop." Boston, Beacon Press, 70.
2. Connolly v. Woolrich and Johnson et al. (1867), 17 R.J.R.Q. 75 (Also reported: 11 L.C. Jur. 197).

3.   S.Prov.C. 1850, c.42.

4.   S.Prov.C.1851, c.59, s.II.

5.   S.Prov.C. 1857, c.26, s.1.

6.   Sykes, J.B. (ed.). 1976. *The Concise Oxford Dictionary*. 6th ed. Oxford University Press.

7.   S.C. 1880, c.28, s.12.

8.   The Royal Proclamation October 7, 1763 R.S.C. 1985, Appendix II, No.1.

9.   S.C.1876, c.18, s.66.

10.   S.Prov.C.1857, c.26.

11.   S.20-29 Indian Act R.S.C. 1985, C.105 as amended, ss. 20-29.

12.   Rigoberta Menchu. 1986. *"An Indian Woman in Guatemala."* Thetford, Norfolk, Ed. Elizabeth Burgos-Debray, Chapter XII, 87.

13.   Littlebear, Leroy, Menno Boltand J., Anthony Long. 1984. "Pathways to Self-Determination/Canadian Indians and the Canadian State." *Traditional Indian Government: Of the People, By the People, For the People*. Toronto: University of Toronto Press, 36.

PART IV — PARTIE IV

Healing Body and Spirit —
Santé du corps et de l'esprit

Elsy Gagné présente un texte qui oscille entre deux questions chères aux femmes canadiennes. À qui appartient-il de décider de la méthodologie à utiliser lorsqu'il s'agit de féminiser l'institution médicale «masculinisée»? À qui appartient-il de se soucier des femmes dont le corps a été amputé suite à une chirurgie majeure et mutilante ? À la première question, l'auteure répond en disant que la recherche médicale, à tendance positiviste, promeut la supériorité des approches quantitatives qui conduisent souvent à des conclusions décontextualisées du vécu des femmes. À la seconde, Gagné indique que l'institution médicale est peu apte à reconnaître les problèmes sociaux vécus par les femmes, tout particulièrement lorsqu'elles ont subi une chirurgie majeure comme la mastectomie.

Pour contrer ces phénomènes, Gagné montre l'importance de faire de la recherche féministe ancrée dans la pratique quotidienne des femmes afin d'humaniser les services et les soins de santé et d'offrir une puissance explicative à un phénomène social complexe. Privées de soutien de la part de l'institution médicale et privées d'une meilleure connaissance de leur qualité de vie de la part de la santé communautaire, les Franco-Manitobaines se sont parlées, regroupées et entraidées afin d'absorber le choc de la maladie et de passer de l'état de maladie à celui de la santé. Gagné offre un bon exemple de la féminisation de la recherche et d'une pratique médicale non traditionnelle et montre que les femmes expliquent l'importance non seulement de se prendre en main, mais surtout d'interpeller l'institution médicale à partir de leurs expériences.

Monique Dumais constate que la tradition religieuse, monopolisée par des ecclésiastiques masculins, est source d'invisibilité et d'inégalité pour les femmes catholiques et que la théologie a déclaré juste et salutaire la condition subalterne des femmes. Historiquement dépossédées de leur propre vécu, elles ont été écartées du discours et, devant l'autorité de la théologie patriarcale, il ne leur restait plus qu'à s'incliner. La prise de parole des femmes dans le domaine des religions et, tout particulièrement au sein de l'église catholique, est le point de départ indispensable afin de les sortir de leur invisibilité millénaire. Relire les écrits théologiques en reconnaissant l'oppression des femmes dans ses multiples formes et donner une interprétation féministe aux paroles

191

bibliques et évangéliques permettent de montrer, comme le souligne Dumais, les distorsions, les perversions ou encore les oppressions pour mieux voir ce dont les femmes doivent être délivrées. Ancrée dans le vécu et les expériences des femmes, la réécriture de ces textes permet de revoir les symboliques phalliques et de dénoncer toute domination des êtres humains à la lumière de nouvelles expériences, de nouvelles évidences et de nouveaux modèles, ceux des femmes. Monique Dumais invite les femmes à contribuer à une nouvelle transmission du sens de la théologie patriarcale par la prise de parole et par l'intégration de thèmes tels autonomie, égalité, solidarité, dignité, identité, croissance et libération, etc., dans la relecture des textes bibliques et évangéliques. Elle les incite aussi à constituer une «ékklèsia de femmes» afin qu'elles puissent accéder à un réel statut d'égalité. Le succès des femmes n'a d'égal que leur vigilance et leur détermination à ne pas céder dans les domaines qui sont d'actualité pour les femmes.

Ineffective social change organizations are the source of women's oppression that educator and researcher Sandra Laiken addresses. Her concern is that, without more effective feminist models, organizational patterns intended as alternatives to hierarchy within non-profit organizations sometimes have the unwanted outcomes of hidden and, therefore, problematic decision-making structures, conflict, and negative self-defeating media attention. Since she is using the example of a particular sexual assault treatment centre, publicly funded but administered by a volunteer board of directors, she is alerting us to oppression in the voluntary sector and the state as well as in families where domestic violence occurs. Her article outlines various program observations and suggestions she made as joint consultant to an urban sexual assault centre.

Coholic and Prévost locate oppression in perpetrators of abuse against children, and in a social system which frequently fails to effectively support and women who are survivors of childhood abuse. A generic community service agency in a Northern Ontario city which failed to identify and provide for the needs of women survivors of childhood abuse is the focus of this article. The authors write as social workers who introduced consciousness-raising and assertiveness training for women survivors of abuse. Their work as insiders, in conjunction with a progressive change in government policy, empowered women and transformed the larger agency within which they were situated.

Feminizing is one outcome of what Black women in Nova Scotia achieved through their work in Baptist churches. Bernice Moreau is a Caribbean-born feminist and religious activist who explored the lives of Black women in Nova Scotia in her doctoral research. She explains how women established ways for members of the Black community to throw off poverty and racism, and, in the process, they empowered themselves. The spiritual elements of their pathway to change were faith, hope, and love. As teachers of reading and leaders of community change, these women used their literacy skills and strong beliefs to educate church leaders, build schools, and improve the lives of Black people in Nova Scotia.

Monique Dumais

Sous le soleil féministe en théologie

Alors que des nuages de dénonciation
obscurcissaient le soleil patriarcal,
l'affirmation des femmes fait luire l'astre féministe.

Depuis plus de 20 ans, des chercheures féministes en théologie et en sciences religieuses se préoccupent d'investir un champ de réflexion qui est notoirement patriarcal, celui de la théologie[1]. Il est en effet apparu et devenu important que les femmes marquent des traces précises et visibles pour manifester qu'elles sont présentes et actives dans le monde de la pensée et de l'action religieuses. La féminisation d'institutions telles que la théologie chrétienne et l'Église catholique est un processus scientifique qui vise à créer et à promouvoir un espace d'expression, de valorisation et d'engagement du potentiel des femmes dans les domaines indiqués. Elle se manifeste, à mon avis, dans la présence d'écrits qui expriment explicitement la place, le rôle et les actions des femmes, dans leur quotidien comme dans leurs gestes exemplaires.

Il est clair que l'introduction du concept «expériences des femmes»[2] est venue interpeller fortement certaines disciplines scientifiques étudiant les systèmes religieux en montrant des aspects nettement misogynes dans les écrits sacrés, notamment ceux de la Bible[3], dans la tradition chrétienne, dans la fabrication d'un discours institutionnel et académique entièrement mâle. Les chercheures féministes ont alors tenté d'entreprendre l'exode nécessaire hors des territoires patriarcaux pour aller vers des terres nouvelles ouvertes aux expériences des femmes. La prise de parole des femmes tant dans la société que dans les églises marque le point de départ indispensable d'un périple au pays de la nouveauté. Au Québec, une «prise de conscience des femmes dans l'Église donne lieu à des prises de parole collectives qui varient en fonction d'analyses plus ou moins radicales et de stratégies d'actions diverses» (Melançon, 1989 : 17).

Des voix de femmes se sont déjà fait entendre; nos mères dans la foi ont témoigné. La bien-aimée du Cantique des Cantiques, Phoebée et les femmes de la Bible, Héloïse, Julienne de Norwich, Hildegarde de Bingen, Thérèse d'Avila et les femmes mystiques, Elisabeth Cady Stanton et les chercheures ont tracé des voies; il s'agit de les retrouver, de les rendre visibles dans le désert de la société contemporaine pour que d'autres femmes puissent les suivre et se réjouir avec toutes celles qui reviennent d'exil.

En effet, il est temps de sortir de l'invisibilité[4]. Des groupes de femmes se sont formés pour étudier la situation des femmes dans le domaine des religions. Dès 1972, surgissent dans les universités américaines, des regroupements de femmes (*women's caucus*), par exemple, à Harvard Divinity School[5]. En 1988, on a mis sur pied le Centre canadien de recherches sur femmes et religions[6], sous la direction de Elisabeth J. Lacelle. Ce Centre, localisé à l'Université d'Ottawa, a vu le jour après dix ans de travaux menés par le Groupe d'études interdisciplinaires sur femmes et religions au Canada du Centre de documentation et de nombreuses recherches à son Département de sciences religieuses. En France, la Faculté de théologie de Lyon, conjointement avec l'association Femmes et Hommes dans l'Église, dispose depuis 1986 d'un centre de recherche et de documentation sur les femmes et le christianisme[7]. Signalons l'existence de l'Association européenne des femmes pour la recherche théologique; ce regroupement tenait en septembre 1989 son troisième congrès à Arnoldsheim, République fédérale allemande, sur les images de Dieu et leur rapport à la critique féministe.

Je tenterai donc de mettre en évidence — sous le soleil — de quelle manière des théologiennes féministes, en faisant entendre leurs voix, ont réussi à tracer des routes bien marquées et significatives pour la pensée et l'action dans le domaine religieux afin d'assurer une mise en évidence fructueuse de leurs travaux. Dans une première étape, j'indiquerai que les expériences des femmes signalent le point de départ des parcours de la théologisation des féministes. Dans une deuxième étape, je montrerai la dimension critique, dénonciatrice, des discours théologiques féministes. Dans une troisième étape, je soulignerai la portée créatrice de ces discours.

Entrée en vigueur des expériences des femmes

Christ avait déjà indiqué en 1977 que «l'expérience devenait une nouvelle norme pour la théologie» (204), pour les chercheures féministes, qu'elles soient considérées réformistes ou révolutionnaires. Schüssler Fiorenza l'a confirmé hautement en 1990 au colloque international de Concilium: «La théologie féministe commence par une réflexion critique sur l'expérience et une analyse systématique de cette même expérience. Elle cherche à écrire la théologie à partir de nos expériences et en faisant retour à nos expériences» (1986 : 21). Cette nécessité de passer par les expériences des femmes m'avait déjà marquée et j'affirmais :

> Dans le domaine de la tradition judéo-chrétienne, de la science théologique, les femmes n'ont pas bénéficié de la possibilité de l'expression directe de la communication de

leurs propres expériences. Elles ont dû se fier aux scribes masculins de leur temps, à une hiérarchie masculine pour découvrir ce qu'elles vivaient dans tout leur être et comment Dieu se révélait en elles et par elles. Des femmes ayant accédé plus nombreuses aux outils de la connaissance et de l'expression ne peuvent plus tolérer cette dépossession de leur propre vécu et se lancent dans la découverte, l'expérimentation et le dévoilement (pour ne pas dire révélation — lever le voile) de leurs propres expériences (Dumais, 1980 : 39).

Dickey (1990) et Leonard (1990), deux théologiennes canadiennes, confirment ce recours aux expériences des femmes. La première tente de préciser ce qu'elle entend par «expériences des femmes». «L'expérience des femmes est la multiplicité de choses que les femmes expérimentent à la fois individuellement et collectivement» (Dickey, 1990 : 49). Elle indique par la suite cinq façons de parler au sujet des expériences des femmes : expérience du corps, expérience socialisée (selon ce que la culture apprend aux femmes), expérience féministe, expérience historique et expériences individuelles (53).

Quant à Leonard, elle soutient que «l'expérience a toujours été utilisée en théologie, même si sa fonction n'a pas toujours été reconnue» (1990 : 143). Cependant, elle souligne qu'un profond changement s'est manifesté dans l'utilisation de l'expérience comme source de la théologie et elle a entraîné «la correction de préjugés (biais). Désormais les expériences autrefois ignorées constituent un lieu de référence (source) pour la réflexion théologique» (146). C'est reconnaître qu'«aucune théologie ne peut revendiquer l'universalité, que toutes les théologies sont politiques, formées par leur propre contexte» (146). À partir de cette nouvelle épistémologie, les expériences des femmes deviennent une importante source pour la théologie; elles sont alors considérées comme l'expérience de l'oppression dans ses multiples formes, incluant les expériences de harcèlement sexuel et de violence, l'expérience d'être une fille, une sœur, une mère, l'expérience d'avoir un corps de femme, avec ses propres rythmes avec les menstruations et la ménopause, l'expérience de la conscientisation croissante de la sororité avec les femmes de partout. Toutes ces expériences sont reconnues comme le lieu du divin et une source d'inspiration pour la théologie (Leonard, 1990).

Pour ma part, ce recours aux expériences des femmes, particulièrement à la réappropriation du corps, m'a conduite à donner une interprétation des paroles de la consécration eucharistique : «ceci est mon corps, ceci est mon sang». Ainsi, j'ai affirmé comment les femmes peuvent expérimenter le «ceci est mon corps» à travers les grandeurs et les limites de leur propre corps, les expériences du corps de l'enfant naissant, du rapprochement avec le corps de l'être bien-aimé. Quant «au ceci est mon sang», il s'interprète aisément pour les femmes comme le sang menstruel, le sang de l'accouchement ainsi que le sang de toute blessure. Cependant, l'association du sang sauveur avec celui des femmes ne va pas de soi, car le *Livre du Lévitique* indique que le sang des règles est un sang impur. Il m'a donc fallu faire une nouvelle interprétation : «Présente à son sang, la femme ressent le versement du sang avec sa fluidité, sa chaleur, sa lourdeur, la valeur du sang, quoi ! Du sang de Jésus au sang menstruel des femmes peut s'établir un cycle rédempteur, régénérateur et porteur de vie» (Dumais, 1983 : 66)[8].

La prise en considération des expériences des femmes constitue une étape incontournable dans l'avènement d'une théologie féministe (Dumais, 1995a) pour que l'herméneutique et l'épistémologie trouvent des pistes nouvelles dans une science déjà constituée dans un système patriarcal. Ainsi s'affirme de façon inéluctable la féminisation de l'institution du savoir qu'est la théologie.

Dimension critique, dénonciatrice

La mise en place des expériences des femmes manifeste déjà l'aspect critique souvent dénonciateur des discours théologiques féministes. Ceux-ci veulent démasquer l'emprise d'une tradition lourdement mâle, voire patriarcale, qui s'affiche dans les discours et les pratiques religieuses. Les femmes s'y perçoivent facilement dans une situation d'enfermement, d'appropriation qui se confond assez souvent avec le refus. Daly (1985), une des penseures américaines les plus critiques vis-à-vis la tradition chrétienne, a tracé une voie pour dénoncer les aspects les plus opprimants pour les femmes. Elle a montré comment les hommes ont exercé un contrôle sur le corps des femmes, comment ils les ont enfermées dans leur définition à eux et comment ils ont sacralisé leur pouvoir pour mieux assurer leur domination. Les expériences féministes des femmes, comme le souligne Dickey (1990), contribuent à remettre en question le statu quo de la théologie traditionnelle. Elles conduisent à se demander si les femmes sont incluses ou non dans les formulations théologiques, si elles sont intégrées dans la recherche anthropologique, soit en étant consultées, soit en étant les auteures des travaux de recherche.

La dénonciation d'un patrimoine religieux uniquement patriarcal — n'est-ce pas le sens du mot «patrimoine» qui n'inclut pas le «matrimoine»? — s'est traduite de façon spectaculaire au Québec par une œuvre dramatique, *Les fées ont soif* de Boucher (1978). Cette pièce de théâtre constitue une critique très vive de l'influence du culte marial tel qu'il a été propagé par des hommes du sacré, des célibataires mâles. L'auteure démontre comment le modèle de Marie, représenté par la statue, a contribué à présenter les femmes à la fois comme des ménagères soumises à leur mari et à leurs enfants, sans une identité bien à elles, et comme des prostituées passives, toujours disponibles pour répondre aux désirs des hommes.

La Statue

Moi, je suis une image. Je suis un portrait.
J'ai les deux pieds dans le plâtre.
Je suis la reine du néant, je suis la porte sur le vide.
Je suis le mariage blanc des prêtres.
Je suis la moutonne blanche jamais tondue.
Je suis l'étoile des amers.
Je suis le rêve de l'eau de Javel.
Je suis le miroir de l'injustice. Je suis le siège de l'esclavage. Je suis le
*   vase sacré introuvable.*
Je suis l'obscurité de l'ignorance.
Je suis la perte blanche et sans profit de toutes les femmes.
Je suis le secours des imbéciles. Je suis le refuge des inutiles.
Je suis l'outil des impuissances.
Je suis le symbole pourri de l'abnégation pourrie.
Je suis un silence plus opprimant et plus oppressant que toutes les paroles.
Je suis le carcan des jaloux de la chair.
Je suis l'image imaginée. Je suis celle qui n'a pas de corps.
Je suis celle qui ne saigne jamais (Boucher, 1978 : 91).

La tâche dénonciatrice de la théologie féministe constitue un premier moment important qui ne peut être escamoté. Il faut montrer les distorsions, les perversions et les oppressions pour mieux voir ce dont nous devons être délivrés, autant les hommes que les femmes. La féminisation de la théologie peut maintenant transparaître dans toutes ses dimensions créatrices.

Dimension créatrice

Un autre moment important pour tout discours théologique féministe, c'est celui de la création. Le recours aux expériences des femmes, en autant qu'elles soient conscientisées et partagées, «fournit de nouveaux modèles, de nouvelles questions et une nouvelle évidence pour la théologie» (Dickey, 1990 : 61). Il faut sortir du silence qui pèse lourdement sur les femmes et se livrer audacieusement à un travail d'innovation. Schüssler Fiorenza, dans *En mémoire d'elle*, évoque le «silence» qui pèse lourdement sur les femmes et qu'il faut rompre en vue d'entreprendre une reconstitution théologique féministe des origines chrétiennes.

Si le silence qui règne à propos de l'expérience historique et théologique des femmes et de leur contribution aux débuts du mouvement chrétien est engendré par les textes historiques et les publications théologiques, nous devons alors trouver le moyen de rompre le silence des textes et de tirer parti de l'historiographie et de la théologie androcentriques. Plutôt que de voir dans le texte un reflet exact de la réalité dont il parle, nous devons chercher des pistes et des allusions qui donnent des indications sur la réalité à propos de laquelle le texte reste silencieux. Plutôt que de prendre les textes androcentriques comme des «données» qui informent et des *rapports* précis, nous devons lire leurs «silences» comme une preuve et un signe de cette réalité dont ils ne parlent pas. Plutôt que de rejeter l'argument du silence comme un argument historique valable, nous devons apprendre à lire les silences des textes androcentriques de telle manière qu'ils nous fournissent des «pistes» qui nous permettent de rejoindre la réalité égalitaire du mouvement chrétien primitif (Schüssler Fiorenza, 1986: 79).

Le travail de création peut s'exercer de différentes manières; je signalerai celle de la réécriture des textes bibliques, puis celle de la mise en place d'une symbolique nouvelle ou réinterprétée. J'ai eu l'occasion d'expérimenter la réécriture des textes bibliques dans la collective *L'autre Parole*[9]. Il s'agit de prendre un texte biblique, de le repenser à travers nos expériences de femmes et de l'écrire dans une nouvelle version. La réécriture des Béatitudes en suivant la structure de Luc 6, 20-25, «Bienheureux… malheureux» a permis de cerner un certain nombre de libérations et d'oppressions vécues par les femmes. Voici, à titre d'exemples, quelques-unes de ces béatitudes[10], avec la mise en parallèle du texte de la Bible[11].

L'autre Parole	*Évangile selon saint Luc, ch. 6, v. 20-26*
Heureuses celles qui travaillent à pétrir le pain de l'autonomie, de l'égalité, de la solidarité,	v. 20 Heureux, vous les pauvres; le Royaume de Dieu est à vous,
Ensemble, elles nourriront la terre.	v. 21 Heureux, vous qui avez faim maintenant : vous serez rassasiés.
Malheureuses celles qui sont facilement rassasiées des miettes qui tombent de la table sacrée,	v. 25 Malheureux, vous qui êtes repus maintenant : vous aurez faim.

Elles paralysent la croissance de l'Église.

Heureuses les femmes audacieusement éprises de l'Évangile de Jésus-Christ qui ont le courage d'y être fidèles plus qu'en verbe ou en pensée, mais en actes véritablement.

Malheureuses celles qui dissocient leurs pensées, le cœur et les actes car elles ternissent la lumière de l'Évangile.

Malheureuses celles qui se taisent pour «avoir la paix»,

Car elles entretiennent l'oppression.

Heureuses les victimes du pouvoir patriarcal qui trouvent dans la violence qu'elles ressentent la force de bâtir la paix.

Heureuses vous les femmes bafouées à cause de vos prises de parole,

Par votre ténacité, la libération se construit.

Malheureuses serez-vous lorsque vous vous laisserez séduire par un discours qui vous dépossédera du sens de votre lutte.

v. 22 Heureux êtes-vous lorsque les hommes vous haïssent, lorsqu'ils vous rejettent, et qu'ils insultent et proscrivent votre nom comme infâme, à cause du Fils de l'homme.

v. 23 Réjouissez-vous ce jour-là et bondissez de joie, car voici, votre récompense est grande dans le ciel; c'est en effet de la même manière que leurs pères traitaient les prophètes.

v. 24 Mais, malheureux, vous les riches, vous tenez votre consolation.

v. 25 Malheureux, vous qui riez maintenant : vous serez dans le deuil et vous pleurerez.

v. 26 Malheureux êtes-vous lorsque tous les hommes disent du bien de vous : c'est en effet de la même manière que leurs pères traitaient les faux prophètes.

Les récits de la création de la Genèse ont été aussi revus par la collective *L'autre Parole*. Les femmes n'ont-elles pas quelque chose à dire sur les débuts du monde, alors que plusieurs d'entre elles connaissent des grossesses et donnent naissance? Il y a deux récits de la création dans la Genèse; nous, nous en avons esquissé quatre selon notre générosité coutumière. Je ne retranscris que l'un[12] de ces quatre récits avec, en parallèle, le texte de la Bible[13].

L'autre Parole	*La Genèse, chap. 1, v. 1-27*
À l'origine est l'Amour cette énergie créatrice cette lumière jaillissante qui anime des femmes, des hommes libres.	v. 1 Lorsque Dieu commença la création du ciel et de la terre, la terre était déserte et vide, et la ténèbre à la surface de l'abîme; le souffle de Dieu planait à la surface des eaux.
	v. 3 et Dieu dit : «Que la lumière soit! Et la lumière fut».
Mais cet amour s'est obscurci, s'est détérioré dans des relations de domination entre les humains, entre les hommes et les femmes.	v. 27 Dieu créa l'homme à son image, à l'image de Dieu il le créa, mâle et femelle il les créa.
Chaque lutte pour recouvrer notre dignité de femme, pour modeler notre identité, pour déployer notre autonomie, annonce une aube nouvelle et ouvre un jardin tout rempli d'arbres chargés des fruits de la plénitude.	(Le deuxième récit, chap. 2, v. 4 à chap. 3, v. 24, raconte la création de l'homme et de la femme, leur faute commune et l'expulsion hors du jardin d'Éden.)

Les symboliques ont besoin d'être repensées et réinventées pour mieux inclure les expériences des femmes et des hommes. La symbolique phallique doit être remise en question; il importe de trouver des voies autres que celles de la compétition, de la rivalité. L'exploration de nouvelles avenues n'est pas si simple. Sur le plan des formes, faut-il privilégier la rondeur plutôt que la hauteur? L'observation de statuettes représentant des déesses-mères nous y inviterait. Une exposition «Idoles» à la galerie *À la reine Margot*, à Paris, du 22 novembre 1990 au 28 février 1991, a mis en valeur cette variété de statuettes qui se sont multipliées vers le troisième millénaire :

> en ces grottes de notre préhistoire, apparaît à Lespugne une «idole» féminine, toute gonflée de multiples fécondités, avec l'amorce de sinuosités rétrécissant le sommet de la tête et le bas des jambes, comme plus tard dans les idoles d'Amlash ou des Cyclades. (…) La plupart de nos idoles évoquent la féminité, par des courbes porteuses de vie ou de lait nourricier» (Lewis-Rodis, 1990 : 4).

La représentation de Dieu est en cause. Dans nos traditions juive, islamique et chrétienne, Dieu est surtout perçu selon des attributs mâles, le monothéisme s'étant érigé en combattant les divinités féminines. Dans tous les écrits qu'elle a consacrés à l'étude des documents primitifs, Stone (1979) a su dénoncer la répression qui a sévi contre toutes indications culturelles de la Grande Déesse. Nous nous sentons maintenant la responsabilité de nous demander : «Comment sortir Dieu du ghetto masculin?» (Dumais, 1989). Déjà des images de Dieu comme une femme se trouvent dans l'Un et l'Autre Testament (belle expression de Beauchamp[14]); il s'agit de leur redonner leur dynamisme vital en même temps que d'élargir leur capacité signifiante. Ramey Mollenkott (1983) a fait un tour remarquable des différentes expressions de Dieu au féminin dans la Bible. D'autres théologiennes féministes, comme Radford Ruether (1987) et Schüssler Fiorenza (1986), ont travaillé «à rendre possible une appropriation de la figure de Jésus de Nazareth qui soit positive pour les femmes» (Melançon, 1990 : 197). Un retour aux sources, au Jésus des Synoptiques, permet de voir qu'il y a eu des altérations importantes dans la tradition : Jésus n'a pas prôné un messianisme davidique, il se situe dans le courant prophétique, dénonçant toute domination sur les êtres humains. Si l'avènement du salut en Jésus était repensé à travers les expériences des femmes, nous pourrions prendre au sérieux que «la souffrance féminine puisse être le lieu de révélation du divin et le paradigme du salut» (Melançon, 1990 : 206). Ainsi, Radford Ruether rapporte le témoignage d'une femme violée qui a expérimenté, à travers l'agonie qu'elle a vécue, la vision du «Christ comme une femme crucifiée» (1987 : 146-147).

Des symboles déjà utilisés, tels que l'eau, la terre, le lait, le miel et les produits de la terre, peuvent être réinvestis d'une manière autre, dans leur force vitale et leur puissance évocatrice à travers les expériences des femmes. Les symboles ont des possibilités multiples de signifier; les femmes sont donc invitées à contribuer à cette transmission de sens.

Conclusion

Un soleil nouveau a resplendi grâce aux paroles
des femmes; une vitalité inédite s'annonce.

Les réflexions et les argumentations des féministes sont entrées dans le champ théologique pour y rester, espérons-le. Elles apportent des transformations importantes dans ce domaine de la pensée qui a été surtout monopolisé par des ecclésiastiques de sexe masculin. Elles ont créé leur espace d'expression : les ouvrages scientifiques sur les femmes et la religion ne cessent de s'accroître, les bibliographies en témoignent largement[15].

Un changement important de paradigme s'est amorcé dans les études contemporaines de la religion à la fois en théologie et dans les études religieuses, affirme King (1995). Il remet en question les prétentions de la connaissance à l'universalité, à l'objectivité et à la neutralité telles que proposées par des millénaires de culture patriarcale. Pour sa part, Veillette (1995) conclut que les femmes, en passant de l'occultation de leur discours à une présence d'influence, «changent la dynamique du champ religieux» (248). Les femmes ont donc osé, de façon audacieuse, parfois intempestive, se frayer des routes. Même si leurs voix sont de plus en plus nombreuses et variées, force est de constater que leur influence n'est pas devenue majeure. Seules la ténacité et la persévérance des femmes pourront assurer l'avènement de voies nouvelles dans l'academia qui a encore des allures majoritairement masculines.

Du côté de l'Église, une étude menée sur les femmes et le pouvoir dans l'Église catholique au Québec (Caron, 1991) a montré que, malgré leur présence très active dans les différentes tâches ecclésiales, les femmes ne participent pas réellement au pouvoir. Celles-ci se limitent souvent à des revendications, qui proviennent surtout de quelques groupes davantage conscientisés et politisés (Caron, 1991)[16]. La voie de salut semble résider particulièrement dans le regroupement des femmes et dans leur communion avec l'ensemble des femmes. En effet, il apparaît que les femmes, en dépit même de leurs qualifications, ne pourront accéder à un réel statut d'égalité dans l'Église que dans la mesure où elles pourront se regrouper entre elles et en communion avec l'ensemble des femmes qui représentent une proportion toujours plus importante des membres actifs de cette institution pour constituer une «ekklèsia des femmes», au sens où l'entend Schüssler Fiorenza (1986 : 250).

Le succès de la féminisation ne sera durable qu'en autant que s'exercera une vigilance constante sur les acquis dans les transformations des discours théologiques et sur les avancées dans les communautés ecclésiales. Il implique aussi une détermination à ne pas céder sur les revendications des femmes qui sont toujours d'une grande actualité.

Quand on parle d'une «synergie entre femmes et religion», c'est toujours en incluant une grande espérance, car les succès demeurent très relatifs : «Argumentations, recherches, publications, colloques, célébrations, engagements, forment un cercle dynamique qui devrait s'inscrire de façon permanente dans les traditions religieuses» (Dumais, 1995b : 64). Ainsi, dans sa *Lettre aux femmes du monde entier*, à l'occasion de la quatrième Conférence mondiale sur les femmes à Beijing, Jean-Paul II rend hommage aux femmes pour leurs contributions qui ne sont pas inférieures à celles des hommes, mais dans des conditions souvent plus difficiles, et il exprime son regret pour la «responsabilité objective de nombreux fils de l'Église» qui a pu entraîner la marginalisation et l'asservissement des femmes[17]. Cette *Lettre* a soulevé diverses réactions chez les chercheures préoccupées de l'avancement des femmes dans l'Église; les quelques pas positifs apparaissent rapidement comme des moyens de modérer les élans des femmes; donc, ils sont jugés non satisfaisants (Couture, 1995 : 11). Il n'en demeure pas moins que le mouvement de reconnaissance effective et efficace de la participation des femmes en théologie et dans l'Église semble enclenché et devrait se poursuivre dans les différentes sphères sociales et ecclésiales.

Bibliographie

Boucher, Denise (1978), *Les fées ont soif*, Montréal, Intermède.

Caron, Anita (collectif sous la dir. de) (1991), *Femmes et pouvoir dans l'Église*, Montréal, VLB, coll. Études québécoises.

Christ, Carol (1977), «The new feminist theology: A review of the literature», *Religious Studies Review*, vol. 3, no. 4, 203-212.

Couture, Denise (sous la direction de) (1995), *Les femmes et l'Église suivi de Lettre du pape Jean-Paul II aux femmes*, Montréal, Fides, (Débats de l'Église).

Daly, Mary (1985), *Beyond God the Father: Toward a Philosophy of Women's Liberation*, Boston, Beacon Press.

Davis Finson, Shelley (1991), *Women and Religion: Bibliographic Guide to Christian Feminist Liberation Theology*, Toronto, University of Toronto.

Dickey Young, Pamela (1990), *Feminist Theology/Christian Theology*, Minneapolis, Fortress Press. Les extraits sont traduits par Monique Dumais.

Dumais, Monique (1980), «Expériences des femmes et théologie», *Women as Persons. La femme en tant que personne, Resources for Feminist Research/Documentation sur la recherche féministe*, Fall 1980, 39-42.

Dumais, Monique (1983), «Femmes faites chair», dans *La femme, son corps, la religion*, sous la dir. de Elisabeth J. Lacelle, 52-70, Montréal, Bellarmin (Femmes et Religions, 2).

Dumais, Monique (1989), «Sortir Dieu du ghetto masculin», *Souffles de femmes. Lectures féministes de la religion*, sous la dir. de Monique Dumais et Marie-Andrée Roy, 135-146, Montréal, Éditions Paulines.

Dumais, Monique (1995a), «Le concept «expériences des femmes» dans l'avènement d'une théologie féministe», dans *Gender, Genre and Religion. Feminist Reflections*, sous la dir. de Morny Joy et Eva K. Neumaier-Dargyay, 83-99, Waterloo, Wilfrid Laurier University Press for the Calgary Institute for the Humanities.

Dumais, Monique (1995b), «Synergie : femmes et religion au Québec depuis 1970», *Religiologiques*, no 11, printemps, 51-64.

King, Ursula (1995) (ed.), «Introduction and the Study of Religion», dans *Religion and Gender*, 31-38, Oxford UK and Cambridge USA, Blackwell.

Leonard, Ellen (1990), «Experience as a source for theology: A Canadian and feminist perspective», *Studies in religion/Sciences religieuses*, vol. 19, no 2, 143-162. Les extraits sont traduits par Monique Dumais.

Lewis-Rodis, Geneviève (1990), *Idoles. Au commencement était l'image*, Paris, À la reine Margot.

Melançon, Louise (1989), «La prise de parole des femmes dans l'Église», dans *Souffles de femmes. Lectures féministes de la religion*, sous la dir. de Monique Dumais et Marie-Andrée Roy, 15-27, Montréal, Éditions Paulines.

Melançon, Louise (1990), «Quelle figure du Christ pour une théologie non-sexiste?» dans *Jésus Christ universel?* sous la dir. de Jean-Claude Petit et Jean-Claude Breton, 197-208, (Héritage et projet, 44), Montréal, Fides.

Radford Ruether, Rosemary (1987), «Feminism and Jewish-Christian Dialogue», dans *The Myth of Christian Uniqueness. Toward a Pluralistic Theology of Religions*, sous la dir. de J. Stick et P.F. Knitter, 140-147, New York, Orbis Books.

Ramey Mollenkott, Virginia (1983), *The Divine Feminine. The Biblical Imagery of God as Female*, New York, Crossroad.

Schüssler Fiorenza, Elisabeth (1986), *En mémoire d'elle. Essai de reconstruction des origines chrétiennes selon la théologie féministe*, Traduction de In Memory of Her par Marcelline Brun, Paris, Cerf.

Stone, Merlin (1976), *The Paradise Papers*, London, Virago Ltd, Traduction en français (1979) sous le titre *Quand Dieu était femme*, Montréal, L'Étincelle.

Veillette, Denise (dir., de publ.) (1995), *Femmes et religions*, collection Études sur les femmes et la religion/Studies in women and religion, no 1, Corporation canadienne des sciences religieuses/Canadian Corporation for Studies in Religion, Québec, Presses de l'Université Laval.

Notes

1. Monique Dumais est professeure de théologie et d'éthique à l'Université du Québec à Rimouski et a mené depuis 20 ans des recherches sur les femmes et la religion ainsi que sur l'éthique dans les discours féministes. Elle a publié, avec Marie-Andrée Roy, *Souffles de femmes* (1989), puis *Lectures féministes de la religion* (1992), *Les droits des femmes* (1992) et *Femmes et pauvreté* (1998) (Montréal, Médiaspaul, coll. Interpellations).

2. Une subvention de recherche du Conseil de recherche en sciences humaines du Canada m'a permis d'explorer l'utilisation du concept «expériences des femmes» en théologie. L'Institut canadien de recherches sur les femmes a publié, en 1993, *Diversité des utilisations féministes du concept expériences des femmes en sciences religieuses*, Ottawa, Les Documents de l'ICREF/The CRIAW Papers, no 32.

3. Je me réfère surtout aux traditions juive et chrétienne.

4. Voir à ce sujet, «Les femmes invisibles dans la théologie et dans l'Église», *Concilium*, no 202 (1985).

5. Voir à ce sujet le document «Ten Years of Women's Studies at HDS», *Harvard Divinity Bulletin*, vol. XIV, no. 2 (déc. 1983-jan. 1984).

6. Le Centre canadien de recherches sur les femmes et les religions publie une *Lettre* d'information bilingue que l'on peut obtenir en écrivant à : Sciences religieuses, 177, Waller, Ottawa, Ontario, K1N 6N5, Canada.

7. Femmes et christianisme, Faculté de théologie, 25, rue du Plat - F-69002 Lyon, France.

8. Luce Irigaray a traité du «Ceci est mon corps, ceci est mon sang» dans *La croyance même*. Paris, Galilée, 1983.

9. La collective *L'autre Parole*, créée au Québec en 1976, regroupe des femmes qui se définissent comme chrétiennes et féministes. Elle publie une revue quatre fois par année, tient un colloque annuel et fête en 1996 son vingtième anniversaire d'existence. J'ai le bonheur d'être une des quatre cofondatrices.

10. *L'autre Parole*, no 22 (octobre 1983).

11. Traduction œcuménique de la Bible, *La Bible*. Paris, Cerf, 1989.

12. *L'autre Parole*, no 31 (décembre 1986).

13. Traduction œcuménique de la Bible. À noter qu'il est difficile de suivre exactement le texte.

14. Voir à ce sujet, Paul Beauchamp, *L'Un et l'Autre Testament*. Essai de lecture. Paris, Seuil, 1979. Expression découverte grâce à Paul Ricoeur, *Soi-même comme un autre*. Paris, Seuil, 1990, p. 36.

15. Dans le livre publié sous la direction de Denise Veillette (1995), nous trouvons 1 328 orientations bibliographiques sur le sujet en titre. Soulignons également le travail de référence bibliographique de Ursula King (1995).

16. Voir Caron (1991). Notons qu'il existe au Québec un regroupement Femmes et ministères qui s'intéresse spécifiquement à la participation des femmes dans l'Église.

17. *Lettre du pape Jean-Paul II aux femmes*, 29 juin 1995.

Elsy Gagné

Réflexion sur les méthodes et la féminisation de l'institution médicale

Dans le domaine de la santé, le développement des méthodes de recherche est un phénomène dont les implications économiques, politiques et sociales sont telles qu'il a, jusqu'à présent, suscité des débats intéressants et passionnés. La majorité des écrits portant sur le sujet repose essentiellement sur une conception technique de la science et de ses méthodes. Les chercheurs ne sont concernés que par les effets physiques des traitements mis en œuvre. Il ne faut donc pas s'étonner que ces analyses, s'appuyant sur des techniques de recherche objectives, attribuent au progrès scientifique une place prépondérante parmi les nombreux facteurs de succès. Mais évoquer le progrès n'a de sens véritable que si l'on se réfère à un changement relatif dans la prise en charge individuelle de sa maladie et dans l'autonomie des ex-patientes dans un contexte non-institutionnel. Et, c'est là le point faible des méthodes quantitatives dominantes basées sur des techniques et des tests statistiques. En effet, on ne dispose pas suffisamment d'instruments qualitatifs pour bien mesurer les transformations relatives à la prise en charge de la santé et du dépassement individuel dans un contexte non-institutionnel. Pour disposer de tels instruments, il importe alors de féminiser la pensée logique de l'institution médicale. Une réflexion critique et l'utilisation de nouvelles méthodes qualitatives permettraient la compréhension et l'explication des effets globaux du traitement médical ou chirurgical et des moyens utilisés pour prévenir le retour de la maladie.

Cet article décrit en quelque sorte une méthode qualitative, une approche, une réflexion, une façon de faire et de penser les mots et les choses qui sont révélatrices d'un autre versant : la signification possible attribuée au cancer du sein vécu par un groupe de Franco-Manitobaines qui adhèrent à leur culture. En somme, il s'agit de décrire une approche de recherche adaptée à l'étude de problématiques qui rejoignent un groupe de femmes et leurs réflexions face au choix proposé par l'institution médicale. Nous verrons comment une telle approche envisage le quotidien, le vécu, le privé, la douleur, le déchirement, l'isolement, la peur, l'incapacité d'exprimer une frustration, l'effet post-opératoire dans leur contexte social plus large. Grâce à cette approche méthodologique, nous verrons qu'il est possible de parler avec les femmes et de les écouter pour mieux comprendre leur discours sur les effets quotidiens du post-traitement institutionnel. L'objectif de ce travail de réflexion montre l'effet positif de l'approche qualitative dans le domaine de la santé communautaire et les multiples informations qui peuvent en découler.

Pour réaliser un tel objectif, nous présenterons d'abord les critères de l'approche traditionnelle de recherche et sa façon de traiter les questions médicales et sociales. Ce faisant, nous préciserons les forces politiques et idéologiques qui soutiennent l'approche traditionnelle dominante, laquelle manifeste encore aujourd'hui une forte résistance à l'égard d'autres approches méthodologiques. Ensuite, nous établirons certains critères de la recherche qualitative utilisés dans le domaine de la santé communautaire et nous montrerons leur intérêt pour les chercheurs et les chercheures dans le domaine de la santé. Finalement, nous illustrerons les mérites de cette approche, en nous appuyant sur une technique qualitative particulière, celle des récits de vie, et nous soulignerons son importance.

Méthodes de recherche et résistance au changement

Bien que les cours de méthodologie soient quelquefois ennuyeux aux yeux de la population estudiantine, les méthodes de recherche sont toujours très populaires. Elles sont un passage obligé. Dans la plupart des universités canadiennes, on forme les étudiants à bien manipuler les méthodes pour mieux expliquer le «social». On étudie les méthodes quantitatives avec leur lot de données chiffrées, l'ordre des variables, les techniques statistiques, les hypothèses et leurs tests d'inférence, la courbe normale, la marge d'erreur, etc. Cette abondance d'informations peut, quelquefois, en dérouter plus d'un et finir par embrouiller les idées. Malgré tout, on retient que l'administration informatisée d'un questionnaire à un échantillon représentatif permet l'inférence statistique des résultats, dernière étape d'un long processus au cours duquel on vérifie les hypothèses élaborées au début de la recherche. Il s'agit là d'une logique développée et intégrée par les universitaires, lesquels promeuvent avec force le discours formel et sans contredit les bienfaits des méthodes quantitatives.

Par «social», il faut entendre un groupe d'individus conçu comme une réalité bien distincte. Or, parler du social sous l'angle des méthodes quantitatives conduit trop souvent à établir la répartition des individus dans la société selon des variables définies telles le sexe, la race, l'âge, l'orientation sexuelle, les classes sociales, la division du travail et ses effets sur les individus, etc. Toujours dans la perspective des méthodes quantitatives, lorsque le social est appréhendé sous l'angle des significations d'un événement, d'une situation, d'une conduite, la réflexion méthodologique qui s'ensuit porte sur le traitement médical ou chirurgical dont les effets auront été vérifiés par des tests statistiques bien définis et dont le cumul des résultats publiés viennent renforcer le discours dominant de ces mêmes méthodes. Or, il faut le dire, les méthodes et les techniques de recherche sont des outils permettant à la science de comprendre davantage le fonctionnement du corps social. La science doit donc avoir une conscience et mesurer l'importance de l'action communautaire. C'est grâce à l'usage des méthodes et à leur application que la science et la technologie dans le domaine médical sont devenues ce qu'elles sont aujourd'hui et ont un tel effet sur le mode de pensée de la société.

Bien que la plupart des méthodes quantitatives gagnent en puissance explicative par le biais de l'informatisation, elles perdent, par leur nature même, un certain nombre d'informations. Cette perte est attribuable, entre autres, à l'exclusion de variables déterminantes qui sont difficilement mesurables ou, encore, qui n'ont aucune raison de l'être à cause du discours dont elles sont porteuses. Songeons ici à l'effet quotidien de la marque corporelle ou du stigmate laissé à la suite de l'ablation du sein, au rejet de la féminité, à l'isolement de la femme, au deuil vécu par cette perte, à la nouvelle façon de s'habiller pour cacher son imperfection corporelle, etc. Il arrive donc que certaines informations liées aux effets dévastateurs de traitements chirurgicaux soient évacuées et deviennent dénuées de sens. Dans l'ensemble, les méthodes quantitatives ne rendent pas toujours compte avec exactitude de la multiplicité et de la complexité des dynamismes sociaux qui sont en jeu lors de la période post-opératoire hors de l'institution hospitalière. Dit autrement, plusieurs chercheures ayant été longtemps sous l'influence du positivisme logique se sont rendu compte, à tort ou à raison, que le modèle statistique risque parfois de n'être que prédictif. Il peut conduire à des conclusions souvent partielles et décontextualisées. Un tel modèle fait abstraction des modifications des structures de groupe ou des représentations de la maladie, lesquelles ne peuvent s'observer qu'à petite échelle (Rivière, 1978 : 159).

Trop souvent, les spécialistes des sciences sociales, sous l'influence des missionnaires influents et acharnés du positivisme logique, supposent qu'il n'y a de science «véritable» et objective que celle qui repose sur le savoir quantitatif. Celui-ci remplace alors le savoir qualitatif, lequel est rabattu au rang de l'expression du «gros bon sens». Mais lorsqu'on manipule les méthodes quantitatives basées sur une multitude de tests statistiques et qu'on les applique à des groupes précis, la situation peut être bien différente. La science de la santé dépend non seulement du savoir quantitatif, mais également du savoir qualitatif qui puise ses premières formulation dans le gros bon sens. Certes, dans les meilleures conditions, le savoir qualitatif cherche à dépasser ce stade par un travail de construction objective théorique élaboré à partir des données obtenues auprès des sujets étudiés (Cook et Reichardt, 1979: 50). Nous n'avons plus besoin de dire et de redire encore une fois que les méthodes qualitatives sont reconnues et qu'elles méritent leurs lettres de noblesse. Nous n'avons plus besoin de démontrer que leur utilisation est nécessaire pour mieux comprendre le social et, par ricochet, l'expliquer plus justement. Il n'y a pas de doute que les méthodes qualitatives vont de pair avec le savoir médical. Incontestablement, elles offrent un complément d'informations à des recherches médicales qui, malgré les avancées réalisées en ce domaine, sont trop souvent réduites aux seules dimensions techniques. En ce sens, les méthodes qualitatives permettent d'appréhender les besoins de femmes aux prises avec les conséquences désastreuses de cet ennemi acharné qu'est le cancer du sein et d'y répondre plus adéquatement. Les conséquences de cette maladie et de son traitement institutionnel se mesurent aux marques sur le corps des femmes et aux handicaps que cela peut représenter dans leur vie quotidienne.

Aujourd'hui, dans les établissements universitaires, on enseigne un peu plus les méthodes qualitatives. À tout le moins, on en souffle un mot ou deux dans divers cours pour sensibiliser les étudiants aux diverses méthodes utilisées pour comprendre le social. Il est ainsi facile de comprendre pourquoi on ne parle pas des conditions dans lesquelles vivent quotidiennement les femmes ayant survécu à la maladie. Toutefois, ce changement d'attitude et de comportement à l'égard des méthodes qualitatives peut s'expliquer par un désenchantement face aux froides études qui relatent l'impact, la probabilité ou les résultats relatifs à une intervention chirurgicale ou médicale (Filstead, 1970b). On veut obtenir plus d'informations que la seule efficacité du traitement médical ou chirurgical pour faire des choix éclairés. On se montre alors un peu plus ouvert aux possibilités offertes par une méthode d'analyse qualitative pour saisir la signification de la maladie ou d'un problème, au lieu de croire que l'analyse factorielle, les tests statistiques, la déduction, la vérification et l'expérimentation sont les seules techniques d'analyse valables pour résoudre ou expliquer les divers problèmes. Par exemple, on invoque moins souvent, auprès des étudiants universitaires, l'unicité de la méthode, de la démarche et de la connaissance scientifique. Plus souvent, on souligne le caractère dual, sinon ternaire des méthodes de recherches, faisant ainsi une place de choix aux méthodes qualitatives dans la construction d'un savoir scientifique reconnu.

Il est inutile de poursuivre des débats souvent stériles portant sur la supériorité des apports des méthodes qualitatives ou quantitatives, tel n'est pas ici notre objectif. Les deux approches méthodologiques constituent les deux faces d'une même médaille. En théorie, le processus et le résultat, l'induction et la déduction sont intimement liés. Ensemble, ils permettent d'expliquer la même chose, soit l'image globale d'une intervention chirurgicale et ses effets dans la vie quotidienne des femmes marquées par le bistouri ou la chimiothérapie et la peur qui l'accompagne. En pratique, une telle polarisation est maintenue pour des raisons politiques et économiques (volonté de contrôler le savoir et de le reproduire) ainsi qu'idéologiques (la science infaillible et impersonnelle). La polarisation se constate davantage par l'usage des méthodes employées pour obtenir l'information nécessaire.

Critères de succès de la recherche qualitative

Les chercheures et les chercheurs qui ancrent leur réflexion sur le travail de terrain font appel à une grande variété de techniques, caractéristiques de la recherche qualitative. Les traditions d'études ethnographiques et monographiques, de récits de vie, d'entrevues en profondeur, d'études de terrain et d'observation participante sont bien connues en anthropologie médicale (Saillant, 1988; DelVecchio-Good, 1993; Good et DelVecchio-Good, 1982), en sociologie (Coulon, 1992)[1], en phénoménologie (Carini, 1966) et en ethnométhodologie (Garfinkel, 1967). Ces traditions font écho à la notion weberienne de *verstehen*, soit la compréhension du sens de l'activité sociale. Chez Weber, la compréhension se voit opposée à l'explication où les faits sociaux sont appréhendés comme des choses[2]. Ce faisant, ces traditions insistent particulièrement sur la signification (le sens de l'expérience), le contexte (en incluant le quotidien[3]) et l'empathie (capacité de l'analyste de ressentir ce que ressent la femme en tant que sujet). Il s'agit là d'une méthode qualitative et objective qui permet de comprendre les phénomènes sociaux au moyen d'une introspection sympathique et d'une réflexion en profondeur à partir de descriptions détaillées et d'études de cas (Glaser et Strauss, 1967).

Comme Filstead (1970a) l'a indiqué, les méthodes qualitatives permettent à l'analyste de donner un sens ancré sur le terrain et un caractère scientifique à son travail de collecte de données. Sur le plan de la validité, il s'agit de faire ressortir l'imaginaire social et le monde empirique à partir du vécu individuel et des moyens de survie individuelle. À titre d'analyste, il importe de respecter l'univers symbolique de ce monde empirique dont le sujet est porteur et de voir comment il vit son organisation selon des variables sociologiques telles la culture, la classe sociale, la région, la culture (langue), le sexe, les habitudes, etc. Pour que ce travail de recherche sur le terrain soit possible, il est nécessaire de bien comprendre le social sous ses différents angles et les phénomènes culturels qui se déroulent dans un contexte précis (Guba, 1978). Une bonne formation académique et une connaissance approfondie des diverses méthodes sont, sans contredit, des conditions de base et des paramètres d'étude fondamentaux pour garantir le succès de la recherche. L'étude des méthodes quantitatives et qualitatives permet de reconnaître les limites de l'une (l'application du test) et les richesses de l'autre (l'appréciation de l'écoute), et vice versa.

Dans l'esprit de la féminisation de l'institution médicale, il est possible de considérer qu'une recherche respectant le sujet doit tenir compte de son témoignage et des moyens de survie. En procédant ainsi, cela permet de saisir davantage le succès de la science et l'avancement des techniques de recherche. Toutefois, il ne faudrait pas considérer les méthodes qualitatives comme une simple étape préparatoire ou exploratoire à une recherche quantitative plus élaborée. Les méthodes qualitatives ne sont aucunement accessoires, elles ont un statut équivalent aux méthodes quantitatives. Malgré le nombre limité de sujets pour réaliser une étude qualitative, il est possible d'obtenir des données révélatrices quant au fonctionnement social et aux effets de la science médicale dans la vie quotidienne des femmes ayant survécu au cancer du sein. Qui plus est, on dira que des conclusions solides, objectives et généralisables peuvent en être tirées. Nous pensons ici à tout ce qui peut conduire à un inventaire plus ou moins structuré d'attitudes, de représentations, de comportements, de motivations, de processus, etc. Mais qu'en est-il du sens individuel que les femmes donnent à l'expérience de la maladie et des effets psychosociologiques de la post-opération ou du traitement médical? Un tel sens ne peut être compris et expliqué par des renseignements chiffrés. Seul le discours qu'en donnent les femmes ayant survécu au cancer du sein peut nous amener à en saisir le sens.

On sait bien que l'exercice structuré de mise en relation logique de catégories de données tente de reproduire un schéma mental de l'expérience sociale du cancer du sein qui est vécu en tant que phénomène du social (Saillant, 1988). Dans un tel contexte et en adhérant à un esprit critique portant sur la féminisation de l'institution médicale, la femme, sujet de son propre milieu, devient un échantillon de son groupe d'appartenance. Par l'observation en milieu naturel, on constate une variation dans le comportement des femmes et on remarque que cela n'entraîne pas les mêmes réactions de l'une à l'autre. Il y a de cela plusieurs décennies, des analystes ont déjà démontré que l'expression de la douleur ou l'expression sociale de la maladie en particulier est modelée par le milieu d'origine (Sborowski, 1952)[4]. C'est grâce à une recherche qualitative comme celle que nous avons effectuée et à toutes les autres qui utilisent les mêmes méthodes qualitatives dans le domaine de la santé, que nous comprenons rapidement que la douleur et le déchirement institutionnel ont l'empreinte du milieu d'origine. On voit que cette expérience sociale et individuelle ne se vit pas de la même façon d'une femme à l'autre, mais qu'il y a des croisements d'expériences quotidiennes quant à la façon de prendre en main sa maladie et de vouloir la contrer. On apprend également que, pour les survivantes du cancer du sein, il s'agit d'une période difficile dans laquelle se côtoient quotidiennement la lutte et le dépassement humain.

Au nombre des techniques de recherche qualitative, les récits de vie doivent être considérés comme des pratiques culturelles (Bertaux, 1976). Les récits de vie et l'analyse du discours des personnes interrogées qui s'ensuit apparaissent comme des moyens de saisir la réalité vécue et distincte par un groupe de femmes. C'est dans une telle perspective que plusieurs études effectuées dans le domaine de la santé ont mis en relation les notions de maladie et de malaise en s'appuyant carrément sur le concept de culture (Herzlich, 1984; Kleinman, 1986). Nous savons déjà qu'il existe dans chaque culture un ensemble de symboles particuliers dont le pouvoir et la charge symbolique sont enseignés et partagés par l'ensemble des membres de la communauté[5]. Cet enseignement, qui correspond à l'aspect sémantique, nous aide à mieux comprendre comment la maladie est associée culturellement à une grande variété de situations. C'est grâce à l'analyse du discours des femmes ayant vécu l'expérience sociale de la maladie que les anthropologues médicaux se sont rendu compte qu'il était possible d'articuler les réseaux sémantiques afin de révéler simplement et ouvertement le vécu des femmes (Good et DelVecchio-Good, 1982).

Plusieurs anthropologues et sociologues intéressés au domaine de la santé ont indiqué que la culture est au centre de toute expérience humaine. Nous dirons que cela inclut aussi, bien sûr, l'expérience de la maladie (Saillant, 1988). L'expérience sociale du cancer du sein se comprend davantage lorsqu'on quitte l'institution médicale, encore trop souvent «masculinisée» et coupée du milieu, pour découvrir dans l'univers des interactions, des organisations parallèles en santé communautaire, des rites culturels et religieux, des symboles porteurs d'un langage, d'un sens conjugué au pluriel (la beauté et la laideur, la perfection et l'imperfection, la santé et la maladie, etc.). C'est suite à un tel effort de rapprochement avec les femmes (un contact social) et à l'usage des méthodes qualitatives que l'institution médicale peut renouer avec ses origines (science/technique et santé communautaire). En procédant ainsi, il va de soi que l'institution médicale doit féminiser ses rapports sociaux et introduire, dans sa production scientifique et technique sur l'expérience de la maladie, un savoir qualitatif alimenté d'un discours *moins* décousu de sens (objet de la science) et *plus* humain (sujet de l'avancement).

Une méthode et une approche qualitative faite auprès des femmes vivant leur culture minoritaire

Nombreuses sont les institutions médicales canadiennes offrant un traitement pour le cancer du sein. Ces institutions spécialisées structurent les relations entre médecins et patientes et organisent les comportements entre les traitants et les traités. Les institutions médicales sont en quelque sorte ce qui stabilise et rend habituel les comportements des médecins envers le traitement de la maladie et les patientes aux prises avec le cancer du sein. Dans ces milieux de santé, la science et les techniques médicales sont utilisées pour sauver la vie *des* malades, contrer la mort *des* personnes ou encore traiter les patientes. Dans les institutions médicales et universitaires, on procède à des expériences médicales et on applique des tests statistiques pour infirmer ou confirmer des hypothèses, et les résultats sont ensuite publiés dans des revues spécialisées. Tout cela représente un ordre, une pensée, une logique, une production scientifique, une expression, une façon d'être et de penser, un moyen par rapport à une fin. Toutefois, un nombre grandissant de médecins et de professionnels de la santé remettent en question cette façon rigide d'être et de faire des institutions médicales. On résiste au *statu quo* et on cherche à insérer de nouvelles techniques pour tenir compte de la logique et de la pensée du patient. Or, lorsque les statistiques démontrent que la science et les techniques échappent au hasard, que tout le crédit de la guérison revient aux médecins et presque pas aux femmes ayant survécu à leur maladie, on doit se poser de sérieuses questions sur l'égocentrisme du système médical. Il est temps de modifier la mentalité du corps médical en y insérant une réflexion critique sur la connaissance utilisée. À titre de chercheur, il ne faut pas avoir peur de remettre en question le savoir médical et l'usage de ses méthodes quantitatives qui laissent trop souvent de côté l'aspect humain de la recherche, soit les sujets. N'est-il pas temps de dire qu'une théorie scientifique et médicale qui tient compte des femmes et de leur vécu est nécessaire pour saper les construits masculins du savoir médical, tel qu'il est appliqué aujourd'hui ? Tel était l'objectif de notre recherche.

Notre recherche qualitative a débuté en 1993 et a été complétée quelques années plus tard. Cette recherche portait sur les récits de vie des femmes francophones en situation minoritaire ayant survécu au cancer du sein. Elle s'est nourrie de la volonté de remettre en cause les méthodes quantitatives utilisées et enseignées dans le système institutionnel médical. Nous voulions comprendre le vécu des femmes aux prises avec la maladie et qui se retrouvent seule à vivre les effets du traitement dans leur milieu naturel. Pour ce faire, nous avions une volonté, une curiosité, un goût de l'aventure, une formation académique et méthodologique, une liste de questions, un carnet, une plume, une carte du Manitoba, un dictaphone et une automobile. Cette expérience sur le terrain et la découverte des discours des femmes sont vite devenues de plus en plus enrichissantes. L'explication du vécu par les femmes francophones vivant en situation minoritaire et dans des régions éloignées des grands centres institutionnels a été des plus révélatrices (Gagné, 1995).

Afin de mieux comprendre la réalité d'un sous-groupe de femmes francophones, nous avons eu recours à une méthode qualitative, soit un exercice structuré de mise en relation logique de variables et de catégories données. Par la suite, nous avons tenté de reproduire logiquement un schéma mental de l'expérience du cancer du sein. C'est grâce à des entrevues en profondeur et à l'observation que nous avons pu vérifier la correspondance entre le niveau de la construction ou la création théorique et le niveau empirique, celui de la maladie et des réalités vécues quotidiennement par les femmes une fois qu'elles ont quitté les murs de l'institution médicale. C'est donc à partir du discours des femmes que nous avons essayé de reconstituer les modèles culturels et d'expliquer un ensemble d'éléments de référence à partir desquels nous sommes parvenus à mieux comprendre l'expérience sociale et individuelle de la maladie. Dans un tel devis de recherche, la femme devient un échantillon de son groupe d'appartenance culturelle. C'est à partir de son expérience, de ses anecdotes, des moindres événements de sa propre quotidienneté que nous avons mis en commun ce qui l'unissait aux autres femmes.

Des faits sociologiques intéressants sont ressortis de cette recherche, comme la place des valeurs religieuses et leur encadrement philosophique dans la représentation sociale du cancer du sein. Nous pensons également à l'usage répétitif des mots dans le discours des femmes tels que la mort et la vie, le passé et le présent, la peur et l'espoir, la perte et la lutte, les enfants et la présence ou non du conjoint, la laideur et la beauté, le couteau et la marque, etc. Grâce au découpage des mots et des choses, des signes et des idiotismes, des valeurs et des pratiques culturelles soulevées lors des entrevues en profondeur, il a été possible de construire les diverses catégories du réseau sémantique des femmes ayant survécu au cancer du sein, de saisir leur réalité quotidienne et ainsi de mieux comprendre le sens de leur expérience.

Une attitude différente de celle qui domine généralement dans la littérature sur le sujet a animé la collecte de données, soit celle d'approcher l'histoire des femmes par leur petite histoire (Le Gall, 1987). Les récits de vie ont permis de présenter cette petite histoire qui se joue au quotidien et ainsi d'approcher les femmes francophones que l'on pense, à tort, sans histoire. Grâce à la technique d'échantillonnage boule de neige, la collecte des récits de vie a été possible, bien qu'il ne s'agissait pas d'une mince tâche. À l'époque, il n'existait pas de données permettant d'identifier, de localiser et de rendre compte de la situation sociale des femmes francophones manitobaines ayant vécu un cancer du sein. Il a fallu être patiente et solliciter constamment l'aide des membres de la communauté francophone pour nous aider à identifier les femmes.

Une vingtaine d'entrevues ont été réalisées auprès de femmes francophones âgées de 36 à 79 ans, dispersées pour la plupart dans la Vallée de la Rivière Rouge au Manitoba. La sélection de l'échantillon a été faite à partir des critères sociologiques suivants : femmes francophones vivant en français (ce qui n'est pas évident en situation minoritaire), ayant survécu au cancer du sein et ayant subi une mastectomie (ablation du sein). Les entrevues en profondeur portaient sur l'expérience institutionnelle de la maladie (symptômes, diagnostic médical, réactions, traitements et réajustement) et le sens que les femmes interrogées donnaient à cette expérience (spirituel ou religieux). Les entrevues en profondeur ont également porté sur la période de réadaptation en milieu naturel (santé, famille, conjoint, groupe de soutien et corps médical).

Points saillants : Expérience sociale de l'institution médicale et système de réseautage

Mon intention n'est pas de présenter en détail les résultats de la recherche, mais d'en récapituler les points saillants (Gagné, 1995). Précisons d'abord que les femmes révèlent que le rôle des médecins est des plus importants, car c'est par eux qu'elles arrivent à comprendre la gravité de la maladie et la nécessité de l'intervention proposée. Que l'intervention médicale soit en cours ou terminée, les femmes ont clairement indiqué le sentiment d'avoir vécu un vide institutionnel médical. En effet, la majorité d'entre elles ont non seulement appris très vite la mauvaise nouvelle, mais ont dû apprendre également qu'il fallait agir rapidement pour contrer la progression de la tumeur. Dans un court laps de temps, les femmes doivent absorber le choc de la maladie, de l'institution médicale, du traitement de la maladie et du retour précipité à la maison, et cela leur paraît très difficile. Toutes ces étapes traversées à toute vitesse ne préparent aucunement les femmes au retour ingrat à la réalité et à l'incapacité immédiate de gérer les effets de la maladie au sein de la famille et du couple.

Nous retenons deux éléments des résultats obtenus. En premier lieu, la sémantique de la maladie est directement associée à une variété de situations, de moments séquentiels vécus par les femmes, d'états affectifs sur le plan psychologique et d'agents stressants sur le plan social. Le sens social et culturel donné au cancer du sein est étroitement lié à des expériences typiques telles que la prise en charge de sa vie, les rencontres avec son médecin, le déchirement psychologique, l'acceptation de la maladie et la lutte pour le retour à la santé malgré le corps marqué par l'institution médicale, etc. Précisons ici le rôle crucial des médecins dans la relation entre médecin et patiente, particulièrement lors de la divulgation de la mauvaise nouvelle. Toutes ont précisé que les médecins les ont invitées à participer activement au processus thérapeutique, ce qui a eu pour effet de créer un climat de confiance entre les parties et d'insuffler de l'espoir dans les récits thérapeutiques. Par ailleurs, les femmes ont clairement indiqué que les oncologistes développent auprès de leurs patientes un rapport plus immédiat. Ce sens de l'immédiateté domine le moment vécu par la patiente dans l'institution médicale et contraste avec celui du dévoilement de la terrible nouvelle par le médecin.

En second lieu, il existe un système informel de réseautage dans les milieux ruraux qui favorise l'autonomie des femmes et la prise en charge de leur maladie et de leur vie. Ce réseau, composé de femmes ayant survécu à la maladie, tente de répondre aux besoins des femmes aux prises avec la maladie et ses traitements. C'est grâce à des moyens d'information portant sur la maladie et à ses effets qu'un tel réseau prend tout son sens auprès des femmes luttant *toujours* contre la maladie. Plusieurs d'entre elles ont clairement indiqué que sans l'existence du réseau, elles se seraient senties bien seules à subir les effets dévastateurs de la maladie. Autrement dit, les groupes de soutien mis sur pied dans la région de l'étude ont permis à plusieurs femmes de traverser moins durement l'expérience sociale de la maladie. Ces groupes de soutien communautaire sont d'autant plus nécessaires qu'ils comblent le vide de l'institution médicale. Ce réseau se distingue des autres réseaux de la francophonie minoritaire manitobaine, car ils sont organisés par des femmes francophones ayant elles-mêmes survécu à l'expérience du cancer du sein.

Les entrevues en profondeur nous ont permis de constater que les groupes de soutien facilitent le passage entre l'état de la maladie et celui de la santé. Par exemple, ce réseau offre aux femmes malades de les conduire à l'hôpital afin de recevoir leurs traitements de chimiothérapie ou, encore, organise des soirées de mode pour pallier les inquiétudes vestimentaires des femmes aux prises avec la maladie. On encourage les femmes à surmonter leur peur de s'afficher publiquement et la pensée que les gens vont se moquer d'elles à cause d'un handicap qui fait dorénavant partie de leur vie. La recherche nous a également appris que plusieurs femmes se définissent en fonction de leur communauté d'appartenance culturelle, et que c'est à l'intérieur de celle-ci qu'elles se retrouvent et partagent leur expérience de la même maladie. Cela dit, les femmes ayant survécu au cancer du sein et faisant partie de notre recherche qualitative se reconnaissent entre elles et se comprennent dans leur rapport au social et au médical. En effet, certaines femmes ont eu le sentiment que l'institution médicale les a utilisées comme des objets de science lors du traitement, puis les a carrément abandonnées à leur sort une fois celui-là terminé (inexistence des contacts humains). D'autres femmes ont utilisé leur expérience pour aider d'autres femmes aux prises avec des problèmes difficiles. Quoi qu'il en soit, les initiatives sociales et communautaires développées *par et pour* les femmes francophones ayant vécu l'expérience de la maladie ont permis de faciliter la prise en charge de leur santé.

Un fait retient notre attention. Toutes les femmes interrogées ont le sentiment d'appartenir à un groupe circonscrit de femmes possédant son propre code culturel en raison de leur expérience et de leurs relations à l'institution médicale. Ce sous-groupe de femmes francophones vivant en situation minoritaire se distingue culturellement de sa propre communauté d'appartenance en raison de son vécu social particulier et de tout ce qui s'y rattache. L'identification de ce sous-groupe s'explique par la sous-culture de la maladie qui est au centre de leur expérience en tant que femme et qui s'enracine au cœur de leur quotidienneté.

Conclusion

Visiblement, la féminisation de l'institution médicale en tant qu'agence de production d'un savoir médico-social est importante, ne serait-ce que pour obtenir de l'information sur les conséquences d'une maladie ou d'un traitement du point de vue des femmes. Plus encore, la féminisation est importante parce qu'elle participe au renouvellement de la production du savoir médical déjà amorcé par le courant de recherche qualitative. En prenant en considération d'autres méthodes de recherche qui permettent l'érudition et qui évitent la distanciation des rapports entre les chercheurs et les chercheures et les sujets de recherche, l'institution médicale poursuivrait une toute autre logique et une nouvelle théorie. Son discours serait basé dorénavant sur la reconnaissance des différences entre les sexes. Sur le plan de l'historicité, en se rapprochant du sujet «femme», le chercheur ou la chercheure accomplit un geste remarquable à cause du succès humain de sa démarche. Le savoir ainsi produit peut apporter une transformation radicale des institutions médicales et, surtout, la féminisation du discours médical.

Dans le domaine des recherches en santé, l'usage des méthodes qualitatives augmente la valeur des recherches épidémiologiques, lesquelles subissent difficilement des transformations matérielles. L'intégration des méthodes qualitatives permet à l'institution médicale de se féminiser en adoptant un discours théorique moins rigide et plus humain dans son contenu et dans sa forme. Comme nous l'avons dit auparavant, l'idéologie dominante de l'institution médicale est la science. Or, la science doit avoir une conscience, à savoir une connaissance approfondie des êtres humains dans leur milieu naturel et, en particulier, une connaissance du corps et des problèmes vécus par les femmes atteintes du cancer du sein. Si la science, aux moyens des méthodes quantitatives, mesure et calcule, en vue de prévoir et d'agir, elle doit aussi tenir compte de la santé des femmes ou valoriser le savoir de ces dernières. En s'insérant dans leur milieu naturel, la science et les méthodes utilisées pour mieux comprendre le social permettent à l'institution médicale de devenir plus humaine. Les femmes contribuent à la transformation de leur situation tout en aidant à transformer leur communauté d'appartenance et l'institution médicale.

En acceptant de partager leurs récits de vie par l'exercice structuré de mise en relation logique et de catégories données, les femmes et les chercheures, travaillant directement sur le terrain, proposent des orientations ou des pistes de recherche pertinentes au domaine de la santé communautaire. Toutefois, le fait de vivre dans des milieux éloignés des grands centres urbains a un impact dans la tentative de réunir les femmes au sein de groupe de soutien. Or, ces derniers jouent un rôle crucial dans la mesure où ils permettent aux femmes d'affronter leur maladie. C'est pourquoi il est important de les reconnaître et de les considérer, surtout lorsque les médecins proposent un traitement médical aux femmes aux prises avec la maladie.

Finalement, une telle analyse permet d'insérer de nouvelles données dans le discours médical et de sensibiliser les institutions médicales à la possibilité du changement. En effet, elle offre aux femmes des moyens concrets de prise en charge individuelle de leur vie quotidienne. Ce faisant, une telle analyse qualifie les femmes et leurs discours, les faisant passer d'objets de science à sujets de connaissance par l'usage des méthodes qualitatives. Elle démontre l'influence et la pertinence de la culture conjuguée au féminin.

Bibliographie

Bertaux, Daniel (1976), *Histoire de vie ou de récit de pratiques? Méthodologie de l'approche biographique en sociologie*, Paris, Rapport du CORDES.

Carini, P.F. (1966), *Observation and Description: An Alternative Methodology for the Investigation of Human Resource*, Englewoods Cliffs, N.J., Prentice-Hall.

Cook, Thomas D. et Charles S. Reichardt (dir. de publ.), (1979), *Qualitative and Quantitative Methods in Evaluation Research*, Beverly Hills, Sage.

Coulon, Alain (1992), «Alfred Schütz. Le chercheur et le quotidien», dans *La sociologie*, sous la dir. de Karl M. Van Meter, Paris, Éditions Larousse, 455-473.

DelVecchio-Good, Mary-Jo (1993), «Oncologie et temps narratif», *Santé et culture*, vol. 9, no 1, 19-40.

Filstead W. S. (dir. de publ.) (1970a), *Qualitative Methodology*, Chicago, Markham.

Filstead, W.S. (1970b), «Qualitative Methods: A Needed Perspective in Evaluation», dans *Qualitative and Quantitative Methods in Evaluation Research*, sous la dir. de T. D. Cook et C. S. Reichardt, Beverly Hills, Sage, 68-86.

Gagné, Elsy (1995), «La réalité des Franco-Manitobaines et le cancer du sein», *Reflets*, vol. 1 no 2, 90-114.

Garfinkel, H. (1967), *Studies in Ethnomethodology*, New York, John Wiley.

Glaser, B.G. et A.L. Strauss (1967), *The Discovery of Grounded Theory: Strategies for Qualitative Research*, Chicago, Illinois, Aldine.

Good, Byron et Mary-Jo DelVecchio-Good (1982), «Toward a Meaning Centered Analysis of Popular Illness Categories: Fright Illness and Heart Distress», dans *Cultural Conception of Mental Health and Therapy*, sous la dir. de Iran A.J. Marsella et G.M. White, Boston, D. Reidel Publishing, 141-146.

Guba, W.G. (1978), *Toward a Methodology of Naturalistic Inquiry in Educational Evaluation*, CSE Monograph Series in Evaluation, no 8, Los Angeles, University of California.

Herzlich, Claudine (1984), *Santé et maladie. Analyse d'une représentation sociale*, Paris, Éditions de Minuit.

Kleinman, Arthur (1986), «Social Origins of Distress and Disease: Depression Neurasthenia and Pain in Modern China», *Current Anthropology*, vol. 27, no 5, 499-509.

Le Gall, Didier (1987), «Les récits de vie : approcher le social par la pratique», dans *Les méthodes de la recherche qualitative*, sous la dir. de Jean-Paul Deslauriers, Sillery, Presses de l'Université du Québec, 35-48.

Rivière, Claude (1978), *L'analyse dynamique en sociologie*, Paris, Les Presses Universitaires de France.

Saillant, Francine (1988), *Culture et cancer*, Montréal, Éditions Saint-Martin.

Sborowski, M. (1952), «Cultural Components in Response to Pain», *Journal of Social Issues*, vol. 8, 16-60.

Weber, Max (1971), *Économie et société*, 5ᵉ édition, Paris, Éditions Plon.

Notes

1. C'est Schütz qui utilisera les concepts de la phénoménologie pour indiquer que le monde de la vie est en soi constitué par les institutions et les événements courants. De plus, ce monde social est travaillé par les personnes ordinaires dans leur vie quotidienne, sans qu'elles en aient réellement conscience. Voir Coulon (1992).

2. Weber (1971) en a souligné l'importance dans sa réflexion sociologique. Toutefois, il n'a pas défini clairement ce que cette notion recouvrait.

3. Le quotidien n'est pas fait par les événements, mais, bien au contraire, par les individus qui ont prise sur eux. Le quotidien ne se construit pas au hasard des choses et du temps. En tant que construit sociologique, le quotidien s'ordonne en regard d'un fil conducteur. Dans un tel contexte d'analyse, les récits de vie sont un matériau de base utile pour la chercheure.

4. Sborowski (1952) a réalisé une étude comparative, aux États-Unis, entre trois groupes ethniques eu égard à leurs réactions à la douleur.

5. Dans le contexte de la maladie, la culture devient un vaste appareil matériel ou humain qui aide la personne à affronter les problèmes qui se posent à elle et donc à trouver des solutions temporelles et partielles.

Marilyn E. Laiken

Alternatives to Hierarchy in Feminist Organizational Design: A Case Study

Introduction

"Many non-profit and social-change organizations, working to make the world a better place, manage to create work environments that are social nightmares for their staffs. The lack of good management in these organizations often drives their most dedicated employees and volunteers away, frustrated and resentful" (Britell 1992, 84).

Beyond management practices, which include issues of power and particular difficulty with the role of executive director (Martin 1990; Ristock 1991), there seem to be many other obstacles to the effective functioning of such organizations. Issues of class, gender, and ethnicity challenge increasingly multi-cultural and mixed economic workforces: "The attempt to replace stultifying hierarchical systems with organizational designs which are structureless produces covert structures which are even more problematic to those whose worklives they define" (Freeman 1974). The scarcity of workable models and a lack of skill in implementing collaborative processes often results in a reversion to traditional designs with ensuing frustration and anger (Greaves 1991). Additionally, I suggest that the very personal investment which most staff in these organizations bring to their work polarizes them from within, if they differ philosophically or politically, and can create factions both among staff and between staff and board members. Finally, these difficulties have been both exposed and fuelled by the fact that many of these organizations, finding themselves in the midst of internal chaos, often become the focus of negative media attention as well (Freedman 1993).

The purpose of this article is to explore each of these issues in some depth, both within the context of recent feminist research, as well as within a specific case organization for which a colleague, Karon West, and I provided consulting services[1]. A year-long review with this organization (hereafter referred to as "The Refuge") included extensive data collection and a variety of interventions with both board and staff members. It resulted in the development of an organizational model which may be unique in producing structures that feature both collaboration and efficiency. Karon and I were co-consultants to the organization, participating equally in all data collection, diagnosis, and intervention roles. The consultation was not conducted for research purposes, but rather at the request of The Refuge in order to help improve organizational functioning.[2]

Apart from exploring the issues which were encountered by The Refuge, this article outlines briefly the interventions which were designed to respond to these issues, and provides an overview of the organizational model which resulted from the consultation and has been in operation for several years. It is hoped that this information will provide, not a "recipe" to be transplanted, but some inspiration and methodological help for other organizations which might be struggling with the challenge of "re-inventing" themselves so that their structure is more consistent with their values. In my view, redesign efforts such as these are a pragmatic enactment of feminist principles in organizational contexts and deserve attention to both their outcomes and their process.

The Refuge

In 1992, when the consultation took place, The Refuge was in its seventh year of operation, with twenty staff members, eight board members, and an operating budget of just under a million dollars from a variety of funding sources. Its stated purpose at the time was to provide, in the organization's words, "legal, counselling, cultural interpretation, community education, and advocacy services for women who are victims of violence." Significantly, the review that we conducted was the second commissioned by the organization within two years. During that period, several key staff members had resigned, including three executive directors, and the board of directors had also experienced a high rate of turnover. Clearly, this was an organization in considerable turmoil. However, the issues identified by the Organization Review Steering Committee as the presenting problems were only the proverbial "tip of the iceberg." They included perceived value differences among board and staff members, resulting in a lack of trust between the groups; decision-making processes which were often dysfunctional; roles which were unclear; and a lack of effective mechanisms for conflict management.

It should be noted here that every organization with which I work experiences difficulties in some or all of these areas. These issues are certainly not restricted to feminist organizations. One might assume that feminist women would be more amenable to collaborative processes, and therefore find implementing alternatives to hierarchy easier than in mixed-gender organizations; however, it appears not to be the case in this particular example. Although the intentions and philosophy of The

Refuge hold collaboration as an ideal, as in all such organizations, in my experience, there is a gap between the vision and the reality. Therefore, based on an initial assessment, we identified, with the Steering Committee (comprised of both board and staff personnel), some preliminary goals for the review. These were the following:

- To assess the internal organizational functioning of The Refuge regarding changes needed in processes and structures;
- To clarify the roles of board and staff groups relative to each other, explore differences in values and approaches, build trust, design mechanisms for dealing with conflict, and address any blocks to clear and constructive communication within and between these groups;
- To assist the board and staff in designing and implementing necessary structural changes, in order to facilitate their determining strategic directions for The Refuge and managing most effectively the day-to-day operations of the organization.

A variety of complex and interrelated issues was unearthed through several data collection methods. These included a thorough review of organizational documentation, as well as focus-group interviews with three separate groups of board and staff members; individual interviews both in person and by telephone; and several follow-up letters written by those who chose the anonymity of this medium to express their concerns. The consultation process was guided throughout by ongoing meetings with the Organization Review Steering Committee and characterized by consistent communication with all staff and board members regarding proposed interventions.

The next section outlines the issues in some detail, relating them to recent feminist research. The purpose here is to explore the hypothesis that the issues which were identified, although enacted in unique ways by different feminist organizations, tend to be generic and therefore predictable. Perhaps some anticipation of these concerns, as well as a recognition that they are both understandable contextually as well as manageable organizationally, will help groups of women experimenting with alternatives to hierarchy to avoid some of the "growing pains" associated with this pursuit.

Key Issues Identified

The Structural Dilemma

A major paradox for organizations such as The Refuge is the fact that their belief system and the context in which they must survive are incongruent. The Refuge espouses "feminist principles" which include the beliefs that

- empowerment and self-determination are at the core of both service provision and organizational functioning;
- collaboration and consensual decision-making are critical for staff motivation and commitment;
- open communication and effective conflict management at all levels of the organization are key goals; and
- leadership serves to coordinate and facilitate ("power with" rather than "power over").

These beliefs imply an organizational form which is collaborative and non-hierarchical. However, funding imperatives force organizations such as these into a more traditional structure, with a board which is fiscally accountable to funders such as the United Way and an Executive Director in the role of "senior manager." The result is on-going board/staff power struggle, as accountability issues cause board members and the executive director to revert to the "default setting" of their traditional social coding ("managers are ultimately accountable for organizational policy," etc.), while staff members alternate between the dependence on authority of their own social coding and the counterdependence which is a predictable response in their struggle for control. As one astute board member at The Refuge noted,

> By giving the responsibility for setting direction, establishing policy and ensuring effective management to the board, a de facto power struggle is set up. 'Maximizing staff input and involvement' just doesn't cut it. The question of accountability has never been clarified — who is accountable for what to whom? (board member, written response)

Another board member reveals her frustration with this dilemma in her comment: "You can't have it both ways — that is, the board has ultimate responsibility for The Refuge, but the board and staff operate as partners...power is power!" (board member, focus-group interview).

The problem is exacerbated when one considers that the board members are volunteers, while the staff members are salaried. This has the potential to create mixed feelings regarding volunteerism among feminists, including perceptions of board members as "exploited labourers," or, alternately, as more politically free because they're not paid. It may also raise the issue of exclusivity in the board membership, given that low-income women might not be able to afford to volunteer their services. Finally, it raises the possibility of resentment among board members that their time isn't being formally "valued."

Another significant issue is the fact that many of the women employed or volunteering in sheltering and anti-violence organizations often, themselves, have been victims of abuse. When survivors of abuse have had the opportunity to work through individual emotional issues, they can perform their roles with tremendous commitment and useful insight into the client's experience. However, when personal issues have not yet been resolved, emotional concerns related to power and control often emerge. These can be difficult to recognize and even more difficult to manage organizationally. Struthers calls women's organizations "the organizational containers of (women's) personal experience" (Struthers 1994, 4). Although issues related to power are generally part of the human condition, Liem and O'Toole (1992) describe research findings which indicate a particularly profound sense of powerlessness in victims of sexual abuse. This is combined with a strong need for power, resulting in extremely conflicted relationships with those who have formal authority in a work setting, "This preoccupation with power can manifest itself both as...an increased desire to exert influence and control over people and outcomes, and as a continuing fear of the power of others" (Liem and O'Toole 1992, 68).

Apart from these concerns, research indicates that a socialized tendency to equate power with "unfeminine" self-interest makes issues of power particularly contentious in an all-woman work environment (Woolsey and McBain 1987; Bardwick 1977; Miller 1982).

At The Refuge, unexplicated and unresolved power relationships were manifested in fear and mistrust on the part of both staff and board groups in relation to each other. Anger, pain and feelings of helplessness were eroding energy. Neither group wanted the board and executive director to have ultimate decision-making authority as in a traditional hierarchical structure. In fact, it was decided that a new executive director would not be hired to replace the third one to leave in two years. However, both groups also rejected a collective structure, recognizing the inefficiency of having thirty people involved in making every decision by consensus. Also, an implicitly defined or structureless design was recognized as potentially dangerous, in view of the conflicted attitudes regarding power previously outlined. The Refuge members would agree with Marilyn Struthers that "Only a relational structure, explicitly defined on the basis of a critical organizational theory, has the ability to alter the default settings of members steeped in the social norms to which they stand in critical opposition" (Struthers 1994, 17). However, the organization saw no alternatives at the time other than the two extremes of collectivity or hierarchy.

With both hierarchy and collectivity rejected as viable options, and no alternatives evident initially, the structural dilemma for The Refuge seemed insurmountable.

Managing Conflict

Although difficulties in managing conflict are not unique to women's organizations (Laiken 1994a; Manz et al. 1990), women tend to be particularly reluctant to identify conflictual issues. Woolsey and McBain (1987) discovered what they term "intransigent conflict" in a large number of women's groups, despite the use of counselling and mediation interventions. Several feminist researchers attribute this phenomenon to a variety of causes: feminist values support affirming and strengthening bonds among women, which inhibits criticism; traditional female values support nurturance and collaboration; the importance to women of their work relationships causes reluctance to express anger directly for fear of abandonment; women's early socialization produces conflict avoidance as a learned behaviour to exact the benevolence of those who control the resources; the traditionally inferior status of women begets self-doubt and low self-esteem, making it difficult to express anger openly and directly; and finally, the fact that various ethnocultural groups experience and deal with conflict in different ways, making conflict management an even more complex process in a multicultural context (Miller 1977; Woolsey and McBain 1987; Bardwick 1977).

The outcome of conflict avoidance for such women's organizations as The Refuge is the presence of resentments which are never acknowledged, along with small annoyances which build disproportionately and eventually become explosive. Alternately, a release of the tension is sought through forming coalitions of potential allies against those who are perceived as threatening. If this is the context within which the issues of power and control raised earlier are also coming to the surface, it is not difficult to imagine an environment in which feelings of trust and group cohesiveness seem like unattainable goals. The intensity of this dilemma is magnified by the fact that it is exactly these issues which many women's organizations are attempting to address in their work and hoping to exemplify positively in their organizational functioning.

Issues of Difference

A third challenge for social-change organizations is to some extent engendered by their political agenda. In their commitment to employment equity and cultural diversity among the workforce, their employees tend to be more intentionally representative of the communities they serve than do those of other organizations. However, if, as in the case of The Refuge, their funding needs require a volunteer board of directors, sheer economics dictate that board members will likely be middle-class white women of privilege, who have both the time and the inclination to voluntarily support social-change projects, as well as having easy access to potential sources of funding. The extent of difference in class, ethnicity, educational background, and lifestyle, within the staff group itself and between the staff and board members, is a certain source of potential conflict.[3]

The Refuge members were fully aware of these concerns, as one staff person pointed out: "We're paying more attention to race, culture and power differences — at least we're acknowledging the issues exist. Now we need to recognize the difficulties as they arise, and be willing to work through them" (staff member, focus-group interview). However, as Argyris (1990) notes, there is often a vast difference in an organization between its "espoused theory" (beliefs and values), and its "theory-in-use" (actual practices).

In the case of The Refuge, both board and staff groups viewed themselves as "different breeds," and basic assumptions about each other's belief systems tended to go unexplored. In fact, so potent was the fear of expressing themselves before the other group (especially among staff who felt less powerful), that it took several months of work with each group separately before they would agree to meet together to discuss their mutual vision for The Refuge. As one board member observed: "Board and staff are different breeds, and the conflicts often do seem to be around values; there may be differences in management philosophy, and board members are not as personally invested in the work of The Refuge (as are the staff)" (board member, focus-group interview). Board members also made assumptions about the staff not perceiving them as "politically correct enough," and staff members admitted that they, too, saw large differences between the groups in terms of political ideology. In fact, they noted that these often "sensitive issues" were rarely dealt with even during staff-only meetings (from board and staff interviews).

Although much of this perception of difference, particularly in philosophy and commitment, was based on assumptions which proved for the most part to be exaggerated, there were some genuine differences which created major gaps in understanding.

The assumption of difference, as well as the reality, created an environment in The Refuge replete with what Argyris (1990) refers to as "defensive routines." These are described by Senge (1990) as habitual ways of interacting which protect us from the pain of appearing uncertain or ignorant. Rather, we polarize around differing and strongly held values, and tend to be without mechanisms to make these polarities discussable. As Audre Lorde points out: "It is not our differences which separate women, but our reluctance to recognize those differences and to deal effectively with the distortions which have resulted from the ignoring and misnaming of those differences" (Lorde 1984, 122).[4]

In order for any of these issues to be managed effectively, deliberate structures and processes need to be included as part of the on-going functioning of the organization. Struthers points out that "Without support, like a tent without a frame, the organizational structure flaps with any gust of contentious wind. Those least marginal, and most personally powerful by virtue of social location, will form its structure by default" (Struthers 1994, 16-17).

In writing about the process of "dialogue" and the concept of "polarity management," Peter Senge (1990) and Barry Johnson (1992) offer procedural structures to help make issues of organizational diversity discussable. Senge encourages both a position of "advocacy" (clarity about one's own opinions) and one of "inquiry" (a willingness to truly attend to the ideas of others) in an environment which promotes, not a "win-lose" debate, but open interaction to identify and hold the differences. The trust that such dialogue engenders helps make possible constructive approaches to highly charged issues.

According to Johnson, issues of diversity are not problems to solve, but polarities to manage. He claims "it is the incompleteness combined with the conviction of rightness (accuracy)...which is the source of a potential problem" (Johnson 1992, 44). His polarity management maps help groups or individuals who stand on opposite sides of a pole to recognize the "up" and "down" sides of both ends of the polarity, and thus appreciate more fully the position of the other, as well as have one's own stance better understood:

> As evidence of the effectiveness of these methods in practice, Laurie Edmiston (1994) cites a detailed case example of a feminist Community Health Centre for immigrant women, where she volunteered as a board member. In this setting, traditional conflict management interventions failed to alleviate the kinds of problems outlined in this paper, while a facilitated dialogue process helped to revive an organization on the verge of extinction. The women Edmiston interviewed said: Whereas the goal of the conflict resolution process was reconciliation, the intent of the dialogue process was simply to get people talking. The premise was that it was okay not to sort out our problems. In the end, everyone became aware of each other's history and perspectives, without the need to agree. We discovered that we have more in common than in diversity (Edmiston 1994, 2 — taken from personal communication with board members).

Although such methods as polarity management and dialogue exist, and have successfully helped organizations to manage in diversity, one of the issues faced by The Refuge was its lack of exposure to or experience with such models.

Scarcity of Workable Models and Lack of Skill in Implementing Alternatives

Much of the recent feminist literature has provided a number of efficient and life-enhancing alternatives to traditional organizational mechanisms. As Struthers says:

> Hierarchy and collectivity are often set as opposite poles of a masculine and feminine dialectic. The misplaced emphasis on collectivity as feminist structural form obscures the manner in which women's organizations are modifying both traditional hierarchical and collective forms to gain efficiency, size, and at the same time, respond to the ideological imperatives of feminism. (Struthers 1994, 14)

As early as 1977, Judith Bardwick was writing about "modified structures" to specify constraints on power and broaden input to decision-making. Even earlier, Jo Freeman railed against "the tyranny of structurelessness" which was resulting from a "pendulum swing" from hierarchy to collectivity (Freeman 1974). More recently, Robin Leidner supports employing some standard organizational practices to overcome the difficulties that have plagued many feminist organizations, such as "overwhelming emotional intensity, ideological factionism, leadership trashing and stifling of dissent" (Leidner 1993, 4). This researcher describes several forms of democratic innovation experimented with in the National Women's Studies Association (Leidner 1991), while Kathleen Iannello writes about three other organizations practising what she terms "modified consensus" in their decision-making process (Iannello 1992). A literature review by Marilyn Struthers suggested five types of alternative and collaborative "structural mechanisms" (Struthers 1994).

Why, then, should there be a paucity of workable models to guide an organization like The Refuge in its quest for a new organizational form? To begin with, the existing literature on organizational change, although helpful to some extent in the private and public sectors, tends to be rejected by feminist organizations as "corporate" and "gendered." As Struthers says: "Existing corporate organizational theory takes into account neither the relational reality of women in organizations, nor the effect of an explicit politics created by a critical perspective" (Struthers 1994, 28). The case in question illustrates the impact of this belief.

As consultants to The Refuge, we were engaged in the second organizational review to have been commissioned within two years. Even though both Karon and I were recognized as feminist in our orientation, as well as experienced organization consultants, our interventions were often met with suspicion and resistance. Interviews and meetings were continually rescheduled or cancelled, and every process proposal was questioned in detail, despite the fact that all proposals resulted from lengthy consultations with the representative Steering Committee. When asked about their desired outcomes for this consultation, several board and staff members expressed the concern that nothing would change, while at the same time assuring us as consultants that our style and methods were credible and acceptable to Refuge personnel.

Beyond the apparent lack of credibility of organizational theory, the theory in practice provides even less help. Feminist organizations, at least in the Toronto area where The Refuge is located, have recently received a plethora of negative media attention (reference the June Callwood story, "White Woman's Burden," in the April 1993 issue of *Saturday Night*). In describing the Nellie's women's hostel story, journalist Adele Freedman says: "The themes were age-old: power, race, justice — with the late-century nuances of personality, feminist teachings and what came to be called the death of liberalism" (40). In response to this article, Anne Melgaard writes a "letter to the editor" in the next issue of the magazine, saying: "I did not need to read the details to know what happened at Nellie's. Many women's organizations, including the one I belong to, are experiencing the same story...There are few rules on how to work together that are not patriarchal" (Melgaard 1993).

At the end of her literature review in search of new organizational forms, Marilyn Struthers concludes that "the literature generally reveals few organizational mechanisms to structure inclusion, and little theory about the effects of the mechanisms used" (Struthers 1994, 25). Furthermore, she notes, significantly, that none of these approaches addresses changing the actual structure of the organization. Therein, of course, lies the problem.

If none of the feminist organizations which have appeared in the literature or in practice successfully demonstrates an actual restructuring of their organizational design, the role models for newer organizations such as the Refuge are non-existent. Furthermore, as Struthers notes, "A structure or structural mechanism cannot be transplanted without adjustment from one location to the other...The process by which a group of people creates and recreates its structure is as important as its form" (Struthers 1994, 20). Therein, of course, lies the possibility.

Refuge members were, by their own admission, lacking in process skills ("even agreed-upon processes are sometimes circumvented" — board member; and "sometimes attention to process is seen as impeding the work of The Refuge" — staff member). However, they were also willing to concede that developing process skills was an important part of the work towards organizational change. The following was noted:

> We need to have clear mechanisms and skills for conflict management, to encourage more productive and less stressful conflict, maybe with the help of a facilitator. We also need to honour people's readiness for confronting conflict to ensure safety, and to help them bring issues to staff meetings for debate. Finally, we need to attend to language and jargon, and learn to give and receive feedback without being defensive. (staff member, written response)

The final section of this paper will illustrate how these processes were enhanced at The Refuge and outline the organizational model which was developed through the consistent and strategic use of these processes by board and staff members.

The Consulting Intervention

The key issues identified through the data collection process, and outlined in this paper, indicated the need and the potential for a radical redesign of The Refuge's organizational structure.[5]

At the same time, it was clear that the process was as critical as the outcome for organizational learning. Assumptions needed to be recognized and clarified. Conflict emanating from diversity, as well as from issues of power and control, needed general acknowledgement and a "safe container" for expression and dialogue. Refuge staff and board members needed an opportunity to consider a variety of options before together creating an organizational form which was consistent with their shared beliefs. Finally, relationships with clients and funders had to be continued in a credible manner while the work of reorganizing was occurring.

Data feedback meetings held with the staff and board groups separately were the first opportunity for us as consultants to verify our findings and to allow the members to publicly acknowledge the issues that were identified. Although the issues were consistent between the two groups, the major concern, especially among the staff members, was ensuring a "safe" enough environment for the groups to meet together to discuss the findings. Two half-day visioning meetings were the venue for this phase of the process, with part of the first one spent in generating an agreed-upon list of guidelines to assist group members in respectful communication and appropriate confrontation. The remaining time in these meetings was spent in identifying individual and then group visions, values, and philosophy regarding The Refuge and its operation. Although a shared "statement of philosophy" was the eventual outcome of these sessions, more critical was the process, which allowed group members to express deeply-held beliefs about their work in an environment which was kept open and positive, despite key differences.

The next full-day planning meeting was scheduled for one month after the visioning process. The intervening period was intended as a learning/reflection phase, in which all group members, as well as we two consultants, committed to "researching," both in the literature and in current practice, organizational models which were felt to be consistent with the now mutually-shared vision for the Refuge. Notes and diagrams were sent or faxed among all of the members, and these were then brought to a daylong "model-building" session, during which the group was to design its "ideal" organizational model.

It was at this point that a minor setback threatened to impede the process. The staff group, in an attempt to empower themselves in their interaction with the board, met separately two days before the planned session and designed their own organizational model, which they intended to present as a proposal to the board group. A board member heard about this "in camera" meeting, phoned the consultants, and complained that the board had not had the same opportunity to meet and design. Somehow, what had felt like "a level playing field" was suddenly tilted. Of course, the staff members might rightfully have claimed that the playing field had never been level, given the power differentials previously outlined in this paper. However, all had committed to a process which had now been usurped, and the board members felt this was simply a reenactment of the board/staff issues which had originally instigated the consultation.

Karon and I agreed that this concern needed to be addressed before planning work could continue. We began the next all-member session by meeting separately with the two groups to discuss the change in dynamics brought about by the new developments. Following this discussion, the staff group apologized to the board for contravening their agreement, and offered their model as one of the many under consideration, promising to allow it to be "dissected" and rebuilt to meet the participants' mutual needs. The board, in turn, acknowledged the staff's concerns regarding power differences and asked the consultants to help keep this issue alive throughout the discussions.

The model-building day was successfully spent in a combination of activities which involved small, mixed board/staff groupings in defined

various aspects of their proposed model, and then presented these to the total group for discussion, approval, and changes before continuing their work. Notes on the "researched" models were posted around the room for reference, as were the philosophy statements, to ensure that all proposals were consistent with The Refuge vision.

The description of the organizational model which follows was the outcome of that day's work. Although it may be unique, and is certainly creative, it does not reflect the most important aspect of the work it represents. That is the richness of the dialogue — including disagreements, clarifications, surfacing of assumptions, and expression of fears and excitement that accompanied each decision made. The model became the framework for continuing project group discussions to refine each specific aspect. In the ensuing months, both board and staff members had ample opportunity to practise the process skills they would need to maintain the trust which was building and to continue communicating across their differences about the operational plans and policies that would drive the future work of their organization.

The Organizational Design: An Alternative to Hierarchy

Figure 1 illustrates the preliminary design which resulted from the model-building process.

Figure 1 — Model Building Process

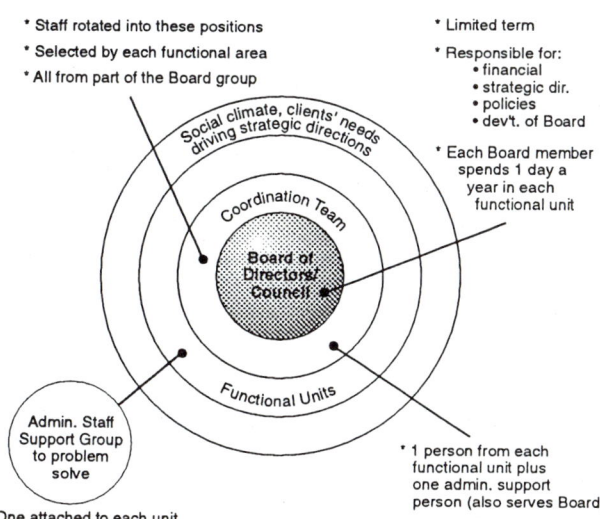

* Staff rotated into these positions
* Selected by each functional area
* All from part of the Board group

* Limited term
* Responsible for:
  • financial
  • strategic dir.
  • policies
  • dev't. of Board
* Each Board member spends 1 day a year in each functional unit

Social climate, clients' needs driving strategic directions

Coordination Team

Board of Directors/ Council

Functional Units

Admin. Staff Support Group to problem solve

* One attached to each unit

* 1 person from each functional unit plus one admin. support person (also serves Board)

Changes to this design continue to this day, as the intention was that the model be viewed as organic rather than static — a responsive structure which would meet the changing needs of an evolving organization.

Before describing the model in detail, I wish to reiterate that it is presented here not as a recommended "ideal" for all organizations of this type, but as one alternative among many which was designed to meet the needs of The Refuge at a specific point in time. I also wish to emphasize my belief, and I think Refuge members would agree, that the process of creating this model was as important as, if not more important, than the outcome.

a) The outer ring is intended to represent the context in which The Refuge operates, including the social climate, trends, and clients' needs that are consistently driving strategic directions and goals. In order to remain connected in an "open system" fashion to this context, the organization is committed to designing mechanisms to continually collect data on the changing needs and impact of this environment.

b) The second ring is entitled "Functional Units," and represents the various units of service provided by The Refuge. Each unit is comprised of staff who are trained in a particular technical skill (i.e., counselling, legal services, etc.), and one support staff person whose time is dedicated to the unit. Cross-functional ad hoc committees are formed as needed to deal with specific Refuge issues, while all support staff from each unit meet weekly as an Administrative Staff Support Team to problem-solve issues specific to their work.

c) The third ring is entitled "Coordination Team" and is intended to provide coordination leadership to all functional units, as well as facilitation within each separate unit. Although this team replaces the role of executive director, the functional units are not accountable to the members of the Coordination Team as they would be to a traditional manager. In fact, the model is based more on an academic-type structure, in which the department Chair is filled by faculty members who are rotated into the position every few years. Similarly, staff from the functional units are chosen by their colleagues to be rotated into the Coordination Team positions and developed in their jobs to be ready for this role at some point in their career with The Refuge. Although the Coordination Team members are paid a higher salary than their colleagues to compensate them for the additional responsibility, every employee has the opportunity to fill this role; the employee's salary is adjusted once he/she leaves it to reassume her/his functional unit membership. An administrative support staff person is chosen by the Support Staff Team to be assigned to this group on a rotational basis; this person also serves a support function for the board of directors.

d) The fourth ring was entitled the "Board of Directors" when the model was first proposed. However, there was discussion about renaming it "The Council," with some concern expressed regarding credibility with funders. This issue was yet to be resolved at the end of the model-building session. The board group is comprised of the members of the Coordination Team, to ensure board familiarity with the work of The Refuge, as well as an equal number of community members selected by a board/staff committee. Each of these members sits on the board for a limited term, and is expected to spend one day a year in each functional unit, to familiarize herself with Refuge realities. The board as a group is responsible for its own development and operation, retains legal and fiscal accountability for The Refuge, and sets strategic directions, policies, and guidelines within which staff can freely and autonomously make operational decisions. It is part of the responsibility of each Coordination Team member to ensure that her functional unit members' input is consistently solicited in the setting of policies and strategic directions.[6]

Conclusion

The case described in this paper and the organizational issues it exemplifies could be dismissed as unique and therefore unimportant in the larger realm of organizational learning and redesign. However, both current research and practice in the world of work provide convincing evidence that the issues are generic. This may be particularly true for organizations with a mandate for social change; it is most commonly demonstrated by those which are feminist in their orientation. However, I maintain that these are bellwether organizations in the truest sense. As employees across sectors become increasingly demanding of alternative work structures which involve participation at all levels of decision-making, the organizations that have been struggling with these alternatives and their consequences will take the lead in providing workable models and process awareness. Kathleen Iannello notes that "in (American auto firms) and other cases, prospects for profit have brought intense attention to the benefits of consensus, which feminists and others have known about for decades" (Iannello 1992, 122), and she emphasizes that "the pervasiveness of this type of organization needs to be documented" (Iannello 1992, 123). It is the intention of this article to contribute to this documentation, by delineating the issues which need consideration and providing a process and a model which may assist other organizations in their quest for innovative forms.

References

Acker, Joan. 1990. "Hierarchies, Jobs, Bodies: A Theory of Gendered Organizations." *Gender and Society*, 4, 2, June, 1990: 139-158.

Argyris, C. 1990. *Overcoming Organizational Defences: Facilitating Organizational Learning.* Harvard University, Boston: Allyn and Bacon.

Bardwick, Judith M. 1977. " Some Notes About Power Relationships Between Women." In Alice Sargent. *Beyond Sex Roles.* St. Paul: West Publishing. 325-335.

Bohm, D. 1989. *On Dialogue.* Edited by Bohm, from meeting transcription, November 6, 1989, Ojal, California.

Britell, J. 1992. "Life at the Bottom: Managing Problems in Social Change Organizations." *Whole Earth Review*, Fall, 1992: 84-91.

Carver, John. 1990. *Boards That Make a Difference.* San Francisco: Jossey-Bass Publishers.

Edmiston, Laurie. 1994. *Dialogue: The Missing Link in Organization Development Efforts?* Toronto: The Ontario Institute for Studies in Education. unpublished paper.

Freedman, Adele. 1993. "White Woman's Burden." *Saturday Night*, April, 1993: 40-84.

Freeman, Jo. 1974. *The Tyranny of Structurelessness in Women in Politics.* Jan Jaguett (Ed.) New York: J. Wiley and Sons. 202-214.

Greaves, Lorraine. 1991. "Reorganizing the National Action Committee on the Status of Women, 1986-1988." *In Women and Social Change: Feminist Activism in Canada.* Toronto: James Lorimer. 101-116.

Iannello, K. 1992. *Decisions Without Hierarchy: Feminist Interventions in Organization Theory and Practice.* New York: Routledge.

Issacs, W. 1993. *Dialogue: The Power of Collective Thinking.* The Systems Thinker. Cambridge, Mass.: Pegasus Communications, April, 1993.

Johnson, Barry. 1992. *Polarity Management: Identifying and Managing Unsolvable Problems.* Amherst, Mass.: HRD Press, Inc.

Katzenstein, Mary Fainsod and Carol M. Mueller (Eds.). 1987. *The Women's Movement of the United States and Western Europe.* Philadelphia: Temple Press.

Kraus, William. 1980. *Collaboration in Organizations: Alternatives to Hierarchy.* New York: Human Sciences Press.

Laiken, Marilyn. 1994a.. "The Myth of the Self-managing Team." *Organization Development Journal* (International Issue) 12, 2, Summer, 1994: 29-34.

Laiken, Marilyn. 1994b. "Conflict in Teams: Problem or Opportunity?" Lectures in Health Promotion Series, # 4, pp.1-12. Centre for Health Promotion, University of Toronto.

Leidner, Robin. 1991. " Stretching the Boundaries of Liberalism, Democratic Innovation in a Feminist Organization." *Signs: Journal of Women in Culture and Society*, 16, 2: 263-289.

Leidner, Robin. 1993. "Constituency, Accountability and Deliberation: Reshaping Democracy in the National Women's Studies Association." *NWSA Journal*, 5, 1, Spring, 1993: 4-27.

Liem, J.H. and J. O'Toole. 1992. "The Need for Power in Women who were Sexually Abused as Children." *Psychology of Women Quarterly*, 16: 467-480.

Lorde, Audre. 1984. *Sister Outsider — Essays and Speeches.* New York: The Crossing Press.

Manz, C., Keating, D. and A. Donnellon. 1990. "Preparing for an Organizational Change to Employee Self-Management: The Managerial Transition." *Organizational Dynamics.* Autumn, 1990: 15-26.

Martin, Patricia Yancey. 1990. "Rethinking Feminist Organizations." *Gender and Society*, 4, 2, June 1992: 182-206.

Melgaard, Anne. 1993. "Balancing Act" (Letter to the Editor). *Saturday Night*, May, 1993.

Miller, Jean Baker. 1977. *Toward a New Psychology of Women*. Boston: Beacon Press.

Miller, Jean Baker. 1982. *Women and Power* (Work in Progress No. 82-01). Wellesley, MA.: Wellesley College, Stone Centre for Developmental Services and Studies.

Moss-Kanter, Rosabeth. 1983. *The Change Masters*. New York: Simon and Schuster.

Riger, Stephanie. 1984. "Vehicles for Empowerment: The Case for Feminist Movement Organizations." In J. Rappaport, C. Swift and R. Hess (Eds.). *Studies in Empowerment*. New York: Hawthorne Press.

Ristock, Janice. 1991. "Feminist Collectives: The Struggles and Contradictions in Our Quest for a 'Uniquely Feminist Structure'." *In Women and Social Change: Feminist Activism in Canada*. Toronto: James Lorimer. 41-55.

Ristock, Janice. 1989. *Feminist Social Service Collectives in Canada: A Viable Force or a Contradictio?* Toronto: OISE Doctoral Thesis.

Senge, Peter. 1990. *The Fifth Discipline: The Art and Practice of the Learning Organization*. New York: Doubleday.

Struthers, Marilyn. 1994. *Organizing in the Perspective of Experience: A Review of Women's Organization Development Literature in Search of Mechanisms of Inclusion*. Toronto: OISE unpublished paper.

Woolsey, Lorette K. and Laura-Lynne McBain. 1987. "Issues of Power and Powerlessness in All-women Groups." *Women's Studies International forum*, 10, 6: 579-588.

Endnotes

1. I am grateful to the following people for their extremely thoughtful comments on this paper: Karen Blackford (Laurentian University) and three anonymous reviewers: OISE graduate students Laurie Edmiston and Ellen Russell; Wendy Weeks (Author of *Women Working Together: Lessons From Feminist Women's Services*); and Jeff Solway, my life partner and best editor. I also wish to acknowledge Karon West, my consulting colleague, and all of the board and staff members of The Refuge who participated with consistent good will in the organizational redesign project described in this paper.

2. Although Karon's role as my partner ended with the close of the project, and I am writing this paper several years later, I am indebted to her for her participation in the original diagnosis and analysis, much of which is incorporated into this article. It should be noted that, as white middle-class women of privilege, Karon and I were aware that we brought a particular perspective to the consulting process. We tried to be consistently conscious of how that perspective might be affecting our understanding of The Refuge. I have also attempted to do so in writing this piece.

3. Organizations do have the option of providing childcare, transportation, and meal funding for board members, which might offer less privileged women the opportunity to join the board. In their final organizational design, The Refuge attempted to respond to this need to have board members be more representative of their client community.

4. This issue is not at all exclusive to women's organizations, but would tend to be true of any politically committed organization with a mandate for social change. It has, in fact, occurred repeatedly in the consulting experience of the author in mixed gender organizations such as environmental groups, housing cooperatives, etc. It seems to be particularly prevalent in organizations with volunteer boards.

5. The consulting intervention was mandated to deal solely with the internal structure and functioning of the organization. A separate study was being conducted simultaneously to solicit client feedback on service delivery.

6. The author and The Refuge are indebted to John Carver 1990; William Kraus 1980; Gareth Morgan 1986; Travis and Callander 1990; Ulrich and Lake 1991; Karon West, Paul Woolner, and various women's organizations in the Toronto area for many of the concepts which helped to create The Refuge's organizational model. It should be noted here that, although this (or any) model may sound workable in theory, it is ultimately the good will of organizational members and their continuous work on resolving problems as they occur that bring a theoretical model to life.

Diana A. Coholic and Colette T. Prévost

Personal and Organizational Change: A Feminist Sexual Assault Program

Sexual Assault Program

Women share the common experience of being treated "differently" from men. What many of us do not share is the experience of being able to articulate how oppression, inequality, and sexism determine our "different" treatment. In general, we are not exposed to environments which can assist us or which encourage us to learn about our unequal status. This is in keeping with a patriarchal culture which dictates what is "normal" for us[1].

In our view, feminizing means two things. First, particular attention will be paid to the sociological and political circumstances and context of women's lives. Feminist action means enabling women to learn about power differences based on gender. As we gain knowledge about the meaning of living in a patriarchy, we become better equipped to contextualize our reality and to work towards change. It is vital for all women to contemplate their place in the world. Thinking through how patriarchy governs our society is of particular importance for sexual abuse survivors who become empowered by understanding that the abuse they have suffered is not their fault. The program we have developed addresses the context of all of our lives. It also aims to empower women by raising their consciousness about that male-dominated context and by giving them tools for resistance and reframing.

Second, feminizing includes recognizing and acknowledging that women are "experts" on their own experience. Therefore, the perspective of women must be taken into account in the provision of any services for women rather than the assumption that we are "sick" and in need of "expert cures." As Hill (1990) states, feminism was born out of a phenomenological philosophy; that is, we know what is real by trusting our own experience and that of other women. Also, feminizing our programs means that we try to balance the power relationships between the women and the facilitators and seek to build egalitarianism based on cooperation and a consumer orientation (Brown and Brodsky 1992; Lundy 1993). Feminist therapy strives to eliminate hierarchical relationships and empowers women by educating them about their choices (Pressman 1989). Armed with a sociopolitical understanding, women will have better resources to demand what they need and want.

241

Background

The development of this counselling program has been a process that has sustained significant systemic impacts. Most agencies such as the Community Counselling Centre of Nipissing were in part created by already-existing government or private structures and institutions, in which patriarchal fibres can still be observed throughout every level of hierarchy. The conception of feminist programming in such structures has not been a natural trend; rather, it has been a culture shock to a system intent on maintaining the status quo.

If not for feminist activism, public policy reform, and eventual government funding for violence against women programs, this agency and other Family Service Ontario member agencies would likely not have adopted programming which takes a feminist perspective into account. Throughout the 1980s, violence against women counselling programs were shaped and formed through the guidance of feminist literature (Sinclair 1985). The ultimate direction of these programs was almost exclusively influenced by women who were dedicated to eradicating violence. As a result, the larger agency system had little directive impact and "allowed" the lead to be taken by women's programs to meet government funding standards for appropriate and current programming. This has been the evolution of certain feminist programs within mainstream agencies. Our violence against women program, which includes a sexual assault counselling program for women who have been abused as children, and a woman abuse (wife assault) counselling program for women abused in a relationship, have recently developed a sociopolitical and educational sexual assault group program.

Program Rationale and Objectives

The overall objectives of this program are to bring women together so that they can meet, learn about, and discuss the sociopolitical factors that influence their lives.

Counselling programs offered within family service or generic counselling agencies typically do not offer group programs explicitly aimed at examining the broader context of women's lives. As a result, the majority of sexual assault programs offered by these types of agencies present women either with long-term individual or group counselling, which may or may not include an analysis of patriarchy. These practices convey the belief that all women require counselling to effect change in their lives. This, in turn, pathologizes women as the assumption is made that all abused women are in need of expert service and guidance. Indeed, as Greenspan (1983) points out, the dominant, male point of view teaches us that female "symptoms," such as passivity and dependence (the way we are socialized to be) are indicators of pathology.

Penfold and Walker (1986), in an examination of the psychiatric paradox and women, point out that feminists believe much of the misery women experience does not require therapy in the "traditional" sense. In fact, consciousness-raising groups may be far more relevant for women. By offering a sociopolitical/educational group program, we convey the belief that not all women need counselling and that knowledge is a powerful tool.

Women who suffer sexual assault often blame themselves for the abuse. The female socialization process teaches women that we are less important than men and that we are to blame for our own victimization. We are socialized to be dependent, passive, and accepting of responsibility for keeping intimate relationships intact (Auerbach Walker and Browne 1985). As a result, throughout history, women have been blamed for the assaults they suffered. These personal struggles are at the same time political issues in that women suffer violence as a result of inequality and oppression (Levine 1982). In the 1960s, it was feminists who began to describe sexual assault as a form of domination and control, as an act of violence, not sex (Donat and D'Emilio 1992).

Therefore, any counselling program that does not address these political issues continues to pathologize women and risks re-victimizing them as well. The sociopolitical/educational group is an excellent forum in which issues of inequality and their relationship to violence can be discussed. Feminist counsellors assist women in recognizing that part of women's pain is a result of being powerless and not a consequence of personal inadequacy (Malmo and Laidlaw 1990).

Indeed, we have observed that women who develop their abilities to analyze their lives within a sociopolitical framework effect positive change more readily than women who have not yet developed this skill. Women who understand that they have been and continue to be victims of violence because they are women can place the blame for the violence where it rests — with the abuser.

It is particularly difficult in rural areas and smaller communities, such as in Northern Ontario, for women to access appropriate forums in which they can discuss their concerns. In many areas, Women's Centres and other resources do not exist or the demand for services outweighs the available resources. Also, transportation to services and resources is an issue for many women who reside in remote or rural areas. It may be more difficult for women in the North to immerse themselves in a "women's community," as the community is often small, difficult to locate, or non-existent. Since our agency is one of the few organizations in our area that offers violence against women counselling programs, we have an even greater responsibility to provide the most helpful services.

An additional rationale for the development of this program arose out of our concern that, within our own agency, women who were abused as children and women who were abused in relationships were being seen in isolation of each other. This led to women's feeling "compartmentalized" and supported the belief that there was, in fact, a distinction between different types of violence. We know this is not the case and that violence against women constitutes systematic oppression; it takes many forms and affects all women to different degrees (Caputi 1991).

Since a sociopolitical/educational group had already been developed for our woman abuse (wife assault) program, the logical next step was to develop a group program specific to women who had been sexually assaulted as children. We support the belief that the causes of violence against women are the same, regardless of when the violence is inflicted during childhood or adulthood. As MacLeod and Sarage (1988) point out, child sexual abuse is one part of a spectrum of male violence against women and children.

Given that women's services are inadequately funded and that women's needs are not identified as priorities, we struggle with long waiting lists for service. Consequently, women are forced to wait unacceptable lengths of time for service. Within our own agency, women have waited for over one year before accessing counselling. Therefore, an objective of our program was to address this issue by offering women prompt service. The group helps women decide if they, in fact, want long-term individual or group counselling and helps them to focus on specific issues for counselling.

Program Description

The group program consists of four sessions in total; each session lasts approximately three hours. The format of the groups is structured with facilitators leading the women in participatory exercises and discussions. Videos and handouts pertinent to the discussions are also utilized throughout the group. A contract espousing confidentiality is signed by each woman before the group begins and each session ends with a closing exercise in which the women share a positive characteristic or strength.

The first session sets the stage for understanding the sociopolitical context of sexual assault. Statistics are examined concerning sexual assault. For example, women learn that some 50 percent of all women in Canada have been victims of an unwanted sexual act (Badgley Report 1984). Various definitions of sexual assault are examined. The myths perpetuated by society concerning women who suffer sexual assaults are analyzed.

The second session examines victimization in a social context. Particular emphasis is placed on the socialization process (how it is damaging to women) and on the media's portrayal of women. The third session focuses on the causes and costs of violence against women and children. The sociopolitical causes are stressed and the costs of violence to society in general are discussed. This discussion helps the women to understand that violence is a societal problem, not an individual problem or a woman's issue.

Finally, the fourth session focuses on the many roles or jobs a woman has, along with her skills and strengths. The women quickly learn that they have an inordinate number of skills, but that these skills have been devalued and taken for granted. During this last session, we have a "celebration" which provides us with time for group closure. We also facilitate an evaluation of the program during this session. We ask: "What would you change? What did you like? What effect has this group had on your understanding?" and similar questions. Initially, when we first began running this group, the facilitators discussed the questions with the group and recorded their responses. We now recognize the importance of having women discuss and record their responses to these questions privately. The women are also offered an opportunity to meet confidentially with a group facilitator to discuss any further concerns or ideas about the group.

Systemic Barriers

The program referred to above has encountered almost no resistance from the larger agency structure. It was introduced to people in other sections of the agency with a feminist analysis, which corresponds with the philosophy of the violence against women counselling program. While there exists some acknowledgement of feminist principles and practice in certain other program-specific areas of the agency, a feminist-driven systems vision is lacking. An objection that we must not "abandon" the entire agency to feminist principles has been expressed by agency administration and by workers in some programs who appear to have an incomplete understanding of the feminist analysis. Much philosophical tension also exists between feminist-driven programs and other agency service areas. The tension is observed particularly at times when the feminist "agenda" is being considered for global agency consideration. A reluctance to adopt a feminist philosophy can best be explained through an analysis of the agency's historical connections. For example, the Community Counselling Centre was founded and developed through years of affiliations and connections to myriad patriarchal systems. The agency's survival and growth often depended on these affiliations. This agency fondly remembers its "forefathers" and their contributions to building an agency that still exists today. In adopting a feminist framework, the agency would have to re-examine history and risk losing past connections.

Program autonomy in the agency continues to be encouraged within the boundaries of feminist programs. This has led to significant developments in the area of feminist programming which are recognized and encouraged. However, service users face a discontinuous service approach when they become involved in more than one agency counselling program. Thus, the effects of the resistance to feminize the entire institution can clearly be observed at various levels. In the following section, program outcomes concerning the sexual assault group and the larger agency system are presented.

Program Outcomes

In evaluating programs, our responsibility is to listen to women. Since our philosophy is that women are experts concerning their own experiences, it is crucial for us to seek this feedback. This assists us in improving our program delivery and provides us with ideas about the future direction our services should take. With regard to the sexual assault group program, women have conveyed to us the following insights.

All women reported that the program had increased their awareness of how society viewed them. Although this increased understanding of our patriarchal society understandably angered and upset them, most of them viewed their growing awareness as positive and strengthening. With respect to program structure, some women stated that they would have preferred to have completed this particular group program before attending individual or longer-term group counselling. They thought that the awareness they gained through the group would have facilitated the counselling process. Further, they also told us that they would have preferred having a longer group experience, given the extensive amount of information presented in four sessions.

Women also shared with us their personal growth experiences resulting from their participation in this group. Some women reported changes in their daily interactions with partners, spouses, and children. They stated that these changes were based on their ability to no longer blame themselves and they were less anxious. They reported that they would without hesitation recommend the group to other women.

Based on the above feedback, we conclude that the group has been a success. The program's objectives have been met and women have benefited from their participation in this particular program. As women developed a conscious understanding of what it means to live in a patriarchy, and as they learned to articulate how they are oppressed and viewed by society, they became able to demand their rights, to feel better about themselves, and to understand their victimization. Clearly, as women came to understand the context of their lives, they became more assertive and more self-aware. This group also provided a base from which service users made informed decisions about their future counselling choices. In addition, the group ensured that participants were not faced with a long wait before service was available.

We have found that, upon completion of this program, many women opt to take part in a counselling group instead of waiting for individual services. Besides the fact that this allows many more women to access our services, some argue that group counselling is the preferred service modality as it lessens dependency on a counsellor and encourages helpful relationships with other women (Pressman 1989).

The development and implementation of this program have been positive not only for the service users but for the larger agency system as well. As we mentioned earlier, concern was felt for the underlying effects of a feminist program not embodied within a feminist agency structure. We had assumed that systemic change needed to be ordered from top down. Without first having a feminist agency structure, we believed we could not successfully ensure the survival of permanent feminist programming. This belief justified continuous challenge of the agency structures to adopt a greater level of feminist analysis. Resistance to these challenges led to much frustration and painstakingly slow progress. Nonetheless, the challenges continued, fueled by the belief that we were having an impact on feminizing our agency. What had not been fully considered was the extent to which the client system could, in fact, impact the organizational structure and, thereby, instigate a shift.

When we consider differential power experienced by individuals at various levels of this hierarchical organization, we begin to observe at which level pressure can be exerted to create change. Board members and managers have power to effect change through policy. Service workers have influence through their practice. Not usually considered are those individuals who articulate a level of power through needs; that is, service users. In keeping with feminist principles, an egalitarian approach to organizational structure must be respected (Pressman 1989). Such an approach is seemingly contradictory to a hierarchical system unless power and power differences are openly acknowledged.

One might assume that policy makers would necessarily be the force behind most structural change. However, this has not been representative of our experience in the violence against women program. Women, when given a forum to do so, express their needs. Based on the needs they articulate, programs are developed. For example, needs expressed by women in an earlier, more heterogeneous group for dealing with violence in the family taught us that we needed to provide services with a more specific focus. Out of the feedback from these women emerged the educational, consciousness-raising group for women who had been abused in relationships (wife assault) and, later, a similar group for women survivors of childhood sexual assault which is the main focus of this paper. Returning to the women involved in evaluating the group's strengths and weaknesses resulted in very positive evaluations. This feedback encourages policy makers to continue in their support of this program's efforts. In turn, board members and managers are also beginning to adopt language and concepts which at least reflect an appreciation of the feminist perspective. What is becoming clear is that the community we serve, if served well, will, in fact, dictate organizational structure as well as individual needs.

Future Directions

One of our next challenges will involve bridging the gap in power between the client system and the organizational structure. In order to meet this challenge, we need to acknowledge the valuable contribution the women's community provides. We need to assure the involvement of women in our programs through various means. For example, input and involvement will be secured through the training of women to act as co-leaders in our groups. These women can provide support to women at beginning levels of counselling. In so doing, service users will be formally recognized for the power they should rightfully hold in the system and will be more systematically included in the decision-making equation.

We also recognize the value of having other members of the agency, with their particular expertise, involved in our programs. Specifically, we have listened to service users and colleagues alike tell us that the language. concepts, and structures of our program are not always clear to outsiders. We are very concerned that our program not be elitist, and we will therefore look to people throughout our generic agency who can assist us in making our language, concepts, and structures more accessible. Through such partnerships, mutual training will be provided with respect for both specific client needs and for the sociopolitical context of program development.

In looking forward to a more feminized organization, we continue to look for direction from those individuals who are accessing our services. In providing them with a forum for concrete input, we will continue to shape our programs to meet their stated needs. As all of our feminist guided programs increasingly respect and report such feedback, the agency will be influenced to support these programs, and policy shifts will thus occur throughout the larger organization.

References

Auerbach Walker, L.E., and A. Browne. 1985. "Gender and Victimization by Intimates." *Journal of Personality*, 53(2), pp. 179-195.

Brown, L.S., and Brodsky, A.M. 1992. "The Future of Feminist Therapy." *Psychotherapy*, 29(1), pp. 51-57.

Caputi, J. 1991. "Men's Violence Against Women: An International Overview." *Current World Leaders*, 34(6), pp. 847-878.

Committee on Sexual Offenses Against Children and Youths. 1984. *Report of the Committee on Sexual Offenses Against Children and Youths, I-II and Summary* (Badgley Report). Ottawa, Ontario: Department of Supply and Services.

Donat, O.L.N., and J. D'Emilio. 1992. "A Feminist Redefinition of Rape and Sexual Assault: Historical Foundations and Change." *Journal of Social Issues*, 48(1), pp. 9-22.

Greenspan, M.C. 1983. *A New Approach to Women and Therapy.* Toronto: McGraw-Hill Book Company.

Hill, M. 1990. "On Creating a Theory of Feminist Therapy." *Women and Therapy*, 9 (1-2), pp. 53-65.

Levine, H. 1982. "The Personal is Political: Feminism and the Helping Professions." *Feminism in Canada: From Pressure to Politics.* Eds. A. Miles and G. Finn. pp. 175-209. Montreal: Black Rose Books.

Lundy, M. 1993. "Explicitness: The Unspoken Mandate of Feminist Social Work." *Affilia*, 8 (2), pp. 184-199.

MacLeod, M., and E. Saraga. 1988. "Challenging the Orthodoxy: Towards a Feminist Theory and Practice." *Feminist Review*, 28, Spring, pp. 16-55.

Malmo, C., and T.A. Laidlaw. 1990. "Afterword: Empowering Women Through the Healing Process." *Healing Voices: Feminist Approaches to Therapy with Women.* Eds. T.A. Laidlaw, C. Malmo and Associates. pp. 320-323. San Francisco: Jossey-Bass.

Penfold, P.S., and G.A. Walker. 1986. "The Psychiatric Paradox and Women." *Canadian Journal of Community Mental Health*, 5 (2), pp. 9-15.

Pressman, B. 1989. "Treatment of Wife Abuse: The Case for Feminist Therapy." *Interviewing with Assaulted Women: Current Theory, Research and Practice.* Eds. B. Pressman, G. Cameron and M. Rothery. pp. 21-45. New Jersey: Laurence Erlbaun Associates.

Sinclair, D. 1985. *Understanding Wife Assault: A Training Manual for Counsellors and Advocates.* Toronto, Ontario.

Endnote

1. We would like to thank all of the women who have participated in our programs and who have provided us with the feedback necessary for the ongoing development of our services. We would like to give credit to Patricia Tobin and Judy Duncan for developing the original sociopolitical/educational group format within the woman abuse (wife assault) program. Jeanette Bélanger and Annette Rondeau must be acknowledged for their contributions to the development of the group for women survivors of childhood sexual assault. Finally, we would like to thank the members of the violence against women program for their relentless dedication to feminizing this organization.

Bernice Moreau

The Feminization of the Black Baptist Church in Nova Scotia

Introduction

I believe that any inquiry into Black Canadian women's tradition could spark controversy and debate over the interpretation of concepts such as spirituality. This paper, an interpretation of the religious or spiritual practices of a group of Black Canadian women in resistance to patriarchal church governance, is no exception. Be that as it may, I will argue that these Black women's religious or spiritual practices, until recently, were not only for their personal satisfaction and empowerment but were also strategies for change in their spiritual community. It is worthy of note that these Christian Baptist women were not unique in their struggle to feminize their religious community. Many women in other oppressed communities have situated their resistance in spiritual beliefs or in religious organizations.

For example, Black women from the Caribbean and North America in the Pentecostal movement have made significant sacrifices in their struggle to bring about change into their Church. As a result, they "have engendered a legacy...they have prayed, pioneered and paved the way, each in her own unique way (has) helped (to) inspire this...rich legacy our foremothers bestowed upon all of us through their individual commitment to God, the church and family" (Marcelle and Robinson 1986, iii). Similar examples of the link between oppressed women's spirituality, empowerment, and feminization may be found among North and South American Aboriginal women (Benecoff 1997). Also, Schussler Fiorenza reminds us that oppressed women of this era, regardless of race, nationality, status, or culture, have found that the Bible

> has provided authorization and legitimization for women who have rejected slavery, racism, anti-Semitism, colonial exploitation, (patriarchy) and misogynism as unbiblical and against God's will. The Bible has inspired and continues to inspire countless women to speak out and to struggle against injustice, exploitation and stereotyping.... It empowers us to survive with dignity and to continue the struggle when there seems to be no hope for success. (Schussler Fiorenza 1984, xiii)

It is interesting to note that Black women's spiritual strength has been evident in their struggle for freedom in every area of their lives from slavery to the present. Wade-Gayles found that "the remarkable spirituality of slave women is the dominant chord in the spiritual singing" (Wade-Gayles 1993, 6). Praying and other activities inspired faith, hope, and love in women like Sojourner Truth, Harriet Tubman (Wade-Gayles 1993, 6,37 and 149), Catherine Abernathy, Violet King, Phillis George, Maude Sparks, Muriel V. States, Ada Simmons, Marie Hamilton, Pearleen Oliver, and countless others (Hamilton 1982, 1994). Black women's harmonization and amplification of these everyday spiritual practices have assisted in feminizing the church, as was/is evident across North America and, more specifically, in the Black Baptist church in Nova Scotia.

The term "feminization," as it is used in this paper, refers to all the formal and informal religious activities initiated, performed, and maintained by women in the Black Baptist churches in Nova Scotia that have led to the achieving of equality with men in the leadership of the Black spiritual community. The literature (Moreau 1996; Boyd 1976 and others) suggests strongly that Black Nova Scotian women's spirituality, like that of other Black women in the Western hemisphere, has always been a significant part of their cultural tradition. Consequently, for over two hundred years, these women, whose stories are encapsulated in the life of their church, have been able to initiate, perform, and affirm meaningful feminist changes in the church community through positive "female traditioning."

Black female spirituality or religiosity, especially the practice of traditional Christianity, is difficult to define. Its broad range of denominational interpretations and differences makes each women's spiritual experience unique. However, in this paper, it refers to a distinct Black community's experience of their deepest religious beliefs, convictions, patterns of thought, emotions, behaviours, and work ethic in respect to what is ultimate, God. Black Nova Scotian Baptist women's spirituality is holistic, encompassing their relationship with God, with one another in the community, with the society at large, and with nature in a fundamentally cultural way. Consequently, Black Nova Scotian women's religiosity is not an orthodox theological belief system or a moral code. It is a lifestyle guided by spiritual Biblical principles such as faith, love, and hope that shaped their everyday lives. This was/is manifested in their sharing, respectful attitude, co-operation, caring, and mutual support. The consistent manifestation of the women's religious practices, through the medium of faith, hope and love for God and others, especially vulnerable others, has had a permanent female influence on the Black Baptist churches in Nova Scotia. Morton (1993) states that the Church provided women opportunity for socially acceptable roles such as Sunday school teachers, musicians, and so forth. I will argue that these women did not wait for the Church to offer them opportunities for service. Their spiritual values led them to initiate work as educators of youth and adults, welfare officers in their community, encouragers, supporters, and counsellors.

Faith, Hope, and Love

Black Canadian female scholars, in addressing various aspects of Black women's experience, focus primarily on Black women's oppression and resistance (Moreau 1996; Brand 1990; 1984; Hamilton 1994; 1982; Cooper 1988; Mannette 1987; Best 1977; Oliver 1953; and others). James informs us that "Black feminist theorizing is rooted in Black communities and nourished by them even as it challenges those very communities to address issues of internal women's experiences of multiple interrelated oppressions....While reflecting the diversity of its many adherents it also struggles to embrace contradictions" and differences (James 1993, 2). Therefore, discussion of the feminization of the patriarchal Black Baptist church traditions is pertinent and timely.

According to Biblical injunction, "faith is being sure of what we hope for, and certain of what we do not see...and without faith (trust) it is impossible to please God, because anyone who comes to God must believe that God exists and He rewards those who earnestly seek Him" (Bible (NIV) 1985: Hebrews Chapter 11: verses 1+6). Similarly, hope is the confidence we have for a positive expectation of the expression of faith even when the situation appears hopeless. Love, which is understood in practical terms as a deep and tender feeling or devotion to someone or something, allows the practice of faith and hope to become a reality through patience, perseverance, and persistence. Moreover, faith, hope and love are spiritual interrelated gifts which make change possible although not painless. When put into practice, they together resist most negative barriers against feminization found in the Church. In active hope, the women exercised their faith through the hard work they performed in love that brought about desired change.

An examination of the literature reveals the power of the women's spiritual gifts, manifested through faith, hope, and love, in the continuous transformation of the Black Baptist Church throughout its history. Hamilton states that "the involvement and presence of Black women vibrates throughout the social, education, cultural, and religious life of the Black community....Women were active in most of the churches where they taught in the Sabbath schools and nearby day schools" (Hamilton 1994, 34). The application of the spiritual practices that reflected Black women's ways of knowing and being must, of necessity, have been centered in Black women's holistic spiritual life-style. Theirs was/is a faith in a God whom they trusted to provide strength, courage, and tenacity for initiating change; strength to resist blatant oppression (i.e., racism, sexism, illiteracy, poverty, and so forth) and the ability to struggle against fatalism, self-destruction, and the like. Theirs was/is a hope in God and in their vision for a progressive and productive community. Theirs was/is a love for God, for themselves, and for their community that inspired and motivated them to resist traditional Christian practices of sexism in the spiritual community and to initiate changes in quiet ways beginning in their homes.

It is commonly said that 'charity or love begins at home' and quickly spreads abroad. I would like to suggest that this love, interrelated with hope and faith, practised by the Black women with patience and perseverance at home, became the element that ignited the feminization process of the Black Baptist church in Nova Scotia. Carrie Best, a Nova Scotian Baptist woman, recalls her mother's way of making a difference in her home that, over time, influenced Best's work in the church. She said:

> My mother was a meticulous home maker...kind, loving and generous...guiding the sanctity of her home and the family's safety like a lioness with her cubs. Black womanhood was held in low esteem during the early part of the twentieth century and only the home (and the church) afforded the protection needed to ensure security from outside influences. (Best 1977, 43)

Best contends further that the only way that our foremothers' dreams for a better life were to become a reality was through their practice of the spirituality which served as a resistance to any form of oppression against positive change. She reminds us of their past actions:

> somehow, though their cups were often empty and battered, these women with their work-scarred hands dared to hope as they dried our tears and rocked us to sleep in the fullness of their bosoms, that their dreams their hope would become reality in us. (Best 1977, 173)

Similarly, these women's concern for their community's welfare, particularly in the early 1900s, was partly responsible for their drive to influence the Black Baptist church to cater to the whole person. Moreover, their involvement in the creation of a continuum of programs offering social, educational, spiritual, financial, recreational, and other services within the Church meant that their recognition as part of the church leadership was inevitable. It is worth repeating that, although women were always the 'backbone' of the church, they were not officially proclaimed leaders until they decided to resist women's absence in church leadership.

Feminization in The Church

In the 1780s, the Black Baptist church in Nova Scotia came into existence as a form of resistance against all types of oppression by white religious groups (Pachai 1987; Williams 1983). This demanded that Black women and men work together for the survival of their community against the onslaught of religious persecution, racism, sexism, and class and colour discrimination. External religious and social persecution of Blacks by Whites motivated not only the unity of Black women and men in spiritual matters but in every other way. We can conclude that the Black Baptist Church in Nova Scotia, for the most part, has always accepted women as a vital part of its existence but that it needed feminization of its leadership.

Pachai informs us that with the arrival of freed Black Christians to Nova Scotia "the existing churches were only prepared to receive them as special members with separate seating facilities" (Pachai 1987, 50). This religious segregation by white churches led to the establishment of the Black Baptist Church. Moreau 1996; Williams 1988; Hamilton 1982; 1994; Walker, 1980; Pachai, 1987; Best 1977; Boyd 1976; Pratt 1972; Oliver 1970; 1969; 1948, and others inform us that Blacks' enslavement was sanctioned and maintained by most of the mainstream white Christian denominations (Hamilton 1994). This imposition of segregation continued after slavery so that Blacks were not readily or willingly admitted to white public places of worship. Pachai claims that Black Nova Scotians

> were denied access to the corridors of real opportunity in the white world of exclusive membership. They set out to create their own opportunities, their own institutions, their own network — not because they loved segregation but because they had to do their utmost to survive. Religion was the centre of survival. (Pachai 1990, 48)

In some instances, Black Christians were openly rejected, ridiculed, and alienated when they attempted to worship with whites. In others, separate sections of white churches were allocated for Blacks only. In response to these inhumane acts, many Blacks established their own churches. In 1784, David George, his wife, and some other Black Christians organized the first Black Baptist Church in Nova Scotia (Pachai 1990). Black men must be given credit for their leadership role in constructing the church, but Hamilton (1982); Best (1977); Oliver

(1953) and others remind us that the wives of those men and other womenfolk also deserve credit. Throughout their history in the province, Black women struggled to provide for their families and communities by changing their barren environments into livable communities, whether in rural settlements or within the margins of white townships and cities (Hooks 1984).

In spite of the establishment of their own churches, the Black community, as recently as the 1950s, was still perceived by the White churches as insignificant. It was in this hostile religious milieu that Black Nova Scotian women, with faith, hope, and love, worked with the men in their homes, schools, and churches to make a difference. This is where the feminizing of the Black Baptist churches in that province had its genesis. As I have indicated earlier, the Black Baptist Church proffered its community opportunities that were denied its members by white society.

For example, Black Nova Scotian women (and men) through the church established the first Black educational system. The literature reveals that, until the 1950s, formal education for Blacks in Nova Scotia was not a legal or civic right (Moreau 1996; Pachai 1987; Boyd 1976; Oliver 1970). As a result, in many parts of the province, Blacks were bluntly refused formal education with Whites. Black women (and men) through their church established "little Black schools" taught mostly by women who saw it as their religious calling to educate community members as best they could. One Black woman had this to say about the way the community tried to meet its desperate need for formal education: "Poor as we were, we were made to build our own schools, hire our own Black teachers, and pay the teachers by community effort" (Moreau 1996, 128).

In the same way, the women, with the help of the Church, established the first welfare agency. They used all the knowledge acquired from their workplaces, their mothers, grandmothers and great grandmothers (Hamilton 1982) and their own experiences, to nurse, teach, and train the youth and one another to meet the needs of the community from the womb to the tomb (Moreau 1996). Also, the women of the community, with the help of the men, made training available to potential leaders including preachers, teachers, politicians, handicraft makers, and domestic workers. The women worked along with the men in preparing the Church to provide a political platform for public discussion of community issues. The Church was also used as the first sports complex and the medium through which young Black people were able to develop their talents and abilities in different areas of life. Black women in the Church worked to create a forum for Black self-expression and to stimulate the development of group and self-identity. They were instrumental in nurturing group and self-respect among young people who might otherwise have been submerged by societal oppression. Pachai supports this discussion with the reminder that this church was more than a religious organization. It was a training ground for generations of Black leaders, followers, preachers and teachers, politicians and professionals (Pachai 1990, 63).

It is interesting to note that, in contrast to the feminization of the Black Baptist churches in Nova Scotia, there are similar churches in North America dominated by Black males. In these churches, Black women's spirituality has not been celebrated or even respected. For example, Martin discusses the sexism prevalent among male ministers of the Black Baptist religion in parts of North America. Historically, Black men dominated and controlled the Baptist convention and missionary outreach: "therefore, it was possible to overlook the presence of women within the African mission movement or to minimize their support for the mission cause" (Martin 1986,16). While the ranks of the women included teachers, leaders, mission organizers, independent missionaries, or co-workers with their husbands, their efforts to feminize the church went unnoticed because of sexism.

In spite of the Black religious male leaders' sexist attitude toward Black women's spirituality, women continued to struggle for the feminization of the Church. Griffin, in her article "A Layin' on of Hands": Organizational Efforts Among Black Americans, 1790-1930," leads us to believe that, from the earliest days of the American slavery era, the feminization of the slaves' environment was continuous. The author points out that "adult female cooperation and interdependence was a fact of female slave life" (Griffin 1988, 23). She notes further that this Black female tradition of cooperation and interdependence, which was an important part of Black women's spiritual expression, was used as an everyday survival strategy. They were always able to utilize their cooperative organizational skills for the benefit of their own community in times of difficulty. Griffin claims that this tradition continued unabated even during the severe depression years of the early 1930s. She concludes that "in some sense, Black women had an advantage of experience over white women because throughout their history they had to rely on the cooperative nature of their families and neighbours to make do" (Griffin 1988, 8).

In Nova Scotia, the same is true of the women's ability to cooperate and thus bring about change. For instance, in the first half of the twentieth century, Black Nova Scotian women were determined to play a more prominent role in the life of their church. In 1917, the women of the African United Baptist Association (AUBA) formed what they called the Ladies Auxiliary of the church during an AUBA meeting in East Preston Baptist church. It is interesting to note that the women chose to hold the first meeting of their Auxiliary at the community well, a biblical symbolic meeting place for women. The "Women at the Well," as they were referred to, organized and cooperated under the leadership of Sister Maude Sparks to implement and administer church programs and the social services needed in the community. Sylvia Hamilton, a Black Nova Scotian scholar, gives us a brief account of what the women did in the early 1900s. She points out that the objective of the Ladies' Auxiliary was stimulation of the spiritual, moral, social, educational, charitable, and financial responsibilities of all the local churches in the AUBA. She further states that

> In 1917 the women of the African Baptist churches in the province...gathered outside around a well in the community of East Preston since the church had no space for them to use. This gathering became know as "Women at the Well." (Hamilton 1982, 35-36)

Williams also gives some insight into the dedication of these women to making things happen. They took on the financial responsibility of the Church and did a better job of raising money for Church programs than the men did. The author claims that financially the Ladies' Auxiliary was and is the strength and backbone of the Association. During various years, the Auxiliary has raised more money than the total receipts of the Association (William 1983, 448). Through this organization, the women of the Church promoted and organized social work programs that provided for the welfare of the orphans, the destitute, and the aged in the community (Winks 1977).

In addition, they worked as equals with the men in administering to the needs of orphans and juvenile delinquents in a Home for Coloured Children. This was a notable accomplishment by the women (and the men) in the Black Baptist church since Nova Scotia's White social services department refused to accept Black orphans and or juvenile delinquents into their institutions. Another history making event was promoted by the women of the Black Baptist Church: "In 1920 for the first time in Canadian history a convention of coloured women was held in Halifax, Nova Scotia" (Hamilton 1982, 36). By this time, women in the Black Baptist church in Nova Scotia were responding to the need for ordained female ministers to serve as official spiritual leaders in various ministries of the church. The women's resistance to patriarchy in their spiritual community through their practice of faith, hope, and love had made inroads in the feminizing of their church.

Conclusion

This brief investigation of the feminization of the Black Baptist Church in Nova Scotia is used as a notable example of the way Black women were/are able to bring about changes in community organizations. I have found that, from the Church's establishment in 1782, feminization has always been in progress. Women's involvement in changing the Church has been an on-going process throughout its history. When the Black Christians responded to White religious persecution by establishing their own Church for spiritual worship, the women played a major role in creating an amicable spiritual and cultural environment in silence (Oliver 1953). They practised a spirituality that was inclusive of culture and religion, and, in their quiet ways, they created the feminization of the Black Baptist Church. It was not accomplished with specific celebration or violent revolution. It was a subtle, almost invisible, continuous process that resisted most efforts by the men of the Church to control the women's creative participation in the organization. We can conclude that Black Baptist Nova Scotian women's spiritual practice of faith, hope, and love, as manifested in their everyday work activities, set the state for feminization in the Black Baptist Church in the early 1900s. Their holistic and inclusive approach to spirituality has motivated them historically to begin the feminization of the early Church. This laid the foundation for the later progress that was made by the "Women at the Well" and others in the early 1900s in the feminization of the Black Baptist Church in Nova Scotia.

We believe that the spiritual principles of faith, hope, and love form the foundation of this feminization process, and, in the context of this study, we make three significant observations. First, any investigation of Black Nova Scotian women's feminization of their Church is an examination of their spiritual behaviour and, as such, should be done holistically. Second, it is important that the investigation be an honest interpretation in order to prevent an underestimation of the women's ability to administer and perform in a spiritual setting. In addition, it must show how the women supported the men in their efforts and accepted the assistance offered by the men but rejected any attempts to hinder initiatives to make the Church "woman-friendly." The discussion demands respect for the women's self-defined meaning of spirituality, thus making a strong case for the inclusion of all their lives' experiences as spiritual. Finally, we believe that the utilization of the women's spiritual principles of faith, hope, and love, as a way of understanding the feminization of the Black Church in Nova Scotia, has given us a clearer understanding of the Black women's ways of implementing visible changes in the Black Baptist Church in Nova Scotia to this day.

References

Best, Carrie M. 1977. *That Lonesome Road: The Autobiography of Carrie Best*. New Glasgow, Nova Scotia: The Clarion Publishing Co. Ltd.

Boyd, Jr. Frank S. ed. 1976. *A Brief History of the Coloured Baptist of Nova Scotia 1783-1895*. Halifax: Afro NS Press.

Brand, Dionne. 1990. *No Burden to Carry Narratives of Black Women in Ontario in 1920s to 1950s*. Toronto: Women's Press.

Cooper, Afua A. 1988. "Black Women in British North America 1760-1867." A Paper Presented at OISE, University of Toronto, Ontario.

Griffin, Farah Jasmine. 1988. "A Layin' on of Hands: Organizational Efforts Among Black American Women, 1790-1930." SAGE: A Scholarly Journal on Black Women, Student Supplement.

Fiorenza, Schussler Elizabeth. 1984. *Bread Not Stone The Challenge of Feminist Biblical Interpretation*. Boston MA: Beacon Press.

Higginbotham, Evelyn Brooks. 1993. *Righteous Discontent The Women's Movement in the Black Baptist Church*, 1880-1920. Cambridge MA: Harvard University Press.

Hamilton, Sylvia. 1982. "Our Mothers Grand and Great: Black Women of Nova Scotia." *Canadian Women Studies*. Vol. 4, N.2, (Winter)m pp. 33-37.

Hamilton, Sylvia. 1994. "Naming Names, Naming Ourselves: A Survey of Early Black Women in Nova Scotia." *We're Rooted Here and They Can't Pull Us Up*. Eds. Peggy Bristow et al. Toronto: University of Toronto Press.

Hooks, Bell. 1984. *Feminist Theory: From Margin to Center*. Boston, MA: South End Press.

Marcelle, Celia and Robinson, Catherine J. 1986. *Black Women in the Church Historical Highlights and Profiles*. Pittsburgh PA: Magna Graphics Inc.

Martin, Sandy D. 1986. Black Baptist Women and African Mission Work, 1870-1925. *SAGE*. Vol. 111, No.1.

Moreau, Bernice. 1982. "Adult Education Among Black Nova Scotians: 1750-1945." *Journal of Education*. N. 400 (April), pp. 29-35.

Moreau, Bernice. 1996. *Black Nova Scotian Women's Educational Experience 1900-1945; -1995; A Study in Race, Gender and Class Relations*. PhD Thesis University of Toronto, Canada.

Morton, Suzanne. 1993. "Separate Spheres in a Separate World: African Nova Scotian Women in late 19th Century Halifax County." *Acadiensis* XXII, 2 (Spring) pp. 61-83.

Oliver, W. P. 1949. "Cultural Progress of the Negro in Nova Scotia." *The Dalhousie Review*. Vol. 49 (June), pp. 293-300.

Oliver, Pearleen. 1953. *A Brief History of the Coloured Baptists in Nova Scotia 1982-1953*. Halifax, Nova Scotia: Cornwallis Baptist Church.

Pachai, Bridglal. 1987a. *Beneath the Clouds of the Promised Land: The Survival of Nova Scotia's Blacks 1600-1800*. Nova Scotia: Black Educators Associations of Nova Scotia.

Pachai, Bridglal. 1987b. *Peoples of the Maritime Black*. Nova Scotia: Four East Publications.

Wades-Gayles. 1995. *My Soul is a Witness African-American Spirituality*. Boston: Beacon Press.

Walker, James St. G. 1980. *A History of Black in Canada*. Québec: Canadian Government Publishing Centre.

Williams, Savannah. 1983. "Two Hundred Years in the Development of Afro-Canadians in Nova Scotia 1782-1982." Jean L. Elliot (ed.), *Two Nations, Many Cultures: Ethnic Groups in Canada*. Toronto.

Winks, Robin. 1977. *The Blacks in Canada A History*. Montreal: McGill and Queen's University Press. (2nd Edition).

PART V — PARTIE V
Caring —
Question de soins et de services

Feminist researchers Baukje Miedema and Nancy Clark describe the lives of working-class women who choose to mother other people's children. This paper leads to an interesting examination of the family, with an exploration of mothering, childhood, and family relations. The New Brunswick foster mothers interviewed in this article must often use their own funds to meet the needs of the children in their care since state support is insufficient. Child care, including the nurturing done by these women, has little status in society. While these social relations oppress foster mothers and the children they care for, the authors report that foster mothers resist the negative definitions of others. Instead, they recognize the difference they make in children's lives as important. They also value the expertise they gain in caring for children whom they come to know well. Miedema and Clark recommend that children, and, indirectly, the state, would benefit if foster mothers were consulted about children's follow-up care, and were provided with adequate funds to provide child care.

Karen Blackford also invites us to examine family life though her specific focus on parenting with a disability. She argues that a caregiving role for women or for anyone can be empowering. What is oppressive is the assumption that caring must be unidirectional rather than reciprocal, and that only women must be caregivers. Based on interviews with parents who have multiple sclerosis and with their children, Blackford cites the strong beliefs we hold about gender, age, bodily condition, and what a family *should be like*, as barriers to women's empowerment and to positive caring relationships. She reports that the onset of chronic illness can, ironically, serve as a catalyst for empowerment of all family members. This is especially true when disability onset triggers a reassessment of family beliefs and a reorganization of family responsibilities.

Poor, proud, and sometimes desperate residents in low-income communities have few and poorly organized networks, little sense of their own power, high rates of unemployment, and low rates of formal education. These are the observations of researcher Marge Reitsma-Street and community activist Pat Rogerson. They found that sole-support mothers and their children — Native, francophone, and visible minority Canadians-living in two northern Ontario neighbourhoods were further oppressed when government and charitable organizations introduced top-down hierarchical redevelopment structures. Agencies with no long-term stake in the community and little understanding of the perspectives of residents *don't work and don't feel good.* These authors describe community residents who vigorously responded when respectfully invited to participate in research. They took part in training, planning, interviewing neighbours, critiquing findings, and creating neighbourhood services. Empowerment for women, for their children, and for these neighbourhoods in general has been the outcome of the program called Better Beginnings Better Futures.

Heather Garrett points out the restrictions faced by women at the beginning of the nineteenth century. Families were sites to which middle class women were restricted, and in which poor women were oppressed by fatigue and inadequate resources for themselves and their children. The economy and the state were also pivotal in maintaining the poverty experienced by underclass women and in restricting women's political participation. A social historian venturing for the first time into an application of feminist analysis, Garrett introduces what she learned from archival sources about the Needlewomen's Guild. This is a Canadian charitable women's group which originated in England. Members, primarily from the middle class, provided hand-made clothing for children who needed clothing. These maternal feminists did not work for political power, nor did they seek to change the class system. However, their enterprise can be seen as a necessary precursor to future change. According to Garrett, this group participation empowered women by offering them a reason to gather outside their homes, to learn new skills, and to experience the satisfaction of having a positive effect on lives beyond those of their family members.

Baukje Miedema and Nancy Nason-Clark

Mothering for the State:
Three Stories of Working Class Foster Mothers

Introduction

Foster mothers are women who enter a contractual relationship with the child welfare system for the care of children who have been apprehended by the state. Foster care can be described as "the provision of planned, preferably short-term, substitute care for children who cannot be adequately maintained at home" (McKenzie 1989,1). In New Brunswick, the role of the foster mother and other foster family members is described as providing the apprehended child with "stability of a substitute family" (New Brunswick Health and Community Services Information Sheet n.d.).[1]

From an outside perspective, foster mothers appear to be exploited by the state: they provide twenty-four hour care to a troubled child for the cost of that child's room and board in the foster family's home; they agree to accept children on short notice (often two to three hours); they receive little information on the child's presenting problems or past difficulties with the law or the education system; they agree to transport and accompany the child to medical and therapeutic services; they provide ongoing academic support to the child including assistance with school work; they offer physical care including the provision of meals, lunches, laundry, and a clean living space; and they agree to provide emotional support and counsel to multi-problem children. However, the relationship between the foster mothers and the state is far more complex than this suggests.

While for most women mothering is relegated to the private sphere, the care provided by the foster mother is strictly supervised by the child welfare system. As such, she is a public mother, mothering on behalf of the state. In this paper, we want to explore, based on the personal stories of three working-class foster mothers in New Brunswick, the central paradox in the way in which the state understands the contribution of women who foster; i.e., the rewards and challenges they attribute to their work. We will discuss the centrality of their personalized concept of "mothering," and how they believe that as mothers they have something important to contribute to children who are in need of safety and stability.

On the one hand, the child welfare system relies almost exclusively on women to provide care and stability for dislocated children for whom the state acts as guardian. The state provides limited reimbursement for the costs these women incur, relying on their volunteer labour to meet a public need. However, while the foster mothers provide twenty-four hour care to foster children, they are not involved in the decision-making processes related to these children. As such, the state depends upon their altruism and their skills for care and nurturance, but appears to disregard that same knowledge and experience when decisions about the future of the foster child need to be made.

Annie, Barbara, and Connie[2], three New Brunswick foster mothers, tell stories of fostering experiences that can be characterized as examples of success in the feminizing of the child welfare system at the level of the individual caretaker/child relationship. These women derive self-worth from their caring and self-esteem from others who acknowledge the important roles they play in the lives of marginalized children. Yet, in their relationship with the state, they are very vulnerable because their mothering knowledge is marginalized and they have no involvement in the foster child's future.

While the system of foster care receives much attention in the social work literature, the lives and experiences of women who foster are often overlooked. Within the debate around foster care, it is assumed that fostering is a family responsibility, affecting the lives of both adults and children who offer their homes as refuge for dislocated children (Cohen and Westhues 1994; Kulp 1993). Yet, the reality of the foster experience is that, while the support of all family members is crucial to the success of the foster placement, it is the lives of foster mothers who are affected the most (Kendrick 1990).

The feminist literature on mothering offers somewhat opposing views of motherhood (cf Everingham 1994; Rossiter 1988). Neo-conservative and liberal feminists argue that women's mothering is inevitable and that society should strive to make mothering as rewarding as possible without changing the social patriarchal structures of contemporary society (Descarries-Bélanger et al. 1991).

On the other hand, feminists grounded in psychoanalysis and radical feminist thought argue that mothering is socially constructed. Nancy Chodorow (1978) believes that mothering is not grounded in biology but emerges as learned activity from a gendered life experience. While radical feminists also see motherhood as socially constructed and the ultimate result of patriarchal society, they advocate the "abolition of motherhood as an institution and the domestic responsibility of women" (Descarries-Bélanger et al. 1991, 16).

Everingham (1994) expresses the struggle between the divergent philosophies of mothering this way:

> How can the fundamental contribution that women-as-women make to society be specified without tying women's identity to some essential notion of what it means to be a woman? Any fixed formulation of women's "nature" has the potential to undermine women's efforts to achieve some measure of personal autonomy. Yet to ignore women's specific experience as women, and their contributions to society as mothers, inhibits our understanding of nurturing activities and the possible development of a socio-political system grounded in an ethic of care. (Everingham 1994, 4)

In other words, if women want to be recognized as mothers, they may be relegated to the domestic sphere almost entirely through the justification that mothering and its associated activities are biologically determined; on the other hand, to ignore women's contribution as mothers to society will render their work and contributions invisible.

Basing her analysis on personal experience, Amy Rossiter (1988) felt uncomfortable with the sharp bifurcation in the theories explaining motherhood. She states:

> I was stuck on the horns of a very painful dilemma: I believe that children's attachment to their mothers was based on their physical relationship to the maternal body; yet I understood that same preferential attachment to be implicated in the maintenance of patriarchy. (Rossiter 1988, 13)

Others have suggested that economic conditions and social class play an important role in how mothering is viewed by women and society:

> That lack of validation for women's caring obscures the work involved and reinforces the idea that this is the natural work of women. In a society that values paid work in the public sphere, the work of women's caring in the private sphere has received little attention. (Baines, Evans and Neysmith 1991, 30)

Many women in the contemporary western world find that mothering produces both incongruence and ambivalence. When a mother chooses to care full-time for her children, she is relegated to a subordinate position in society and her life is determined by the domestic sphere. If she chooses to be childless and to participate in the public sphere fully, she is questioned about her choices and often meets with criticism. If she chooses to participate both in the domestic sphere as a mother and in the public sphere as a worker, she has to carry out a delicate juggling act (Nason-Clark and Bélanger 1993; Hochschild 1989), one for which there is no clear-cut solution.

An added quandary in the early as well as recent works on mothering is that they deal with women who mother their own children (Chodorow 1978; Trebilcot 1983; Wearing 1984; Rossiter 1988; Kaplan 1992; Everingham 1994). Furthermore, much of this literature understands mothering from a middle-class vantage point. But what about the experiences of working class women who choose to mother other women's children?

Dorothy Smith (1987) has created a "map" to analyze "the work of mothering in a complex of relations that organizes its social and material character" (1987, 170). In a similar fashion, we analyze the daily experiences of women who have chosen to mother children who are not their own. The complex of relations for these mothers involves relationships with the state, personified in various social workers, medical, educational, and therapeutic professionals dealing with foster child and the biological family of the foster child. Mothering for foster mothers, therefore, is not a private matter but a very public one. As public mothers, these women fulfil many of the responsibilities associated with mother care yet they are deprived of several rewards (i.e., seeing their children grow up, making decisions in early childhood that have the potential to affect their later lives).

The narratives of the three foster mothers presented here are part of a larger study on foster care in New Brunswick. The initial research sent a survey to all 650 foster families in New Brunswick (one survey per foster family), but, of the returned surveys (47% response rate), 93% were completed by women. Exactly half of the foster mothers themselves reported that their partners shared in the provision of care for the foster child. However, upon further analysis, it was revealed women were far more involved in the practical day-to-day physical activities, such as assisting with homework and providing transportation. The majority (55%) of the foster mothers were full-time, stay-at-home moms; a further 20% worked full-time; and 20% worked part-time outside the home.[3] Those working for pay tended to be involved in jobs that mirrored women's work in the home, e.g., cooking, baking, personal care. By contrast, the majority of their male spouses had obtained full-time employment or were seasonal workers. A very small percentage of the male spouses did not have employment outside the home.

Providing a family for a troubled child was reported as one of the primary motives for entering into a contractual relationship with the child welfare system. As we shall see, providing a family environment centres around the role of mother and her provision of love and care to children in need.

266

While the purpose of the first phase of this research was to sketch a profile of foster parents in New Brunswick, the second phase focused on the experiences of foster mothers, through twenty in-depth interviews in various geographical locations around the province. To illustrate the complexities of foster mothers' decisions and the impact of fostering on women's daily lives, we have chosen three interviews as the foundation for this paper.

A Window Into the Lives of Foster Mothers

The main goal of the narrative approach is to take seriously "what people say about their lives rather than treating their words simply as an illustration of some other process" (Cruikshank 1990,1). Through presenting three foster mothers' own stories, we hope to provide these foster mothers with "the opportunity to present themselves and their lives as they would want them presented" (Cole 1991, 40).

The three foster mothers described in this chapter were chosen out of the twenty foster mothers interviewed for the study (Miedema 1999). The sole criteria for including these three women in this chapter was the concept that they illustrate a wide variety of fostering experiences based on the ages of the foster children and the purpose of fostering. One foster mother fostered only teenaged children; the second foster mother fostered an infant with the hope of being able to adopt the child in the near future; and the third foster mother fostered a handicapped child. The foster mother's stories are neither typical nor atypical fostering experiences; each story was unique to the individual foster mother. Although the fostering experience was framed by a complex set of relationships between the foster mother, her family, the state, the foster child, and the foster child's family, this article illustrates that one foster mother's story alone cannot embody the fostering experience. These three stories, then, illustrate, from the perspective of the foster mothers, the impact of various aspects of fostering on these women's daily lives.

Annie's Story[4]

Annie was a heavy-set, middle-aged woman with a grandmotherly demeanour and a warm, friendly personality. She lived in a small village of rural New Brunswick in a large, well-kept house from which she ran a seasonal business. She also cared for an elderly father.

With her two grown children on their own, eight years previous, Annie decided to become a foster mother. Since that time, she has provided care for sixty children. At present, Annie is fostering four teenage children, two of whom are young offenders.

The interview with Annie was rather chaotic: her partner entered and retrieved items from the kitchen on several occasions; curious foster children poked their heads in from time to time; the phone rang, and the dog barked. This was a snapshot of Annie's life.

On the decision to foster...

We both made the decision to become foster parents. I fostered before [another province] when my boys were younger. When we moved here, I had [own seasonal business], so in the winter I said: "I will foster." It sort of grows on you. If you don't have kids, the house is empty. It gives me something to do. A little bit of income and...I enjoy it. You do see the rewards. You see the rewards. Maybe not right away but you do see the rewards. It makes you feel good.

On the impact of fostering...

The foster children come here with no rules...most of them who come here they don't know what it is to sit down and have supper at the same time every night, go to bed at the same time, to have a shower at the same time. A lot of them don't have any morals; like respect for other people's stuff; not to take stuff that does not belong to them.

House rules, normal house rules, every house has them but they are not written down. Mine are written down....The first two weeks, the angel period, the children are really, really good. Then they become normal kids again and they try to do what they did at home and stuff like that. Then you have to teach them, what you think is right as a foster parent.

On attachment...

I have to be careful you know, I really like him. In fact, I feel so sorry for him that it is not funny. Like they have been dragging this case for six years. Now that he is fourteen, they realize, I think it was a month or two months ago, just before he came here, one month and half, and they just found out that it is the mother who does not want him. It is hard...the kid has been trying and trying and I don't know....

When [B] left his mom came and got him. She said: "You will probably see him again, it will not be long." No social worker and nothing. I felt happy and hurt.... Not very many will say thank you even when the parents come and get them, half of the parents will not say a boo. Then you do have the odd ones. Like I got a book with cards and stuff like that.

I have a lot of contact when the kids leave. [A foster girl] moved to Ontario. She phones me. Wherever she moves, like she is a little gypsy, but wherever she is, she phones. Mother's Day she will never forget. I get cards, she sends me pictures of her kids. I have [P] another girl from [city]. She phones me three times a week. Another one would bring the adoption papers. That is the reward. The kid is still thinking of you. That contact means a lot to me. I like cards and stuff like that. Then the others, you don't hear, you wonder about them.

On the type of care Annie provides...

Family care. It is like I said before, showing the kid what a normal family is. I am not saying that all foster children are street children. Some of them, like I say, they don't know what utensils to use, they don't know that you have to take a bath every day. Things like that. Just normal family behaviour. Professional [care]?[5] What I meant maybe was, how can I say? It is like a profession, you are like a teacher and for girls, teaching them how to sew, how to cook and clean and taking care of children. You teach them how to cope, how to take care of kids.

On the rewards...

I enjoy the kids and I really like doing it. I would be very lost if I did not have it. I enjoy cooking for them and enjoy taking care of them.

Others think I am up too much. Especially with four teenagers. They think I am crazy. A lot of people think I am crazy. They say: "You got four teenagers? Are you crazy?" They don't understand.

I often pay stuff out of my own pocket. Lots of stuff. I am not saying big things because I cannot afford it. But little odds and ends. It is very unfair, there should be, you know, a scale, not depending on the mood or the feeling of the social worker if the child comes into care.... It is bad enough that they are away from their family. They should have their needs met.

On the relationship between the Department of Health and Community Services and Annie...

It is sometimes hard to get in contact with the social worker. It depends again, it depends on the worker. Sometimes the worker is too busy, they are really busy, I should not say too busy, but they are really busy because they have a heavy case load.

The thing that really concerns me is the aftercare for the kids when they leave. Like they sometimes...the kid has been in care for six months, he should be doing okay and they take him and put him back, you know, there should be more closer contact. I think even more so after they leave here. Because they are floating, they are not sure if they want to go for the good or the bad.

Annie's story mirrors the experience of foster women around the province in that she sees traditional domestic and mothering responsibilities as critical components in the care she offers to the foster children. Her story differs from others in that she chooses to look after teenagers, which in the minds of many foster mothers is considered the most challenging or difficult age group. Central to Annie's fostering experience is her goal to provide a family and to mother children in need of care, stability, and safety. As a result, it is the traditional domestic labour responsibilities that Annie sees as the expertise she brings to fostering.

Barbara's Story

Barbara lives on the outskirts of a small town in a new house with a large live-in kitchen. Barbara is thirty-four years of age, a university educated stay-at-home mother, married to a tradesman with a highschool diploma.

Initially, Barbara became a foster mother because she was involuntarily childless. For the last six years, she has taken care of nine foster children of varying ages. After fostering for six years, Barbara and her husband decided to adopt one of the children for whom they cared.

At the time of the interview, Barbara had an eight-year-old daughter she had adopted, and two other foster children (an eight-year-old and an infant whom she was planning to adopt). The interview atmosphere was quiet because the baby slept almost all the time and the other children were in school.

On the decision to foster...

...we had just found out that we couldn't have any children of our own. That was very difficult for myself more than my husband because I was very hurt, very angry. I felt that I didn't want to bring up other people's children, if I couldn't have my own. So with the support of my husband and sitting down talking about it, this is something we thought that we should try….We had put a lot of thought into this. This is something that you can't just jump into. You need to have a lot of time to think this out.

On the impact of fostering…

It has changed our lives. By now we have adopted one. We used to be able to get up and go before as we felt free but now children come first and we just take one day at a time. We can't plan ahead like before.

I wondered if it was good, because I was used to being able to go wherever I wanted. But I wouldn't change that for anything now because it is really a great experience. We do a lot of family things together which is nice and we do take the time to do things, just my husband and I by ourselves.

I knew it would be a lot of our time spent with the children, because with your own children you know what they are like right from a young age. When you get older children, they are set in their ways, you don't know a lot about them so you really have to work with these children more. I find with the little one that we have now, we had him since birth, it made it easier on us than the other [foster] children.

On attachment…

…if they are here for a long period of time, it makes it harder to see them leave. Even I found, we have had a couple of cases where it has been overnight to maybe just a few days or a week, it has been hard to see them go.

…[It] was very difficult for us to decide for her [current foster child] not to stay with us. She is at a very difficult age and has a lot of problems in her background. We have two other children, we feel that this is our family right now, we like to have a time to be with our family. We did tell her that she was going to leave and she dealt with it very, very well. Children can deal with things very quickly when they are leaving, or if they are staying. They learn to adjust very well. She has her moments when she doesn't want to leave us but we are going to be like an extended family to her, she'll never lose contact, she'll pick the phone and call us.

271

Or she'll come up different times, when she wants to call us and ask to come up she can and we will do some special things with her. We have been like parents that she never had before and to make it a lot easier on her, we agreed to be an extended family for her which is nice that you are able to do that.

On the type of care provided...

Well it is family care because it is not just the foster parents that have to deal with it. It is their family members too. Like my mom and dad and his [husband] parents, brothers and sisters and that. It was not on very good terms at first for his side but on my side it was just wonderful because they knew that we wanted children so much and they were really happy for us. But we had to deal with both sides. Now that we have fostered for a few years and have had children, they know that we really do a lot of good for these kids. They may not be our own but they feel very special to us and we try to make them fit in to the family.

On fostering and rewards...

...with the baby we had, we went and got the baby at the hospital and it was just a matter of three days because the baby had to stay in hospital until things were checked out. That is the thing about children, babies are usually placed on adoptive placements. We had our name on the adoption list before we started fostering. We thought well maybe it could be quite a while down the road before we have a chance to adopt any babies.

We decided yes, it worked out well. We still kept our name on the list for a baby and it wasn't until last year that we got a call....We had the opportunity of going to see the baby. We went shopping, got clothes and stuff for the baby and took them to the hospital and got him dressed and brought him home the next day. It was nice to be able to go because it was something I wanted always to experience. I mean, that is about the newest you could get a child.

On the relationship between the Department of Health and Community Services and Barbara...

No, I think it is great the way it is. I have never had any problem.

Barbara's story is centred around her own voluntary childlessness. She enters into fostering as a vehicle to become a real mother of an infant child. Like the majority of women who choose to foster, Barbara's philosophy of caring is rooted in traditional notions of mothering. Unlike other foster mothers, however, Barbara has some very specific goals about her fostering experience. She had indicated her desire to adopt children before her involvement with the foster care system and foster care in New Brunswick provides foster families with priority adoption. Clearly, one expedient way to adopt a child is to volunteer to become a foster parent. Barbara was successful in her efforts to adopt. In the beginning, she adopted a school-aged child and now she is in the process of adopting an infant. The adoption of the infant fulfilled her desire to construct an experience of attachment with a foster child that imitates as much as possible the experience of birth mothers.

Connie's Story

Connie, forty-two years old, lives in a small two-storey house approximately twenty kilometres out of a major town. She lives with her husband, a grown son, and one two-year-old special needs, foster child. While neither Connie nor her husband completed high school, she has attained a GED Diploma. He is employed full-time as a mechanic.

Connie has been a foster mother for more than eleven years and has taken care of a total of seven foster children. For more than six years, she fostered a severely handicapped child who needed twenty-four-hour care. Eventually, the child died, leaving emptiness in Connie's life.

The interview with Connie was interrupted a number of times by phone calls, a knock on the door, and the waking up of the young foster child.

On the decision to foster...

I got lonely and I missed having kids. I missed feeling needed, that was my main thing. I enjoy having kids around and I found it very lonely in the house. So I just said: "That's it, I'll take another one."

On the impact of fostering...

It was hard to get babysitters so we had to stay home. One of us was more used to him so one of us would go and the other would stay home. Now it is fairly easy to get babysitters. I used to get frustrated but my husband was a great sitter. He supported me a hundred percent. Like the little guy that we had a while ago, we had him for a little over six years, and he was total care. Six years and then he died. He couldn't even sit up on his own. He had spastic.

273

You had to be able to know how to handle him. A lot of people were scared of him. See we got used to him because he was with us.

But I did have babysitters come in you know like every week and I went for groceries and stuff like that but we just didn't go out as a couple, as a husband and wife team very often.

Family care I would say it is more like the closeness of the family unit. The time for playing and helping him learn a little bit. The professional care is the therapy and stuff. That is how I looked at it. To me, I feel I can do just as good as anybody else under the circumstances with the child I had because I had been taught enough about how to look after them. A lot of the kids, the other little guy, everybody used to say I was around him enough that I knew more about him that they did. Which is true because we as foster parents are around these children twenty-four hours a day so we know.

On attachment...

[But now] I have a little boy that is two-and-a-half, but he is tiny, tiny, he was born at a pound and a half and he is only twenty pounds. So he is special needs. We are going to adopt this little guy.

Well, I think it is the idea that I've had him so long that I'm scared that they would take him out of my home. I brought him home from the hospital. He was six months old when they got him out of the hospital and I brought him home.

On rewards...

You make fairly good on special needs, [but on regular foster children] maybe $4.00 a day, that's all you get. I think the last time, I can't be quoted, but it was about $120.00 to $150.00 a month, that's not much for buying baby food and milk. Like I mean they had to go buy Pampers, they have changed that now, Pampers are no longer under them.

I feel they are losing their foster parents because of it. Because I mean people take kids because they want to but they don't need to go into the hole for it. I mean you are allowed so much for maintenance and clothing and stuff but I mean that doesn't go no where. I mean the cost of living goes up, okay we get a raise maybe $4.00 a year, that's not going to buy nothing. They don't realize what it cost to look after the child. I mean you can go out and babysit and make three times the amount of money a month as what when you are looking after a child twenty-four hours a day. Even the chances of having teenagers, they could burn your house down. Social Services will reimburse you so much. No, it is not enough.

On the relationship between the Department of Health and Community Services and Connie...

You shouldn't have to go ask [concerning information]. They should just bring it all out in the open. Because I mean you are taking the child. I mean you have to know whether that child has got AIDS or has been tested, I think anyway. They've never brought stuff like that. I mean it is something that not everybody needs to be checked on but it don't hurt.

I felt that the worker thought that I didn't know nothing. But really after I got to know her, I could see where she was coming from but I just felt that they aren't reading their paperwork or whatever because I had other kids and like, the special needs was really special needs. I thought if I can look after him, I can look after anybody. I felt all they had to do was look back in my files and see that. But she was a new worker and she didn't know me. So I could see where she was coming from but I didn't like it.

Connie's experience of fostering is also rooted in notions that the best care children can receive comes from mothers. But, in Connie's case, she has chosen children who are in need of constant care, thus intensifying both the skills and endurance required of the foster mother. For six years, she provided around-the-clock nurturance for a severely handicapped child until his death in the early 1990s. At the moment, she is both caring for a special needs child and considering adoption of that child because she is worried about his future.

Understanding Foster Mothers' Stories

Embedded within each of the stories that Annie, Barbara, and Connie have told of their fostering experience is the centrality of mothering. For these women, their motherhood was not rooted in their biological experiences, though two were indeed biological mothers. Nor was their mothering simply a function of expressing a need to be needed, although that motive too can be gleaned from the stories. Rather, it is an interweaving of the notion that children need to be raised by a mother in a family setting, that their personal skills as mothers qualify them to look after

275

children who have been apprehended by the state, and that what they impart to these children is the experience of a woman who cares for them to the point of irrationality as a mother is supposed to do. In a retroactive fashion, these foster women strive to overcome the limitations that dislocated children experience: not having a mother to provide care, security, stability, and love.

So what does motherhood include? Mothering demands a "single-minded passion" for a child (Roth 1994). It includes irrational giving (Aaker 1994), "24-hour duty" (Luxton 1980), and "playing, talking, reading and generally worrying about them" (Luxton 1980). From the perspective of the twenty foster mothers in our study, success in fostering is defined as a woman who can act out her mothering role for a child who has been taken from its own mother. As with the working-class women in Wearing's 1984 Australian study, money and education are less important to their sense of self-worth than are the roles of wife and mother: in fact, it was their opinions and ideas as mothers that caused other people to pay attention and admire them. In a similar vein, the women in our foster care study report that their success derives from the fact that as mothers they can make a difference in the life of a child, a child who for whatever reason has been deprived of continued mother-care.

Relying on the feelings of the foster mothers concerning care, the state uses these women's altruism (foster care is the backbone of the child welfare system in New Brunswick) and benefits from their volunteer labour. However, at the same time, the state appears unwilling to tap into their knowledge and experience at the level of the child welfare system as a whole. Rather, the state depends almost entirely on the advice of "professionals," who may have had limited contact with the foster children. In fact, the state considers fostering as something for which "no special skills [are] required" exposing the state's understanding of what mother care is (New Brunswick foster care pamphlet). The New Brunswick Foster Care Pamphlet goes on to state that "if you are able to love children you would make a good foster parent."

The three foster mothers whose stories are told in this article illustrate several contradictions inherent in the "web of relationships" between foster mothers, foster children, and the social workers employed by the state for the purpose of child welfare (Smart 1987; Luxton 1980). First, there is the value of *mother-love*. On the one hand, it is the love of children and the value a woman places on mother love that prompts a woman to consider foster care. Yet, the state does not value such a commitment enough to include foster mothers as part of the foster child's decision-making team. Second, consider the importance of *mother-care*. While the state upholds the desirability of providing a child's care in a home setting, indeed expects foster mothers to take children at short notice (under circumstances that are often fraught with tension and conflict), it also removes children from the foster care environment without adequate preparation for the separation of foster mother and child. Third, there is the importance of *mother-contact*. Although the state requires the provision of physical and emotional care for the foster children by the foster mothers, as soon as the foster child has left, foster mothers are not encouraged to remain in contact with the foster child; in fact, they are often actively discouraged. The result is that many foster mothers still worry about the children who once lived with them.

Thus, foster care is a prime example of the success of feminization of care at the individual level (for both foster mother and foster child), without necessarily demonstrating success at the level of broader structural changes to the institution and society. In essence, the foster mother provides the foster child with the most essential aspect of fostering (love and care) at a personal level that an impersonal system is unable to do. The irrational mother-love, the desire for mother-contact, and the perpetual mother-care of foster women bridges the gap between the multiple needs of children in care and the inflexible bureaucratic nature of the state. Surely, this is one of the central paradoxes of the role of the foster mother: at the point of her greatest irrationality (be it economic, time, or affection), she is most successful to her foster child.

References

Aaker, Linda P. 1994. "Birthing Death." *Mother Journeys: Feminists Write About Mothering*, eds. M.T. Reddy, M. Roth and A. Sheldon. Minneapolis, MN: Spinsters Ink.

Baines, Carol, Patricia Evans and Sheila Neysmith eds. 1991. *Women's Caring*. Toronto: McClelland and Stewart.

Chodorow, Nancy. 1978. *The Reproduction of Mothering: Psychoanalysis and the Sociology of Gender*. London: University of California.

Chruikshank, Julie. 1990. *Life Lived Like a Story*. London: University of Nebraska Press.

Cole, Sally. 1991. *Women of the Praia*. Princeton: University Press.

Cohen, Joyce S. and Westhues Anne. 1990. *Well-functioning Families for Adoptive and Foster Children*. Toronto: University of Toronto Press.

Descarries-Bélanger, Francine and Roy, Shirley. 1991. *The Women's Movement and Its Currents of Thought: A Typological Essay*. Ottawa: CRIAW/ICREF.

Everingham, Christine. 1994. *Motherhood and Modernity*. Philadelphia: Open University Press.

Hochschild, Arlie. 1989. *The Second Shift: Working Parents and the Revolution at Home*. New York: Viking Penguin.

Kaplan, Meryle Mahrer. 1992. *Mother's Images of Motherhood*. London: Routledge.

Kendrick, Martin. 1991. *Nobody's Children*. Toronto: MacMillan of Canada.

Kulp, Jodee. 1993. *Families at Risk*. Minneapolis: Better Endings, New Beginnings.

Luxton, Meg. 1980. *More than a Labour of Love*. Toronto: The Women's Press.

McKenzie, Brad eds. 1989. *Current Perspectives on Foster Care*. Toronto: Wall and Emmerson, Inc.

Miedema, Baukje. 1999. *Mothering for the State: The Paradox of Fostering*. Halifax: Fernwood Publishing.

Nason-Clark, Nancy and Brenda Bélanger. October, 1993. "Jugglers for Jesus: Identifying Career and Family Juggling Patterns Amongst Conservative Religious Women". Paper presented at the Annual Meetings of the Society Study of Religion, Raleigh, North Carolina.

Nelson, Margaret K. 1990. "Mothering Other's Children: The Experiences of Family Day-Care Providers." *Ties That Bind,* eds. Jean Barr, DeBorah Pope and Mary Wyer. Chicago: The University of Chicago Press.

Nelson, Margaret K. 1994. "Family Day Care Providers: Dilemmas of Daily Practice." *Mothering, Ideology, Experience, and Agency,* eds. Evelyn Nakano Glenn, Grace Chang and Linda Rennie Forcey. New York: Routledge.

New Brunswick Health and Community Services. Information Sheet for Potential Foster Families.

Rossiter, Amy. 1988. *From Private to Public.* Toronto: The Women's Press.

Roth, Martha. 1994. "Beneath the Skin." *Mother Journeys: Feminists Write About Mothering,* eds. M.T. Reddy, M. Roth and A. Sheldon. Minneapolis, MN: Spinsters Ink.

Smith, Dorothy. 1987. *The Everyday World as Problematic.* Toronto: University of Toronto Press.

Trebilcot, Joyce ed. 1983. *Mothering: Essays in Feminist Theory.* Toronto: Rowman and Allanheld.

Wearing, Betsy. 1984. *The Ideology of Motherhood.* London: George Allen and Unwin.

Endnotes

1. I would like to thank the Nels Anderson Fund, the Canadian Federation of University Women, and the Social Sciences and Humanities Research Council of Canada for their support.
2. These are fictious names.
3. Some women had retired from the workforce.
4. The original transcript text has been presented in tact, except for some minor editing. All names and personal information have been changed to protect the foster mother's identity.
5. All interviewed foster mothers were asked if they felt that the care they provide was professional or family-based care.

Karen A. Blackford

Caring to Overcome Differences, Inequities, and Lifestyle Pressures:
When a Parent Has a Disability

Introducing Transformation into
Discussions of Disability

This article discusses disability and family life, arguing that living with disability can heighten one's appreciation for and practice of the feminist principles of equity, dailiness, and respect of difference. This article is based on findings from a study of 18 Ontario families in which a parent has multiple sclerosis.

My personal experience as a mother with a chronic illness initially provided the insight that the rights of people living with disability needs to be addressed. Disablist oppression touches all family members and usually includes stigma, economic hardship, isolation, and inadequate access (Abberley 1987). However, as I interviewed each family member in the study individually, it became clear that while oppression certainly exists, there are also strengths to be gained from living with disability. In organizing the social relations of family life when a parent has a chronic illness like multiple sclerosis, family members often learn to do it differently.

Details of the study's method and results are available elsewhere (Blackford 1995). The intent here is to discuss some of the theoretical implications that the study results hold for feminist thinking about the institution of the family and about the practice of caring. I begin with a very brief introduction of how the theorizing and the experience of women with disabilities have enriched the Canadian women's movement.

Women with Disabilities and Feminism in Canada

Canadian feminists were forced to recognize the concerns of those fifteen percent of Canadian women who have disabilities when the Disabled Women's Network (DAWN) formed in 1985. Until that time, the issues of greatest importance to disabled women had been ignored for the most part by the disability movement and by the women's movement (Israel and Odette 1993). As an awareness of similarity in concerns between women with disabilities and other women grew, both groups benefited. They could articulate a clearer understanding of how the ideal female body image and social expectation of female dependency result in powerlessness and violations of the rights of all women (Mathews 1983; Fine and Asch 1988).

Since then, the issue of reproductive rights has emerged as one area of contention. The general philosophy of the women's movement is that a woman has a right to choose when and to whom she gives birth. The position of many disabled girls and women is that their lives are as worthy as other lives. This situation means that abortion on the grounds of potential disability in a foetus presents a problem (Doe and Ladouceur 1993; Saxton 1984). A major concern for disabled women is that they have commonly been denied the opportunity to conceive (Finger 1983). Many could support a woman's right to choose an abortion so long as abortion policy did not include mandatory prenatal testing or limitations on medical coverage needed for the care of babies with disabilities. Ora Prilleltensky (1997) expresses the ironies clearly. The feminist struggle has been defined only as the woman's right to prevent or terminate unwanted pregnancy. In contrast, women with disabilities seek the right to have children.

Women with disabilities have also raised questions about the feminist celebration of embodiment. There is a contrast between the unequivocal celebration of women's bodies advocated by most feminists and the experience of some women with disabilities whose bodies are often too tired or painful to celebrate. For example, philosopher Susan Wendell (1995) advises that feminist dismissal of objectivity and praise of the subjective fail to recognize the benefits of distancing oneself at times from the here and now. She describes benefits for disabled women in theorizing about some more ideal state or as a means of finding temporary relief from a painful body. Wendell's ideas prod feminist thinkers to broaden their definitions of women.

A clarification of this discussion of disability should be added since the term disability will be used in this article to refer mostly to the chronic illness called multiple sclerosis. Multiple sclerosis involves remissions and exacerbations of spastic, painful, and weak muscles; vision loss, mood swings; and fatigue related to lesions in the white myelin covering of the nerves and spinal chord (Roger and Matsumura 1991). This chronic illness tends to affect women of childbearing age. Chronic illnesses such as lupus, multiple sclerosis, and Crohn's disease have in common their age of onset, unpredictability, and invisibility. I learned at a 1994 Disabled Women's Network (Ontario) conference on mothering that the maternity experiences of women who have disabilities from birth or childhood and those of women whose physical or mental situation are relatively stable may vary considerably from those of chronically ill women.

This paper invites reassessment of feminist assumptions about girls' socialization in the context of the family and about family life generally. I identify how disability of a parent can alter the social relations of caring and can modify the cycle of oppression which family life often constitutes for girls and women. In short, the article studies the potential for feminizing family life in the context of disability.

Women, the Family, and the Social Relations of Caring

Critics of family policy such as Margaret Eichler, Karen Anderson, and Meg Luxton have questioned the viability and fairness of a nuclear family form for women and girls. The oppression of restrictive ideas about what families should be like, termed "familialism" by Meg Luxton or "familism" by Lesley Bella, has often resulted in women's being forced to care for themselves, their spouses, their aging parents, and their children (Neysmith 1991; Luxton 1988; Eichler 1988; Bullock 1990).

Caring is usually performed in the context of personal relationships and has unfortunately been understood to be unidirectional. That is, whether we are referring to 'caring for' or 'caring about,' it is assumed that it will be mothers who are the actors, naturally both loving and labouring for their children (Swift 1995). According to this view, one is either a caregiver or a recipient of care. This dualistic male view leaves no room for interdependence. When women take on caring roles, they are often seen (and many come to see themselves) as nurturers, rather than as partners in the family. Neglected or overlooked is the reality that women also have needs and deserve support.

Like other women, women with disabilities are also "forced to care" within a traditionally-organized nuclear family made up of one or two parents and their children. The pressures presented by familialism on mothers with disabilities cannot be appreciated without some consideration of the broader issues associated with disabled mothers.

Motherhood is an issue of unique magnitude for women with disabilities since disabled women are often oppressed by socially-mandated celibacy (Fine and Ashe 1988), restrictions against adoption (Doe 1997), sterilization (Roeher Institute 1995), and other stringent forms of birth control (Blackford 1993). Because of the widespread prejudice against parenting with a disability, mothering or even fathering with a disability is assumed to be potentially 'damaging' for children. In the event of a parent with a disability, family 'dysfunction' is presumed to be inevitable. For example, even charitable organizations whose mandate is to advocate for people with disabilities, such as the MS Society of Canada, have only recently come to recognize needs associated with parenting and multiple sclerosis (Blackford 1993; Fraser 1986).

As a result, in dealing with the traditional expectations of how families *should* be, mothers with disabilities have had little support or even recognition from the women's movement; the male-dominated, self-help disability movement; or health-related organizations. They face barriers such as low income' lone parenting; inadequate access at home, at work, or at their children's schools; inappropriate medical equipment; and poorly-adapted baby furniture. Only recently have the Independent Living Movement, the Disabled Women's Network, and the women's caucus committees within the Council of Canadians with Disabilities and within Disabled People's International begun to address these concerns.

This summary provides a background against which to understand the historic and recent barriers and concerns associated with parenting and with disability. Given the obvious oppression women face associated with both familialism and disability, it could easily be assumed that women with disabilities are victims. Ironically, my purpose here is to discuss from a fresh perspective children and parents in families in which a parent has multiple sclerosis. In contrast to this idea of victimization, I focus on opportunities.

This article complements others in this text on feminist change (Reitsma-Street and Rogerson; Medina and Nason-Clark; Parsons and Goggins) which also note that feminist values of equity, respecting difference, and taking time to care can be hallmarks of everyday living with disability. I argue here that a learned respect for difference, along with equity in the distribution of responsibility and in the practice of taking time for each other, sometimes frees family members from restrictive traditional expectations. Through the intimate experience of caring for and knowing a person with a disability, and through feeling cared-for and understood by a person with a disability, oppression associated with disability prejudice and with familialism is reduced.

I also argue that although caring responsibilities can be oppressive when they are borne by women alone, caring is an enlivening experience when such responsibilities are shared. Feminists can learn from the lives of mothers with disabilities and from the lives of family members who live with a parent's disability that while inequities in responsibility are oppressive, caring *when supported and shared* makes us more human.

Respecting Difference

Lack of accessible transportation, housing, and employment can be as instructive as name-calling for family members as they learn that a parent with a disability is not respected or included in the community. However, within families in which parents reject the notion that only stereotypical body images and functions are valuable, there are many examples that disability is not a reason for exclusion from everyday life.

When a parent has a disability, spouses and children care for that individual and learn to appreciate the caring they receive in return. Through such caring practices, all family members gain intimate knowledge of the details and the reality of disability and achieve a closeness with an understanding of the person who has a disability.

In her consideration of race and representation, Bell Hooks (1992) helps us to understand the importance of this closeness in overcoming stereotypical attitudes: "Stereotypes, however inaccurate, are one form of representation. Like fictions, they are created to serve as substitutions, standing in for what is real. They are a fantasy, a projection onto the other that makes them less threatening. Stereotypes abound when there is distance. They are an invention, a pretence that one knows, when the steps that would make real knowing possible cannot be taken or are not allowed" (170).

The importance of knowing and respecting difference through closeness was made evident in the study through contrasts among situations I observed. Children in the study who were 'protected' from the 'burden' of caring for a disabled parent or sibling appeared to maintain stereotypical expectations of the body. In one such family, a boy ignored his mother in her wheelchair when he encountered her on the street. In a similar family, a daughter wished her father would stop visiting her on parents' weekend at summer camp and a son derisively imitated his father's tremor.

In contrast, children who were permitted to help others overcome impairments and to really get to know a disabled person were remarkable in their acceptance of disability as well as of other characteristics usually seen as 'different' from the norm.

One eleven-year-old girl assists her father when he repairs equipment at home and has learned to operate the lift he needs since his muscle strength is impaired by multiple sclerosis. Now that his employment has been relocated to the home, she appreciates his company at home and respects her Dad's advice about homework. She also helps her younger brother with bed-making because he has "poor balance" and visits this brother whenever he requires hospitalization for a neurological condition.

In another family, a sixteen-year-old who accompanies his mother to hospital examinations, helps his mother onto x-ray tables and regularly cooks supper after school states that he does not know that his life would be better if his mother did not have MS.

Children who came to know and respect a parents with a disability through the intimacy of caring then appeared to extend this respect to other areas usually labelled as 'different.' For example, stigma has historically been a problem for children who are adopted, and their origins have often been couched in secrecy. One boy in the study who is frequently sent outside when his mother is tired or not feeling well but is excluded from meal preparation because of his young age and male gender, carries conformity into his social relations about adoption. Knowing that he is adopted and that adoption is 'different,' he has denied that he is adopted in classroom discussion.

However, in another family where disability stereotypes had been cast aside, attitudes toward adoption were open and accepting. For example, Nathan reported that "half the school knows I'm adopted," and his friends know that his mother has MS "because I tell them." Nathan tends to get his own snack after school. He teases his mother and makes her laugh on days when her multiple sclerosis causes her to feel depressed, and is careful to assist her when the snow makes walking hazardous. Loving his mother and knowing her and her disability have taken the fear out of 'difference.'

Equity

Findings suggest that when a mother or father has a disability such as multiple sclerosis, traditional family expectations of hierarchy and division of labour based on age, bodily condition, and gender are challenged. In a number of families, boys and girls as well as men and women functioned in a relatively egalitarian fashion, with flexibility and pragmatism determining work responsibilities.

Alain at ten years of age appears initially to hold stereotypical ideas about gender. The greatest praise he has for his father is his father's company at hockey practices and fishing. He even aspires to be a professional hockey player. However, Alain also expresses pride in the fact that he cooks and does the family laundry since his dad's MS causes fatigue. According to Alain

> Everyone has a fair right. Men clean, you know, same as women. You see my dad cleans. Women do too. You do your equal part. I know a[nother] family, they all do equal work. They all so some work and pitch in. It's two kids, two parents. Both parents go out to work and make money. Both kids do the house chores, same as their parents.

Nathan, aged 12, is another example of how contributions to the family cross traditional gender and age lines. He helps with the building of an electronic cellar at home, clears the table after meals, puts out the garbage, vacuums, shovels snow, and occasionally cooks supper.

In assisting her brother, her father, and her mother, Penny shows that children sometimes care for siblings and for people older than themselves. She negates the mythology that children are helpless recipients of unidirectional caring. In her discussions about the future, Penny expects that her husband will do his share of household chores and childcare. She also plans to include her children in task allocation: "If I have any kids, when they grow, I'll leave it to them to pick up something that's around the house."

Dailiness

Many family members in the study provided stories which emphasized the importance of taking time for and with each other. In learning to respond spontaneously to the needs of a disabled parent as these needs occurred, the need to respond flexibly to everyone became apparent. Dailiness is the feminist recognition of the spaces and bodies in which we live, and through which we experience both tragedies and joys sometimes simultaneously (Aptheker, 1989; see also Reitsma-Street and Rogerson in this text).

Brian's mother uses a scooter. He describes how difficult and painful it is for her to move her body onto an x-ray table or upstairs. His sister comments grimly on the barriers presented by curbs at street corners and by stairs in their local highschool. The children also see humour when their mother and her scooter race past the surprised faces of car drivers in the 'drive-through' line-up at a fast-food restaurant. Sandra loves the smell of cookies when her mother gives her a baking lesson. Brian thoroughly enjoys the feelings associated with swim practice. Each is aware of the need to enjoy or help when and as the body demands. As Sandra reports, "If anything happens in the morning, she calls me. The dog's crying, she calls me... She can't get out of bed, she calls me, but it's OK."

Conclusion

Three ironies emerge from these considerations. First, since the world is not universally accessible, vacations and even visits to children's schools must be planned well in advance if the parent has a disability. Careful scheduling and attendance to organization is necessary. The spaces and bodies in life to which Aptheker (1989) refers must also be allowed to catch our attention from moment to moment so that we can respond to each other spontaneously.

Second, mothers with disabilities are at greater risk than most women to the oppression associated with familialism. Because of inadequate supports and recognition for parenting with a disability, there are often too few available within a nuclear family to fulfill the required tasks (Ridington 1989). Yet, families who live within the context of disability and who put aside stigma and stereotypical ideals about who should care can at least provide freedom to care without the bondage of rigid roles.

Third, in our legitimate protests against women's being forced to provide informal care, we sometimes imply a denigration of the value of such caring. Examining families in which a parent has a disability helps us to identify more clearly the sources of our oppression and to recall the very positive and human outcomes that caring which is mutual and sufficiently supported can cause for all parties involved. For both women and vulnerable populations such as families living with disability, there are many serious obstacles to liberation, but these do not include caring *per se.*

In summary, feminist family critics have identified the family as a site of oppression for women. They have uncovered three reasons that lie behind this oppression: inflexible patriarchal expectations of what a family *should* be like (Luxton 1988); an unfair burden on women who are expected to take sole responsibility for domestic caring (Neysmith 1991); and the demands of a capitalist economy (Armstrong and Armstrong 1990; Eichler 1988). Economic pressure shapes family schedules and values and reduces the will and the power of the state to provide support to families.

I would argue that many families living with disability have "feminized" family life by addressing these concerns. They have moved beyond the notions of what families and family members should be like by respecting characteristics commonly labelled as differences. By sharing responsibilities in a relatively egalitarian fashion, they have altered the practice of assuming that women will do all the family caring. Finally, by taking time for each other when time is needed, they are resisting the demands of the competitive economy and its values.

These subtle alterations to living family life may be radical. They certainly are pathways toward greater humanness. As families living with disability model for our society some pathways out of familialism, the oppression associated with disablism now needs to be addressed.

References

Abberley, P. 1987. The Concept of Oppression and the Development of a Social Theory of Disability. *Disability, Handicap and Society,* 2 (1), pp. 5-19.

Aptheker, B. 1989. *Tapestries of Life: Women's Work,* Women's Consciousness, and the *Meaning of Daily Life.* Amherst, Massachusetts: University of Massachusetts Press.

Blackford, K.A. 1993. Feminizing the Multiple Sclerosis Society of Canada. *Canadian Woman Studies,* (13) 4, Summer. pp. 124-131.

Bullock, A. 1990. *Community Care: Ideology and Lived Experience.* Community Organization and the Canadian State. Eds. R. Ng, G. Walker, and J. Muller. Toronto: Garamond Press.

Eichler, M. 1988. Family Change and Social Policies. *Family Matters*. pp. 63-86.

Fine, M. and Asch, A. Eds. 1988. *Women with Disabilities*. Philadelphia: Temple University Press.

Finger, A. 1983. Disability and Reproductive Rights. *Off Our Backs*, 113 (9): p. 5.

Fraser, R. 1986. *Volunteers in Action - A Brief History of the Multiple Sclerosis Society of Canada*. Toronto: Multiple Sclerosis Society of Canada.

Hooks, B. 1992. *Black Looks*. Toronto: Between the Lines.

Luxton, M. 1988. Thinking about the Future. *Family Matters*. Eds. K. Anderson et al. Scarborough, Nelson Canada. pp. 237-257.

Mathews, G.P. 1983. *Voices from the Shadows: Women with Disabilities Speak Out*. Toronto: Women's Press.

Neysmith, S.M. 1991. From Community Care to a Social Model of Caring. Women's Caring. Eds. C. Baines, P. Evans, and S.M. Neysmith. Toronto: McClelland and Stewart Inc.

Prilleltensky, O. 1997. *Women at the Intersection of Physical Disability and Motherhood*. Paper presented at the Mothers and Daughters Conference, York Centre for Feminist Research, North York, September.

Rogers, and Matsumura. 1991. *A Guide to Pregnancy and Birth for Women with Disabilities*. New York: Demos Publications.

Ridington, J. 1989. *The Only Parent in the Neighbourhood: Mothering and Women with Disabilities*. Vancouver: Disabled Women's Network.

Rioux, M.H. and Crawford, C. 1994. *The Canadian Disability Resource Program: Offsetting Costs of Disability and Assuring Access to Disability-related Supports. An Occasional Paper*. L'Institut Roeher Institute, York University, North York, Ontario.

Roeher Institute. 1995. *In Harm's Way*. North York, Ontario: Roeher Institute.

Scott, K.J. 1995. *Manufacturing 'Bad Mothers.'* Toronto: University of Toronto Press.

Wendell, S. 1993. "Feminism, Disability and Transcendence of the Body." *Canadian Woman Studies*, 13 (4), pp. 116-122.

Endnote

1.   I am grateful to the children and parents who agreed to allow me to record and interpret their stories. My son Chris Blackford, my mother Freda Sawyer, and York University faculty advisors Gordon Darroch, Françoise Boudreau, Livy Visano, and Penny Stewart provided support. The Ontario Ministry of Health sponsored the research described here, while content and analysis are my own responsibility.

Marge Reitsma-Street and Pat Rogerson

Implementing Principles:
An Alternative Community Organization for
Children

Introduction

The purpose of this article is to describe the principles that guided the development of a community organization serving children. The following is a brief description of the context for the organization. Six categories of principles are described; these principles, expressed as objectives, are as follows:

- To promote active participation of members;
- To create egalitarian work relationships;
- To nourish dailiness;
- To care for the caregivers;
- To expand the capacity to act powerfully;
- To nurture partners and networks.

Examples that illustrate implementation of these principles are presented throughout the article. Specific detail is included to reveal one effort to create a less hierarchical and possibly more feminist organization. Illustrations are drawn from the three historical stages in the development of the organization: from 1989 to 1990, the period during which funding was obtained; from 1991-1994, the period during which the organization and its programs/services were developed; and from 1994 through 1995, the period during which the organization incorporated. In the discussion, we reflect on several issues raised by this case study that are relevant to developing feminist institutions.

Sources for the case study include extensive, weekly minutes of meetings beginning in December 1989 to incorporation in the spring of 1995; interview transcripts with key informants in the organization; and published documents (Reitsma-Street 1992; Reitsma-Street and Arnold 1995; Diallo 1996). Data were collected largely by funded research staff. The authors also draw from their memories, personal experiences, and diaries: both were part of the original group of twelve who worked one day per week in 1990 to organize the Association; the authors continue to be actively involved one day per month.

The Better Beginnings, Better Futures Research Demonstration Project

The organization described in this article is called the Sudbury Better Beginnings, Better Futures/Partir d'un bon pas pour un avenir meilleur/ Nigan Bemaadizidwiina Association, hereafter Sudbury BBBF or the Association. It is one of the eleven sites in the five-year Better Beginnings, Better Futures Research Demonstration Project funded by three Ontario ministries and a federal ministry. The research project aims to evaluate whether holistic, high quality, integrated, and accessible programming for children ages 0 to 8 living in low-income communities presents behavioural and emotional problems and promotes the development of community institutions (Ontario, MCSS 1989).

An essential feature of the BBBF project model is the participation of community members in its design and management. The funders hypothesize that community participation in project management increases the likelihood of the project continuing after funding ends in five years.

Researchers are funded to follow the development of the programs, children, families, and neighbourhoods in the eleven experimental sites and to compare these developments to those in matched comparison communities without Better Beginning programming (Peters 1994). The research aims to follow the children for 20 years after the project ends.

Sudbury is a city of 91 000 located in Northeastern Ontario. The Sudbury BBBF site is located in two adjacent, multicultural neighbourhoods in the heart of the city. Of the 1000 children under ten years of age in the two neighbourhoods in 1990, one-third lived in families dependent on social assistance for everyday expenses. One-quarter of grade four students demonstrated low academic performance, compared to 15% in other schools on similar measures. In a spring 1990 needs survey, 303 parents and children reported that there were few safe places to play in their neighbourhoods and a limited number of culturally sensitive programs.

By 1995, the Sudbury BBBF had created free and interesting daily activities for over 300 children in four community sites, with weekly cultural and peacemaking initiatives in the five neighbourhood schools. Over 250 adults have become members of the Association and are actively learning the skills of participation, including election of a Council to manage the organization. Almost all full- and part-time staff are hired from the community with their earnings and skills remaining in the neighbourhoods. Researchers are currently engaged in analyzing results of the early impact of the programs in Sudbury and the other

290

experimental and comparison sites on indicators such as child development, parental stress, school performance, and behavioural problems.

The Development of Principles to Guide the Organization

Several principles were drafted in the early days of the Association to help create a democratic and comfortable atmosphere, and to guide proposal development (Sudbury, BBBF 1990). The fundamental principle was that the organization must ensure participation of native, francophone, and multicultural groups within its structure and programming. After one year of funding, the principles and project vision were revised. These 1991 revised principles were included in Sudbury BBBF brochures and in all the wallet-size membership cards. The principles were used to guide the development of structures and programs throughout the years, and to shape the deliberations of committees responsible for creating an independent organization. The vision and revised principles make up the preamble to the 1994 by-laws of the independent Sudbury BBBF (Diallo 1996).

We are writing this chapter in response to comments made in 1994 by colleagues that the organizational processes used by the Sudbury BBBF seemed remarkably similar to those envisioned by feminists. These comments spurred us to analyze the organization of the Sudbury BBBF. Our focus is the implementation of six categories of principles that appear most relevant to theorizing feminist institutions. It is not the intent of this paper to evaluate the impact of these principles. That question, however, may be pursued in the future.

The majority of the original team of twelve who developed the initial principles were women as were most of the 35 permanent staff hired between 1991 and 1995 to implement the revised principles. Some were committed to exploring a feminist approach to building an organization. To most members of the Sudbury BBBF Association, however, an explicitly feminist analysis was neither central nor conscious. In the words of one key organizer:

> I had never considered that the style of management I used was a feminist style. I know I am female. I picked and packaged a process of management that felt good and worked with my community and our agency.

There was intense interest in developing an alternative organization that "felt good and worked." The original team members and later the project coordinator and the community workers had many years of community development experience, mostly in anti-poverty, native, women, and children organizations. They did not want a traditional, impersonal hierarchical agency with an English-speaking white, professional, male elite. The alternative was less clear, but the search for an alternative was central to the development of the Sudbury BBBF. Discussion of the elements considered to be important to that development follows:

(1) Promoting Active Participation

The first principle is development of opportunities that promote participation in the activities and decision-making of the BBBF project. This principle meant creating processes to respect diverse traditions of participation of the native, francophone, and visible minorities in the BBBF neighbourhoods. The principle of participation also meant uncovering ways of reducing the multiple threats to participation encountered by poor, proud, and sometimes desperate residents.

Representatives of three cultural communities, along with education and children's mental health services, met in December 1989 at the invitation of two organizers to begin shaping the Sudbury BBBF Association. Later, members of public housing projects in the neighbourhoods and several service agencies joined in. The initial venue for participating in decisions included three-hour weekly Association meetings. Members took turns taking notes and chairing the meetings, using whatever language or style they were most comfortable with. The recorder for one week became the chair the following week, with more experienced people helping those less experienced.

Participation was also encouraged early in the life of the organization through the use of small time-limited action research activities such as collecting and analyzing data of immediate relevance to organizational development (Reitsma-Street and Arnold 1994). For instance, in the spring of 1990, Association members went into two neighbourhoods to find out people's needs and desires. Clear questions were asked, including "What would you do for yourself and the children in your neighbourhood if you won a million dollars?" In three weeks, Association members interviewed 363 children, parents, and agency people who lived or worked in the two neighbourhoods. During a long afternoon session and evening potluck, members searched for themes in the interview data. The four themes that emerged from this piece of action research gave specific directions for project development: the need for safe places to play; good schools; a neighbourhood centre; and more culturally appropriate services.

Following funding approval in January 1991, the weekly Association meetings were expanded to include all those who were interested. Average attendance grew to 15, doubling to 30 when key decisions were discussed. Meetings were held in community buildings with access to childcare and travel monies were supplied to those who requested help. The criteria for membership was deliberately very broad. People who came at least several times to meetings and who accepted the vision and principles of the Association could participate and make decisions.

In 1993, to further promote participation of community residents, a membership coordinator was hired. A simple orientation manual with pictures was created. Throughout 1994 and 1995, community workers and the membership coordinator — all of whom lived in the neighbourhoods involved — frequently visited community residents' neighbourhoods. Membership increased to 250 by the second annual meeting of the Sudbury BBBF Association.[1]

It is not easy, however, to promote and maintain the participation of people with limited incomes who have good reasons to be sceptical of another new organization. Therefore, priority was given to creating and funding avenues for accessible and enjoyable participation *as quickly as possible*, starting with the Hallow'een Party of 1991. Before-and after-school children's programs with food, cooperative games, and art were initiated as well as regular potlucks, feasts, celebrations, and holiday activities for people of all ages. These events take place in four community buildings situated in the two neighbourhoods. *All events are free.* Community members are encouraged to help out with children's activities, or just to drop in. There are also free and frequent activities for adults, such as mediation and racial-awareness workshops. Childcare services are provided.

The Sudbury Association uses staff hiring as one of the most important ways to develop leaders who will maintain community participation. The majority of people on hiring committees are representatives of the community. Priority is given to hiring and training people who have intimate knowledge and commitment to the BBBF neighbourhoods. By hiring neighbourhood people, the Association helps to ensure that staff wages, training, energy, and leadership remain in the community after work hours, and/or after contracts end. Over the past five years, 35 full-and part-time staff have been hired, many of whom live in the project's neighbourhoods. In addition, training opportunities and some wages have been given to 111 people in summer and contract positions; many of these short-term workers also live in or have family in the neighbourhoods.

The last approach used to promote the principle of participation in decision-making is the creation of caucuses or working groups, attentive to the diverse needs of the multicultural neighbourhoods

(Diallo and Reitsma-Street 1995; Reitsma-Street and Arnold 1994). Early in 1991, semi-autonomous caucuses were invented and they have evolved with need and interest. Caucus members are expected to support the vision and principles of the Sudbury Better Beginnings Association, and to come to the Association for budget approval of new activities. Each caucus, however, such as the Research Caucus launched in April 1991 and the Staff Caucus developed in 1994, selects its own language, style of working, links to the community and goals. For instance, the Francophone Caucus initially concentrated on creating a supportive atmosphere for adults and children so they could play in French in their own small community building, and to resurrect French local festivals. Because the caucuses have proved their value in promoting participation of the various cultural constituencies in the BBBF neighbourhoods, the caucus was enshrined in the May 1994 constitution of Sudbury Better Beginnings Section 11.1.

In sum, many initiatives were launched to promote the principle of participation in this community organization for children's programs. Members of the community could participate in the frequent, free activities; become members; or help out with events. They could also hire staff, approve programs, develop their cultural caucus, and elect councillors.

(2) Creating Egalitarian Work Relationships

To implement the second principle of egalitarian work relationships, the Sudbury BBBF chose its sponsoring agency, the Native Friendship Centre, carefully. This Centre had policies, principles, and history that encouraged a holistic response to community needs, and an atmosphere that welcomed cultural diversity and low-income people. The Native Friendship Centre's Board of Directors was ultimately responsible for hiring, contracts, and reports until Sudbury BBBF became a corporation. It did not, however, veto or hold back recommendations that had been fully discussed and decided upon by consensus within the BBBF Association.

Two key procedures used in the Native Friendship Centre were adopted and developed by Sudbury BBBF to promote egalitarian work relationships: consensus decision-making and a flat salary structure.

Although consensus decision-making was strange to some within the agency and to community people who joined the Association, no one could join without agreeing to this consensual approach to decision-making. "Decisions by members at meetings of members shall be made by consensus" is enshrined in the 1995 General Organizational By-law 6 of the incorporated Sudbury Better Beginnings, Better Futures Association. Consensus decision-making is used at the weekly or bi-weekly Association meetings (1990-1994),[2] the monthly meetings of the

Council elected by the Association (1994 to now), and in caucuses, committees, and team working groups.

Over the years, workshops have been held on how to build consensus and many meetings and discussions about what consensus means have occurred. Whether the decisions deal with hiring, firing, contracts, new programs, or the selection of symbols and principles, there is time to discuss and reflect. When a decision is to be made, the chair of a meeting gives everyone in the room an opportunity to comment on his or her willingness to live with the decision or to ask for more time and information. A consensus approach to decision-making helps to minimize the dominance of a few individuals or one constituency. Reducing the propensity of a few to dominate is particularly important when working with people who feel powerful, or when there are constituencies such as women or visible minorities who have had painful histories of exclusion.

There are times when consensus is not achieved; more time is needed; or new proposals must be debated. A member can choose to stand aside or pass or have his or her concern recorded when the person's turn to comment comes. Sometimes the people with the most opposing views go away with the responsibility to come back with a compromise recommendation that they can agree with. The disagreeing parties can ask to agree on a local or outside mediator. If the mediator cannot achieve an agreement, an arbitrator is selected by both sides. The arbitrator's decision is final. To date, mediation has been used several times, arbitration not at all.

Besides using consensus decision-making to encourage egalitarian work relationships, the Sudbury BBBF chose a relatively flat salary to pay its staff. Annually, the coordinator earns only $7,000 more than the community workers. Provincial pay equity legislation boosted everyone's salary in 1995 as listed in Table 1.

Table 1 — 1995 Hourly Wage

$11.65 — short-term contract
$12.15 — childcare workers
$16.84 — community workers, office coordinator
$19.25 — program coordinator

The flat salary structure helps to avoid significant inequalities within the staff group, and between the staff and the community members, most of whom are neighbours. The Association also wanted to hire as many people from the neighbourhoods as possible. This decision meant money, expertise, and ownership of the project would remain in the neighbourhoods. The consensus approach to decision-making and the flat salary structure continue to contribute to egalitarian working relationships as we write this article.

(3) Nourishing Dailiness

Holistic organizations assume that many aspects of people and their communities must be taken into account when services are developed. Feminism adds a sharper focus to holism and speaks of dailiness; the spaces and bodies that people actually live in where tragedies, joys, and contradictions converge in everyday moments (Aptheker 1989). Organizational processes attentive to dailiness start with the bodies, fears, and uniqueness of people within the minutiae of an encounter — this includes meetings, events, workplaces, and long-term planning exercises.

Concrete attention to dailiness is expressed through food, space, and time for visiting. Family events and children's activities include substantial, free snacks, not just for nourishment but also for comfort and sociability. When the Association designed its physical space, there was systematic attention to creating welcoming space that "did not look like agency offices." The program centres are in simple community spaces, such as church basements, recreation centres, and schools, within walking distance for older children and adults. Within the centres, there are no individual offices and closed doors. Desks are placed in backrooms or at edges of rooms, with paintings, couches, plants, and coffee welcoming people as they come through the door.

The Association imbibed the sponsoring agency's policy on "visiting" that acknowledges the importance of spending time with colleagues and neighbourhood residents, chatting about joys and troubles, and asking about friends and family. Visiting makes the moment important; it is not just a means to an efficient end.

An invention to nourish dailiness, called "circling in," developed early in 1990: at the beginning or end of each meeting or event, members and guests take a moment to reflect, to ask questions, to add to the agenda, to seek solace or advice, to share a story, or to pass in silence. If there are more than 20 people or many newcomers in a meeting, the focus of circling is on introductions at the beginning; at the end of the meeting, people are asked to break up into small groups for a moment of reflection and sharing. Throughout the years, we have heard members exclaim: "At least I am not treated as a machine in these meetings. There is always some time for me." This circling process is not unfamiliar to people from feminist and native traditions; it is an important practice that has been taken up by most of the caucuses, small teams, and committees developed after 1990.

The systematic attention to colour, texture, comfort, and celebration of success helps to nourish a sense of delight in the day. Food, music, ceremonies, awards, art, plants, and stories are used to build and maintain an organizational culture that expresses appreciation of effort, and honours the achievements that every member makes, no matter how small. In May 1995, the first year of independence and Council elections were celebrated with a potluck and dance attended by people of all ages: appreciation awards were given to 60 volunteers. Throughout the years, there has been particular attention given to choosing vivid colours for brochures and lively paint for walls, to designing attractive, artful, and simple membership booklets, and to selecting the Association's logo of four children holding hands looking towards the tree of peace presented in Figure 1. Good-quality paint and materials are purchased for use in the child activity programs, and the concrete blocks and pipe-filled ceilings of the four simple program centres are covered in crafts by the children as well as work by local artists. Additional grants have been sought to plant trees and build gardens.

Figure 1 — *Logo of Sudbury's Better Beginnings Better Futures*
Partir d'un bon pas pour un avenir meilleur
Nishin Aagi Maagitang Wii Niigan Bemaadiziwiina

The final approach to nourishing dailiness is an organizational culture that supports cooperation and creative risk-taking. There are no competitive sports or games in the children's programs. Staff are hired and trained to build a cooperative sense of adventure and problem-solving. Members and staff rotate to try out new jobs and roles. The Sudbury BBBF supports risks: for instance, in 1994, members of the street theatre group sponsored by BBBF joined with other social justice groups in Sudbury to protest a welfare snitch line.

Nourishing dailiness has moved beyond principle; there is continuous attention to the daily needs and strengths of those who participate in BBBF through the presence of food at events, welcoming space arrangements, "circling in" at meetings, time for visiting, and use of colour and celebrations.

(4) Caring for the Caregivers

To implement the caring principle means the BBBF Association had to design processes that support its members, especially those giving care to others whether as staff, parents, or volunteers. Section 2.8 of By-Law Number 1 explicitly states this intent: To care for members of the Corporation and its partners by providing mutual support, learning and personal development opportunities.

"Caring for the caregivers" has solid roots in human services organizational research (Berry 1975; Street, Vinter, and Perrow 1966; Ontario, MCSS, 1989). Feminist scholarship gives additional attention to building processes in organizations that care fully for the range of caregiver strengths and needs (Finch and Groves, 1983; Weeks, 1994). Persons who perform paid or unpaid caring work for children and adults inside the family home or in social service and educational centres have social, emotional, problem-solving, and organizational skills that too often are devalued or made invisible; these competencies could and do add valuable strengths to organizations. Because those who give care are often devalued, caregivers may become overworked, anxious, unwell, and unproductive, especially when they do not receive financial, emotional, and social support (Baines et al. 1991). Female caregivers, in particular, are expected by others to perform unpaid and paid caregiving work *at the same time*, or for many long hours per day with little time off (Oakley 1981; Armstrong and Armstrong 1990). In an organization, attention to "caring for the caregivers" therefore, means developing an environment and policies that attend to the multiple tasks, demands, and needs of people who care for others.

From 1992 to 1994, there were free bi-weekly workshops — often led by highly-skilled professionals versed in progressive adult learning methods — for members to learn about consensus building, mediation, welfare appeals, architect designs for the community gardens, and voting procedures. Since 1994, the training has been tied more closely to the monthly staff meetings and semi-annual retreats. Several programs have developed to help parents achieve literacy and complete high school credits. Hiring, training, and supervising students are crucial procedures used to promote leadership that people can use in their own lives and for their communities. Adding up full-time, part-time, contract staff, and placement students, 171 adults[3] have gained training and experience through the Better Beginnings Association in the last five years. This figure *excludes* the more than 50 human service and educational professionals who have contributed to Better Beginnings during these same years.[4]

298

Children of members are not welcome only at meetings or events. There is an assumption that childcare needs to be provided, although in the early years procedures were clumsy and members had to request money to reimburse babysitters or to cover travel costs.

Sick leave policies are similar to the city's Board of Education, 1.25 days per month. Vacation time is not so generous. Staff members who have worked for one year are entitled to 2 weeks off. The pattern continues as follows: 3 weeks for 2-5 years of service, 4 weeks per year for 6-10 years of service, and 5 weeks per year for more than 10 years of service. Part-time staff have less time off.

Additional time, however, can be taken off to stay home with sick children or for mental health reasons without pretence. Compassionate and court leave to sort out family concerns is not uncommon nor is it frowned upon. Sick time has averaged two days per year per staff, excluding extended periods for major illnesses or pregnancies. In the contracts of full-time staff, it is written that they neither lose their jobs nor their positions if they are on leave for extended periods of time.

The learning is not a one-way street. The principle of caring for caregivers assumes that people know things and bring skills to the project. The Association, therefore, finds opportunities and gives encouragement to people so they will give what they can and so they will learn more. In reflecting on her four years with the project, one woman said:

> Before I just sat and listened, or I didn't come to meetings. But here, it's such as surprise. People want to hear what I have to say. Sometimes my ideas are used. Makes me want to say more. I use what I learn at home, and in my other part-time job.

A final implication of the caring for caregivers principle is the awareness that people are not machines nor are they unidimensional and limited to just one role or task. The Association assumes that members are learners and family members at the same time that they are workers or volunteers. It is not uncommon for Association members to know and care about each other's children and family members; to use work time to call home or have family visit at work; to organize an Association workshop or bake pies for events at home. Caring means helping people find a balance between members' private home and public worlds, rather than leaving the difficult task of balancing up to individuals.

Are there some members more responsible for this principle of caring? What happens to them? The practices of sharing work with a buddy, rotating jobs and responsibilities, and taking time off help to ensure that no one person is overwhelmed and that the work of the Association can carry on without her (or him). For instance, five of the original team members took several months off from BBBF in 1990-1991, while, during 1994-95, three of the full-time staff took long leaves to renew themselves.

(5) Expanding the Capacity to Act Powerfully

Power is seen by Sudbury BBBF as the capacity to achieve objectives that are cooperatively devised and revisited. Power is not limited to a few people in management.

The organizational diagram in the original 1990 proposal was that of a large circle symbolizing the Association, with small intercepting circles each of which had specific tasks and interests, such as the Research Caucus, the Native Working Group, the sponsoring agencies, and the Community Advisory Committee. The 1994 organizational diagram presented in Figure 2 features the expansion of forums in which BBBF members can discharge power on behalf of their neighbourhoods. In the middle is the Council, made up of volunteer members who live in the Better Beginnings neighbourhoods and who are elected annually by the Caucuses and Association members at large (By-Laws 12 and 17). The By-laws formalize the power of the people who live in the neighbourhoods to "manage and direct the affairs of the Corporation, borrow money, and sign contracts that affect the direction of the Sudbury Better Beginnings activities."

Figure 2 — 1994 Organization Chart of Sudbury Better Beginnings, Better Futures

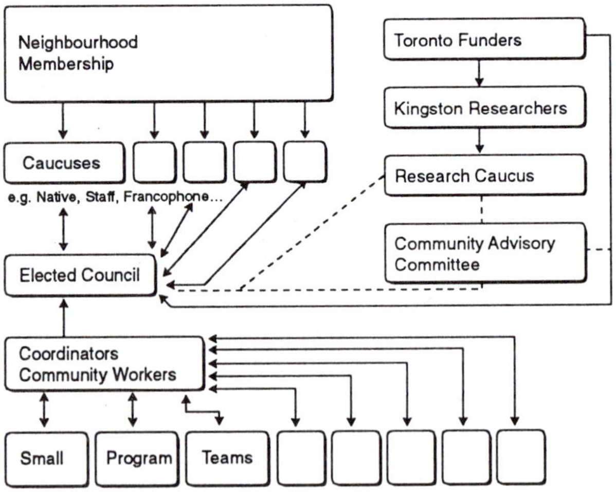

The early creation of cultural caucuses and the later development of many small self-directed teams for each program/activity help to implement the principle of expanding the capacity of people to learn skills, to make decisions, and to influence outcomes.

The self-directed teams are scattered throughout the various services and components of the Association. There is, for instance, a team for each of the Early Bird and after-school programs offered at three locations, the cultural programs and peaceful playgrounds within the five neighbourhood schools, and the summer native camp. The paid and volunteer community members associated with a service or job become a team. They meet regularly, usually weekly, to sort out their activities and problems.

To help small teams commit to a common vision, a full-day staff meeting and workshops happen every month. Twice a year, there are week-long training and planning sessions for all Association staff. New staff are given orientation sessions by senior staff who emphasize the overall vision, the specific tasks, and the stories and legends of the Association. Annually, staff have a job review with the Coordinator. The review emphasizes the gifts each staff member brings to the job, as well as strengths, accomplishments, and plans to address any difficulties.

In a Spring 1995 interview, a staff member summed up the long process to expanding the power of Association members:

> I don't know if it was accidental or on purpose. We were
> pushed to take charge of our own services and responsibilities
> in small groups, and we learned how to develop our own
> power.

(6) Nurturing Partners and Networks

From the beginning the principle of nurturing partners was pursued. Network building with human service organizations started with the original organizers who were lent to the Association for one day per week from their agencies, such as the Children's Mental Health Centre, John Howard Society, the Board of Education, and the Native Friendship Centre.

In February 1990, meetings and workshops were organized to invite interested human service agency people in the city to learn about the BBBF model of prevention, and to ask for assistance in the creation of the new organization. An Agency Caucus started in the spring of 1991. Middle managers and senior front-line people in health, educational, and recreational organizations met to discuss partnering, integration, and prevention. The Agency Caucus met monthly for two years and then disbanded. Although the agency people were not successful in finding terms of reference for tasks they felt comfortable carrying out, they did share and learn from each other.

In the 1994 Constitution of BBBF, there is no provision for agency representatives on the Council or in the Association. There are, however, several formal agreements with various groups such as churches, recreation departments, and schools for renting inexpensive space in community buildings, along with many informal connections with human services agencies and organizations through frequent workshops, professional development days, and some purchase of service arrangements.

Several other systematic attempts to nurture networks have also occurred. In 1990, official leaders in the community, including the Chief of Police and the Medical Health Officer as well as spiritual and labour leaders, were invited to become members of the Community Advisory Committee to the BBBF (See Figure 2 presented earlier). Since funding, this Committee continues to meet annually to support the Association, and to contribute expertise to problem-solving and vision-building.

A second approach is the development of ties to the local university and college so that up to five students annually can complete educational placements within Sudbury's BBBF Association. In addition, each year the Association successfully finds summer and short-term funding for over 20 people. Successful applications for funds from other sources, such as the Bronfman Foundation for inner-city environmental regeneration, also expand the network of people and agencies associated with Better Beginnings.

The third avenue to help implement the principle of nurturing networks is the secondment and voluntary contributions of Association staff and members to other neighbourhood organizations or committees, such as *la Caisse populaire* and a native business. As of 1993, the Association devoted approximately one day per week of one staff member's time to work with other agencies on job creation proposals and the creation of GEODE — a new, non-profit grassroots organization committed to economic development through small lending circles, small loans, a cashless green barter system, and small business ventures.

Discussion

Although Sudbury BBBF does not call itself feminist or emerge from the women's movements, we argue that six principles, especially "nourishing dailiness" and "caring for the caregivers," are infused with the feminist ideals of participation, humanism, and cooperation (Ferguson 1984; Riger 1994; Weeks 1994). Given some of the similarities between feminist principles and those pursued by the Sudbury BBBF, the specific details association with implementation of the principles through three stages of organizational growth may help others to learn or replicate these efforts. As participants, we see these details as evidence of strengths and successes. As observers, we see several issues that challenge BBBF and other feminist organizations.

The use of principles, consensus decision-making, and small teams does not prevent dissent, nor always resolve it. The hope is that, with these three organizational structures, dissent does not explode destructively but becomes a source for growth, creativity, and change.

For instance, the dissent between the neighbourhood residents and professional agency representatives was never resolved to everyone's satisfaction. Developing egalitarian participation in the face of substantial inequality in power and resources is difficult. People in the Better Beginnings neighbourhoods report they feel less powerful in their speech, knowledge, resources, and connections than professionals (Diallo 1994). Carefully-picked professionals and agencies who were committed to consensus decision-making and community participation gave generously of their paid and unpaid time and expertise in the first years of the project; some continue to do so at the time of writing. Nonetheless, these professionals, female and male, continued to dominate in Association meetings and decision-making. The Community Advisory Committee captured the expertise and support of agency directors, but it met annually and was not directly involved in the BBBF organization or integration efforts. A BBBF agency caucus started in 1991 to give professionals their own space and to decrease their dominant participation in the Association. The agency professionals could not find an institutionalized role within BBBF that they were comfortable with, nor did the community members feel confident with agency representatives in the decision-making circles of BBBF. In 1994, the agencies were disappointed to find that they did not get the anticipated one-quarter of the seats on BBBF Council.[5]

In our opinion, the attempts used over the years to resolve the differences between neighbourhood members and professionals have sparked greater interest in community development and a shrewder appreciation of partnership and power. Different processes and strategies need to be explored to implement the principle of nurturing networks when there is significant inequality among people. To date, Sudbury BBBF has chosen to emphasize the principle of promoting the participation of neighbourhood residents over nurturing formal agency partnership.

Differences and controversies continue, particularly over culture and language (Reitsma-Street 1992; Diallo 1996). The domination of English as a language of decision within meetings and buildings is most difficult problem to solve. The francophones are more bilingual than those of other cultures, but they also know that use of the French language is central to their cultural identity. Implementation of the six principles described in this article has helped to create some compromises and solutions, such as creation of a francophone caucus, several rooms

303

within one building dedicated to francophone programs, and multi-cultural workshops. However, cultural tensions tend to flare up during the current formalization stage of organizational development in which policies and procedures become routine (Riger 1994). The principles of participation and caring will be tested again as new forms of compromise are sought.

The precarious financial health and fragile reserves of families within the neighbourhoods and the members of Sudbury BBBF pose the greatest challenge to the principles, magnifying not only cultural and policy tensions, but also threatening livelihoods. Using a flat salary scale to promote the principle of egalitarian working relations can mean that everyone is paid poorly. The egalitarian approach reduces inequity and envy; it cannot ensure adequacy. In Sudbury's BBBF, there are few staff people earning sufficient money from their paid work to actually meet the needs of their own families. Many neighbourhood people are hired, and salaries are not lower than community standards, but individuals, especially single parents, are still left with the problem of making ends meet.

In March 1995, the Sudbury Better Beginnings Association received an additional two years of funding. After 1997, the Association is expected to find money to meet neighbourhood needs. At the same time, there are substantial cut-backs in all social services, increasing unemployment, and decreasing levels of political and economic power at the local level. As of October 1, 1995, members on social assistance, including one-third of BBBF neighbourhoods, faced 21% reductions in their cheques with no changes in the costs of shelter or other necessities.

It may be time to develop several new principles, or to revisit old principles that give greater priority to the skills needed for the upcoming struggles against cutbacks, inequality, and oppression. This may not be the task or responsibility of a community organization serving children, such as BBBF, but there is a need to theorize what types of principles and organizations can help to change the rules of a game that so unfairly dispossesses people. The trust necessary for implementing consensus, cooperation, and egalitarian principles within an organization may need to be tempered with a scepticism that can fuel the risk-taking and militancy for conflict work outside the organization. Larger networks, more resources, and political action may develop from a principled commitment to fight the structures that disadvantage people (Irwin 1994; Ng 1990).

Organizational principles that help to overcome oppression will not be feminist or freeing; this is especially true if they are implemented on the backs of the invisible work and energies of women or poor people.

We found in the BBBF work that promoting participation meant people put a great deal of themselves into their work, including many unpaid hours. On the one hand, energy is released when there is a serious sharing of power with dispossessed groups and there are opportunities to learn new skills. On the other, will the government and leaders ignore the need for substantial resources for children's services and argue that poor neighbourhoods can maintain these services using just volunteers? In addition, when does the promotion of participation and egalitarian work relationships demand that people give their organization more than what is personally healthy? Future research is pending on the volunteer hours and "in kind" contributions donated by neighbourhood people to the Better Beginnings, Better Futures projects. Initial conservative estimates suggest that these voluntary contributions add up to one-half of the Better Beginnings' annual budgets (Mione, Neysmith, and Reitsma-Street 1995). It is impossible to understand what it truly costs to launch comparable community programs or social justice struggles without acknowledging invisible energies and costs.

The one thing that does not depend upon further funding or research, however, is our awareness that another vision of organization is possible, a vision rooted in union, native, and feminist traditions. The personal skills and knowledge gained are owned and will remain in the Sudbury Better Beginnings, Better Futures neighbourhoods. The sense that there is another way to manage is also being discussed by educational and service agencies who have worked with the BBBF Association. Six years of contact have piqued an interest; high levels of serious community participation in low-income neighbourhoods are not impossible.

References

Aptheker, Bettina. 1989. *Tapestries of Life: Women's Work, Women's Consciousness, and the Meaning of Daily Life*. Amherst, M.A.: University of Massachusetts Press.

Armstrong, Pat and Hugh Armstrong. 1990. *Theorizing Women's Work*. Toronto: Garamond Press.

Baines, Carol, Pat Evans, and Sheila Neysmith (eds.). 1991. *Women's Caring*. Toronto: McClelland and Stewart.

Barnsley, Jane. 1988. "Feminist Action, Institutional Reaction." *Resources for Feminist Research*. pp. 17, 3, 18-21.

Berry, Juliet. 1975. *Daily Experience in Residential Life: A Study of Children and their Caregivers*. London: Routledge and Kegan Paul.

Bopp, J. 1984. *Community Development*. Discussion Paper no. 8. Lethbridge, Alberta: Four Worlds Development Project, University of Lethbridge.

Diallo, Lamine. 1994. *Integration*. Sudbury Better Beginnings, Better Futures Report.

Diallo, Lamine and Marge Reitsma-Street. 1995. "Stratégies de survie et d'identité: les dynamiques culturelles dans un projet d'intervention en prévention communautaire." *Reflets: Revenue ontaroise d'intervention sociale et communautaire* 1 (1)m pp. 43-69.

Diallo, Lamine. 1996. *Report on Management and Organization of Better Beginnings Better Futures*. Sudbury Better Beginnings, Better Futures Report.

Ferguson, Kathy E. 1984. *The Feminist Case Against Bureaucracy*. Philadelphia: Temple University Press.

Finch, Janet and Dulcie Groves (eds.). 1983. *A Labour of Love: Women, Work and Caring*. London: Routledge and Kegan Paul.

Irwin, Jude. 1994. "The Empty Promise of Multiculturalism for Women." *Women Working Together*. ed. by Wendy Weeks, Longman Cheshire. pp. 103-116.

Mione, Angela, Sheila Neysmith, and Marge Reitsma-Street. 1995. *Services in Kind*. Unpublished report.

Ng, Roxanna, Gillian Walker, Jacob Muller eds. 1990. *Community Organization and the Canadian State*. Toronto: Garamond Press.

Oakley, Ann. 1981. *Subject Women*. Oxford: Martin Robertson.

Ontario Ministry of Community and Social Services. 1989. *Better Beginnings, Better Futures: An Integrated Model of Primary Prevention of Emotional and Behavioural Problems*. Toronto: Author.

Peters, Ray DeV. 1994. "Better Beginnings, Better Futures: A Community-based Approach to Primary Prevention." *Canadian Journal of Community Mental Health*, 13 (2)m pp. 183-188.

Reitsma-Street, Marge. 1992 *Community Coming Together: Development of the Sudbury Better Beginnings*, Better Futures Project. Report.

Reitsma-Street, Marge and Bob Arnold. 1994. "Community-based Action Research in a Multi-site Prevention Project: Challenges and Resolutions" *Canadian Journal of Community Mental Health*, 13 (2), pp. 229-240.

Riger, Stephanie. 1994. "Challenges of Success: Stages of Growth in Feminist Organizations" *Feminist Studies*, 20 (2), pp. 275-300.

Ristock, Janice L. 1991. "Feminist Collectives: The Struggles and Contradictions in our Quest for a 'Uniquely Feminist Structure'" *Women and Social Change*. eds. Jeri Dawn Wine and Janice L. Ristock. pp. 41-55. Toronto: James Lorimer.

Street, David, Robert P. Vinter and Charles Perrow. 1966. *Organization for Treatment: A Comparative Study of Institutions for Delinquents*. New York: The Free Press.

Sudbury Better Beginnings, Better Futures Association. July 1990. *Proposal to Implement the Integrated Prevention Model*.

Weeks, Wendy. 1994. *Women Working Together: Lessons from Feminist Women's Services*. Melbourne: Longman Cheshire.

Endnotes

1. As of 1994, membership is divided into two categories: "regular members" who live in the two neighbourhoods and "associate members" who live elsewhere but who are sponsored by a regular member and have had a community involvement in the neighbourhoods. Associate members are restricted to 25% of total membership.

2. With incorporation, the Association meets up to three times per year, while the thirteen member Council elected by the Association meets monthly (By-Law 8.3).

3. 35 full-time staff; 111 on various contracts; five students for each of the five years for total of 171.

4. This conservative figure includes the 51 people whose attendance was recorded several times in minutes of Association, Agency Caucus, or Community Advisory meetings, or at training workshops.

5. Other Better Beginnings sites had 50% of their Steering Committees reserved for agency representatives.

Heather L. Garrett

Feminizing Social Welfare:
The Needlework Guild of Canada, 1892-1995

Feminizing Social Welfare:
The Needlework Guild of Canada, 1892-1995[1]

The formation of women's organizations was a widespread phenomenon in the mid-nineteenth century. Many of these women's groups began in churches and were committed to charity work. It has been argued that toward the end of the nineteenth century, there was an increase in women's organizations committed to social reform (Baines 1988). Some women's groups which have been studied are the Young Women's Christian Association (YWCA), the Women's Christian Temperance Union (WCTU), and the National Council of the Women of Canada (NCWC). Historians connect the groups' emergence with a series of fundamental changes in the late nineteenth century: the entry of women in the workforce, lower fertility rates, expansion of towns and cities, immigration, industrialization, changes in transportation and schooling, and the migration of young workers into the city (Mitchinson 1982).

It can be argued that one of the main consequences of the growth of women's clubs was the extent to which they encouraged women to come out of the domestic, private sphere and into the public sphere. They also provided women with the chance to learn from each other. Although much of what was learned was an extension of their domestic role, the association enabled some women to develop skills that could be used in the public sphere, such as managing finances, organizing meetings, and preparing reports. These were skills they were unlikely to learn in the home. Almost all of these groups were restricted to women and provided them with a chance to develop friendships and take on leadership roles otherwise normally denied to them. Moreover, some of the groups such as the YWCA are still in operation today.

One group which formed during this period and is still in operation today is the Needlework Guild of Canada. The Guild's main aim was the collection and distribution of new handmade garments and household linens for adults and children. Similar to the original Needlework Guild of England, whose mandate was to make articles of clothing for state-run orphanages in order to "bridge the Island of Waste and the Island of Want," the Canadian Guild used the goods it collected to meet the needs of state-operated hospitals, homes, and charities.

This paper will show how the voluntary work engaged in by the members of the Needlework Guild of Canada exemplifies the feminization of the social system. It will be argued that this women's reform group can be considered an example of the successful feminization of an institution in the sense that success means the following:

1. providing women with a chance to meet and socialize outside of the domestic realm
2. providing women with a chance to make use of domestic skills which gave them a sense of self-worth
3. providing women with a chance to learn new skills and exposing them to new ideas
4. providing a service to others in need in the absence of state agencies

If successful feminization of an institution is defined in terms of breaking down patriarchal power relationships and class privilege, the Guild does not qualify. However, it was a product of its historical time, and its maternal feminism cannot be dismissed simply in the light of future events. By locating these women historically, it will be argued that the organization of the Needlework Guild enabled its members to undertake social reform successfully, as well as create a support network sufficiently meaningful to some women that it is still in operation today.

To set the context, I briefly discuss the ideology of maternal feminism, followed by a brief history of the original Needlework Guild of England and of the Toronto Branch. Finally, evidence gleaned from Annual Reports, Minute Books from business meetings, and newspaper reports chronicling the work of the Guild over 100 years will be analyzed to show how its members were maternal feminists and how the group can be in this context considered successfully feminized.

Maternal Feminism

The ideology of maternal feminism (Kealy 1979) is associated with the literature on the emergence of national women's organizations. It incorporates the ideas from both social feminism (Kraditor 1968; O'Neill 1969) and domestic feminism (Smith 1974). Maternal feminism draws from social feminism the idea that women should have the right to engage in social reform in the public sphere because of their special characteristics as women. The term social feminism was coined by O'Neill (1969) in order to distinguish extreme or hard-core feminists who were specifically concerned with women's rights from those women, called social feminists, whose main concern was social reform. This term has been closely linked to women's role in the suffrage movement.

From domestic feminism, maternal feminism draws the claim to greater women's autonomy inside the family, but not beyond it in the public realm. The term "domestic feminism" was developed by (Smith 1974) in his work on the limitation of family size and sexual control during the Victorian era in America. He argues that it is inappropriate in understanding women's historic position to separate public and private in this period since so few women had the opportunity to participate in the public sphere at all.

Drawing on Kealy (1979), I adopt the perspective of maternal feminism in this paper:

> Building from the term "social feminist" and incorporating the important role played by domestic ideology, "maternal feminism" refers to the conviction that women's special role as mother gives her the duty and the right to participate in the public sphere. (Kealy 1979, 7)

The key tenet of the ideology is that not only married women but all women possess the special characteristics and virtues that qualify them for reform of the public sphere. It is also assumed that women are normally superior to men because of their special characteristics. Hence, only women can effectively address those uniquely "domestic" problems fostered by industrialization such as poverty, crime, child welfare, child labour, infant mortality, working girls, public health, intemperance, prostitution, morality, social purity, housing, juvenile delinquency, concerns with food and milk contamination, demand for education, and perceived lack of cultural standards. Thus, as Brandt (1985) notes, women's reform organizations developed in response to the lack of success in handling societal problems experienced by state agencies headed by male governmental officials (Brandt 1985).

This public reform activity was legitimated because it was built upon the existing, accepted role of women in the domestic sphere. Brandt notes that "the acknowledgement of women's special attributes made maternal feminism seem reasonable and acceptable because it provided a respectable, non-threatening rationale for female activism" (1985, 87). The Needlework Guild can be examined in the context of the ideology of maternal feminism.

Origin of the Needlework Guild

> It might amaze many women to be told that there are women, bringing a little new life to birth, who shiver every night in cold beds.... But a motherly, tender-hearted woman, able to project herself into the lives of others, came to realize these things and so she founded the Needlework Guild in

London Eng., as long ago as 1883 (Mail and Empire, November 14, 1927).

The original Needlework Guild was founded in 1882 in Irwene, Dorsetshire, by Lady Giana Wolverton. Lady Wolverton founded an orphanage that became a refuge for hundreds of children who were orphaned in the 1882 mine disaster in Wales. She soon found that the needs of the orphaned children were greater than her institution could provide. The funds were too limited to pay for clothing for the children and "nakedness or near-nakedness remained" (MacArthur 1955,23). She turned to her close friends, asking them to provide clothing for the orphans in her charge.

Since Lady Wolverton apparently could have afforded to pay for the clothing herself, why did she call upon her middle-class friends? In his book on the Needlework Guild of America, MacArthur suggests one reason:

> Lady Wolverton might have herself supplied the emergency needs of the influx of orphans. That might perhaps have been the easier way. She could have provided ample money. Just to give money, if one has it is the easiest way to "give to charity," and as even the giver knows. the coldest way. It provides for human needs but leaves the spirit of the recipient empty, and with-holds the heart of the giver. (MacArthur 1955, 22)

There was another reason. It seems that she noticed that many of her friends were unhappy with their lives and had time on their hands. Though the cult of domesticity was as much or more ideology as reality, these well-to-do women were often confined to the private, domestic sphere (Cott 1977; Welter 1966).

Moreover, according to MacArthur, Lady Wolverton regularly thought about "all the women she knew whose hands were so often idle, whose spirits were unhappy, whose lives were filled with boredom" (MacArthur 1955, 23), and she worried as much about "the women whose hands were NOT idle, whose hands were, indeed, very busy, doing both useful things and very aimless, time-filling things" (MacArthur 1955, 23). Knowing that many of her friends would have clothing in their homes suitable for the orphans, or if they did not, could easily make the clothing themselves, she recognized the opportunity to serve both the 'less fortunate' and her middle-class friends.

Apparently, Lady Wolverton shared the common upper-middle-class concern with the problems of those 'less fortunate' than herself. She wrote, "If only a little bridge could be thrown from the Island of Waste to the Island of Want, how both would benefit!" (cited in

310

MacArthur 1955, 23). The bridge was her effort to engage her friends' help in providing clothing for her orphanage. Thus, not only was she able to provide clothing for those in need but also provide her friends with worthwhile and meaningful work which they could do in their homes. According to MacArthur, Lady Wolverton asked for her friends' help in a precise way:

> "I'm asking each of you," she told her friends, "for two new articles of clothing. They must be new. They must be exactly alike. They must not be expensive. They will be better for the children for whom they are intended, and even better for you, if you make them yourselves. As the work of your own hands they are part of you."
> "But why two garments?" Lady Wolverton was asked.
> "What does the child wear," replied Lady Wolverton, "while what he has been wearing is being laundered?"
> Thus the slogan which has since been used by millions of women — and of men and children — came into existence: "one to wear, and one to wash" (MacArthur 1955, 24).

Lady Wolverton had, indeed, recognized an opportunity to bridge two social worlds. Initially, she was very successful in obtaining handmade garments for the orphanage. Her local success became an international movement: by 1892, other branches of the Needlework Guild (NWG) had been formed by word of mouth in Ireland, Scotland, England, Wales, France, Italy, Switzerland, the USA, and Canada.

The Needlework Guild of Canada, Toronto Branch

The first meeting held to organize the Needlework Guild of Canada took place on December 1, 1892, at the YWCA in Toronto. The group was founded by Mrs. Irving Cameron and Mrs. J. K. Kerr, who served as the Guild's first president. At this meeting, Mrs. Cameron gave a brief history of the object of the Guild, its work, and the successful growth of the Guild in England and the United States. The origins of the groups are chronicled in the Annual Report for 1935 in the following way:

> It is interesting to note that the Needlework Guild was really started here by an American woman, a Mrs. Arthur Dodge of New York, who used to spend her summers at the Georgian Bay, and there she met and interested Mrs. Irving Cameron in the work. Mrs. Cameron got together a group of women here in Toronto to hear Mrs. Dodge speak on the work done in the States and so it was in this manner that our branch came into existence (Annual Report 1935).

I have traced some of the members who were present at the first meeting using the Annual Reports of the Needlework Guild and biographical dictionaries edited by Rose (1886) and Morgan (1912). The search revealed that the backgrounds of the founding mothers were middle-to upper-class, with a common Anglo-Saxon heritage and religious affiliations which were mainly Methodist, Presbyterian, Anglican, or the smaller Protestant Churches. In these respects, the women tended to fit the model of those who were part of the late nineteenth-century suffragist and reform club movements. Like others in those movements, many were members of more than one group (Bacci 1983, 5).

The commitment to prayer exemplifies the influence of the Social Gospel at work in the Needlework Guild (Allen 1975). Needlework Guild membership, like membership in other reform clubs, was a way to demonstrate social salvation through 'good works.' The Constitution of the Toronto Branch of The Needlework Guild states that the group is non-sectarian. In this respect, it is similar to the National Council of Women; however, as in the Local Council in the Toronto Branch of the Needlework Guild, prayer was a part of the meetings (Strong-Boag 1976). In fact, at the beginning of the Executive business meetings, prayers were given by various members of the Guild. For example, the minutes taken on April 6, 1898, state that "the secretary opened the meeting, reading short prayers." This tradition still continues today as the Needlework Guild Prayer is printed in the Guild's most current Annual Report:

> Direct us, O Lord, in all our doings with thy most
> gracious favour, and further us with thy continual help.
> That in all our work begun, continued and ended in thee.
> That we may glorify thy holy name. Amen.
> (Annual Report 1993)

The Minute Book reflects the depth of the religious commitment when the secretary was writing about which hospitals should be given articles of clothing from the Guild:

> It is always a difficult matter to keep Personality out of a
> Work, such as the Guild. We have, naturally more sympathy
> for one Home or Hosp. than another but working as we all
> do, for the one dear Lord, we must lay aside any private
> wishes, or prejudices, and so bring a Blessing on our Guild
> (Minutes, November 21, 1901).

The actual 'good works' which the women accomplished are outlined in the Constitution and the Annual Reports. The first object of the Guild was to "distribute new, suitable articles of clothing among the Hospitals, Homes and needy Institutions of Toronto" (Annual Report 1984). This has not changed much over the last hundred years. The rules of membership were elegantly simple: "All members were required to contribute two or more new garments every year" one for wash and one for wear (Annual Report 1894). In 1892, 456 articles were collected and distributed; in 1993, the number was over 5000.

One aspect of the Guild's work was the making of the two new articles of clothing. The rationale for the requirement reflects maternal feminist ideology; sewing clothes is one of women's special capacities. Sewing for the Needlework Guild was synonymous with being a true woman (Welter 1966). Lady Wolverton expressed the ideology thus:

> There must be thousands in England 'plying the needle' — the most womanly of all occupations; to everyone I say, you are doing a Divine work; you are helping to carry out the divine mission to 'clothe the naked'; you are benefitting, by association, thousands of your fellow-creatures; you are benefitting yourselves in the best possible way, by learning to be active, unselfish, sympathetic, and economical (MacArthur 1955,43).

As for the virtues the Guild fostered, she was equally enthusiastic:

> The virtues I see coming out of the Guild are, first, industry; second, the twins: Patience and Perseverance. Patience, for one garment finished, you begin another. Perseverance, because you will not begin Number 2 before Number 1 is finished. Third, another twin, Economy and Ingenuity. Perhaps you hardly call these virtues. To me Economy is a Divine virtue, and Ingenuity the use man makes of it. Fourth, Sympathy. Working for an object gives you sympathy with an object, and this is the Mainspring of the Guild (MacArthur 1955,44).

These maternal virtues were not only confined to the Guild, of course, but to the wider society through the Guild's distribution of quality clothing to state hospitals, homes, and charities.

Feminizing Social Welfare

Does the Guild exemplify the successful feminization of social welfare? According to Lady Wolverton, the two main objectives of the Guild were to provide 'benefit to workers' and to 'benefit from work.' Although clearly founded on a maternalistic ideology, the Guild had at least five significant social and political consequences for its middle-class members.

313

First, it enabled women to meet other women outside their homes and develop new social networks and friendships. For example, tea was often served after the meetings and the women socialized. As the minutes reflect for April 28, 1909, "the meeting adjourned, after a very sociable cup of tea, kindly provided by Mrs. Blackwood."

Second, it enabled these middle-class women to make wider use of their domestic skills, engendering a sense of self-worth and status. In the early days of the Guild, the heightened sense of self-worth drew on the religious link between salvation and 'good works.' Moreover, when the women sewed together, the older generation transmitted domestic skills to younger women and deepened friendships:

> Older women know when younger ones do not know, but wish to know. They smile, and explain, naturally and simply, and two people of different ages — or comparable ages — become friends for all the rest of their lives. If they are already friends, their friendships deepen because of the inspiration of their concerted effort (MacArthur 1955, 57).

Third, the Guild enabled women to learn new organizational skills that drew them out of the domestic sphere. As the Annual Reports show, even in a relatively simple organization, there were a variety of formal procedures and practices to be followed, such as taking minutes, collecting articles, managing finances, organizing and running meetings, distributing articles, and advertising for the Distribution Day.

Fourth, it exposed the women to a wide network of other women's organizations such as the WCTU, YWCA, IODE, Local Council of Women, Aberdeen Association, and the Women's Welcome Hostel. The Annual Reports and Minute Books show that the Guild Executive was offered the use of the WCTU rooms for their distribution meetings (Minutes, November 21, 1900); that it provided the WCTU with clothing in 1899 and 1900 (Annual Reports 1899, 1900); that it supported the IODE in 1914, and that held its annual distribution for 1914 at 599 Sherbourne Street, the Headquarters for the Women's Patriotic League (Annual Report 1914). The Minute Book also records the discussion surrounding entry into the Local Council of Women in 1905. Speakers were often invited to Executive meetings, exposing women to new ideas and reform issues, though normally limited to those compatible with the maternalist ideology of the time. At one meeting, representatives from institutions that had received packages of clothing discussed how the Needlework Guild had helped their particular institution:

> Miss Campbell gave a vivid picture of distress amongst the poor where her work lies chiefly with unprepared mothers and newborn babies (Minutes, April 28, 1921).

Miss H. D. McCollum re-iterated the same appeal, and also showed how the decency of being able to wear clothing such as that furnished to her society by the Guild for many years past, often saved the self-respect of growing boys and girls who otherwise would have slunk away into undesirable or depraved bypaths (Minutes, April 28, 1921).

Finally, the Guild provided a service to others in need, a service which the state was not providing. This is reflected in this excerpt from the Guild's 100th Anniversary Speech by Madelaine Bain:

> Toronto, 100 years ago, was a very different place than it is today. The population was under 200,000 and mainly Protestant of British stock. There was no OHIP, no baby bonus, Old Age or Canada Pension, no unemployment insurance. If you didn't work, or were ill, there was very little government assistance. However, there were many people, men and women, with a dedicated sense of social responsibility. many of the social agencies in Toronto today which are funded by Community and Social Service were founded by people who felt they had a duty to help those less fortunate than themselves. (Annual Report 1993).

As Baines (1991) notes, women's groups like the Needlework Guild were the forerunners to contemporary social welfare institutions. The Needlework Guild is still in operation, providing a service to those whom they see as needy. and for whom the state is providing. As Bain noted in her 100th Anniversary speech, Toronto now has "good government-funded social agencies, but in these days of recession, these agencies have a hard time supplying the most basic needs, and rely on volunteer efforts." She also stated that "as long as there is a need…the Needlework Guild will be there" (Annual Report 1993).

Considered in historical context, the Needlework Guild was part of the thorough feminization of welfare institutions in the nineteenth century. Moreover, whereas many of the women's groups which emerged during the club movement of the last century are no longer in existence, the Needlework Guild recently celebrated its 100th anniversary:

> The Needlework Guild of Canada, Toronto Branch, is 100 years old. All members have a right to be very proud of this milestone. We have planned three social activities which will give everyone an opportunity to meet other Guild members, renew acquaintances, and let the public know that we represent a group of people dedicated to helping the needy. (Annual Report 1991)

Today, many of the women of the Guild knit blankets, booties, and bonnets following a pattern for Toronto hospitals with premature baby units. However, the group surely would not survive if it did not continue to fulfil a contemporary form of the maternal feminist aspirations of its members-finding part of their identity in serving those in need through 'useful work.'

References

Allen, Richard. (ed). 1975. *The Social Gospel in Canada.* Ottawa: National Museums of Canada.

Bacci, Carol. 1985. *Liberation Deferred: The Ideas of the English Canadian Suffragists,* 1877-1918. Toronto: University of Toronto Press.

Baines, Carol. 1988. *Women's Reform Organizations in Canada 1870-1930: A Historical Perspective.* Toronto, Faculty of Social Work: University of Toronto.

Brandt, Gail Cuthbert. 1985. *"Organizations in Canada: The English Protestant Tradition."* pp. 79-98 in Paula Bourne ed. Women's paid and Unpaid Work: Historical and Contemporary Perspectives. Toronto: New Hogtown Press.

Cott, Nancy, F. 1977. *The Bonds of Womanhood: "Woman's Sphere"*in New England, 1780-1835. New Haven: Yale University Press.

Kealy, Linda. (ed.). 1979. *A Not Unreasonable Claim: Women and Reform in Canada,* 1880's-1920's. Toronto: Women's Educational Press.

Kraditor, Aileen. (ed.). 1968. *Up From The Pedestal: Selected Writings in the History of Feminism.* Chicago: Quadrangle Books.

Morgan, Henry James. 1912. *The Canadian Men and Women of the Time: A Handbook of Canadian Biography of Living Characters.* 2nd ed. Toronto: William Briggs.

MacArthur, Burke. 1955. United Littles: The Story of the Needlework Guild of America. New York: Coward-McCann, Inc.

Mitchinson, Wendy. 1982. *'The WCTU:"For God, Home and Native Land":* A Study in Nineteenth-Century Feminism'. Pp.190-209 in Michael S. Cross and Gregory S. Kealy eds. Canada's Age of Industry 1849-1896: Readings in Canadian Social History. vol.3. Toronto: McClelland and Stewart.

O'Neill, William L. 1969. *Everyone Was Brave: The Rise and Fall of Feminism in America.* Chicago: Quadrangle Books.

Rose, George Maclean (ed.). 1886. *A Cyclopaedia of Canadian Biography Being Chiefly Men of the Time.* Toronto: Rose Publishing Company.

Smith, Daniel Scott. 1974. *'Family Limitation, Sexual Control, and Domestic Feminism in Victorian America'.* Pp.119-137 in Mary Hartmann and Lois Banner eds. Clio's Consciousness Raised. New York: Harper.

Strong-Boag, Veronica. 1977 *"Setting the Stage': National Organization and the Women's Movement in the Late 19th Century'.* pp. 87-103 in Susan Mann Trofimenkoff and Alison Prentice eds. The Neglected Majority: Essays in Canadian Women's History. 1st ed. Toronto: McClelland and Stewart.

Welter, Barbara. 1966. *"The Cult of True Womanhood,* 1820-1860". American Quarterly XVIII: 151-174.

Archival Sources

Archives of Ontario, F828 Needlework Guild of Canada Papers, Annual Reports, 1892-1990. MU 4696, Folders 1-8.

Archives of Ontario, F828 Needlework Guild of Canada Papers, United Littles, The Story of the Needlework Guild. MU 4697, Folder 12.

Archives of Ontario, F828 Needlework Guild of Canada Papers, Constitution. MU 4697, Folder 20.

Archives of Ontario, F828 Needlework Guild of Canada Papers, Minutes of the First Meeting of the Needlework Guild of Canada, Minutes of 1892 (read at 50th Anniversary, 1942). MY 4698, Folder 40.

Archives of Ontario, F828 Needlework Guild of Canada Papers, Minutes of Annual, Business and Distribution Meetings and Newspapers Clippings 1892-1918. MU 4698, Folder 41.

Archives of Ontario, F828 Needlework Guild of Canada Papers, Minutes of Annual Meeting, 1919-1927, Executive and General Meetings 1921-1927, Management Meeting, 1921 (includes newspaper clippings). MU 4698, Folder 41.

Needlework Guild of Canada, Annual Reports, 1991-1993. Personal Correspondence with Mrs. Elizabeth James, President of the Needlework Guild of Canada.

Endnote

1. A version of this paper was presented at the CSAA Conference, Carlton University, Ottawa, Ontario in June 1993. I have appreciated the comments of Pat Armstrong, Karen Blackford, and Gordon Darroch on earlier drafts.

Karen Blackford, Marie-Luce Garceau, Sandra Kirby

PART VI — PARTIE VI
What We Have Learned
Leçons de nos expériences

In the opening chapter of this book, we reviewed Rosemarie Tong's (1989) idea that feminist theory is demonstrated by action imbedded in particular locations and identities. From this starting point, we introduced each of the sections of the book to highlight the diverse identities and locations of Canadian authors and their various approaches to creating change.

In each chapter, authors presented their explanations of why and how women are oppressed. Now, in this final chapter of *Feminist Success Stories*, we review where this text has taken us and identify the collective lessons we have learned.

Our first major lesson involves the practical experiences the authors have shared as they clarify the areas in which Canadian women are oppressed. These areas include educational systems, patriarchal traditions, institutional processes, individual attitudes, cultural controls, and both written and verbal communication situations.

Secondly, the authors have also described principles, actions, and strategies that they and other women have used to claim or reclaim power. All of these elements

Dans le chapitre d'introduction, nous présentions l'idée développée par Rosemarie Tong (1989) selon laquelle la théorie féministe se caractérise davantage par une action qui porte le sceau de son enracinement local et de son identité. Ce point de vue ayant servi de canevas aux différentes parties du livre, il servira aussi à élaborer ce dernier chapitre.

Chacune des auteures présente, à sa manière, les différentes identités des femmes, les multiples lieux de leur oppression, les raisons pour lesquelles l'oppression s'exerce, la façon dont elle le fait et, enfin, les moyens mis en place pour obtenir des changements. Ainsi, dans ce chapitre de *Célébrons nos réussites féministes*, nous débuterons en montrant certains des lieux communs de l'oppression des femmes : le système d'éducation, le patriarcat, les institutions, les attitudes individuelles et collectives ou le contrôle culturel, etc.

Deuxièmement, nous décrirons les principes, les stratégies et les actions adoptés par les auteures et les femmes afin d'acquérir plus de pouvoir et d'obtenir des changements sociaux. L'ensemble de ces éléments sont fondamentaux à la

are fundamental to the feminization of institutions in Canada.

Next, we noted the many themes of Canadian women's oppression addressed in the articles. As each theme was identified, women's ways of overcoming particular situations of oppression were also highlighted. In spite of variety in emphasis and differences in worldview, similar themes of oppression and resistance run through every chapter. These themes include the socialization of women and girls, the power of the written and spoken word, the Canadian economy, and human rights and responsibilities.

The outcomes of feminist change were discussed and include improvements in the lives of women and transformations in many of the organizations and institutions in which they work and live. Given that many improvements and transformations have occurred, it is important to create tools to measure these changes. To ensure that the evidence we provide of feminist success is strong enough to empower future feminist action and thought, we have summarized a number of recurring indicators of success in the process of "feminizing". Prominent among these indicators are feminist process, education as consciousness raising, respect for diversity, historical context, evaluation, and women-centeredness.

In our final reflections, we conclude that, in spite of variation related to location, identity, and

féminisation des institutions canadiennes.

Troisièmement, en parcourant l'ensemble des chapitres, il est possible de tirer certaines leçons concernant l'oppression des femmes et la façon féministe de concevoir le changement social. On trouvera ainsi de courtes discussions ayant pour thèmes la socialisation, le pouvoir symbolique, l'économie canadienne ou les droits et les responsabilités.

Finalement, même si la moindre transformation des conditions de vie des femmes ou des organisations dans lesquelles elles œuvrent constitue une réussite, celle-ci revêt souvent un caractère mitigé dans une société patriarcale. Il faut donc créer des instruments propres à mesurer les changements accomplis afin que toutes les femmes puissent en bénéficier et qu'ils puissent stimuler les théories et les pratiques en s'appuyant sur des faits et des expériences robustes. En ce sens, les auteures ont proposé un certain nombre d'indicateurs rendant possible la mesure des réussites des femmes. Parmi ceux-ci, certains ressortent de façon plus particulière : les stratégies féministes, la prise de conscience au moyen de l'éducation, le respect de la diversité, le contexte historique, l'évaluation critique et l'approche centrée sur les femmes.

De ces chapitres, nous pouvons d'ores et déjà conclure que les luttes des femmes, qu'elles soient du domaine privé ou public, sont importantes au plan individuel et collectif. Elles sont importantes parce que chacune des auteures précise, à sa

action, there are many common ideas and theories about the nature of feminism across Canada.

façon, ce qu'elle entend par une pratique féministe marquée du sceau de la réussite.

Sites of Oppression and Feminist Processes
Lieux de l'oppression et stratégies féministes

Uncovering the various sites of oppression involving any aggregate demonstrates that social change is never a direct or obvious enterprise. Working alone or in concert, the many facets of oppression comprise enormous barriers to women's efforts to improve the quality of their lives and their status.

This is true for women in their views of themselves; it is also reflected in societal and physical norms, in homes, in workplaces, and in communities in which women work as volunteers or for wages. For example, organizational and research practices based on the modern ideals of rationality, individuality, and objectivity have created hierarchies and inflexible arrangements which oppress women and girls in the educational system (Epp). These oppressive practices are also evident in research funding institutes and methods (Christiansen-Ruffman et al ; Garceau), in political life (Garrett); and in the workforce (Hare and Corbiere, Parsons and Goggins, Briskin). Sexist, disablist, racist, homophobic, Eurocentric, ageist attitudes emerging from these modern values counteract the efforts by women to be in control of important aspects of their lives (Bouchard et Cholette). Women's bodies (Blackford, Gordon), the family (Miedema and Nason-Clark, Blackford), medical institutions (Blackford; Gagné), the church (Dumas) are likewise sites of oppression. Cultural assimilation has the effect of severing historic connections with religion, language, and other identity and contextual concerns important to women's cultural origins and strengths (Hébert; Hare and Corbiere). Words, as instruments for communicating knowledge and values (Whitney), are also often sites of women's oppression. Taken together, these multiple sites of oppression impede efforts made by women to bring about change. For progressive change to occur, it is important that women, both individually and collectively, identify oppression as it exists in their own locations and see themselves as capable of making feminist change as individuals and in concert with other women.

Principles of Change
Principes du changement

We have chosen seven articles to demonstrate how explicit and implicit principles have guided feminist change. Fulfilment of these same principles serves as measures of success in bringing about feminist change.

The members of the Better Beginnings, Better Futures project (Reitsma-Street and Rogerson) decided that success for their neighbourhood organization should include achievement of the following six principles: active member participation, egalitarian work relations, dailiness, care for the caregivers, empowerment, and networking. This organization has literally changed whole neighbourhoods by developing affirming and respectful processes through which women along with others have been able to work together and with others. Assessment efforts have always included feedback from the neighbourhood as well as participant involvement.

Gordon describes a community dance school committed to consensus and cooperation in both its internal and external activities. The inclusive nature of the school means that instructors, volunteers, and girls attending the school have a sense of ownership of the school and that no sharp divisions exist among the three groups. The accomplishments of this organization include valuing and recognition of women's paid and unpaid work and fostering of communication in spite of age differences.

Parsons and Goggins provide an example of the importance of feminist process at the local level. Innovative approaches including that of decision-making by consensus which eventually transformed both the women's caucus, and, subsequently, an entire educators' union. Working through problems associated with diversity and solidarity strengthened women in their efforts to raise bargaining issues with union executives and with employers; these issues included work-site standards, childcare, benefits for dependents, and accommodation for working union members with disabilities.

Briskin tells how rank-and-file women gained a voice in Canadian unions through a participatory approach on the part of female union staff. The context of affirmative action legislation, in conjunction with these advances, Briskin argues, placed discussion of representation and shared power at the forefront of the union agenda across Canada.

Whitney writes that both the process and outcomes of change were integral to the organization of the Girl Guides. Consensus was achieved through negotiations at rallies across the country. Guides as well as their leaders were included in decision-making. While Whitney acknowledges that more changes in these directions are warranted, she likewise remarks that increased democratization of the organization and enhancement of guiders' self-esteem and self-determination were important feminist goals achieved through these processes.

La féminisation des institutions canadiennes, particulièrement au chapitre des coopératives, repose sur l'analyse des multiples formes d'oppression des femmes et la lutte qu'elles mènent pour y mettre fin.

Le succès de *La coopérative Convergence*, étayé par Bouchard et Cholette, montre que la féminisation d'une institution est chose possible, malgré les embûches et les difficultés que rencontrent les coopérantes. Ces auteures soulignent que la féminisation des structures, dans lesquelles elles travaillent depuis maintenant quelques années, se fonde sur quelques principes cardinaux : partage des pouvoirs, environnement de travail flexible, inclusion de personnes possédant le moins de privilèges et autonomie des femmes. Toutefois, elles mentionnent également que les acquis des femmes demeurent fragiles. Plusieurs iniquités subsistent encore aujourd'hui. C'est pourquoi Bouchard et Cholette en appellent à la solidarité des femmes et des exclues et à leur commune volonté de changer les rapports sociaux de domination.

Success for Laiken lies in processes involving clear communication, broad input into decision-making and policy implementation, and milieux supportive of women. In other words, measures of success are tied to emergence and expression of individual participants' philosophies, followed by negotiation of a group philosophy and construction of an organizational model. Most important is the development of participants' process skills, safe environments for dialogue, and clearly understood and accepted mechanisms for conflict resolution. Effective decision-making is only possible in the context of long term commitment to an organization, effective communication, and accountability. Together, these factors lead to decision-making through consensus.

Strategies for Bringing about Change
Stratégies pour le changement

In this book, authors identify a variety of strategies for bringing about change. These strategies include placing women at the centre, partnerships, education including consciousness-raising, respect for diversity, recollection of historical context, and critical evaluation of outcomes. The relationship between sites of oppression and where feminists have chosen to focus their efforts to bring about change are clearly described.

Placing Women at the Centre — Approche centrée sur les femmes

Kirby, in her analysis of the development of the Canadian Sport Council, highlights the value of placing women at the centre of training opportunities and in positions as spokespersons and government policy-makers. When the climate of change becomes positive, success can be measured by how effectively well-informed well-positioned women contribute. It can also be measured by the existence of gender equity and participant-centredness in mandates, goals, objectives, and policies of organizations. To determine whether women-centred changes have occurred, evaluation is a necessary and long-term activity for the organization. That is, an organization must determine whether its planning outcomes are "window dressing" or catalysts for real change.

Women are at the core of the Aboriginal community development program described by Hare and Day-Corbiere. They cite women-led meetings as an important aspect of the project.

Miedema and Nason-Clark demonstrate that it is empowering for foster mothers to describe their situations and perspectives and to voice their recommendations for change. Women-centred approaches are valuable in unravelling state oppression when it involves inadequate funding and consultation with women on the one hand and proof of successful parenting on the other. Miedema and Nason-Clark argue that foster mothers succeed in making an important contribution to society in spite of, rather than with the support of, the social welfare system.

Bouchard et Cholette montrent l'importance que l'on devrait accorder aux valeurs féministes telles l'absence de hiérarchie, la flexibilité, l'inclusion et l'autonomie dans le développement de nouvelles structures du travail susceptibles de répondre aux besoins des femmes. Leurs expériences comme coopérantes viennent étayer la façon dont ces valeurs changent la structure quotidienne du travail et les relations qu'entretient l'organisation avec l'extérieur.

Aux valeurs développées par Bouchard et Cholette viennent s'ajouter celles de Garceau : motivation, respect, souplesse, bonne communication, confiance mutuelle, échange, reconnaissance des compétences, partage d'une vision commune. Celles-ci sont autant de gages de réussites individuelles et collectives pour les femmes participant à un processus de recherche-action. Pourtant, on ne saurait trop insister sur l'importance de partager une vision commune centrée sur les problèmes d'un groupe précis de femmes. Pour Garceau, il s'agit de celle des Franco-Ontariennes de 45 à 64 ans, car c'est leur vision commune qui est à l'origine de la transformation de leurs multiples réalités.

Coholic and Prévost highlight the innovative approaches possible when programs for adult survivors of sexual abuse are women-centred. They describe how counselling on an individual and group basis can move beyond healing of trauma to an examination of sexism in society. Participants' altered worldviews with regard to power and gender help to strengthen women for the tasks of reframing their experiences and of eliminating self-blame and guilt. Success is evidenced in participants' heightened self-esteem, their ability to deconstruct and analyze the events in their everyday lives, and their ability to reconstruct social relations.

Successful change can come from the bottom up or the top down. As Coholic and Prévost illustrate, one of the by-products of a women-centred approach is the ripple effect that feminist change has within an organization. A successful women-centred program can modify policy directions of its "parent" organization so that issues of importance to women are given priority. On the other hand, progressive women-centered state policies, even though they may be federal or provincial/territorial, can also have a strong influence at the level of municipal program implementation. Success emerges when optimal conditions for change exist; these conditions can be created by individual women or state policy.

Partnerships — Partenariats

Le partenariat est une composante essentielle du changement social féministe. À partir d'une recherche-action, Garceau présente certains éléments propres à façonner ce genre d'expérience partenariale. D'abord, une telle démarche s'appuie sur l'initiative des femmes qui, en collaboration avec des chercheures, apprennent à valoriser leurs expériences et leurs compétences mutuelles. Dès lors, pour Garceau, les rapports entre les partenaires doivent s'inscrire dans une logique d'égalité respectueuse des différences. Cette égalité implique que les femmes doivent avoir le contrôle sur le déroulement de l'enquête. Celui-ci s'obtient d'abord par la présence et la participation des femmes aux discussions et décisions. Cette prise de parole atteint son apogée lorsque leurs préoccupations deviennent centrales à la fois au processus de recherche et aux stratégies d'actions. La recherche-action devient alors une démarche féconde, malgré ses exigences et ses contraintes, parce qu'elle s'effectue à l'instant et au lieu même où les femmes se trouvent.

Garceau montre la dimension fort importante du temps qu'il faut accorder à un projet de recherche en partenariat. Ce temps permet aux femmes de se connaître afin que s'établissent des bases solides et nécessaires à toutes les étapes subséquentes de la recherche. Par ailleurs, malgré les difficultés inhérentes à un tel projet, il doit permettre de valider le savoir expérientiel des femmes et leur vision du monde à partir de leur position d'actrices sociales. L'idée défendue est que les femmes, après avoir exploré leur privé, sont capables de s'en abstraire pour construire un pan de la réalité sociale intersubjective et transubjective. Finalement, pour Garceau, le changement social doit être au centre de la motivation et des préoccupations des partenaires.

Partnerships are a critical component of feminist change. They can be formed to undertake research that has a wide scope; the results of this kind of research have a broad impact (Reitsma-Street and Rogerson; Christiansen-Ruffman et al.). Partnerships can be alliances between academics and community activists. Such partnership ensure that those involved in change are as fully informed about issues and strategies as possible (Reitsma-Street and Rogerson). Partnership can also be formed between organizations and their particular caucuses or committees to bring about change within organizations (Briskin; Moreau; Parsons and Goggins). The most difficult, perhaps, are partnerships formed between women's groups and/or government or business (Hare and Day-Corbiere, Reitsma-Street and Rogerson; Christiansen-Ruffman et al.). In this last case, the power differential between partners is great. Furthermore, the outcomes of change in such situations may be more direct and salient for the women than for their partners.

Paid and unpaid individuals often work together to bring about change (Laiken; Reitsma-Street and Rogerson). Artificial divisions based on pay or status or exclusivity need to be carefully factored into the creation of partnerships. This is necessary to ensure that the partnerships are equal in how women are valued, respected, and empowered to participate in decision-making. To be productive and satisfying, partnerships need to be based on a fair sharing of resources, negotiation of desired direction, commitment to tasks at hand, and shared responsibility for outcomes.

Significantly, some women prefer to act alone. However, when social change involves the work of groups of women, the processes of group interaction are critically important. Some have suggested that the longer it takes to effect a change, the more important it is that egalitarian processes be observed. Others have suggested that process is always important, maybe even more important than outcome.

Education Which Includes Consciousness Raising — Éducation, formation et prise de conscience

Epp sees how valuable outcomes emerged from the efforts of the feminist faculty network at the university in which she was situated. Although she emphasizes the ongoing need for further education about sexism and women's issues, she likewise recounts how a Women's Studies area of study, initially established as a minor elective, has grown to include a Master's Degree Program. Some faculty members experienced a change in worldview. This new worldview includes a sense of empowerment and belief that change is possible. Although Epp indicates that no radical paradigm shift occurred across her campus, passage of an affirmative action policy is a concrete indicator of feminist change.

The safety and separate spaces provided by support groups for women survivors of childhood sexual abuse (Coholic and Prévost), a union women's caucus (Parsons and Goggins), Women's Studies classes (Epp), and an association of sporting women (Kirby) provide opportunities to revise women's views of the gendered world (Dumais). Similarly, consciousness raising has occurred at countrywide rallies of Girl Guides and in Guiding executive meetings (Whitney). Even the privacy of family life can provide a space in which to reframe social relations when a parent has a disability (Blackford). These opportunities bring improved understanding of how male-centered political, social, and economic power has been maintained by assumptions about biological differences and socialized roles.

Selon Garceau, dans toute recherche-action, les femmes arrivent avec des connaissances issues de leurs expériences et méconnaissent le plus souvent le processus de recherche. La recherche peut devenir alors un instrument de distanciation entre les partenaires plutôt qu'un lieu de convergence. C'est pourquoi les chercheures doivent transmettre les principales étapes de ce processus dans un langage clair et accessible et échanger sur l'état actuel de la théorie, de façon à permettre aux femmes de s'approprier elles-mêmes la démarche de recherche qui leur convient. L'idée sous-jacente est de permettre aux femmes d'expliquer elles-mêmes les causes et les mécanismes à l'origine de leur oppression. La formation prend alors une importance capitale.

Par ailleurs, Garceau insiste sur l'importance d'une prise de conscience des différents enjeux afin de pouvoir agir : prise de conscience réalisable au moyen de la formation et de l'éducation. Du même souffle, elle affirme que cette prise de conscience repose sur le partage et le choc des savoirs et des expériences pour en arriver à l'obtention d'un savoir collectif sur certains aspects de la réalité.

To empower women to bring about change, the very ways in which we work become critical. Many authors highlight the need for creative environments in which involvement, inclusion, visibility, assertiveness training, consciousness raising, consensus, and cohesiveness are maximized. To establish such practices, discussion of both women's differences and similarities needs to occur. Some call this consciousness raising. Others call this negotiation of the process of working together. This emergence of female issues needs to occur in safe and fertile environments.

Women need supports to enable them to act. They need assistance in the forms of increased education (Hare and Day-Corbiere) as well as training in issues that are the focus of change (Kirby) and active participation. They need encouragement to "get to the sites of change." It also helps greatly if women have good role models and some experience in role-modelling for others.

Respecting Diversity — Respect de la diversité

Although virtually all authors highlighted the need for equity in the ways women work together, such equity does not mean that all women need to be included in the same manner or that they must undertake equal portions of the social change work. Sameness of treatment is not the issue here. When women work in groups marked by diversity of membership and concerns, the need to negotiate differences is paramount. While every woman should be supported in her ability to participate fully, each may undertake this participation in a different way. Emphasis needs to be upon diversity, openness, respect, maintenance of room for individual differences, and shared efforts and responsibilities in bringing about change.

Affirmation of diversity among participants, their contributions, and their ways of working together has been basic to the operation of the Better Beginnings, Better Futures project (Reitsma-Street and Rogerson). Whitney points out the efforts made by the Canadian Girl Guides to include diversity in the processes of change. Traditional labour values of equality have been transformed into those of equity by feminists (Bouchard et Cholette).

La critique féministe des classes sociales et des catégories de sexe s'est aussi attaquée au racisme et à l'ethnicité. Les textes de Bouchard et Cholette, Hébert, Gagné et Garceau en sont des exemples éloquents. Ils montrent certaines facettes de la situation des femmes francophones vivant en milieu minoritaire. Leur présence dans ce livre et leurs propos témoignent de l'importance d'inclure, au sein du mouvement des femmes au Canada, leur vision du monde, leurs projets et leurs réalisations, pour rapprocher les deux solitudes qui existent au sein même du mouvement féministe canadien. Dans tous les cas, ces auteures s'interrogent sur les rapports d'oppression à partir du vécu des femmes francophones. Elles revendiquent, à partir de leurs expériences ou de leurs recherches, leur francité, leur existence comme sujets francophones.

Our authors critiques have also identified the issues of sexual orientation, physical and mental health, family composition, age, and religion. Questions of workplace unanimity and equality have led to pursuit of equity and broad consciousness raising.

Remembering the Historical Context — Contexte historique

Pour Hébert, les succès des femmes dans le milieu de l'éducation doivent s'accompagner d'une compréhension historique et culturelle. En effet, pour Hébert, si le Manitoba francophone contemporain possède un réseau d'institutions scolaires offrant une éducation en français, la situation n'est pas étrangère à la lutte quotidienne, souvent vécue dans l'isolement, des «maîtresses d'école». Durant la période étudiée par Hébert, les pressions gouvernementales sont fortes pour imposer l'anglais comme langue officielle d'éducation. Or, ces femmes ont joué un rôle considérable pour le maintien et la survie des écoles françaises au

Manitoba. C'est grâce aux «maîtresses d'écoles» qu'on peut aujourd'hui envisager leur gestion et poursuivre la lutte pour la protection des droits linguistiques et religieux des francophones. C'est là que réside la réussite des institutrices franco-manitobaines. Paradoxalement, l'évocation des femmes francophones comme gardiennes de la culture, de la foi et de la famille, souvent envisagée de façon négative parce que célébrant les rôles traditionnels des femmes, prend ici l'allure d'une forme de résistance de ces dernières contre l'assimilation de la francophonie en milieu scolaire dans une province majoritairement anglophone. De la recherche de Monique Hébert, on retiendra l'influence des «maîtresses d'école» qui se transmet de génération en génération, permettant aux plus jeunes, à leurs étudiantes et étudiants, de garder cette fierté d'être francophones dans cet archipel manitobain.

Whitney and the Girl Guides of Canada attended to the historical roots of the Girl Guides of Canada, while removing some of the organization's historical "baggage".

Garrett suggest that the organization she describes in her article about the Needle Women's Guild should be evaluated within its historical context. The mandate of the Guild was to provide women with the benefits of work as well as enormous quantities of clothing, bedding, and household goods for impoverished women and their families. Garrett argues that the Guild was successful in maintaining distribution of provisions even in times of economic depression, war-time rationing, and public spending cuts. Like other charitable organizations, the Guild filled the gap between what families needed and what was available to them through earned wages and the state. Garrett further acknowledges that a lifestyle of poverty, affecting both mothers and their children, was reproduced within the system of charity. Likewise, the social and charitable associations to which middle-class and upper-class women belonged sometimes reinforced differences between these women and poor women who were on the receiving end of "good works." Still, the Guild benefited its early members by providing them a vision of the world outside their class location and outside of the home. As well, it provided women with contact with the economic, social, and political issues of the days.

Pour Dumais, une institution aussi misogyne que l'Église et la théologie qui la soutient a entraîné une marginalisation et un asservissement des femmes depuis des siècles. Elle convie donc les femmes à une communion qui permettra, à force de courage et de persévérance, de transformer cette théologie. Elle invite, par la prise de parole et l'intégration, les femmes à contribuer à l'élaboration d'un renouveau théologique autour des notions que sont l'autonomie, l'égalité, la solidarité, la dignité, l'identité, la croissance, la libération, et ce, au moyen d'une relecture des textes bibliques et évangéliques. Elle les incite à construire une «ekklesia de femmes» afin qu'elles puissent accéder à un réel statut d'égalité. Finalement, elle indique que les femmes, individuellement et surtout collectivement, doivent continuer leurs efforts de conscientisation et de politisation. Leurs réussites seront à la mesure de leur vigilance et de leur détermination à ne rien céder dans les domaines qui sont d'actualité pour les femmes.

Hare and Day-Corbiere describe the cultural history of Aboriginal women as an important source of their strength. Cherishing the past and learning wisdom from female elders comprise the platform on which the present day entrepreneurship program for Aboriginal women at West Bay is founded.

Critical Evaluation of Outcomes — Évaluation critique des résultats

To be effective, we must evaluate what has been accomplished. Hare and Day-Corbiere recognize that indicators of the outcomes from their project are important. However, because these outcomes include personal confidence and hopefulness, indicators are difficult to define. They have, however, identified three specific goals: development of the individual, maintenance of Ojibwe community culture, and self-sustaining self-employment. The more general goal set for women in the program cannot be measured in finite terms. Instead, success for Aboriginal women in the program is measured "by what an individual can contribute to the community and how 'good' that individual can become while walking this path called earth."

The evaluation provided by Christiansen-Ruffman, Descarries, and Stewart of the Social Science and Humanities Federation of Canada's Women and Work Strategic Grant initiative points out uneven outcomes. The benefits of the program varied from project to project and from one geographic location to another, with large universities in Quebec, southern Ontario, and British Columbia receiving the bulk of research funding. Acknowledging these inconsistencies in "success," the authors explain that clearly positive outcomes for women include an increase in the number of studies focused on women, and a greater number of women among the successful grant recipients. In addition, approval of partnership grants involving academic and community-based researchers meant funding for independent researchers. This meant the practical advantages for recent doctoral graduates and researchers unconnected with academic institutions where research and publishing generally occur. Such post-graduate opportunities were often followed by academic appointments for these women. SSHRC also opened research funds outside the Women and Work Strategic Grant Area for independent researchers.

Women researchers, the authors argue, gained significant symbolic power through the legitimation of women's lives as subjects worthy of academic study. The creation of Women and Change, a new Strategic Grant Area, was a critically important outcome. Although other symbolic gains in legitimation of women's ways of theorizing, methodological innovations, and collaborative techniques were anticipated, Christiansen-Ruffman et al. argue that these were sometimes lost when researchers tailored their research proposals to meet SSHRC's approval criteria. They also suggest that more innovative feminist research proposals were screened out. Finally, the potential of the Women and Work Strategic Grant for enhancing the development of Women's Studies as a discipline in Canada was limited because proposals and innovations recommended by Women's Studies scholars were not accepted by SSHRC. In fact, the authors conclude, the policy of non-sexist research was eventually dropped.

Gagné apporte une contribution additionnelle à la recherche et à l'évaluation. Dénonçant le vide institutionnel médical qui laisse les Franco-Manitobaines à elles-mêmes après avoir subi une mastectomie, Gagné montre que la réussite des femmes est à l'image de leur vie quotidienne dans leurs communautés d'appartenance. Privées du soutien de l'institution médicale et privées d'informations des départements de santé communautaire sur les conséquences d'une telle chirurgie et ses effets sur leur qualité de vie, les Franco-Manitobaines de régions rurales se sont regroupées, entraidées et ont échangé afin de transgresser le choc de la maladie et retrouver le chemin de la santé.

Pour Gagné, si la science médicale mesure et calcule, elle doit aussi tenir compte de la santé des femmes comme sujets. La féminisation de l'institution médicale est donc incontournable et passe par une politique qui, contre l'idéologie fonctionnaliste dominante de l'institution médicale, misera sur l'humanisation des soins de santé. Par ailleurs, Gagné illustre bien le caractère critique que revêt la féminisation, notamment des pratiques médicales traditionnelles, en montrant que les femmes sujets veulent se prendre en main et interpeller l'institution médicale à partir de leurs expériences.

These different articles portray what is meant by successful feminist change. We now turn to theories about how change occurs as identified by our authors.

Current Discussions in Canadian Feminist Thought
Thèmes actuels du féminisme canadien

Review of the papers in this book suggests that a number of discussions are currently of interest to

Ce livre présente un certain nombre de thèmes actuels du féminisme au Canada. Ceux-ci

feminists in Canada. In this section, we identify and discuss the various themes of women's oppression our authors have explored. Among them are the following: the socialization of women; symbolic power; the Canadian economy; human rights; and leadership.

Although our analysis has shown that these themes are threaded throughout all chapters, we do not mean to imply that they are defined, or experienced, or even priorized in a similar fashion by each author. Instead, we respect the unique perspective with which each author comes to these various ideas. Differences in language, geography, ethnicity, and other demographic characteristics blend into but are not lost within the rich culture of feminism in Canada.

The following is a description of each of these issues. As well, the strategies which different authors have applied relative to each of these areas will be identified.

forment la trame du livre et parcourent l'ensemble des chapitres. Ils ne sont pas toujours explicites ou définis clairement, ni classés hiérarchiquement de la même façon par chacune des auteures. Témoignant de la perspective unique de chacune et du caractère ethnique, culturel, géographique ou démographique particulier de leurs propos, ces thèmes illustrent la richesse du féminisme canadien.

Nous avons regroupé ces thèmes sous quatre rubriques : la socialisation, le pouvoir de la parole, les femmes et l'économie et, finalement, les responsabilités et les droits.

Dans cette section, nous présenterons les différents lieux où s'exerce l'oppression des femmes tels que décrits par les auteures et nous verrons comment les femmes ont cherché à transformer leur situation.

The Theme of Socialization
La socialisation

Many authors in this text identify feminine socialization as a major contributor to women's oppression. When they are well learned, stereotypical feminine attributes such as fragility, passivity, and humility have kept many women out of physically competitive sports and out of prominent positions when they have entered sports (Kirby). These notions have also precluded many women from leadership in industry and in the labour movement (Bouchard et Cholette, Briskin, Parsons and Goggins). Internalized caring roles have taught some women to police themselves so that they stay in abusive marriages to carry out their duties as wives (Coholic and Prévost). Women and girls keep secret their experiences of sexual assault by family members out of shame and a need for social acceptance. In some dance schools, the stereotype of the waif-like prima donna ballerina encourages girls to maintain undernourished bodies (Gordon). Certainly, domestic feminine stereotypes kept women in the home and out of public life until the turn of the century in Canada (Garceau, Garrett). Most women in Canada remained disenfranchised until the early part of the twentieth century. We learn from Hare and Day-Corbiere about the irony of Aboriginal women who finally enfranchised within the Dominion of Canada but then lost their rights within First Nations communities.

The authors also discuss strategies which Canadian feminists have used for counteracting the oppressive effects of socialization. These include modelling, mentoring, assertiveness training, and feminist language and definitions. Each of these strategies merits further description.

Action: Transforming the Process of Socialization — Socialisation en changement

Modelling and Mentoring — *Modélisation et mentorat*

Some authors have suggested ways of providing girls and women with alternate and/or expanded roles after which to model themselves (Dumais, Gordon). Historically, middle-class women modelled themselves after a few women leaders who were active in community groups (Garrett), in the church (Moreau), and in other social reform movements. Mentoring involving women elders played an important role in the determination and achievements of native women both historically and in present time (Hare and Day-Corbiere). Informal leaders at the local level are encouraged by union staff women who serve as models of assertiveness (Briskin). In turn, local leaders in a women's caucus inspire other union members (Parsons and Goggins).

En théologie, selon Dumais, les femmes tentent de sortir du silence millénaire qui les entoure. Elles ont recours aux expériences des femmes afin de présenter de nouveaux modèles. Et l'une des forces de ces femmes est dans l'expérimentation d'une prise de parole qui réinterprète les textes bibliques afin d'y déceler les oppressions vécues par les femmes et qui cherche à promouvoir la transformation d'une pensée trop longtemps monopolisée par les ecclésiastiques masculins.

Assertiveness Training — *Affirmation politique*

Political analysis empowers women with knowledge; it also provides them with tools to create change through individual and collective action. Most women's lives consist of daily events and relationships to which they must apply their analytic skills. Assertiveness training is a method of providing women and girls with opportunities to see links between stereotypic feminine roles and the oppression they may experience in their everyday lives.

Our authors have noted that assertiveness training has been useful to many groups, such as staff and board members in sexual assault centres (Laiken), adult survivors of sexual abuse (Coholic and Prévost), and union members within a women's caucus (Parsons and Goggins). These approaches to modifying women's expectations of themselves and others on an everyday basis brings general feminist principles into specific action.

Dans le milieu du travail, la création d'institutions qui répond aux besoins des femmes doit assurer leur développement et leur épanouissement et lutter contre les inégalités sociales. Pour ce faire, certaines travailleuses ont choisi de s'impliquer activement, non seulement dans leur milieu de travail mais aussi dans la communauté des femmes afin de favoriser une prise de conscience et une formation continue concernant les diverses formes d'oppression et les problèmes vécus par les femmes (Cholette et Bouchard, Garceau). De cette façon, elles sont mieux outillées pour prendre la parole et lutter contre ces inégalités.

The Theme of Symbolic Power
Le pouvoir symbolique

Language plays an important part in the identity politics that keep women and other less powerful groups invisible. Les femmes francophones vivant en milieu minoritaire sont des exemples de l'oppression linguistique. Et elles réclament de plus en plus qu'on reconnaisse leurs droits de vivre dans leur langue et leur culture. L'isolement et la réalité d'être francophone en milieu minoritaire sont des éléments particuliers qui ont un impact sur la perception qu'elles ont d'elles-mêmes (Garceau, Hébert, Gagné). Another powerful example of oppression through language is provided by Hare and Day-Corbiere. These authors explain the crude obliteration of Aboriginal identity which resulted from rules against speaking the Ojibwe language in residential schools. While the legal terms in which Aboriginal women are defined are more complex than school yard rules, they are equally powerful in erasing the identity and rights of Aboriginal women.

Au sein de la francophonie manitobaine, les «maîtresses d'écoles» ont historiquement, mais toujours dans le silence et sans pouvoir, orienté leurs pratiques vers la préservation et, à plus long terme, vers l'épaississement d'une trame sociale nécessaire à la négociation avec la société dominante (Hébert). Toujours au Manitoba, les femmes francophones sont aux prises avec une institution médicale dominée par une approche traditionnelle qui la rend sourde aux besoins des femmes et les laisse démunies devant l'obligation de survivre à de graves maladies (Gagné). En Ontario français, les femmes sont aussi invisibles et on méconnaît largement les problèmes auxquels elles sont confrontées quotidiennement, tout particulièrement

334

lorsqu'il s'agit des femmes plus âgées (Garceau). Dans l'Église, des siècles se sont écoulés sans que l'on prenne en considération la parole des femmes (Dumais). Dans tous ces cas, les femmes sont soit invisibles, soit l'objet d'une secrète indifférence à l'égard de leurs situations réelles. Pourtant, dans tous les cas, ces femmes se sont données les moyens pour sortir de l'invisibilité et avoir du pouvoir dans leur vie.

Government funding bodies, publishers, professional associations and universities have all used their power to ignore feminist scholarship until the relatively recent establishment of Women's Studies programs in specific academic environments (Epp, Christiansen-Ruffman et al.).

Miedema and Nason-Clark point out the oppression of foster mothers by state agents who refused to recognize foster mothers' knowledge about the children in their care. Although these foster mothers wish to contribute to the plans made for the children, they have come to know that the social welfare system has not been organized to include them in consultations about programming for these children.

Attitudes and practices which oppress the members of a family in which a parent has a disability are based on particular definitions. This is especially true when the disabled parent is a mother. The term 'proper mother' implies 'perfect' genetic makeup which, in turn, guarantees procreation of 'healthy' children. It further suggests a feminine monopoly on family caring. In contrast, the term 'disability' frequently implies dependency which some equate with non-human status. Words and definitions such as these make it impossible to bring the concepts mother and disability together. When there is no language which identifies mothers with disabilities, these women and their children are erased from public consciousness.

Action: Gaining and Regaining Symbolic Power — Lutte symbolique et prise de pouvoir

Identified below are some strategies feminists have employed for taking charge of language both in civil society and in their social relations with the state.

Using Words to Gain Power in Civil Society — Prendre la parole comme moyen d'acquérir du pouvoir dans la société civile
The Canadian Girl Guides' decision to modify their law and promise is an excellent example of the power of language (Whitney). Previous wording which had established the social expectation of girls in a serving role has been replaced with phrases which foster girls' individual levels of growth and leadership.

Miedema and Nason-Clark provide an example of validation for women who do work that is often undervalued. Through the experience of reviewing their ideas with these authors and knowing respect from this academic audience, foster mothers gain symbolic capital. They describe their experiences in their own words and in their own ways.

According to Miedema and Nason-Clark, previous feminist authors have sometimes contributed unknowingly to the oppression of foster mothers by describing them in simplistic terms as victims of the state. Instead, Miedema and Nason-Clark emphasize that these women are empowered by an opportunity to define their own tasks, purposes, and outcomes.

We have only a glimpse of the historical experiences of Black women in Nova Scotia because few of their stories have been recorded in written text. However, Bernice Moreau tells how Black women sometimes learned how to read when the white middle-class women for whom they worked wanted someone to help with children's homework. Or, they learned to read recipes. After gaining the power of the written word, Black Baptist women transmitted this power to others in the Black community. Aboriginal women, in both informal and formal social relations, are regaining power by attaining formal education while honouring their Ojibwe language and ways of knowing (Hare and Day-Corbiere).

Ce qui caractérise la réussite de la recherche-action discutée par Garceau est le fait que les participantes ont d'abord pris la parole pour produire des changements individuels et sociaux. L'absence de connaissances sur les Franco-Ontariennes de 45 à 64 ans était telle qu'elles ont eu recours à une approche fondée sur leur propre reconnaissance comme sujet porteur d'histoires spécifiques pour pallier ce manque. Appartenant à ce groupe d'âge, c'est par la mise en commun de leurs expériences personnelles que les femmes ont pu construire collectivement les aires de vie sur lesquelles elles ont enquêté dans les étapes subséquentes de la recherche-action. Elles ont donc déconstruit les fondements de leur exclusion pour se mettre en évidence et forcer la création d'un savoir rendant compte de leur présence.

A concrete symbol of women's success in a union women's caucus is the significant role of women played in the design, revisions, and distribution of a union poster representing inclusiveness. This poster design became a rallying point for women mobilizing against what they viewed as the informal oppressive communication patterns which governed much of the social relations in their union. Taking charge of words and images in this manner is an excellent demonstration of women gaining symbolic power.

Using Words to Gain Power in Relations with the State — La parole comme moyen d'acquérir du pouvoir face à l'État

The major critique of treaties and other legislation related to the Indian

Act provided by Hare, Day-Corbiere, and other Aboriginal legal experts exposes state oppression embedded in public documents. Moves toward the empowerment of First Nations and Aboriginal women have emerged from the work of these women.

In their discussion of federal research funding, Christiansen-Ruffman et al. provide an example of the power of language. They identify the symbolic importance of recognition from the Social Sciences and Humanities Research Council of research by, for, and about women.

The language commonly encouraged by government in proposals for funding of sexual assault centres has discouraged organizational structures that vary from traditional boards of directors and management hierarchies (Laiken). Reitsma-Street and Rogerson point out that research fund holders have the power to accept or reject research reports written collectively and reflecting participatory research, such as the report from Better Beginnings, Better Futures. The power to define and constitute as authentic various feminist contributions relates to the use of particular language. An analysis of discourse has aided women in understanding and, in some cases, altering gendered balances of power.

Les institutions traditionnelles avec leur mode de fonctionnement spécifique et leur vision du travail ne répondent pas aux besoins et aux aspirations des femmes. Afin que les femmes qui y travaillent aient des structures qui leur ressemblent, elles doivent, selon Bouchard et Cholette, mener de l'intérieur la lutte pour et par la féminisation. Pour ce faire, elles doivent utiliser des stratégies telles la prise de parole, la participation active, la culture de la mémoire et la prise de pouvoir.

The Theme of the Canadian Economy
L'économie canadienne

Oppression of women at the economic level is exemplified in the low incomes of artists and dancers (Gordon), of foster mothers (Miedema and Nason-Clark), of sole support mothers, and of disabled parents (Blackford). Lack of job security, inadequate occupational health and safety programs, inequity in hiring and promotion, and unequal power within labour groups are all facets of the workforce for many Canadian women (Parsons and Goggins; Briskin). The rates of poverty and unemployment among the disabled women and Aboriginal women to which Hare and Day-Corbiere and then Blackford refer are the highest in the country. The inequity of who does unpaid work in terms of race (Moreau), gender, and disability (Blackford) are other feminist economic concerns raised by articles in this text.

Epp's description of the pressure under which women faculty work points out how budgetary constraints have overloaded women in their occupational responsibilities, and drawn energy and attention from their efforts to make feminist change. While Epp describes women in a university setting, preoccupation with occupational expectations affects women in most work settings.

Male dominated administrative responses have meant reduced resources for women. This includes less spending on children's daycare centres and attendant care facilities at work sites. Such facilities can make employment possible for women and people with disabilities by recognizing the additional caring roles and needs they may have.

Action: Transforming the Economy — *Transformer l'économie*

Women in the Workplace — Femmes et travail rémunéré

Briskin provides an overview of women and Canadian unions, and explains the background and circumstances in which women have chosen to make alliances. She also makes clear how women have chosen to organize as separate groups or caucuses within unions. She describes the struggle of women workers which continues in the present day. Some of the goals they have achieved include acceptance in the workplace, membership in unions, legislated pay for equal work, benefits equal to those of men who perform comparable jobs, and, more recently, a voice in union leadership.

Parsons and Goggins provide a more specific and personal account of achievement by a women's caucus in an educational sector union of contract employees. They reveal their success in maintaining mutual respect and unanimity among a diverse group of women's caucus union members, in spite of an environment dominated by the oppressive and competative social relations of male dominated union executives and employers.

À partir de leurs expériences, Cholette et Bouchard montrent qu'une coopérative gérée entièrement par des femmes peut adopter une structure fondée sur le partage des pouvoirs et des avoirs. En adoptant le principe de flexibilité, les coopérantes peuvent s'entraider et partager tout en étant sensibles aux transformations qui s'opèrent à l'intérieur du groupe de travail. Elles montrent aussi qu'une structure favorisant l'autonomie permet aux femmes de se développer personnellement et professionnellement.

The success of Ojibwe women (Hare and Day-Corbiere) in establishing an employment development project tailored to the specific situation and culture of Aboriginal women will make an important positive economic change in the lives of these women and in their communities.

338

Recognition for Women's Unpaid Work — Femmes et travail non rémunéré
One outcome of the Women and Work SSHRC Strategic Grant was
the public and formal acknowledgement that women are a large part of
the paid workforce. More radical was the insight that women's work at
home and elsewhere is also worthy of recognition and study. Though
unpaid, this work makes an important contribution to the economy
and to society in general.

Gordon identifies the unpaid work of volunteers in a dance school
as important to the school's function. She describes the school's policy
of recognizing the volunteer labour provided by the mothers and friends
of dancers as feminist work.

In order to acknowledge the value and impact of unpaid work,
the Better Beginnings/Better Futures Project has chosen the unpaid
contributions of its volunteers as the focus of a research study (Reitsma-
Street and Rogerson). The study will 'cost out' unpaid contributions
and make visible what is usually hidden in economic reports.

The goals of women in unions (Parsons and Goggins, Briskin)
include achievement of benefits such as sick leave for a family member,
workplace childcare opportunities, and job sharing options. These goals
are premised on the belief that women's unpaid work in the family, as
much as their paid work in the employment setting, is of value. Women's
work in charitable and voluntary organizations such as the Needle
Women's Guild (Garrett), la Fédération des femmes canadiennes-
françaises de l'Ontario (Garceau), the Girl Guides of Canada (Whitney),
and the Canadian Sport Council (Kirby) are evidence of the benefits of
unpaid work and of the high quality and volume of volunteer work
which Canadian women undertake.

*Fighting Against Cut Backs and Privatisation — Lutte aux compressions
budgétaires et à la privatisation*
Laiken raises the question of the effects that economic factors will have
on feminist organizing. Laiken argues that women, by acting collectively,
are bringing private troubles into the public sphere. She, along with
protesters in Child Care Advocacy groups, Women's Centres, and Sexual
Assault Centres, brings to the public information that is needed to
organize against government financial 'cut backs', 'claw backs', and other
reductions in services. She points out that accomplishing goals using a
consensus model is made almost impossible when time and financial
resources are not sufficient to guarantee long term continuity in staff or
board member participation. Economic down turns have increasing
constrained voluntary non-profit boards and contract workers in terms
of time and resources.

Early attempts by women in Canada to ameliorate the poverty
they observed have resulted in the formation of charitable organizations

such as the Needle Women's Guild. This organization placed concern about individual children's and families' poverty in the domain of public concern. Subsequent efforts involving taxation and income supplement have made poverty an official concern for all Canadians. In calling for equality and then for equity and in exposing the public/private dichotomy as a myth, feminists now see a need to end poverty and lifestyles impoverished by the threat of unemployment and reduced local decision-making. Poverty and multinational power are now seen as barriers to health and to the liberation of women.

The Theme of Women's Leadership
Femmes et leadership

The authors of this book almost unanimously identify leadership as essential to the creation of feminist social change. Labour unions (Briskin; Parsons and Goggins), business firms (Cholette et Bouchard), social service administration (Gagné, Coholic and Prévost), women's organizations (Garceau), schools (Hébert), and churches (Dumais, Moreau) have all, historically, been dominated by men. Male visions of what should be and patriarchal ways of organizing in the world of work have restricted union demands for childcare and work sharing and have perpetuated hierarchical workplace decision-making (Briskin; Parsons and Goggins). For exemple, Black women in Nova Scotia were invisible within Baptist male-led churches (Moreau). Middle-class Canadian women were not accepted as contributors in public social matters (Garceau, Garrett). The theme of women in leadership positions is prominent among the issues raised by the authors in this book.

Action: Establishing Women's as Leaders — Femmes de tête et modèles

Preparing Girls and Women for Leadership — Former les femmes au leadership
Self-esteem and assertiveness are characteristics which progressive community dance schools (Gordon) and Girl Guide troops (Whitney) promote so that girls will grow in leadership ability. Teaching by and role modelling of experienced women have been important to the development of women Aboriginal leaders (Hare and Day-Corbiere) and Women's Studies faculty members (Epp). Out of the mutual support women gained as they drew together at a public well in Nova Scotia, Black Baptist women leaders emerged and won the respect of a male dominated clergy and congregation (Moreau). In similar fashion, the provision of education for women union members at the local level has prepared women to take leadership roles in labour organizations at the national level (Briskin).

La prise de conscience menant à l'action, l'estime et l'affirmation de soi sont les résultats tangibles liés au processus d'empowerment vécu par un groupe de femmes de l'Ontario français. Ces acquis ont propulsé à l'avant-scène certaines d'entre elles et leur ont permis d'occuper subséquemment des postes de pouvoir et de responsabilités dans leur communauté respective. Depuis, ces femmes n'ont de cesse que de continuer à s'affirmer socialement (Garceau).

Outcomes of Women's Leadership — Leadership des femmes et résultats
Briskin describes the progressive transformation of labour organizations as a whole through informal and formal leadership of women at the local level. Coholic and Prévost point out the organizational effects on a generic family service agency because of the impact of feminist leadership within one of the agency's sexual assault counselling department. Two whole neighbourhoods in a northern Ontario city have been revitalized by a woman leader modelling consensus decision-making in the Better Beginning, Better Futures program. There is shared vision for a more just society for low income families (Reitsma-Street and Rogerson). The outcomes of Black women's organizing in Nova Scotia include improved education and economic opportunities for people in the Black community (Moreau).

The Theme of Human Rights and Responsibilities
Droits et responsabilités

The theme of human rights and responsibilities speaks directly to disability-related issues. The Charter of Rights and Freedoms protects women with disabilities who choose to have children in spite of prejudice against their parenting capacities, parents with disabilities who seek access to teacher/parent interviews related to their children's school progress, and parents who wish to accompany their children in accessible leisure activities (Blackford). Rights, such as those to a formal education (Moreau) or to an education which reflects one's own language and culture (Hare and Day-Corbiere; Hébert), have been denied to large number of women. Furthermore, what has becomes clear in the articles is that, along with rights, the personhood and the humanity of women in these groups have been repressed. Women, along with people of colour (Moreau), Aboriginal people (Hare and Day-Corbiere), and disabled persons (Blackford) have during various historical periods been treated as non-persons. They have been seen either as unworthy of recognition or citizenship, or incapable of holding office.

Other ways by which the personhood and humanness of women have been ignored are related to our previous discussion of invisible, domestic work. Women are expected to be caregivers to others, often caring for others at work and later the same day at home. Often, their own needs are overlooked. Important concepts such as human interdependence, mutual caring, and spirituality or harmony with nature have been overlooked in the quest for patriarchal social relations and individual goals.

Action: Claiming Human Rights and Responsibilities — Réclamer nos droits

Valuing Caring and Interdependence — Interdépendance et soutien mutuel Gagné montre comment le quotidien des femmes ayant subi une mastectomie suite à un cancer du sein est marqué du sceau de l'entraide et du soutien des autres femmes partageant un vécu similaire. Comme elles ne trouvent pas, au sein des institutions médicales et communautaires, le support et les ressources nécessaires leur permettant d'affronter la maladie, elles les développent en échangeant leurs expériences et en se transmettant l'information. En ce sens, ces femmes deviennent un modèle pour le développement des programmes de santé communautaire.

Miedema and Nason-Clark indicate that foster mothers are fully aware of injustices due to inadequate provincial funding. They see that much of society fails to recognize the high value of the work done by foster care mothers. Yet, these authors are adamant that, in spite of lack of recognition by others, the women they interviewed have a sense of personal empowerment because of their relationships with the children entrusted to them. Foster mothers are hopeful about the future and certain of their competence; they know they have had an important and positive impact on the lives of children. In spite of injustices which need correcting, these women do not deserve the misnomer of "victim." Rather, they should be identified as richly human. The complexities of caring for and about others, mutual respect, and shared responsibilities are what Miedema and Nason-Clark challenge us, as feminists in Canada, to consider.

Garrett points out that, although women, as members of the Needlewomen's Guild, did not play a public and formal role in reducing child poverty historically, they gained a strong sense of purpose and a positive sense of worth sewing and knitting garments for impoverished children and their mothers. Their personal contributions of time and labour were important steps toward creating a more humane society.

While the group action and interaction of the Aboriginal women's economic renewal project benefits individuals, there is also great benefit to other group members and to the First Nations community (Hare and Day-Corbiere). This situation brings to native women a strong sense of community as well as respect from others for their work as leaders.

Dailiness — Quotidienneté

Reitsma-Street and Rogerson describe dailiness as taking time and acknowledging one's feelings during everyday work and in community interaction. The process of beginning group meetings with "circling in" shows respect for individual intentions and concerns. This practice acknowledges that it is the whole person who makes a contribution to a group. The group, therefore, takes responsibility for recognizing the humanity and the reality of each community member.

The practice of "circling in" which allows time for acknowledgement of all group members originated in traditional Aboriginal social relations. The practice remains part of the economic development project currently in place in northern Ontario. This practice is part of what Hare and Day-Corbiere call an "enabling environment" for the women in their project.

Taking time for others in the family often becomes part of family social relations when a parent has a disability. The age, physical condition, and circumstances of each member requires that time, attention, caring for, and caring about are made available for all family members (Blackford).

Clarifying Responsibility Within an Organization — Rôles et responsabilités dans les organisations

Women know that with rights come responsibilities. Laiken feels that feminist work will not be done effectively unless the ideal of shared decision-making is balanced with clarity about who is responsible for initiating and carrying out decisions. Her emphasis is accountability in the context of open communication and mutual respect.

Foster mothers in Nova Scotia express a strong sense of responsibility for the children in their care. As caring mothers, they also feel a responsibility to contribute to the future of the children (Miedema and Nason-Clark). Thus, they wish to contribute their ideas and knowledge as program plans are developed about the future of these children.

First Nations women have a keen understanding of the close tie between responsibility and rights. They underscore the responsibility of the Canadian government to honour treaty agreements and to return land and resources to First Nations people. At the same time, they take pride in knowing that they share responsibility for other community members. It is "Aboriginal women who maintain the life and stability of their people..." (Hare and Day-Corbiere). Aboriginal women see themselves as "keepers of the cultures so that the culture will survive within the changes of modern times. For, it is the Ojibwe women who breathe the air for each life that only they as women carry within. Their responsibility goes unchanged from one generation to the next, for the nurturing of a healthy people" (Hare and Day-Corbiere).

Pursuing Harmony with Nature — L'écologie

Women's rights to health and a healthy environment are perhaps the most overt connections among the various issues raised by the authors in this book. Also of particular importance is recognition of the body in all its variations and the physical contexts in which women are situated. Hare and Day-Corbiere protest articulately against destruction and pollution of First Nations land by colonists. The argument they present about rights to and responsibilities for land and people shows a link with spirituality and a sense of working in harmony with nature. Native spirituality is based on honouring nature. Moreau also notes that the spiritual pathway of Black women includes a relationship with nature.

The idea of working together with nature rather than controlling it is a cornerstone of what has been called ecofeminism. The idea of ecofeminism is also connected to this book's discussions of respecting the body in its diversity. This diversity includes disability (Blackford), race (Moreau), and the "ideal body image" in dance (Gordon) and in sport (Kirby). Ecofeminism contributes to the notion that our responsibility extends beyond today and further than ourselves.

Reference

Tong, R. 1989. *Feminist Thought: A Comprehensive Introduction.* Boulder: Westview Press.

Karen Blackford, Marie-Luce Garceau, Sandra Kirby

CONCLUSION

The Faces of Feminist Change —
Les multiples visages du changement féministe

In the preceding chapter, we have analyzed what constitutes success in making feminist change. Our analysis has shown that, although some authors emphasize certain themes more than others, each author's work contributes in some way to our understanding of all the identified themes. In other words, there is a shared understanding of how feminism is defined across many Canadian constituencies. At the same time, the constituencies represented in this book vary by bodily condition/disability/ability, geographical location, class, race, age, and ethnicity. Thus, while there is a shared sense of what feminism is, it is not surprising to find that feminist change comes with many faces and many unique challenges.

Feminist change clearly has a human face; this affects our ways of seeing, ways of acting, and ways of acknowledging the body. A philosophy of human rights is intertwined with one of reciprocal humane caring among ourselves and with others. To produce feminist change, care must be taken to ensure that all participants are enabled to fully and actively participate.

These human and humane philosophies are enacted though feminist process. This process includes negotiation of everything from what changes are to be undertaken to who will undertake what responsibilities along the way. For effective change, the feminist process must include ways to improve the capacities of women and their sense of self-esteem, which, in turn, positions women to have more strength to deconstruct and analyze the events of their everyday lives and to reconstruct their social relations over time (Garceau, Coholic and Prévost).

A second face of change is its economy. Innovation in economy is a key characteristic of feminist change. Women produced dramatic outcomes even in the absence of basic resources, and in spite of a financially strong patriarchal status quo. This financial frugality is balanced by the tremendous generosity of many women who contribute their valuable time and efforts, usually as volunteers, to make the world a better place.

A third face of feminist change is its shared nature. Even though the outcomes may be uneven for various participants and/or partners (Christiansen-Ruffman et al.), there are major efforts being made to reach out to girls and women outside the immediate circle. This process involves mentoring women as activists (Briskin, Miedema and Nason-Clark, Kirby) and women researchers (Gagné, Hébert, Garceau, Christiansen-Ruffman et al.). These efforts result in ongoing re-creation of the ways in which activists work and re-making of the feminist research process (Gagné, Garceau).

A fourth face of feminist change is the reality that it is informed. Information travels from expression of the experiences of a single woman to corporate analysis of the effect of a policy, from researchers' reports on issues of concern to women to the writings of a local community group about an issue important to the group. Feminists see such information, based on measurable evidence, as vital to good decision-making and necessary to commitment to action. The authors have identified that further education is needed on the particular issues of the day, as well as sexism and its interrelation with women's issues (Dumais, Epp, Kirby), bodily condition/disability/ability (Blackford), feminizing success stories (Blackford, Gagné, Garceau, Dumais and Kirby), culture and history (Hébert, Whitney), family (Blackford, Miedema and Nason-Clark) and community (Bouchard et Cholette), economy (Briskin), and research processes (Gagné, Christiansen-Ruffman et al.).

L'implication de chacune des auteures dans le mouvement des femmes est une expérience précieuse dans l'émergence des savoirs sur les femmes. Chacune, explorant sa réalité, montre les conflits sociaux qui la traversent afin d'ouvrir et de poursuivre le débat-combat qui permettra en bout de ligne leur résolution. Féminiser est un processus dynamique, comme le montrent les exemples présentés dans ce livre. Et ce processus ne s'accomplit pas sans rencontrer sur sa route de multiples résistances des institutions en place. Nous espérons que ce livre contribuera, ne fut-ce que modestement, à la féminisation d'autres institutions. Si nous apprenons de nos réussites et de nos erreurs, le féminisme, qui est une pensée et une pratique en mouvement, continuera de puiser dans ses expériences la source de ses futurs pas.

Today, feminism in Canada reflects the influence of current and former women leaders. It is also characterized by its redefinition and reassertion of itself by women in all parts of the country. Feminizing, like all change, is a dynamic process energized by some and resisted by others. As this book exemplifies, feminizing is always in transition, and process is as important as outcome. This realization is itself feminist. Just as there is a need for this book at this time, we look forward knowing that, as the process of feminist change continues, there will soon be the need for another.

Contributors
Collaboratrices

Karen A. Blackford, Royal Bank Research Chair in Disability Studies, Canadian Centre on Disability Studies, Winnipeg; Adjunct Professor in Sociology, University of Manitoba; Associate Professor on Leave, School of Nursing, Laurentian University, Sudbury, Ontario.

Lyne Bouchard, La coopérative Convergence, Ottawa.

Linda Briskin, Ph. D., Associate Professor in the Social Science Division, York University.

Chantal Cholette, La coopérative Convergence, Ottawa.

Nancy Nason-Clark, Professor, Sociology Department, University of New Brunswick.

Diana A. Coholic, Social Work Practitioner, Doctoral Candidate in Social Work, University of New South Wales, Sydney, Australia.

Laura Day-Corbiere, Project Coordinator, Women's Group, M'Chigeeng First Nation.

Francine Descarries, professeure, département de sociologie, Université du Québec à Montréal, membre de l'Institut de recherches et d'études féministes, IREF.

Monique Dumais, professeure de théologie et d'éthique, Université du Québec à Rimouski.

Juanita Ross Epp, Associate Professor, Faculty of Education, Lakehead University.

Elsy Gagné, Ph.D., LL.B., Pitblado Buchwald Asper, Winnipeg.

Marie-Luce Garceau, professeure agrégée, École de service social, Université Laurentienne.

Heather L. Garrett, Part time Faculty, Department of Sociology, York University.

Starla Goggins, Research Coordinator, Princess Margaret Hospital Lodge; Doctoral Candidate, Graduate Program in Sociology, York University.

Jane Gordon, Associate Professor of Sociology and Anthropology, Mount Saint Vincent University.

Susan Hare, LL.B. Barrister and Solicitor, M'Chigeeng First Nation.

Monique Hébert, Ph. D., féministe et militante active, Aylmer.

Sandra Kirby, Chair, Department of Sociology, University of Winnipeg.

Marilyn E. Laiken, Associate Professor, Ontario Institute for Studies in Education or the University of Toronto.

Baukje Miedema, Research Associate, Family Medicine Unit (Dalhousie), Fredericton.

Bernice Moreau, Assistant Professor, School of Social Work, Carleton University.

Marianne Parsons, Part-time Faculty Member, Sociology and Criminology, St. Mary's University; Doctoral Candidate, Graduate Program in Sociology, York University.

Colette T. Prévost, Director of Research and Development, Community Counselling Center of Nippissing, North Bay.

Pat Rogerson, Former Assistant Director, N'Swakamok Friendship Centre, Sudbury.

Linda Christiansen-Ruffman, Professor of Sociology and Women's Studies, Saint Mary's University.

Mary Lynn Stewart, Professor of History and Women's Studies, Simon Fraser University.

Marge Reitsma-Street, Associate Professor, Multidisciplinary Master's Program in Policy and Practice, Faculty of Human and Social Development, University of Victoria.

Patricia Whitney, Coordinator of the Women's Studies Program, University of Prince Edward Island.

AGMV
MARQUIS
Québec, Canada
1999